D·I·V·I·N·E
INVASIONS

D·I·V·I·N·E
INVASIONS
A LIFE OF
PHILIP K. DICK

LAWRENCE SUTIN

HARMONY BOOKS / NEW YORK

Published by Harmony Books, a division of Crown Publishers, Inc., 201 East 50th Street, New York, New York 10022

HARMONY and colophon are trademarks of Crown Publishers, Inc.
Printed in the U.S.A.

Library of Congress Cataloging-in-Publication Data

Sutin, Lawrence, 1951–
   Divine invasions: a life of Philip K. Dick / by Lawrence Sutin.
      p. cm.
   1. Dick, Philip K.—Biography. 2. Authors, American—20th
century—Biography. I. Title.
PS3554.I3Z89 1989
813'. 54—dc19
[B]   89-2014

ISBN 0-517-57204-4

Book design by Jennifer Harper

First Edition

10 9 8 7 6 5 4 3 2 1

To my good and loving parents,
Jack and Rochelle Sutin

ACKNOWLEDGMENTS

The research and writing of this book proved to be an adventure beyond all initial expectations. Those who regard Philip K. Dick's probings into "What is Real?" as mere metaphysical quibblings have never undertaken to write a full account of a life.

I am indebted to so many persons who extended me time and consideration that it seems ungrateful to single out a few for special thanks. But I must mention those whose support was most vital. My agent, Dorothy Pittman, diligently marketed my proposal at a time when those "in the know" declared that a biography of Philip K. Dick was a commercial impossibility. Dorothy was also, for me, the perfect reader— one who dreams along with the text. My editor, Michael Pietsch, took the risk of purchasing the book and, in his labors on the manuscript, respected my style and intentions while constantly spurring me to greater clarity and depth. Paul Williams, the literary executor of the Philip K. Dick Estate, provided all the cooperation a biographer could ask for; his sole concern was that, insofar as possible, the truth be told. Anne Dick gave vital support by granting me numerous long interview sessions and access to her excellent book *Search for Philip K. Dick*. Tessa Dick, Nancy Hackett, and Kleo Mini all graciously responded to my interview queries on their married lives with Phil. Laura Coehlo and Isa Hackett, Phil's daughters, similarly extended their cooperation. Tim Powers, Phil's good and true friend, unstintingly shared his memories, journals, and personal contacts. Joseph Morris, my good and true friend, shared the vision of this book with me throughout.

I interviewed well over one hundred persons who knew Phil or possessed information about him, and I thank all who—out of love and respect for Phil—took the time to talk or write to me. A few of these persons shall, by their own wishes, go nameless here. All errors and omissions in the text are, of course, solely my responsibility. But I can extend my most heartfelt thanks to: Gerald Ackerman, Karen and Poul Anderson, D. Scott Apel, Alexandra Apostolides, Chris and Greg Arena, Lawrence Ashmead, Charles Bennett, James Blaylock, Hatte Blejer, Charles Brown, Jayne Brown, Mildred Downey Broxon, Dr. Harry E. Bryan, Harry and Nita Busby, Carol Carr, the late Terry Carr, Loren

Cavit, Lynne Cecil, Richard Daniels, Grania Davis, Thomas Disch, Dick Ellington, Harlan Ellison, Gladys Fabun, Hampton Fancher, Tim Finney, Pat Flannery, James Frenkel, Russell Galen, Evelyn Glaubman, Cynthia Goldstone, Sherry Gottlieb, Ron Goulart, Iskandar Guy, Michael Hackett, Linda Hartinian, David Hartwell, Linda Herman (Librarian, Special Collections, California State University at Fullerton), Neil Hudner, Mark Hurst, Honor Jackson, K. W. Jeter, Dr. George Kohler, Jerry Knight, Dean Koontz, Jerry Kresy, Gwen Lee, Ursula K. Le Guin, Linda Levy/Taylor, Miriam Lloyd, Richard Lupoff, Vincent and Virginia Lusby, Michelle McFadden, Willis McNelly, Steve Malk, Merry Lou Malone, Barry Malzberg, David May, Ann Montbriand, Bernie Montbriand, Margaret Nearing, Kirsten Nelson, J. G. Newkom, Nicole Panter, David Peoples, Juan and Su Perez, Serena Powers, J. B. Reynolds, Alan Rich, Gregg Rickman, Leon Rimov, Betty Jo Rivers, Gregory Sandow, William Sarill, Doris Sauter, Donald Schenker, Tom Schmidt, Robert Silverberg, Joan Simpson, John Sladek, Barry Spatz, Art Spiegelman, Norman Spinrad, Nit Sprague, the late Roy Squires, Lou Stathis, E. M. Terwilliger, J'Ann Tolman, Ray Torrence, Jeff Wagner, Michael and Susan Walsh, Mary Wilson, Robert Anton Wilson, William Wolfson, Richard Wolinsky, Donald Wollheim, and Roger Zelazny.

My greatest debt is to the courageous spirit of Philip K. Dick.

Lawrence Sutin
Minneapolis
May 1989

CONTENTS

FOREWORD BY PAUL WILLIAMS

Philip K. Dick died on March 2, 1982, and the excellent biography you hold in your hands ends, appropriately, with the man's death. But one of the great attractions of the writing life, as Will Shakespeare was fond of telling us, is that it allows a person to extend his or her personality beyond the grave; the writer goes right on showing off, seducing, complaining, bragging, commiserating, demanding and receiving attention, even when his heart no longer pumps. As editor of an odd publication called *The Philip K. Dick Society Newsletter*, I get letters every week from readers who have just recently entered into intense and intimate relationships with the man; often they insist on telling me (a perfect stranger) that he has become their best or in some cases only friend in the world. Phew.

What most impresses me about Larry Sutin's biography of Phil Dick is that I have no quarrel with either its facts or its imputations. This will seem faint praise, unless you have ever read a newspaper story about an event you were actually involved in, or read a biography of someone you know personally. Biography is a kind of fiction, necessarily a weaving of a story; but because it purports to be the truth about a person, it is a slippery kind of fiction indeed, and very seldom can one read the biography of a friend and even recognize the person described therein. I am pleased to say that not only do I recognize my friend in this book, I know him better for having read it. Sutin's narrative violates neither my head's knowledge nor my heart's sense of who Philip K. Dick was, and by adding a perspective on his life that I as friend and, now, literary executor, could never achieve (too close to the subject matter), it puts me in a position to offer it the best testimonial one can give a friend's biography: this is the man I knew.

Philip K. Dick's success in the years since his death is ironic, given the financial and professional struggles he was faced with for most of his life. In a novel written in 1976, *Radio Free Albemuth*, Dick (who is a character in the book) is told by his jailer (he's a political prisoner in an overtly fascist America) that the government is now writing his books and that they will continue to appear, with pro-government propaganda woven in, even if he is executed. This novel was itself published posthumously, and indeed new books by Dick have continued to appear at an alarming rate: eight previously unpublished novels (all hardcovers) in seven years, plus a children's book, a screenplay, four books of interviews, a collection of nonfiction, and two new story collections (in English; dozens more in other languages), as well as a very impressive five-volume, 900,000-word set of *The Collected Stories of Philip K. Dick*.

There have been twenty issues of the *PKDS Newsletter* so far (we have about a thousand subscribers around the world); what surprises me is that there continues to be so much "PKD-related" news to write about. In particular, creative artists of all kinds are drawn to Dick's writings and constantly find ways to adapt his work for and/or include his presence in their creations. In addition to being a character in his own later novels, Dick is one of the protagonists in (and primary inspiration for) Michael Bishop's 1987 novel *The Secret Ascension* (published in Britain as *Philip K. Dick Is Dead, Alas*). He is also the central character in a dozen different short stories written since his death. Young filmmakers acknowledge him in their films (Subiela's *Man Facing Southeast*, Walkow's *The Trouble with Dick*), rock and roll and avant-garde musicians talk about him in interviews (R.E.M., Elvis Costello, Sonic Youth, Guns n' Roses, Stuart Hamm, the Fall) and sometimes name their albums after his books. Composer Tod Machover created an opera based on Dick's novel *VALIS*, which premiered at the Pompidou Centre in Paris in 1987, has been well received in compact disc and cassette form, and is to be performed in Japan and the United States in 1990. Off-Broadway veterans Mabou Mines staged a mixed-media drama based on Dick's *Flow My Tears, the Policeman Said* in New York and Boston; other theater groups in Chicago, Paris, Tokyo, and London have also mounted Dick adaptations. France's best-known designer, Philippe Starck, is a passionate PKD reader; the individual pieces in his popular line of new wave furniture are named after characters in Dick's novel *Ubik*. American comic artist R. Crumb has rendered part of Dick's personal story in illustrated form, "The Religious Experience of Philip K. Dick."

And so forth. Dick died shortly before the release of *Blade Runner*, Ridley Scott's film based on Dick's novel *Do Androids Dream of Electric Sheep?* The film has been extremely popular and influential around the world and contributed greatly to Dick's present status as one of the best-known (and read) American novelists in Japan. Dick is also a major literary figure in Great Britain and in France; books of his are published and republished constantly in these countries, where there are usually more than forty PKD books in print at any one time. Germany, Spain, and Brazil lag only slightly behind. Dick's vision of twentieth-century reality (as projected onto science-fictional landscapes) obviously speaks to readers across national and language boundaries; in fact, it is in his native country (the U.S.) that Dick has had the most trouble finding a mass audience.

And this interesting life-after-life of P. K. Dick shows no sign of slowing its pace. *The Collected Letters of Philip K. Dick* (he was an articulate, compulsive, very funny letter writer) are in preparation and will probably run to at least four volumes. A first volume of selections from Dick's philosophical/theological journals, his *Exegesis*, has also been announced. Two more unpublished novels will be released by 1991. One of the big summer movies of 1990 is expected to be *Total Recall*, directed by Paul Verhoeven and starring Arnold Schwarzenegger, based on PKD's short story "We Can Remember It for You Wholesale." Studios big and small have three or four other Dick projects in preparation.

Dick spin-offs proliferate and his bizarre personality insinuates itself into consciousnesses everywhere and yet Dick is not yet a "famous" person and his writings, though written about in the press frequently and studied by academics obsessively, cannot yet be said to have been accepted by the literary establishment, at least not in the United States. There are advantages to this. You want to get out there and cause as much trouble as you can before they pigeonhole you, mount and stuff you, freeze your myth in stone, chain you to your pedestal. Every reader who discovers Dick seems to feel they've found something unknown and very special; he is not yet public property.

Perhaps, just possibly, he (if we can speak of him as though he really were still alive, still conscious, breathing through all those books and adaptations and translations) will find a way to avoid the trap of outright public and literary acceptance, fame, immortality. Perhaps this present volume will be read not as the life story of a great American (or twentieth-century) novelist but as the tale of an interesting oddball, a California character, creator of junk masterpieces whose life somehow expresses the passions and eccentricity inside each one of us. If so, literature's loss could be the reader's gain. Wouldn't it be nice if in the twenty-first century *Martian Time-Slip* and *The Man in the High Castle* and *The Transmigration of Timothy Archer* are not taught in the schools at all, but still passed around furtively in beat-up old paperback editions with lurid covers (or holographic reproductions of same, suitable to look at while microchips whisper the text in your ear or print it out on the back of your hand)?

I don't know. I do know Larry Sutin has told a good story here, a story that has continued to stimulate, surprise, and bemuse me long after I would have expected to have worn it out. (I have a short attention span.) If you already know Philip K. Dick, have already encountered him through his novels, this biography will fascinate you, fill in the gaps, and leave you with more and better and more difficult questions than the ones you came in with. If you haven't made the man's acquaintance yet, welcome. You're in for a wild ride. Don't figure on coming out unscathed.

Paul Williams
Glen Ellen, California
June 1989

D·I·V·I·N·E
INVASIONS

INTRODUCTION If Heraclitus Is Right—And "The Nature Of Things Is In The Habit Of Concealing Itself"—Then Where Better To Look For Great Art Than In A Trash Genre?

For without a doubt there is a difference between science fiction and all the neighboring, often closely related, types of trivial literature. It is a whore, but quite a bashful one at that; moreover, a whore with an angel face. . . . The best science fiction novels want to smuggle themselves into the Upper Realm [of the mainstream]—but in 99.9 percent of cases, they do not succeed. The best authors behave like schizophrenics; they want to—and at the same time they do not want to—belong to the [Lower] Realm of Science Fiction. . . . For this reason science fiction is such a remarkable phenomenon. It comes from a whorehouse but it wants to break into the palace where the most sublime thoughts of human history are stored.

STANISLAW LEM

. . . what he [the science fiction writer] wishes to capture on paper is different from writers in other fields. . . . There is no actual boyhood world once extant but now only a moment, gnawing at him; he is free and glad to write about an infinity of worlds. . . .

PHILIP K. DICK, 198(

PHILIP K. Dick (1928–82) remains a hidden treasure of American liter; ture because the majority of his works were produced for a genre— science fiction—that almost invariably wards off serious attention.

You can't write about rocket ships *and* be serious, can you? A gr white whale serves as a literary symbol, but surely the same can't be t of a telepathic Ganymedean slime mold.

Phil Dick used the junk props of the SF genre—the tentacled ali alternate worlds, and gee-whiz high-tech gimmickry—to fashion most intensely visionary fiction written by an American in this cen In Europe and Japan, Phil is widely regarded as one of our most ori novelists, *period*—SF and mainstream labels be damned.

1

But somehow, in his native land, Phil's books continue to be shelved in the whorehouse.

The problem is that Phil's best work—*The Man in the High Castle* (1962), *The Three Stigmata of Palmer Eldritch* (1964), *Martian Time-Slip* (1964), *Ubik* (1969), *A Scanner Darkly* (1977), and the aforementioned *Valis*—comes under the heading of SF if it comes under any heading at all. And SF makes most serious-minded Americans smirk: Ray guns wielded by guys with ripped shirts and rippling pecs, bug-eyed monsters (BEMs) distressing damsels in brass brassieres—all set in "bold new worlds of tomorrow" that remind you more of dreary B movies with flying saucers dangling on strings over toy cities, or of the sappy superhero comics you read as a kid. And speaking of kids, it is an obvious unsubstantiated fact that most SF readers—and writers (including Phil Dick)—first became fans well before they graduated from high school. What do you make of a genre that seldom attracts new readers who are self-supporting?

Some SF readers who tire of the smirks point out that certain Higher Realm official classics, such as Sir Thomas More's *Utopia* (1516), come within the genre because an alternative world is logically extrapolated from hypothetical societal innovations. They claim Edgar Allan Poe as the founding father of modern SF—forty years in advance of Frenchman Jules Verne—on the basis of stories such as "The Case of M. Valdemar" and "The Mystification." They cite the proud British SF tradition, which includes works by certifiable Higher Realm names such as H. G. Wells, Aldous Huxley, C. S. Lewis, George Orwell, Kingsley Amis, Anthony Burgess, Colin Wilson, and Doris Lessing.

But most American fans of SF scoff at such tortured scholarly apologetics. They know damn well what SF is and where it came from, and here's the story they'll tell you:

First off, SF wasn't born in the mind of More, who wrote in Latin, for chrissake, or in the mind of Poe or Wells or Verne, or even, for that matter, between the covers of any respectable *bound* book. SF grew like a rocket-finned silver orchid out of the rich mulch of the pulps that covered American newsstands from the end of World War I through the early fifties (when Phil's writing career began—he had stories in seven different pulp magazines in June 1953). As the pulps receded, the rise of paperback publishers revived the genre. SF sold and continues to sell to this day because its best writers know what writers in all great popular genres— detective story, western, true romance—know: The imagination can be an incredibly simple lock to pick if you know how to employ the tried and true rules.

In the case of the SF genre, the basic rule was, is, and always has been: Come up with a *startling* idea and set it loose in astonishing ways in a future world. The pulps didn't pay well but just enough . . . if you had consistently startling ideas and could churn the stuff out at breakneck speed.

2

Phil was the man for the job. No one in the history of the SF genre—in which amazement alone buys new shoes for writers' kids—has been able to "What If?" as widely, wildly, and convincingly as Philip K. Dick.

He loved to tell the story of how he discovered SF:

> I was twelve [in 1940] when I read my first sf magazine . . . it was called STIRRING SCIENCE STORIES and ran, I think, four issues. The editor was Don Wollheim, who later on (1954) bought my first novel . . . and many since. I came across the magazine quite by accident; I was actually looking for POPULAR SCIENCE. I was most amazed. Stories about science? At once I recognized the magic which I had found, in earlier times, in the Oz books—this magic now coupled not with magic wands but with science. . . . In any case my view became magic equals science . . . and science (of the future) equals magic.

Phil read James Joyce's *Finnegans Wake* several times in his early twenties. Throughout his life the range of his reading was virtually limitless, from technical papers on physics to Binswanger's *daseinanalyse* to Jung, Kant, William Burroughs, the Bible, the Dead Sea Scrolls, the Bhagavad Gita. Influences on his work? Phil would frequently cite—before getting around to any SF authors—Stendhal, Flaubert, and especially Maupassant, whose tales, along with those of James T. Farrell, taught him how to structure the stories he sold for his livelihood in the early fifties: over seventy in three years, before the novels took precedence.

What I mean to say is that Phil was smart as a whip and fully capable of appreciating the finer literary things of life. So what did he need with the Lower Realm?

It was the SF genre, with its hospitable tenet of astonishment above all, that set Phil the writer free.

From what? The art of biography consists in tackling impossible questions about your subject that you couldn't answer about yourself, and I'll do my best to do that by book's end. But for now, just imagine yourself as a young writer able to type at an amazing 120 words per minute—and you can barely keep up with yourself when you're hot. Now consider the possibilities of a genre in which any psychological, political, sexual, or evolutionary premise is allowable so long as readers keep laying down cold cash for the lure of unknown worlds.

Phil wanted badly into the mainstream. As the years went on he knew damn well he was writing brilliant books that no one else could about his two obsessions: "What is Real?" and its frightening corollary, "What is Human?" But he also knew that the mainstream rules didn't much allow for the kinds of possibilities that tended to come to his mind. Knowing those things could make him feel outcast, angry, and blessed all at once:

I want to write about people I love, and put them into a fictional world spun out of my own mind, not the world we actually have, because the world we actually have does not meet my standards. Okay, so I should revise my standards; I'm out of step. I should yield to reality. I have never yielded to reality. That's what SF is all about. If you wish to yield to reality, go read Philip Roth; read the New York literary establishment mainstream bestselling writers. [. . .] This is why I love SF. I love to read it; I love to write it. The SF writer sees not just possibilities but *wild* possibilities. It's not just "What if—" It's "*My God*; what if—" In frenzy and hysteria. The Martians are always coming.

But only in the pulps ("trashy pulps," as they are usually called). In April 1911, Hugo Gernsback wrote and serialized a novella, *Ralph 124C41 +: Novel of the Year 1966*, in his own magazine, *Modern Electrics*. The futuristic adventure tinctured by wild "What If?" extrapolations went over surprisingly well in a magazine previously devoted exclusively to practical fact. But it took until April 1926 for Hugo Gernsback to seize the idea of founding the first all-SF pulp in the English language: *Amazing Stories*. And it was Gernsback who, starting with the term *scientifiction*, at last anointed SF with the name that stuck.

Amazing was an enormous success until the Depression hit and Gernsback found himself in receivership. He lost control of *Amazing*— others bought him out and carried it on—and Gernsback never again set the course for SF. He has, however, been duly immortalized through the Hugo Awards, the highest SF literary honor, awarded by fan vote at annual Worldcons.

Phil Dick won the Hugo in 1963 for *The Man in the High Castle*, a novel that was published by Putnam with a dust jacket that betrayed no SF content within. It posits a post–World War II world in which Japan and Germany are the victors and the continental United States is roughly divided between them; Japan governs the western half, which includes the nominally futuristic San Francisco in which the novel is set. Phil devised the plot by consulting the *I Ching*, and several of the novel's characters—Japanese and conquered, culturally cowed Americans alike—consult that divinatory text, marking its debut in American fiction.

Phil thought, after over a decade of writing effort that had produced eleven mainstream novels (none published at that point) and seven SF novels (all but one published in pulpy-looking paperback by bottom-of-the-line Ace Books), that at last, with *The Man in the High Castle*, he had merged the best of the Lower and Higher Realms by telling a very serious, beautifully written story about the nature of fascism and the Tao and (as SF allowed) reality going quietly haywire. But the Higher Realm turned its head away—there was no mainstream recognition for *High Castle*—even as the Lower Realm bestowed its Hugo honors.

Categories . . . Phil never fit well into any of them, nor could he fit what he thought might be Real into them. This is not to say that Phil was impractical or otherworldly. The novels and stories testify to his detailed, sympathetic understanding of everyday work and marital woes and the value of craft in the former, of love despite all in the latter. And Phil managed, mark you, to make a living for thirty years writing books he *wanted* to write. He was a consummate professional.

But you can't make an omelette without cracking eggs, and you can't write of Mr. Tagomi seeing through a glass darkly in *The Man in the High Castle*—or of Barney Mayerson pleading with Mr. Smile the suitcase psychiatrist in *The Three Stigmata of Palmer Eldritch*, or of Joe Chip warding off retrograde time with a handy spray can in *Ubik*, or of Fred/Robert Arctor the brain-damaged undercover narc informing on himself in A *Scanner Darkly*, or of Horselover Fat in *Valis* explaining to character Phil Dick (both know that they are really one and the same person) just how he encountered a vast One Mind that might be God or something else (". . . Fat must have come up with more theories than there are stars in the universe. Every day he developed a new one, more cunning, more exciting and more fucked")—you can't write of any of these souls without first confronting the terror and shaky hilarity of a world that cannot cohere. In 1981, looking back on his efforts, Phil wrote:

> I am a fictionalizing philosopher, not a novelist; my novel & story-writing ability is employed as a means to formulate my perception. The core of my writing is not art but *truth*. Thus what I tell is the truth, yet I can do nothing to alleviate it, either by deed or explanation. Yet this seems somehow to help a certain kind of sensitive troubled person, for whom I speak. I think I understand the common ingredient in those whom my writing helps: they cannot or will not blunt their own intimations about the irrational, mysterious nature of reality, &, for them, my corpus of writing is one long ratiocination regarding this inexplicable reality, an integration & presentation, analysis & response & personal history.

Unsurprisingly, then, strict categories worked against Phil. Take novels like A *Scanner Darkly* and *Valis*. They were marketed as SF, but if, say, William Burroughs and Thomas Pynchon, respectively, had written them, they would have been mainstream. Why? Categories. Borges's frequently anthologized story "Tlon, Uqbar, Orbis Tertius" (about an imaginary planet that gradually becomes our world) would be SF if Phil had written it.

Another Borges story, "Pierre Menard, Author of Don Quixote," offers a way out of the categorical maze. Menard, in the twentieth century, is writing an original work entitled *Don Quixote* in the exact same Spanish that Cervantes employed. Since Menard's is a different

5

(modern) consciousness from Cervantes's, the effect of Menard's duplicate *Quixote* text upon the reader must be entirely other. Borges explains:

> Menard (perhaps without wishing to) has enriched, by a new technique, the hesitant and rudimentary art of reading: the technique is one of deliberate anachronism and erroneous attributions. This technique, with its infinite applications, urges us to run through the *Odyssey* as if it were written after the *Aeneid*. [. . .] This technique would fill the dullest books with adventure. Would not the attributing of *The Imitation of Christ* to Louis-Ferdinand Céline or James Joyce be a sufficient renovation of its tenuous spiritual counsels?

All very well and good. But whom, in light of Borges's "deliberate anachronism" method, shall we posit as the author of the works of Philip K. Dick, in order to obtain for them the respect they deserve?

Phil would have enjoyed that question. Hell, he asked something very much like it often enough in the eight-thousand-page *Exegesis* (subtitled by him *Apologia Pro Mia Vita* to emphasize its central importance) he wrote night after night for nearly eight years in an attempt to explain to his own satisfaction (he never succeeded) a series of visions and auditions that seized his soul in February–March 1974 and held it to the end of his life. This biography incorporates the results of the first study ever made of the *Exegesis* in its entirety.

The 2-3-74* experiences posed, one might say, the ultimate startling "What If?"—or rather, a new and infinite range of them. On March 21, 1975, one year later, Phil wrote as concise and radiant a summary of the visions as he ever achieved:

I speak of The Restorer of What Was Lost
      The Mender of What Was Broken

March 16, 1974: It appeared—in vivid fire, with shining colors and balanced patterns—and released me from every thrall, inner and outer.

March 18, 1974: It, from inside me, looked out and saw the world did not compute, that I—and it—had been lied to. It denied the reality, and power, and authenticity of the world, saying, "This cannot exist; it cannot exist."

March 20, 1974: It seized me entirely, lifting me from the limitations of the space-time matrix; it mastered me as, at the same time, I knew that the world around me was cardboard, a fake. Through its power of perception I saw what

---

*As Phil himself utilized the form 2-3-74 to refer to the experiences of February–March 1974, it shall be followed here.

really existed,, and through its power of no-thought decision, I acted to *free myself*. It took on in battle, as a champion of all human spirits in thrall, every evil, every Iron Imprisoning thing. [. . . .]

The 2-3-74 experiences, which so influenced Phil's final novels, are a rare and remarkable event in American literary history; how often has an American writer of any stature confessed to, and been obsessed by, such a subject? The title of this biography—*Divine Invasions: A Life of Philip K. Dick*—pays homage to Phil's 1981 novel *The Divine Invasion* and, further, underscores the signal importance to his life and work of the above events. I do not wish to imply that any particular term (such as *God*) exclusively describes what Phil encountered in 2-3-74, nor that a Saint Phil emerged at last; Phil himself would have rejected both these notions.

But the core of the difficult truths that Phil held dear in his last years lay in 2-3-74. No one can pass upon the unanswerable question: Were those events *real*? Phil himself had no doubt that *something* had happened, though he always retained as a possibility—as his friend and fellow SF writer K. W. Jeter observes—the "minimum hypothesis" that they were self-delusion. But for readers who would, in this skeptical age, readily leap to that conclusion, the cautionary words of William James in *The Varieties of Religious Experience* may be of value:

> We are all surely familiar in a general way with this method of discrediting states of mind for which we have an antipathy. We all use it to some degree in criticizing persons whose states of mind we regard as overstrained. But when other people criticize our own more exalted soul-flights by calling them "nothing but" expressions of our organic disposition, we feel outraged and hurt, for we know that, whatever be our organism's peculiarities, our mental states have their substantive value as revelations of the living truth; and we wish that all this medical materialism could be made to hold its tongue.

Returning to the "deliberate anachronism" suggested by Borges, let us, for purposes of this biography, arbitrarily settle on Philip K. Dick himself as the author of numerous brilliant works that are SF or mainstream, as you prefer. And let us further, for the sake of clarity and courtesy, briefly set forth the rules of this biographical road for the gentle reader contemplating its course.

First off, Phil—who will, of course, be quoted more often and lengthily than anyone else as to the events of his life—was very fond of elaboration, extrapolation, reinterpretation, and outright putting people on. This is agreed upon by all who knew him. Now Phil placed a fierce value upon truth in both his writings and his personal relations. But he never was one to resist the fascination of a new, brilliant, complex theory of 2-3-74, or of anything else, and his capacity for generating such theories was limitless. In addition, being gracious and gregarious (when he was not in the throes of extreme depression and despair), Phil loved to tell stories and write letters that pleased—or matched the preconceptions of—the person addressed.

I am well aware that many of the quoted accounts by Phil of his life are very likely a mixture of fable and fact; but I am not unsympathetic to the value of fable in casting light upon Phil's spirit and character. My biographical approach must be, then, to provide alternative or clarifying accounts when I can, and for the rest, to let the reader (who may have some personal familiarity with the emotional magnifications—and deletions—of memory) beware and enjoy.

Second, let me confess that in this narrative I am arguing on behalf both of a life that I believe to have been remarkable and of a unique body of literary work that has been unjustly neglected. Much of this neglect is due to Phil's SF-genre identification and his prolific (and, admittedly, highly uneven) output. There is, however, a more personal negative factor at work: the reputation Phil acquired, particularly within SF circles, of being—to state it unadornedly—a drug-addled nut.

Phil was fully aware of this reputation. Indeed, he actively fostered it on many occasions, particularly during the sixties, when weird excess was the fashion even for far more respectable types than SF writers. But in the last decade of his life he came—not without humor—to regret it. His novel *A Scanner Darkly* (1977), a coda to the most painful years of his life, is a vehement antidrug testament that contains, in his typical way, some of the most hilarious scenes he ever wrote. Such as when Charles Freck, Substance D (Death) addict, decides to end it all by downing an overdose of reds with an expensive bottle of 1971 Mondavi Cabernet Sauvignon. But Freck is burned by his dealer, who instead passes him a weird new psychedelic:

Instead of quietly suffocating, Charles Freck began to hallucinate. Well, he thought philosophically, this is the story of my life. Always ripped off. He had to face the fact—considering how many of the capsules he had swallowed—that he was in for some trip.

The next thing he knew, a creature from between dimensions was standing beside his bed looking down at him disapprovingly.

The creature had many eyes, all over it, ultra-modern expensive-looking clothing, and rose up eight feet high. Also, it carried an enormous scroll.

"You're going to read me my sins," Charles Freck said.

The creature nodded and unsealed the scroll.

Freck said, lying helpless on his bed, "and it's going to take a hundred thousand hours."

Fixing its many compound eyes on him, the creature from between dimensions said, "We are no longer in the mundane universe. Lower-plane categories of material existence such as 'space' and 'time' no longer apply to you. You have been elevated to the transcendent realm. Your sins will be read to you ceaselessly, in shifts, throughout eternity. The list will never end."

Know your dealer, Charles Freck thought, and wished he could take back the last half-hour of his life. [. . .]

Ten thousand years later they had reached the sixth grade.

The year he had discovered masturbation.

He shut his eyes, but he could still see the multi-eyed, eight-foot-high being with its endless scroll reading on and on.

"And next—" it was saying.

Charles Freck thought, At least I got a good wine.

Despite *Scanner* (or perhaps because of its pervasive humor and love, for all its antidrug vehemence), the reputation persisted. In a January 1981 letter, Phil accurately appraised the damage: " 'He's crazy,' will be the response. Took drugs, saw God. BFD [big fucking deal]."

Phil was surely not crazy by any standard that I would dare apply. For what it's worth, I have interviewed a psychiatrist and a psychologist who saw Phil during two of the most difficult periods of his life, and both declare him to have been as fully sane as the rest of us. In addition, it sticks in the craw to indulge in psychological name-calling in the case of a productive and disciplined artist who demonstrated an intelligence and imagination well beyond those of any of his detractors.

Phil's emotional and behavioral difficulties were, at times, extremely severe—causing considerable pain and suffering to himself and to others—and led him to write, at times, of his "three nervous breakdowns" and to level against himself diagnoses of "schizophrenia" and "psychosis." (On other occasions, he would vehemently deny that such terms had any bearing upon his life.) Phil's inner life was unremittingly intense. Perhaps he utilized extreme psychological terms to lend maximum drama to the forces that fueled him as a writer. Perhaps he said simply and directly what he believed, at certain times, to be the truth.

I am left with this compromise: to quote him faithfully, to acknowledge and probe the painful difficulties, but also to avoid, at all times, passing judgment on the basis of a simplistic and patronizing sane/insane dualism that would make a mockery of Phil's artistic and spiritual vision, and an ass of his biographer.

Finally, a note on the organization of the book. The sheer bulk of Phil's work—over forty novels and two hundred stories—makes detailed examination of the whole a practical impossibility. I have therefore focused, in the main narrative, on only the best of the stories and on those eleven novels—*Eye in the Sky* (1957), *Time Out of Joint* (1959), *Confessions of a Crap Artist* (w. 1959, p. 1975), *The Man in the High*

9

Castle (1962), *Martian Time-Slip* (1964), *The Three Stigmata of Palmer Eldritch* (1965), *Ubik* (1969), *Flow My Tears, The Policeman Said* (1974), *A Scanner Darkly* (1977), *Valis* (1981), and *The Transmigration of Timothy Archer* (1982)—that are most exemplary of his themes. In addition, in the Chronological Survey I provide (in capsule review form) a guide to Phil's entire *oeuvre* in order of composition, affording the interested reader a tour of the themes weaving through the whole.

◆

And now, returning to the quote of Phil's that opens this Introduction, let us—with every effort at retaining an objectivity Phil's own novels call into question—proceed to imagine the life of a writer "free and glad to write about an infinity of worlds."

Beginning, of course, with that "actual boyhood world" the power of which Phil sought to deny.

1 *This Mortal Coil (December 1928–January 1929)*

I can only be safe when sheltered by a woman. Why? Safe against what? What enemies, dangers? It is that I fear I will simply die. My breath, my heart will stop. I will expire like an exposed baby. Jane, it happened to you and I am still afraid it will happen to me. They can't protect us. . . .

PHIL, journal entry, c. 1971

"Now here's a number for Phil and Jane. . . ."

Car radio in A *Scanner Darkly* (1977)

PHILIP Kindred Dick and his fraternal-twin sister, Jane Charlotte, were born six weeks prematurely, on December 16, 1928.

As was typical for her time, their mother, Dorothy, had no idea she was carrying twins. She and their father, Edgar, had just moved from Washington, D.C., to Chicago to accommodate Edgar's transfer within the U.S. Department of Agriculture. The birthing took place in their new apartment at 7812 Emerald Avenue. It was the dead of a very cold winter. The attending physician, chosen by Dorothy, was a doctor who lived down the street.

Phil was born at noon, twenty minutes ahead of his sister. Edgar, who had attended at many farmyard animal births, wiped the mucus from the babies' faces. They were frail things. Phil weighed four and one-quarter pounds and squawled loudly. Jane, a mere three and one-half pounds, was quieter and darker than her blond-haired brother.

Dorothy, tall and gaunt, could hear the babies' cries but did not have enough milk for twins. Edgar kept busy at work and, in off hours, drew Dorothy's ire by joining a men's club to escape the domestic upheaval. But escape there was none: The twins grew more sickly by the day.

Nearly five decades later, in an August 1975 letter to Phil, Dorothy recalled the mounting horror of that winter:

> For the first six weeks of your life, you were both starving to death because the (incompetent) doctor I had could not find the right formula for your food and

11

because I was so ignorant I did not know how desperate your condition was. I did know things weren't right, but I didn't know how to get other help.

At the turn of New Year's 1929, Dorothy's mother, Edna Matilda Archer Kindred (known as Meemaw), came from Colorado to help the new parents. Meemaw was wonderful with young children, having raised three of her own, but the difficulties posed by two-week-old premature twins were unfamiliar and frightening to her. And then Dorothy, while attempting to warm the crib, accidentally burned Jane's leg with a hot-water bottle.

They learned, by chance, of a life insurance policy for the children that would cover the costs of an immediate home visit by a nurse. Dorothy's August 1975 letter to Phil continues:

She came with a doctor in a taxi, with a heated crib, and the doctor said at once that Jane would have to be taken to the hospital. Then she asked to see "the other baby." I went to get you. Meemaw snatched you up and ran in the bathroom and locked the door; it was a while before we could persuade her to open the door. The doctor and nurse left with both babies; Jane died on the way to the hospital; you were put into the incubator and given a special formula [. . .] You were within a day or so of death, but you began to gain at once, and when you weighed 5 pounds I was able to take you home. I could visit you every day in the incubator, and during the periods I was there I was given instruction in making up the very complicated formula.

Dorothy's letter is a self-termed *"mea culpa"* for maternal sins that Phil could not forget and would not forgive. The greatest of these sins, in Phil's view, was her negligence, or worse, leading to Jane's death on January 26, 1929.

When Phil was still very young, Dorothy tried to explain to him what had happened. Twin sister Jane, of whom Phil had no conscious memory, took vivid life within the boy by way of these explanations. Always they were colored by the anguish that shows through in her letter: It wasn't lack of love but ignorance, horrible ignorance, she hadn't been around little babies much, didn't know Phil and his little twin sister were starving away. Three decades later, Phil would confide to his third wife, Anne, that "I heard about Jane a lot and it wasn't good for me. I felt guilty—somehow I got all the milk."

The trauma of Jane's death remained the central event of Phil's psychic life. The torment extended throughout his life, manifesting itself in difficult relations with women and a fascination with resolving dualist (twin-poled) dilemmas—SF/mainstream, real/fake, human/android, and at last (in as near an integration of intellect and emotion as Phil ever achieved) in the two-source cosmology described in his masterwork *Valis* (1981).

Jane's death shadowed, and ultimately shattered, the newly created family of three. The marriage of Edgar and Dorothy—at one time the seemingly perfect couple, each tall, slender, and with sharp, intelligent features—would not long survive. And the divorce would take Phil's father away.

◆

Joseph Edgar Dick was born in 1899, the second oldest of fourteen brothers and sisters in a Scotch-Irish family. He spent his first sixteen years on two different small farms in southwestern Pennsylvania. In 1969, when he was seventy, Edgar wrote an autobiographical reminiscence, *As I Remember Them*, which includes careful character studies of his parents.

Edgar clearly preferred the warmth of his mother, Bessie, to the hard lessons of his father, William, who once whipped Edgar and fellow siblings for mimicking the way he gargled to treat a cold. Of Bessie, Edgar wrote like a son in love: "She would cry and laugh at the same time, just like an April shower when the sun was shining." Bessie's love for animals became a guiding principle for Edgar—after World War II, as a lobbyist in the California legislature, he would sponsor important animal protection legislation.

Did the young Phil hear, through Edgar, rhapsodic tales of this ideal mother who through the hard times managed to keep her many children healthy and well fed? Bessie's influence can be seen in the ideals of motherhood that Edgar and Phil shared, and in their judgment of Dorothy as falling short of them.

From his father, Edgar received the American work ethic tinged with fear and hellfire. The Bible according to William taught that it was a sin not only to be lazy but also to be poor, like the neighboring coal-mining families. But Edgar outgrew any belief in hell, and he never cared for the churches that spread fear of damnation while doing nothing for the needy in their midst.

Discomfort with religious institutions, the exaltation of simple human kindness over the uncaring functionary—these impulses, fundamentals of identity, Edgar passed on to his son. And something more.

There is, in the midst of Edgar's settled narrative, a single sentence that mirrors the worlds of Phil's SF novels—novels that Edgar never much cared for. "We had a difficult time," he recalls, "learning to know and understand the strange actions of creatures called people." You can see it in the struggles Edgar had with the church—with the world as it was, compared to the world insisted upon by his father. A sense of strangeness. Nothing could be assumed. Reality had to be eyed carefully.

Edgar enlisted shortly after America entered the war in 1916. The previous year the family had moved from Pennsylvania to homestead dusty government land at Cedarwood, Colorado. At seventeen, Edgar was fed up with farm chores and eager to see the world. Just before going off to Europe, he met Dorothy Kindred, from the nearby town of Greeley. There was a spark of sorts, but Edgar and Dorothy didn't correspond during the war. "You kind of got away from civilian life entirely," he later said. "I did."

Edgar described himself in Europe as "a corporal like Napoleon and Hitler." He showed considerable heroism carrying messages by night within range of the front lines. His Fifth Marines were the shock troops, Edgar recalled proudly, and he had marvelous stories to tell. Though he conscientiously avoided gore, he showed young Phil his military souvenirs: his uniform and gas mask, sundry photographs. These stories, reinforced by Edgar's taking him to the 1931 film *All Quiet on the Western Front*, struck Phil deeply:

> [Edgar] told me how the soldiers became panicstricken during gas attacks as the charcoal in their filtration systems became saturated, and how sometimes a soldier would freak and tear off his mask and run. As a child I felt a lot of anxiety listening to my father's war stories and looking at and playing with the gasmask and helmet; but what scared me the most was when my father would put on the gasmask. His face would disappear. This was not my father any longer. This was not a human being at all.

Edgar returned to Colorado after demobbing in 1918, and he and Dorothy renewed their courtship. Dorothy was the middle child of three in a family of English descent. (As an adult, Phil would sometimes claim to be one-quarter German, due to his love for German opera and poetry, but Scotch-Irish-English is his lineage.) Earl Grant Kindred, Dorothy's father, was a lawyer whose financial fortunes fluctuated wildly. Earl's boom-or-bust economics could trigger drastic consequences for his children; in two different downswings he had their pets shot to save on feed money.

Edna Matilda Archer—the Meemaw who hid with baby Phil in the bathroom when the nurse came to visit—married Earl in 1892. Dorothy was born in 1899. When Dorothy was in her early teens, Earl announced that to make his fortune he would have to travel. What it boiled down to was walking out on his family. When he did circle back now and then, Meemaw took him in gladly, which disgusted Dorothy. When Earl was gone, Meemaw and Dorothy's younger sister, Marion, looked to Dorothy for support, both psychological and economic. Harold, her older brother, who was considered the wild one in the family, ran away at this time. At fifteen she went to work. A year later she met Edgar, and while he was off to war Dorothy grappled with a family in disarray. Throughout her life Dorothy would rue how she constantly found herself having to take care of people.

Edgar was likely a welcome source of support when he came home from the war. They married in September 1920, then moved to Washington, D.C. After graduating from Georgetown University in 1927, Edgar took a livestock inspection job with the Department of Agriculture. During this time, Dorothy's health began to deteriorate badly. Just after the move, she had come down with typhoid fever. Then came the onset of Bright's disease. One doctor told her she hadn't long to live. Dorothy survived to age seventy-nine, but suffered from kidney problems for the rest of her life. Later years brought on circulatory ailments and a consciousness of illness that some found obsessive or hypochondriacal (complaints Phil did not raise against her, perhaps because too often he found himself fending off similar charges).

The Department offered Edgar a post in Chicago, and, though both he and Dorothy hated Chicago winters, he took it. It was an advancement of sorts, and with Dorothy expecting, it seemed time to build for the future.

◆

It is common medical knowledge today, as it was not in 1928, that of all the risks posed by a multiple pregnancy, premature birth is the leading cause of death of one or both twins. Psychological studies made in the past decade have further confirmed that, for parents and the surviving sibling alike, the death of a twin is a trauma with unique dimensions.

For the parents, the grief, guilt, and anger may be intensified due to the emotional magnitude of giving birth to twins. Researcher Elizabeth Bryan notes that society treats the birth of twins as a "special event," and cites findings that "a prolonged or abnormal grief reaction was more common amongst those mothers who had a single surviving twin than amongst those who had lost their only baby." Part of the anguish lies in "the difficulty of mourning a death and celebrating a birth at the same time." Overprotective fears can arise with respect to caring for the surviving twin. And there may be resentment, conscious or not, in the feelings of the parents toward the surviving child.

What is known of Edgar and Dorothy's reactions to Jane's death does correlate with these findings.

In Edgar's case, overprotectiveness showed in what Dorothy called his "germ phobias." He forbade Dorothy to kiss the baby or to allow him to crawl outside of his crib for his first eleven months. Dorothy sought to evade the first prohibition by kissing Phil "in places I thought I couldn't contaminate, like the back of the neck." She managed to obtain crawling freedom for Phil by agreeing to Edgar's condition that it be limited to an hour in the morning and an hour in the afternoon—if the entire apartment was first thoroughly vacuumed.

In Dorothy's case, the grief reaction was pronounced. In the first months of Phil's life, she kept a journal on his growth and behavior that

15

testifies to her love for the baby and nowhere focuses upon the death of the twin. But Dorothy's enduring anguish showed clearly in letters and conversations over the years dwelling on Jane's death and her role in it.

The relationship between Phil and his mother, in its painful duality of extreme, dependent closeness and rage over errors and omissions in loving, was mirrored in every love relationship Phil ever had with a woman. Those who saw Phil and Dorothy together were often struck by the degree of resemblance between them—both were at home in self-fashioned systems of abstract thought, both read voraciously and felt the writer's vocation (though Dorothy failed at her efforts at a writer's career). Throughout his life Phil turned to her for money, advice, even critical response to his manuscripts, and Dorothy never faltered in her encouragement of Phil the artist.

But Dorothy was a difficult mother for Phil to bear: physically undemonstrative, emotionally constrained, watchful and reproving, forbidding all demonstrations of anger, weak from pain and often bed-ridden. She gave Phil, as he grew, a respectful individual freedom, treating him like a little adult (by his early teenage years he called her "Dorothy"), yet somehow—in Phil's sense of things—she withheld approval, warmth, maternal affection, and protection from the world.

She was incapable of loving her children, Phil believed. She had proved that by letting Jane die. Later in life he accused Dorothy of having tried to poison him and so complete the destruction of her children.

Studies of surviving twins point to a sense of incompleteness that can make relationships, particularly with the opposite sex, very difficult. There is also the guilt of having survived, and a fear of death that causes the survivors to be overly concerned with health and safety or, paradoxically, to place themselves in difficult situations. These are all generalities that could be applied to Phil (including, of course, *both* of the paradoxical choices). What the studies fail to touch upon is the possibility of dwelling upon how it could have been different—to the point of sheer rage.

Cut to: Phil on the couch during a November 1974 interview with writer Paul Williams for *Rolling Stone:*

PKD: Yes. I get very mad when I think about my dead sister.
PW: Really?
PKD: That she died of neglect and starvation. Injury, neglect and starvation.
PW: How do you know?
PKD: My mother told me. I get very hostile when I think of it. [. . .] 'Cause I was a very lonely child, and I would love to have had my sister with me, all these years. But my mother says, "Well, it's just as well she died, she would have been lame anyway, from being burned by us with the hot-water bottle." In which case I suppose— It's like Heinrich Himmler saying, "Well

16

. . . she made a good lampshade, you know, so I guess it worked out all right."
You see what I mean?

In his grade school years, Phil invented an imaginary playmate—a girl named "Teddy" (according to fifth wife Tessa) or "Becky" (according to third wife Anne)—or perhaps there were two, or more. He played with them because he knew of Jane and yearned for her to be there, and if that seems strange—how could what happened at his birth affect him so?—it can be corroborated by the testimony of anyone who has lost a twin. It is a bond that causes nontwins to be skeptical because it is, in truth, a bond beyond the telling.

Jane's death was a tragic affair, which neither Dorothy nor Edgar intended and from which both suffered. The facts as known do not serve to explain Phil's exclusive focus on Dorothy as the guilty party, if guilty party there must (for Phil) be. His feelings toward Edgar were attenuated—even resentful—for most of Phil's life. But he placed the responsibility for practical *nurture* upon women. It was only the love of a woman that could quell Phil's fears and, more basically, render the world safe and *real*. Dorothy failed to provide such a love, as would, ultimately and perhaps inevitably, every woman in Phil's life. In a 1975 *Exegesis* entry he wrote:

I think I fear that death is something one allows to happen more than it being something one does, i.e. one does not kill but fails to provide life. Thus I must think that life comes to one (to me) from outside, a child's view; I am not yet on homeostasis, on intrinsic. Of course, life originally comes from the mother; but this symbiosis ends. After that, life is sustained from God, not through any woman. Tessa is right; I am still a child.

This bitter "symbiosis" with the female must continue throughout his life, drawing Phil at times to the verge of suicide. Again from a 1975 *Exegesis* entry:

[I]t is Jane-in-me-now, the anima or female principle, which is the lachrymose side, which is ailing and now seeks hospitalization [. . . .] It is Jane trying to die. Or rather, it is a rerun of Jane who actually died, the steps repeated by my anima again and again, that fatal trip due to negligence. It is Jane-in-me who is afraid now and depressed. But if Jane-in-me dies, she will carry me (the male twin) with her, so I must not succumb. [. . .] Jane must live on a vestigial existence in me on this side, but be beyond on the other side. [. . .]

The obsession, found in twins, with dualities—as complementary and conflicting at once—has been termed *twinning* by Dr. George Engel ("The drive is always to be two, yet unique from all others"). This "twinning" motif found expression in a number of Phil's stories and

17

novels, notably *Dr. Bloodmoney* (1965), *Flow My Tears, The Policeman Said* (1974), *A Scanner Darkly* (1977), *Valis* (1981), and *The Divine Invasion* (1981).

In *Dr. Bloodmoney* there is a fictionalized depiction of Jane's ongoing "vestigial experience" as Phil felt it inside him. The novel is set in the post–nuclear holocaust world of 1981. The story focuses on the survival efforts of a small population living in rural Marin County. The effects of radioactive mutation are omnipresent, and that is how Edie Keller's condition is explained for purposes of the plot.

Seven-year-old Edie actually carries within her (in her left side, near the appendix) a twin brother named Bill. "Someday the girl would die and they would open her body, perform an autopsy; they would find a little wrinkled male figure, perhaps with a snowy white beard and blind eyes . . . her brother, still no larger than a baby rabbit." Bill talks to Edie through an inner voice that only she can hear. But Bill wants to be able to see, to move about; the summaries of reality provided him by Edie will no longer do:

> "I wish I could come out," Bill said plaintively. "I wish I could be born like everybody else. Can't I be born later on?"
> "Doctor Stockstill said you couldn't."
> "Then can't he make it so I could be? I thought you said—"
> "I was wrong," Edie said. "I thought he could cut a little round hole and that would do it, but he said no."
> Her brother, deep within her, was silent, then.

Edie and Bill are triumphs of Phil's art of characterization. They are believably wayward, willful children whose love and fierce loyalty for each other are mingled with casual cruelty. Bill possesses the ability to project his soul into any living creature held near him; Edie tricks him, at one point, by making blind Bill project into a blind worm. In one scene, brother and sister discuss, in a perfectly rendered childlike tone, the karmic cycle of existence. Bill possesses the strange power to talk with the dead—he can imitate their voices perfectly. Edie grows curious:

> "Do me," Edie said. "Imitate me."
> "How can I?" Bill said. "You're not dead yet."
> Edie said, "What's it like to be dead? I'm going to be someday so I want to know."
> "It's funny. You're down in a hole looking up. And you're all flat like— well, like you're empty. And, you know what? Then after a while you come back. You blow away and where you get blown away to is back again! Did you know that? I mean, back where you are right now. All fat and alive."

The fictional twins in *Dr. Bloodmoney* vividly embody the bonds and conflicts that Phil felt by virtue of his ongoing psychic contacts with Jane.

18

The struggle with his twin lay at the root of his fiction and of his determination to probe the nature of reality. In the *Exegesis*, near the end of his life, Phil wrote:

She (Jane) fights for my life & I for hers, eternally

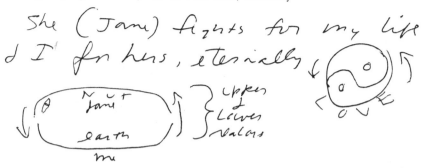

My sister is *everything* to me. I am damned always to be separated from her/& with her, in an oscillation. Very fast. Both: I have her in me, and often outside me, but I have lost her; 2 realities at once yin/yang.

Two realities, out of which, as from rich loam, the multiverses of the stories, the novels, and the *Exegesis* blossomed. But always the loss of Jane hovered in Phil's soul. That loss is at the heart of the difficulties—the toppling, twisting universes, death-dealing wives, desperate loves—that his fictional characters must always overcome.

And toward the end of his life, Phil's yearning for his twin—melded with the events of 2-3-74—became the basis for a divine cosmogony that attempts to explain the despair and persistent hope that mark our lives. In the "Tractates Cryptica Scriptura" that concludes *Valis*, Passage No. 32 reads:

The changing information which we experience as world is an unfolding narrative. It tells about the death of a woman. This woman, who died long ago, was one of the primordial twins. She was half of the divine syzygy. The purpose of the narrative is the recollection of her and of her death. The Mind does not wish to forget her. Thus the ratiocination of the Brain consists of a permanent record of her existence, and, if read, will be understood that way. All the information processed by the Brain—experienced by us as the arranging and rearranging of physical objects—is an attempt at this preservation of her; stones and rocks and sticks and amoebae are traces of her. The record of her existence and passing is ordered onto the meanest level of reality by the suffering Mind which is now alone.

2 Coming Of Age And The Onset Of Vertigo (1929–1944)

I suppose that you can see by [my] letters that I am very changeable, but I can't help it. Sometimes I am sure I want to go home, sometimes I am doubtful, sometimes I am sure that I want to stay. I just don't know what to do, but I'm not doing anything for a while.

PHIL, age thirteen, letter to Dorothy from the California Preparatory School, Ojai, California, November 1942

The pre-schizoid personality is generally called "schizoid effective," which means that as an adolescent he still hopes that he won't have to ask the cute chick (or boy) in the next row for a date. Speaking in terms of my own schizoid effective experience, one gazes at her for a year or so, mentally detailing all possible outcomes; the good ones go under the rubric "daydreams," the bad ones under "phobia." [. . .] If the phobias win out (Suppose I ask her and she says "with you?" etc.), then the schizoid effective kid physically bolts from the classroom with agoraphobia that gradually widens into true schizophrenic avoidance of all human contact, or withdraws into phantasy, becomes, so to speak, his own Abe Merritt [popular SF/fantasy writer of the twenties]—or, if things go further wrong, his own H. P. Lovecraft.

PHIL, 1965 essay "Schizophrenia & The Book of Changes"

JANE'S body was transported to Colorado, where Edgar's family conducted a graveside funeral service in the Fort Morgan cemetery.

When Phil returned from the hospital, the family hired a wet nurse and he recovered rapidly. Nonetheless, as winter abated, Dorothy and Edgar were in full agreement that Chicago was not for them.

That summer they took a vacation trip to Colorado to visit their families. When Edgar returned to his job, Dorothy stayed on with Phil in Johnstown, Colorado. She was delighted that by the age of eight months Phil was already using words like "g'acious," his rendering of Dorothy's favorite exclamation. She conscientiously applied the favored behaviorist theories of the time to combat Phil's thumb sucking. These theories,

20

coupled with Edgar's germ phobias, still further limited her own physical contact with the baby, much to Dorothy's later regret:

The idea was that the infant was a healthy animal that should be cared for physically and left alone. [. . .] Cuddling, rocking, kissing were frowned on. [. . .] Pediatricians made an ignorant young mother feel that to violate any of the rules would cause irreparable damage to the child. [. . .]

Added to that really important prevailing thought about infant care was my own nature: I had been brought up in an undemonstrative household among people who kissed members of the family only on departing and returning from a trip. At least, that was the way I was treated. I do remember when I was seven and up, watching Mother kiss, rock, and cuddle Marion and call her pet names; and I remember wishing she would just once call *me* sweetheart or hug me.

In late 1929, a livestock market news service position opened up in the Department of Agriculture's San Francisco office, and Edgar jumped at the chance. The family moved to the Bay Area—first Sausalito, where they stayed with Meemaw and Marion, and then the Peninsula and Alameda before finally, in 1931, settling in Berkeley. There Phil attended the Bruce Tatlock School, an experimental nursery school.

Phil was a leader among his schoolmates. He also took to chatting with their parents on the school phone. At play Phil was a proud child who, if he fell down and hurt himself, would cry behind a tree rather than out in the open. Records for the 1931 summer session provide this portrait of Phil at age two:

Philip is a very friendly and happy youngster. [. . .] He is a lover of peace and often steps aside rather than have an argument. This is a very natural, normal behavior and should cause no concern, for when Philip feels his rights have been encroached upon he is very capable of protecting them. [. . .] He talks remarkably well for his years, has an intellectual curiosity and a keen interest in everything about him. He cooperates well with both children and adults and is, withal, a splendidly adjusted child.

You can't do much better than that in nursery school. Indeed, it was the apex of Phil's academic life. The report lends credibility to Edgar's gushing boast that back then Phil was "the most handsome little fellow I ever saw in my life. He just bubbled with life." But as relations between Edgar and Dorothy grew strained, the "splendidly adjusted child" took on new complexities. A Mental Test Report compiled when Phil was four rated him "Definitely Above" average in intelligence. The accompanying "Comments" show that the child had become father to the man— conceptually adept and fluid, emotionally wayward and yearning:

21

His highest scores are for memory, language and tests in manual coordination. His reactions are quickly displayed, and just as quickly reversed. His independent initiative and executive ability are shown in rapidly varying techniques which are frequently replaced with strongly contrasting dependence. It might be well to guard against the development of this degree of versatility at his age by encouraging the frequent repetition of very simple situations which demand uniformity of behavior on the part of any or all participants.

If anyone did, in fact, attempt to discourage Phil's "degree of versatility," they failed resoundingly. Instead, the tensions between Edgar and Dorothy—which would lead shortly to divorce—encouraged the boy to develop "versatile" strategies to retain the love of each. Phil's strategies for seeking out affection were not confined to the home. Forbidden by his parents to cross the street during his playtime, he would walk around the block, getting to know the elderly neighbors, who would make him little toys that he brought back proudly to the house. Edgar recalled this as exemplifying Phil the "promoter."

But Phil's consuming playtime passion was the all-American choice: cowboys. His parents bought him a complete cowboy outfit: hat, vest, chaps, holster, gun, and boots. They must have made mention by this time, in some manner, of Jane's death, for Tessa Dick, Phil's fifth wife, relates that during his cowboy games

> [Phil] used to pretend he had a sister named Jane, and she was a cowgirl. He would dress up in his cowboy suit and "ride horses" with Jane. Jane was small, with dark eyes and long dark hair. She was also very gutsy, always daring Phil to do things he was afraid of, helping him to get into trouble.

Bear in mind this description of cowgirl Jane. It embodies the look and character of the "dark-haired girl"—Phil's anima and obsession—that guided him persistently in his choice of wives and lovers and in his depiction of the ambiguous (fiercely brave/waywardly evil) heroines that appear in so many of his novels.

Neither Edgar nor Dorothy regarded themselves as religious, but they did send Phil to Sunday school for a time. Phil's stubborn insistence on understanding just what was being said, even in that pious setting, gratified his father. Edgar recalled that during a group sing Phil "got out of his seat and walked up and asked for a psalm book. He said he couldn't sing unless he had a book. Right in the church . . . it shows how natural he was."

Formal religion was not important to Phil in his boyhood. But one incident—an act of spontaneous kindness, and of faith—stayed with him always. While out for a walk with his parents, they met a "great bearded white-haired old beggar." Edgar gave four-year-old Phil a nickel to give to the poor man, who in turn pressed upon the boy "a little pamphlet about God." In the Prologue to *Radio Free Albemuth* (written in 1976), Phil retold this incident with the intent of identifying this beggar with the prophet Elijah.

As to more everyday questions of right and wrong, Edgar prided himself on dealing with Phil on an "adult" basis. "If I scolded Philip, he'd analyze it and come back and tell me. We'd talk it over. I'd admit it when I was wrong." Phil was "irritable" as a boy, and Edgar felt that his calm approach—as opposed to Dorothy's stricter style—gave the boy "a little lift." Between Phil and his father grew a conspiratorial bond against the mother. Even before the divorce, Edgar feared that Dorothy was some-how seeking to exclude him from Phil's upbringing, so he fought back by courting the boy with movies and trips to the country. When Dorothy would come along on trips, Phil would lock the car doors and urge his father to drive off before she could get in. And there were strictly father-son events—such as trips to nearby ranches that Edgar knew through his work—that promised, and sometimes delivered, adventure.

Edgar was afraid of rattlesnakes and taught Phil how to recognize them. One day they visited a friend of Edgar's with a pet bull snake that slept on the open front porch. While the adults were talking inside, Phil came in to announce a "jingle snake on porch." Assured that it was a bull snake, Phil kept to his story. At last the two men checked—and found a thirteen-rattler, the largest ever seen in that area, which they killed. On another nearby ranch, Edgar had noticed rabbits kept in an exposed cage without food or water. One Sunday, while the ranch owners were off at church, he and Phil freed the rabbits. Of their own volition, the rabbits returned to their cage. Undaunted, the two engineered a second great escape, this time transporting the rabbits by car twenty miles away.

But Edgar failed flat out in his attempt to win Phil over to football. Unlike Edgar in his youth, Phil was not an active boy. Together they attended a U Cal football game when Phil was about six (the divorce was final by this time). Recalled Edgar: "That was a show in itself, him [Phil] seeing those people running and chasing each other. He thought they were chasing each other and it was hard for him to see why in the world they were doing things like that."

Underlying the affection between father and son was a persistent ambivalence in both. Edgar saw Phil as "physically lazy" and perhaps resented his son's status as Dorothy's possession. Phil was often sick—he had asthma attacks throughout his childhood—and, for the most part, Edgar left the health concerns of the child to his mother. "Dorothy took great care of Philip, though she was too involved with Phil's glasses and his teeth and various medicines," Edgar recalled. Among Phil's medi-cines was aphedrine (an amphetamine) in pill form, which he took for the asthma.

Phil's own ambivalence is manifest in a much-anthologized 1954 short story, "The Father-thing." The basic plot: A young boy, Charles, discovers that his father, Ted (Edgar's familiar name), has been killed and replaced by a malignant alien life form:

> He was a good-looking man in his early thirties: thick blond hair, strong arms, competent hands, square face and flashing brown eyes. [. . .]
> Ted jerked. A strange expression flitted across his face. It vanished at once; but in the brief instant Ted Walton's face lost all familiarity. Something alien and cold gleamed out, a twisting, wriggling mass. The eyes blurred and receded, as an archaic sheen filmed over them. The ordinary look of a tired, middle-aged husband was gone.

The new Ted—unlike Edgar with his alleged "adult" approach to child discipline—has no qualms about spanking young boys who are overly quizzical of apparent reality. Phil later wrote of "The Father-thing": "I always had the impression, when I was very small, that my father was two people, one good, one bad. The good father goes away and the bad father replaces him. I guess many kids have this feeling. What if it were so?"

One strange aspect of the story is Charles's composure: After a brief cry, the eight-year-old becomes a methodical avenger. The "good" father is innocent of the deeds of the "bad" alien impostor—a device that not only skirts anger (implicit in the killing of the alien) but also parallels the Gnostic view that our world is created by an evil demiurge—and not by the benign supreme deity who has cosmically absconded. Phil's adult fascination with Gnosticism may have stemmed in part from a need to make intellectual sense of the enduring pain caused by Edgar's flashes of anger and his all but total departure (absconding) from Phil's life.

Edgar and Dorothy were divorced in 1933, at the height of the Depression. The National Recovery Administration had asked Edgar to open an office in Reno, Nevada. Dorothy refused to move and consulted a psychiatrist, who assured her that divorce would not have a detrimental effect upon Phil. The psychiatrist was dead wrong: To Phil it felt as if his father had abandoned him, and the scar endured. As for Edgar, his first response was incomprehension. "It came out of the clear blue sky," he recalled fifty years later.

What finally drove the couple apart? Lynne Cecil, later Dorothy's stepdaughter, observes: "Part of the problem was that as Dorothy grew up she just 'matured away.' But the main reason was that Edgar was extremely jealous. She couldn't stand it—he would be jealous if somebody looked at her." At this time, Dorothy was slender, with shoulder-length brown hair and features resembling those of the cinema's reigning beauty, Greta Garbo. But Phil never spoke of Dorothy's having lovers during his childhood and adolescence, or even of any polite courtships.

The freedom Dorothy craved was not sexual but psychological: autonomy, the right to raise her son by her own lights.

After their separation, Dorothy moved into a Berkeley apartment with Meemaw (again on hand in time of crisis) and Marion. For a year, Edgar would pay regular visits there to see Phil. But then the battle for control over their son broke out in full force. In 1934, Edgar threatened to seek sole custody of Phil on the grounds, as Dorothy explained it, "that he was better off financially and could 'do more' for you. When I refused to give you up he wrote that he would forget you, then, and wanted nothing more to do with either of us. [. . .] I made a colossal mistake, taking the advice of a psychiatrist who told me to let you forget your father, never to mention him at all, to ignore his existence."

Dorothy had her reasons for fearing Edgar's legal threats. With a newly found secretarial job, she could barely provide an adequate livelihood for the new household; of necessity, Meemaw took over full-time care of Phil. Dorothy saw that Meemaw "supplied the kissing and cuddling, the indulgence, and the cookies that I withheld." Tessa Dick relates that "When Phil got into trouble, she [Meemaw] would shake her head and say, 'Oh, Philip,' very quietly. That used to have more effect on Phil than all his mother's scolding."

But there was a darker side to the new living arrangement. Meemaw's husband, Earl, had, at this time, circled back to his wife to stay (he died three years later, in 1937). Phil recalled him as "a big man with flaming red hair" who "used to go around the house, waving his belt and saying, 'I'm going to whip that boy.'" During or shortly after his stay in Earl and Meemaw's home, Phil developed severe swallowing difficulties. Barry Spatz, a psychologist who worked with Phil in the late seventies and early eighties, speculates in interview that those symptoms may have been induced by physical abuse or sexual molestation on Earl's part. Phil drew a blank when asked by Spatz, during therapy, if he could recall such incidents.

Spatz points out that Phil's life history shows tendencies characteristic of child incest victims, such as difficult relations with family; drug abuse; repeated suicide attempts; significant memory gaps; low self-esteem accompanied by guilt; a chaotic, crisis-oriented lifestyle; and pervasive mistrust, especially toward the opposite sex, alternating with strong attachments. These are certainly descriptive of aspects of Phil's life that will be detailed in this book. But such tendencies can and do manifest themselves in persons who have not suffered from abuse.

The evidence simply does not allow for certainty. Almost forty years later, in 1964, Phil broached the subject with his third wife, Anne, during the worst of their marital difficulties:

[O]ne day, just before going to church, Phil said he had something very serious to tell me; something that would explain why he couldn't function properly in life. [. . .] He could function just fine. Why did he have to go on as if he couldn't? [. . .] Phil told me, "When I was quite small I was molested by a homosexual neighbor. This is what has made me so inadequate." I told him he should tell this to his psychotherapist.

In this version, a neighbor—not Earl—is the abuser. Was it a ploy for sympathy, as Anne took it at the time? Why didn't Phil tell Spatz about it during their lengthy sessions? To Tessa Dick, Phil recalled being sent, at age six, to a psychiatrist who suggested that his problems had to do with homosexuality. Tessa states that at one of the boarding schools Phil attended (Countryside in 1935, or Ojai in 1942–43) there was a molestation incident that worried Dorothy. But Phil was not personally involved.

Ultimately, one can do no more than to raise the possibility—and to duly note that eating and swallowing phobias remained with Phil, intermittently, throughout his life.

Whether or not molestation occurred, there can be no doubt that at that time Phil was beset by intense insecurity. He especially liked to play inside boxes and cartons, enjoying the sense of safety they provided. This foreshadows the agoraphobia that would emerge in Phil's high school years. It also parallels the yearnings of Mike Foster, the boy in Phil's excellent 1955 story "Foster, You're Dead." (Edgar had an infant brother, Foster, who died at age one.) In this story, Phil modified the anxieties of his own childhood to render an intensely believable portrait of a boy who is shaken to his soul by the psychological terrors of the cold war.

Mike Foster lives in a world (Phil's own fifties recast in an SF "future") in which every child is taught to expect imminent nuclear attack. When Mike's father scrapes up the money to buy a heavily advertised bomb shelter, Mike can feel safe at last:

He sat down on the floor, knees drawn up, face solemn, eyes wide. [. . .] He was in a little self-contained cosmos; everything needed was here—or would be here, soon: food, water, air, things to do. Nothing else was wanted. [. . .]

Suddenly he shouted, a loud jubilant shout that echoed and bounced from wall to wall. He was deafened by the reverberation. He shut his eyes tight and clenched his fists. Joy filled him.

In early 1935, spurred by a desire to escape Edgar's custody threats, Dorothy moved with Phil back to Washington, D.C., and took an editorial job with the Federal Children's Bureau. For Phil, the separation from Meemaw was wrenching. Dorothy deplored that "you had at 4 the loss of your original mother because I went to work and at barely 6 the loss of the loving mother, Meemaw." But as a strategy to retain custody of Phil, the cross-continent move had its desired effect. Within two years, Edgar remarried. Dorothy remained single for eighteen years, though she confided on occasion that, had she known what poverty she and Phil would face, she would never have divorced Edgar.

Her editorial job with the Children's Bureau paid poorly. But she enjoyed the task of writing pamphlets on child care. In the sixties, Phil spotted one on a neighbor's bookshelf. "My mother wrote this book," Phil told her. "Ironic, isn't it, that she was a rotten mother and didn't like kids at all."

Dorothy enrolled Phil in the Countryside School in nearby Silver Spring, Maryland, which promised the "Newest methods and equipment in a charming home environment." Here he spent at least part of the 1935–36 year in first grade. (Phil would later describe it as a "Quaker" boarding school, an affiliation not stated in the school's brochure.) A "Self Portrait" written by Phil in 1968 gives this account of why Dorothy saw boarding school as necessary:

> In Washington, summer is a horror beyond the telling of it. I think it warped my mind—warped that in a fine conjunction of the fact that my mother and I had nowhere to live. We stayed with friends. Year in, year out. I did not do well (what seven-year-old child would?) and so I was sent to a school specializing in "disturbed" children. I was disturbed in regard to the fact that I was afraid of eating. The boarding school could not handle me because I weighed less each month, and was never seen to eat a string bean. My literary career, however, began to emerge, in the form of poetry. I wrote my first poem thus:
>
>> I saw a little birdy
>> Sitting in the tree.
>> I saw a little birdy
>> looking out at me.
>> Then the kitty saw the birdy and there wasn't none to see,
>> For the cat ate him up in the morning.
>
> This poem was enthusiastically received on Parent's Day, and my future was assured (although, of course, no one knew it. Not then, anyhow.)

That little poem already displays the humor and the edge that merge in Phil's finest fiction. But at this point, in the boy, the edge was dominant. He had lost Meemaw, his father, and his sister. He had nothing resembling a stable home, and now was forced to endure a strange new boarding school environment. Swallowing food was especially difficult for him in public places like the school cafeteria. Phil later attributed his eating difficulties at this time to "grief and loneliness."

Whether the above-quoted poem is actually Phil's first literary work is doubtful. Other poems (typed out and preserved by Dorothy) contend for the honor. A "Song of Philip—Five years old" (which places it in 1934, prior to the move to Washington) is remarkable for its subtle distinction between "God" and "spirit":

The spirit of God is a nice old man
Who lived when the days were young.
But when the prince comes riding by
God is nowhere to be seen.

God is the spirit of you and me
And when the God is gone you will see him no more
But the life of the spirit will go in the morning sun.

The poem attests to Phil's unusual independence of spirit—most children cling to God the "nice old man."

In two of his novels, *Puttering About in a Small Land* (written 1957, published 1985) and *Now Wait for Last Year* (written 1963–65 and published in 1966), Phil utilized the Washington, D.C., of his childhood as a significant setting. In *Now Wait*, the stress-ridden Virgil Ackerman, owner of the Tijuana Fur & Dye Corporation, has specially constructed a retreat called "Wash-35" (for Washington, D.C., 1935), which allows Ackerman to return to the world of his childhood. The "omphalos" of that world is 3039 McComb Street (Phil's address for most of his stay in the capital). Playing at the Uptown Theatre is *Hell's Angels* with Jean Harlow (with a negligee scene that jolted young Phil when first he saw it). Fondly remembered details abound in Wash-35, but the context in which they are placed—a "regressive babyland" designed to prop up the psyche of a war-profiteering industrialist—underscore Phil's disdain for a rosy-hued re-creation of his boyhood world.

Phil was deeply unhappy at the Countryside School, so for the 1936–37 school year Dorothy transferred him to the John Eaton School, part of the D.C. public school system. In addition, she hired a series of housekeepers who cared for the boy. A black woman named Lula remained in the household for two years. But Phil would often stand forlornly by the window, watching for the first glimpse of his mother returning home from work.

His feelings toward Dorothy at this point were necessarily complex. He blamed her for driving his father away and destroying the family. And Dorothy's efforts to ease the trauma of Jane's death were backfiring badly. Kleo Mini, Phil's second wife, recalls, "Phil said to me on several occasions that Dorothy had told him, as a child, that the wrong one had died. Now, she may or may not have actually said that—I find it hard to believe—but that *was* the feeling Phil got from her, whether she said it or not."

On a more immediate level, Phil resented Dorothy for packing him off to the Countryside School and then leaving him in the care of housekeepers. And when she *was* in the house, Phil found her a difficult mother to please. If he resorted to tantrums, she confined him to his bedroom—where he could vent his rage by tearing the place apart. But Phil was drawn to Dorothy's brilliance and composure. Later in life he would cite favorably her insistence on his accepting the consequences of his actions.

Their bond was intense, full of a feeling that the hateful denunciations of his later years cannot obscure. After all, Dorothy raised him after Edgar was gone. Phil would later avow: "I have a lot of faith in women. Perhaps because of that. My father was weak; my mother was strong." Dorothy taught him to "admire writing," while Edgar "viewed football games as transcending everything else."

But the conflict between them endured. Dorothy's own lack of writing success—she wrote copiously but published only a single piece in *Family Circle* magazine—must ultimately have provided Phil with a sense of achievement that Dorothy could not dispute. It was never enough. He wrestled tirelessly with her power.

Phil attended the John Eaton School from 1936 to 1938, for grades two through four. He was absent often, a pattern condoned by Dorothy. His report cards reflect good academic work on the whole, with one of his lowest marks, a C, coming in written composition. But a comment by his fourth-grade teacher was admirably prophetic: "Shows interest and ability in story telling."

One incident from Phil's third-grade year impressed the boy deeply. Indeed, one could say that by sheer empathic force it forged the soul of the writer-to-be, appearing in countless thematic guises in the stories and novels. Little boy Phil was tormenting a beetle that had hidden itself in a snail shell. But then, as Phil forced the beetle from its haven, the urge to cruelty subsided, replaced by the sense—the certainty!—that all life was one, and that all depends on kindness:

And he came out, and all of a sudden I realized—it was total satori, just infinite, that this beetle was like I was. There was an understanding. He wanted to live just like I was, and I was hurting him. For a moment—it was like Siddhartha does, was like that dead jackal in the ditch—I was that beetle. Immediately I was different. I was never the same again.

The satori was a window to a world Phil could not yet inhabit. The boy was drawn to things of the spirit, but not at the expense of the dazzling trashy lures of American pop culture. It would be Phil's achievement to forge a bridge between the two. But for now the child prevailed:

There then followed a long period in which I did nothing in particular except go to school—which I loathed—and fiddle with my stamp collection (which I still have), plus other boywise activities such as marbles, flipcards, bolobats, and the newly invented comic books, such as Tip Top Comics, King Comics and Popular Comics. My ten-cent allowance each week went first to candy (Necco wafers, chocolate bar and jujubes), and, after that, Tip Top Comics. Comic books were scorned by adults, who assumed and hoped they, as a literary medium, would soon disappear. They did not. And then there was the lurid section of the Hearst newspapers which on Sunday told of mummies still alive in caves, and lost Atlantis, and the Sargasso Sea. The American Weekly, this quasi-magazine was called. Today we would dismiss it as "pseudo-science," but in those days, the mid-thirties, it was quite convincing. I dreamed of finding the Sargasso Sea and all the ships tangled up there, their corpses dangling over the rails and their coffers filled with pirate gold. I realize now that I was doomed to failure by the very fact that the Sargasso Sea did not exist—or anyhow it did not capture many Spanish gold-bearing ships-of-the-line. So much for childhood dreams.

But one childhood dream remained, intensifying through the years. Comic books and *The American Weekly* were Phil's first introduction to wild pulp "pseudo-science" adventure. If the beetle satori awakened his spirit, this heady mixture set that spirit on fire. Listen to the triumphant scorn Phil directs at "adults" who thought comics would "disappear." He took the same tone in defending SF against its intellectual detractors. Phil didn't read his first SF magazine until he was twelve, but he had already found the "literary medium" that was home to him.

In this medium the tyranny of imposed consciousness is overthrown. Anything can happen, the quicker and stranger the better. Spiraling dreams are as real as former wives lost in alternate worlds or God the Logos in the guise of your boss doing a TV spot for Ubik instant coffee. Characters can be saintly, silly, lonely, horny, brilliant, and crazed all at once in the same story, and you can't prove it isn't true. Just look around you.

◆

In June 1938 mother and son returned to Berkeley. Except for a few very brief forays, Phil would remain in California for the rest of his life.

Dorothy's decision to leave the capital was an impetuous one. Sent off by the Children's Bureau to a meeting in Kansas City, she took Phil along and fit in a vacation to California. Once back in the Bay Area, she resolved to stay and arranged a transfer to the U.S. Forestry Department office in Berkeley. Dorothy then took an apartment at 560 Colusa Avenue, where Meemaw and Marion were again regular visitors: Marion painted pictures that delighted Phil and gave him books—notably, the verse of Irish poet James Stephens—that fostered Phil's lifelong passion for lyric poetry.

The timing of Dorothy's return was likely influenced by Edgar's relocation to Pasadena, well to the south, where he seemed to pose less of a custody threat. But Phil took great joy in being able—however occasionally—to visit with his father for the first time in four years. Dorothy was uncomfortable with these visits, still fearing Edgar would steal the boy away. Father and son attended the 1938 World's Fair in San Francisco together—Phil going to the science exhibition recommended by Dorothy while Edgar eyed the performance of stripteaser Sally Rand. And there was a day of fishing along the San Joaquin and Sacramento rivers, during which Edgar taught him to clean fish. Despite the joy Phil took in these outings, Edgar emphasized that "you could see that a great change had taken place . . . she [Dorothy] sort of ruled with an iron hand." Phil was a "lively" child, Edgar insisted, but "I want to use the right word . . . he didn't seem to have that life in him, enjoyment of life. He had slowed down a lot, I thought. . . . I'll tell you the word I'd like to use. He gave me the feeling that he was *trapped* . . . that he couldn't break out."

Even with Edgar's threatening presence to the south, Dorothy must have found Berkeley a sort of haven after life in the socially conservative capital. Granted, Berkeley in the late thirties and forties was not yet the "Berserkeley" of the sixties and after. It was still a small town, but it had an outsized percentage of freethinking academics and bohemians who thrived within the U Cal radius. Dorothy's feminism and pacifism fit right in. Black-sheep refugees from respectable eastern families took up the artistic life in Berkeley—supported by their moneyed parents—in much the same manner as their counterparts had done in the Paris of the twenties. A trolley car passed up and down Telegraph Avenue, which was lined with elegant little shops and restaurants catering to the cosmopolitan tastes of the university intelligentsia.

But there was also a substantial working-class population, which had little to do with campus life. Down by the bay, in the vicinity of San Pablo Avenue, were the used-car lots, greasy-spoon cafés, repair shops, and bars where blue-collar workers (including black and Japanese populations) and their hard-pressed families passed their lives. It would be the Berkeley working-class milieu, not its academic circles, that provided the settings and characters for so many of Phil's stories and novels. The economic strata of Berkeley life were heightened by the city's topography: The poorer families lived on the flatlands, the more well-to-do in the Berkeley hills, with their terraces, parks, and creeks. *Goats* was young Phil's slang term for those wealthier students who lived in the hills and were able to coast on their bikes on the way to school.

In the autumn of 1938, Phil was enrolled in the high fourth grade of the Hillside School in Berkeley. He remained at Hillside through the spring of 1939, completing the lower fifth grade, and then moved on in the 1939–40 academic year to the Oxford School, another Berkeley public school, for sixth grade. During his Hillside year Phil, with Dorothy's permission, went by the name of "Jim," but by the time he transferred to Oxford he had switched back to Phil again. The reasons for this name change remain unclear. Pat Flannery, a junior high school friend, recalls that Phil was fond of casually tagging acquaintances "Jim." Perhaps Phil took up that name for the regular-guy tone it gave to a new kid in town.

If acceptance was what "Jim" sought, he achieved it. Grades at Hillside were on a Satisfactory (S)/Unsatisfactory (U) basis; Jim earned all S's plus accolades on his report cards. His fourth-grade teacher noted that "Jim has made quite a place for himself in our group. He is quite popular with his playmates. He has a fine sense of 'right' and they seem to realize it." In the fifth grade it was noted, "He has a great deal of poise and self-possession for a boy of his age." In the sixth grade, at the Oxford School, and going by Phil again, he served as a junior traffic patrolman.

But the pattern of frequent absences continued at the Hillside School—for example, Phil missed nearly a quarter of the 1939 spring term schooldays. Dorothy recalled that "he was so bored in public school—from the beginning—that he didn't work at all and seized every opportunity to stay at home with whatever illness was handy." Some of these absences may have been due to illnesses that were far from merely "handy." Phil's asthma attacks continued to be severe. He had never been an avid athlete, but now even relatively mild boyhood activities— running, biking, hide-and-go-seek—became more of a strain than a pleasure. Young Phil was self-conscious and proud, and the humiliation of coming to a wheezing halt kept him away from the playgrounds where friendships might have been made. In addition, he began to experience brief but frightening attacks of paroxysmal tachycardia (sudden, rapid beating of the heart—a condition from which Edgar also suffered), along with bouts of eczema. The tachycardia would remain a lifelong condition. These physical ailments surely took their psychological toll. But it is also true that Phil never felt at home at Hillside or Oxford, not even in the sedentary classrooms. Later Phil would recall having been diagnosed in the sixth grade as having a "learning disability." Whether or not this diagnosis was made, it reflects the boy's sense of himself in academic confines.

Phil's "self-possession" manifested itself not only in his schoolwork but in his relations with Dorothy, who treated Phil like the little man of the house—subject to responsibilities but also worthy of considerable respect. And Phil, though inwardly he longed for affection, was drawn to this flattering view and conducted himself with as much dignity as a boy could muster. Once Dorothy considered buying property in nearby Concord. Anne Dick writes: "Philip had a fit. He said he wouldn't ever live out there! Dorothy lost a million dollar opportunity."

As Jim, at age nine, he tried his hand at selling magazine subscriptions; his solicitation letter scrupulously specified his own profit margin. Discontented with mere marketing, he established a periodical of

...ıs own. The *Daily Dick* cost one cent and was printed on a
that reproduced Jim's handwriting and tiny masthead draw
issues survive from December 1938. There is a brief, poignant a
a neighborhood dog:

> Friday 23. Mickey, a fox terrier was taken to the city pound yesterday. He
> caught without a license. He has no owner. The dog catcher caught him w
> a rope. It was a long battle. Finally the dog catcher caught him. Mickey crie
> and cried.

A crudely drawn comic strip—"Copper"—prefigures the mature
Phil's fascination with fake-real puzzles and the ambiguous role of Authority in distinguishing between the two. A policeman is hot on the trail
of "Looie the Counterfeiter" and questions a filling station attendant who
may have been passed a fake five-dollar bill. "Give it here!" the policeman demands. "Why? Do you think it's counterfeit?" asks the attendant.
"Of course!" the policeman responds. "Why else would I want it?" The
final frame belongs to the attendant, who is not quite suppressing a thin
smile as he answers: "To spend it sir!"

In 1940 Edgar moved to the Los Angeles office of the Department of
Commerce and became a regular on a local radio program: *This Is Your
Government*. Twelve-year-old Phil paid a visit to Edgar and his wife in
May; his pride in his father—and fear of losing him—show in this letter
to Dorothy:

> Dad thought it would be a good idea if I was to stay here until *Monday
> morning* and then leave on the train. It would mean the miss of 1 day of
> school—but that is not importen [sic] since I have so little time down here. . . .
> How about it? I think it would be good: Dad may go to Washington—Frisco—
> or someplace else. I may not see him for a long time. That is why I would like
> to stay here. Hows [sic] it?
> Dad says I am growing to his size. I am almost as tall as him!

Of course, Phil, just about five-three at the time, with blue eyes and
sandy brown hair, didn't approach Edgar's six-foot height. But his excite-
ment here contrasts markedly with other letters to Dorothy from this
time—dutiful summaries, pained explanations of academic woes. And
Phil's fears concerning a job transfer proved accurate. When America
joined World War II, Edgar became a regional business consultant for
the Federal Reserve in Cleveland, then moved to a similar post in
Richmond, Virginia. They did not see each other again until the late
forties, after Phil had graduated from high school. Phil's second wife,
Kleo Mini, stresses that loss of contact with Edgar—not troubles with
Dorothy or the death of Jane—marked Phil most profoundly:

33

:d that his dad had abandoned them. It was a hurt that influen.
, he ever did. A primary aspect of Philip's orientation to the world
.ess—along with a tremendous sense of humor—of the unbalance of
, which was the most endearing thing about him. But he was perpetually
.nd I think the father is why. At the same time, he felt his father was his
.ther's intellectual inferior. Dorothy was a strident feminist and Philip
.ways got a real put-down description of his father from her at the same time
as he missed having him around.

During the spring 1940 visit to his father, it was art—not writing—
that was his primary enthusiasm. Phil had drawn the cover for the Oxford
School yearbook that June, a turbaned crystal gazer foretelling his classmates' futures. There also survive pages of sketches and doodles—of
Nazis, slouched men, dolled-up women, and even a stern SF-like alien
labeled "4162 F"—that demonstrate how seriously he took his drawing for
a time. When, a decade later, Phil began his writing career in earnest,
Edgar was surprised that he had not become an artist instead.

This was for Phil, a time of exploration of all the arts. That summer,
while attending camp in Cazadero, California, he appeared in three
plays. (Also at this camp he learned to swim, but shortly thereafter nearly
drowned—a scare that left him with a lasting aversion to the water.) As for
music, Phil had commenced piano lessons in earnest and provided
Dorothy with a Christmas want list of 78s, including the "Turkish
March" from Beethoven's *Ruins of Athens*, the "Largo El Factotum"
from Rossini's *Barber of Seville*, and Wagner's *Tannhäuser* Overture.
(Quotations from operatic libretti, particularly Wagner and Gilbert and
Sullivan, abound in the SF novels.) He also continued to write poetry. A
poem from November 1940, "He's Dead," is a rhymed elegy to the late
family dog. The final two lines: "No longer shall he scorn his bed./Alas
for us! Our dog is dead." The poem was published, in October 1942, in
the "Young Authors' Club" column of the *Berkeley Gazette*, edited by
one "Aunt Flo."

Of Aunt Flo and her role as Phil's first editor, more shortly. For now,
bear in mind that Phil dated the start of his writing career at age
twelve—which he reached on December 16, 1940 (a birth date Phil was
pleased to share with his idol, Beethoven). At twelve he taught himself to
type, in recognition of his vocation. He also read his first SF magazine:
Stirring Science Stories. SF linked perfectly with his prior discovery of the
Oz fantasies of Frank Baum: "It seemed like a small matter, my utter
avidity to read each and every *Oz* book. Librarians haughtily told me that
they 'did not stock fantastic material,' their reasoning being that books of
fantasy led a child into a dreamworld and made it difficult for him to
adjust properly to the 'real' world. But my interest in the *Oz* books was, in
point of fact, the beginning of my love for fantasy, and, by extension,
science fiction."

Phil became a voracious collector of SF pulps, haunting the second-hand bookstores of Berkeley. By the time he entered Garfield Junior High in 1941, Phil owned stacks of *Astounding*, *Amazing*, *Unknown*, and *Unknown Worlds*. He also regularly took in the Buck Rogers serials. Friend George Kohler recalls that Phil was a "selective" reader whose recall of stories he liked was flawless. Phil the artist would copy the pictures of sleek-finned rocket ships. Throughout his life Phil continued to cherish his pulp collections. In a 1968 essay he wrote:

What is it about sf that draws us? What is sf anyhow? It grips fans; it grips editors; it grips writers. And none make any money. When I ponder this I see always in my mind Henry Kuttner's [a prominent thirties and forties writer of SF and "weird" stories] FAIRY CHESSMEN with its opening paragraph, the doorknob that winks at the protagonist. When I ponder this I also see—outside my mind, right beside my desk—a complete file of UNKNOWN and UN-KNOWN WORLDS, plus Astounding back to October 1933 . . . these being guarded by a nine-hundred-pound fireproof file cabinet, separated from the world, separated from life. Hence separated from decay and wear. Hence separated from time. I paid $390 for this fireproof file which protects these magazines. After my wife and daughter these mean more to me than anything else I own—or hope to own.

Young Phil was also a regular reader of *Life* and *National Geographic*, and followed closely the radio news concerning the Nazi menace and the outbreak of World War II. In a 1979 letter, he linked his memory of Pearl Harbor to the persistent anger he bore his parents. The idealization of youth is typical:

I phoned my mother to tell her. "We're at war with Germany, Italy and Japan!" I yelled, to which she replied calmly, "No, I don't think so, Philip," and went back to her gardening. I was 12 years old and I was more in touch than a grown person. [. . .] This maybe is one reason I get along so well with people a lot younger than me; I have little respect for the opinions of people my own age. I think the older you get the dumber you get. [. . .] You start losing touch with reality by subtle, gradual degrees until you wind up puttering around with your flowers in the backyard while World War Three breaks out. This is how I imagine my father, assuming he's still alive: out in his backyard unaware of the world and, worse, *wanting* to be unaware of the world.

As the war proceeded in earnest, Phil and Dorothy settled into an economically constrained life in their cottage (in the backyard of a larger house) at 1212 Walnut Street. Early on, unaware of the atrocities, Phil wholeheartedly sided with the Allies but was duly fascinated by the Nazis—their outsized "Bismarck" battleship and goose-stepping discipline (viewed in newsreel footage narrated by Edward R. Murrow). He enjoyed imagining superweapons: fighters faster than German Messerschmitts, cannons larger than the Japanese twenty-inchers (from the hills Phil could see the U.S. gun emplacements guarding the Bay). But Phil was very aware that much of the war news—from both sides—was not necessarily what it seemed. He admired the propaganda skills of Goebbels and speculated with friends as to similar Allied ploys. FDR in particular earned his suspicion. (Phil would later put these boyish fantasies and suspicions to hilarious use in *The Zap Gun* (1967), an exposé of cold war neuroses set in the twenty-first century.)

It was relatively easy to figure out propaganda. How to get girls to notice him was the real mystery. Leon Rimov, a junior high friend, recalls that Phil had "fantasies of relating to all the girls in the room, wherever he was," but that the girls were "indifferent." At dances "Phil would line up on one side, the girls would line up on the other, he'd maybe ask for a dance or two and then go home and fantasize what was going to happen and then he'd want to talk to me about it." What attracted Phil to a girl? "Pure looks."

But George Kohler recalls a less inept young Phil whose awareness of realities testified to a liberal sex education policy on Dorothy's part. In eighth grade, Kohler and Phil saw a used condom while walking through a park. Kohler wanted to touch it, but Phil stopped him and proceeded to deliver a "discourse" on what the condom was and the health hazards it might pose. On another occasion, Phil explained to his friend what a homosexual was. On still another occasion, Phil enlightened his friend even more dramatically at a neighborhood party: "Phil was more advanced then the rest of us and was feeling the breasts of one of the girls."

Kohler also confirms that Phil tended to "moon after the neighborhood girls" from an adoring distance. But Phil did ask at least one junior high crush for a date, the memory of which endured. From a 1974 letter to his daughter Laura:

> Laura, honey, did you know that (I never told anybody this before. Get ready. Be cool, baby). Laura, when you were born, neither your mother [Anne] nor I had a name for you. [. . .] The nurse said to me, "What are you going to call her?" I admitted I didn't know. The nurse frowned at me; she was very pretty and I almost said, "What's your name?"—but wisely I didn't. I then remembered—it flashed into my mind—the name of the first girl I ever dated, back in junior high school, a really foxy chick named Lora Heims. So I called you Laura, after her, and never told anybody until now.
>
> If you tell that, you die.

Phil's sexual fantasies—and occasional small triumphs—were part and parcel of the coming of age of most boys. But there was a darker side to his growing psychic self-awareness. During this period, Dorothy decided that her son's academic apathy and anxieties might be dispelled by psychiatric therapy. Phil likely saw more than one psychiatrist during his late elementary and junior high years; little can be said as to the specifics of their treatments. But one thing is certain—the therapy left in Phil a deep sense of tragic *difference* between himself and his peers. Kohler recalls Phil discoursing on Rorschach tests as a seventh-grader: "Phil, in fact, made up his own and he and I played Rorschach test. Phil knew all about the Thematic Apperception Test too. He knew the names of various phobias. He told me, 'I have some I can't fight.' "

But Phil did have one comforting means of breaking out of his introverted woes—writing. Kohler had a tiny printing press, which Phil commandeered for a second brief attempt—this time, in collaboration with Pat Flannery—at a self-published newspaper. *The Truth* made its debut in August 1943 and went for two cents. ("However, if we start to show a huge profit, we'll bring it down to one cent.") Its motto: "A Democratic Paper With A Democratic Principle." The writing was nearly all Phil's, including this fervid pronouncement: "This paper is sworn to print only that which is beyond doubt the TRUTH." It featured a serial story, "Stratosphere Betsy" (about a daring test pilot), and a comic strip hero, "Future-Human," who was Phil's first full-fledged SF creation:

Future-Human, champion of right, defender of the oppressed. Few gangsters dare to oppose him; and when they do they are soon vanquished.

Future-Human lives in the year 3869. Using his super-science for the welfare of humanity, he pits his strength against the underworld of the future. Appearing each issue in:

THE TRUTH!

At thirteen, *Truth* editor Phil was pale, slightly overweight, and often coughing or snuffling due to his asthma. Necessarily, he was contemptuous of team sports. When, rarely, he played games with his friends, he was ungainly and even dangerous, once hitting Flannery with a dart and drawing blood, another time shoving him into a bramble bush. With Kohler, Phil did take rambling walks up the Berkeley hills to Tilden Park (passing the newly constructed cyclotron). But he was delighted when Garfield Junior High reduced phys ed class hours.

Dorothy came home late from work and was soon upstairs in bed reading from piles of books—mostly best sellers, but also works on nutrition and healing. Her nightstand was covered with prescription medications for kidney and other ailments. This home atmosphere of illness was difficult for Phil, who was coping with his own physical and phobic woes. He could be moody, but his outbursts of sharp anger were vanquished by Dorothy's calm. Most often, mother and son spoke formally, using "Philip" and "Dorothy." One can imagine them passing the nights reading fervently in separate bedrooms. But the bond between them was growing—and Edgar was far away. During this period Phil considered dropping "Dick" in favor of his mother's maiden name, Kindred.

Dorothy was polite but taciturn to Phil's chums, seldom engaging them in conversation or inviting them for supper. Those suppers seldom varied from night to night: ground round, peas, mashed potatoes. Phil welcomed dinner invitations from Kohler's grandmother, who provided decadent delights denied to Phil at home, such as chocolate milk and soda pop. He always left a tiny bit of food on his plate, in respect for the Depression custom of showing you'd been fed enough not to require seconds.

Dorothy's upstairs seclusion did allow Phil and visiting friends un-interrupted confidential talks, toy-soldier battles, classical music listening sessions, and chess matches (in which Phil invariably trounced his pals). Phil could fashion Rube Goldberg–like circuitry: a light switch to turn on the Victrola, tiny electrical boxes for show-and-tell that scared his teachers. His musical abilities surprised even close friends. Once he sat Kohler down and played first a Chopin funeral march and then what Kohler recalls as a "macabre kind of thing." When Phil asked which he preferred, Kohler chose the second. Phil played it over and over to make sure his friend really liked it—and only then confided that it was his own composition.

Phil's bedroom was a clutter: records, model airplanes, stamp albums, a microscope, a portrait of the German kaiser. There was also a secret compartment in his desk in which Phil kept a little Kodak camera, nudist magazines, and a teaser known as "Captain Billy's Whiz Bang." He invited Kohler to join him in masturbation sessions in the bedroom, with the blinds drawn. Kohler also slept over on occasion, and naturally they discussed sex. There were no overtures: Kohler recalls that Phil regarded "homosexual" as a derogatory term.

Dorothy offered freedom and privacy, which fostered the adolescent's intense existence. Some idea of it is afforded by his early (circa 1949) unpublished mainstream novel *Gather Yourselves Together*. One character, a young man named Carl, bears a striking resemblance to Phil—including a passionate interest in philosophy (Carl's lengthy journal writings on truth and reality prefigure the *Exegesis*) and in dark-haired girls. In the following passage Carl, secluded in his room, copies a picture he has torn from a magazine:

> The original, the print torn from the magazine, fell from his lap, skidding into the corner. He did not notice or care. This girl, emerging on his drawing paper, did not come from any magazine. She came from inside him, from his own body. From the plump, white body of the boy this embryonic woman was rising, brought forth by the charcoal, the paper, the rapid strokes. [. . .]

In the steamy, musky room the boy was much like a kind of plant, growing and expanding, white and soft, his fleshy arms reaching into everything, devouring, examining, possessing, digesting. But at the windows and doors of the room he stopped. He did not go beyond them. [. . .]

Like a plant, he fed on things brought to him. He did not go and get them for himself. Living in this room he was a plant that fed on its own self, eating at its own body. What came forth from his own vitals, these lines and forms generated onto paper, were exciting and maddening. He was trapped, held tight.

Recall that Edgar described Phil as seeming "trapped" at this time.

Leon Rimov recalls Phil as essentially an "introvert" who lacked self-confidence. "He had a waddle and his head was always down." When he was in a sociable mood, Phil could be charming, "but it was like passing a car in high gear—he'd only go fast for a short time." He notes Phil's futile efforts to found the Rocky Creek Club (after the creek in nearby Live Oak Park) after having been rejected by another neighborhood social club. Phil gathered his pals together, declared himself president, but failed to hold his audience. "He was constantly delaying things, saying let's not make a decision now but instead get together again and talk about it some more. After a few times people were scratching their heads, and finally they moved on." Rimov believes that Phil "would have liked to have been a politician, to have manipulated situations, but he wasn't able to get people to follow him."

In junior high Phil proclaimed himself an atheist, since no one could prove God existed. He also asked Rimov to join a Bible Club he was attempting to found. In Rimov's view Phil wasn't religious, but rather "a devil's advocate for many things—and searching." Phil often adopted an air of authority with friends—it was Phil who found the best reference source, *Jane's Fighting Ships*, on naval warfare. But one topic he seldom discussed was his own writing. Occasionally he showed stories to friends—to Pat Flannery, a modern setting of the Faust legend—but none sensed in Phil a writer, as opposed to a paleontologist or a politician. The one sign of his future vocation was Phil's own disciplined efforts.

At fourteen, he completed his first novel, *Return to Lilliput*, loosely inspired by Jonathan Swift's *Gulliver's Travels*. The manuscript is lost. Phil's humorous account of it in a 1976 interview does no justice to the dreams of his younger self:

PKD: [T]hey had rediscovered Lilliput, in the modern world, you know, like rediscovering Atlantis, these guys report they've discovered Lilliput. But it's only accessible by submarine because it's sunk under the water. You'd think even a fourteen year old kid would have a more original idea than that. I even can tell you the numbers on the submarines, I have so vivid a memory. It was A101, B202, C303, were the numbers and names, the designations, of the submarines.

In addition, he regularly published stories and poems in the *Berkeley Gazette*'s "Young Authors' Club" column. Between 1942 and 1944, from eighth grade through his sophomore year, Phil's work appeared fifteen times. The stories easily exceed the poems in quality. The prose is polished and economical; the plots are derivative but fully imagined. In "Le Diable," set in a French village, wicked Pierre Mechant burgles the castle of a dead Count. The action is fluid, cinematic: "And that night, if there had been anyone around to see it, he would have seen fat little Pierre carrying a candle and climbing up one of the castle walls. They might have seen the candle bob and weave about the castle until it eventually found its way, with Pierre's help, into the wine cellars." Pierre encounters the Devil, who wins his soul in exchange for the Count's gold. Pierre's fatal end in the dank wine cellar was surely inspired by Poe's "A Cask of Amantillado."

"The Slave Race" is the only SF story in the group. In the future, androids created to ease humans' toil have overthrown their lazy masters. Explains the android narrator: "And his science we added to ours, and we passed on to greater heights. We explored the stars, and worlds un-dreamed of." But at the story's end the same cycle of expansive energy followed by sybaritic idleness that doomed the human race threatens the androids as well:

> But at last we wearied, and looked to our relaxation and pleasure. But not all could cease work to find enjoyment, and those who still worked on looked about them for a way to end their toil.
> There is talk of creating a new slave race.
> I am afraid.

The rise and fall of civilizations pursuant to cyclical laws and limits of human (and artificial) intelligence was a favorite SF theme in the forties. Phil's extensive pulp reading had already linked him to the key concerns of the genre.

Phil writhed under the editorial predilictions of the *Gazette*'s "Aunt Flo." Evidence for this comes from Phil's written asides in the notebook into which he carefully pasted his contributions to the "Young Authors' Club." Aunt Flo—pictured with a black hat and generic Betty Crocker features—rendered judgment on each published piece. On "He's Dead" (the poem on the death of Phil's dog) she waxed effusive: "Pathos walks in every line of this poem—and I'm not sure my eyes weren't a trifle moist when I'd finished reading them." Praise like this was hard enough to bear. But when "The Visitation" (Beethoven's ghost returns to compose one last piece) won only second place in her "Senior Day" contest, Phil fumed that Aunt Flo "said it was written well, but 'little authors' shouldn't write about the big unknown—just things they know about!'" On Aunt Flo's behalf, it must be allowed that her strictures on keeping to known reality were echoed by a number of Phil's later editors and critics. Phil's frustration and defiance were constants as well—thirty years later, he would fulminate over Ace editor Terry Carr's suggestion that he move on from the "What is Reality?" theme that dominated his work. As if—Phil would complain—there was a *real* reality out there ready to hand.

The break with Aunt Flo came when Phil, age fifteen, published "Program Notes On A Great Composer," a faint satire on solemn record dust jacket biographies, using the invented composer William Friedrich Motehaven. When Aunt Flo termed the piece a not "strictly creative" factual essay, Phil fumed in his notebook:

> Fooled her completely on this one—knew I would, she doesn't know a satire from a hole in the ground. I hoped she'd say something foolish in her comments, and she did. Made her apologize right out in our paper, too!
>
> Last contribution, I think. Have gotten to the point where she doesn't understand my pieces. No point in sending in any more.
>
> *Don't think she ever did!*

While Phil showed considerable passion as to writing, he continued to be desultory in his schoolwork. His grades at Garfield Junior High were good, but he was coasting and bored with his teachers. To spur him, Dorothy decided upon a boarding school—the California Preparatory School in Ojai, to the south. The Ojai catalogue was plainspoken: "[P]ersistent, down-right hard work and close attention to the main purpose of the School is rigidly insisted upon for every boy." Kitchen duties and weekly church attendance were mandatory.

Phil responded by earning a "cum laude" class rank for the 1942–43 prep school year; other than C's in phys ed, he did well in all subjects. Minor disciplinary infractions included swearing and using a curtain rod as a peashooter. But the strain of the new daily regimen quickly showed. His letters to Dorothy from Ojai show Phil's remarkable capacity—which he would utilize to great advantage in the SF novels—to turn a single set of facts (in this case, life at Ojai) into the basis for constantly shifting and equally credible or incredible conclusions.

Early on Phil complained that kitchen duties interfered with his studies and so he was failing math; his belongings were being stolen; he was bullied by eighteen-year-olds; he was losing weight because he declined the potatoes served twice a day. But he was affronted when Dorothy suggested that he come home—he was a man, not a homesick boy. She must have found it difficult to keep track of which shell the pea was under. From a letter by Phil of October 1942:

41

As soon as I mailed the [previous] letter I sent you I was sorry that I had done it. I realize now what a cruel thing it was to do, and I thought that *you would realize* that I was so *homesick* the *first week* that you would expect a letter like that. Surely the fact that you would want me to come home because you missed me wouldn't overpower your logic in realizing that I would not mean what I said. [. . .] Here is what I think we should do: Don't send Dr. Brush [the headmaster] any kind of a letter; don't send for me; don't decide that I don't like it here. I do not like it here *too* much, but I like it alot better than when I wrote that letter. Then, somewhere around Oct. 23, if I still don't like it, I will come home.

A week or so later:

I do not *like* working, but I do not think that it makes any difference to whether I stay or not. I like it here now, as much as I would if I did not have to work. [. . .]
I will not stay here if I do not have to work, because everyone would say, "What a sissy he is." If you think that being behind in my classes is reason enough for coming home, then I had better do so. Other than that I like it swell here.

By October 22, he was back to tangled reassessments:

For goodness sake, don't tell me that I can come home, because it is just like when you would say "All right, you don't have to go to school today." [. . . .] I hope that the fact that you miss me does not influence your judgment. If you want me to be a spoiled brat, then just let me come home. That would be admitting defeat, and I am going to prove that I am just as much a man as any boy here.

In this same letter, Phil triumphantly informed his mother of his A-grade English paper on a cat, which his teacher read aloud to the class "because they begged him to read it after he had read the first paragraph out loud to make a correction on it." Phil added, "I think that my writing is O.K."

Phil's final letter to Dorothy, in May 1943, declared: "As long as I live I will never make the mistake again of going to a boarding school." He returned to Garfield for ninth grade in the autumn of 1943; in February 1944 he advanced to Berkeley High School. But his difficulties did not end with escape from Ojai. There was something visceral in his hatred of academic structure. In a 1974 letter to his fourteen-year-old daughter Laura:

Around the time I was your age I went exactly one half the time and stayed home the other half. School systems have been shown [. . .] to isolate kids from the real world, to teach them skills no longer needed, to ill-equip them to handle life when or if they ever emerge from the school. In a sense, the better you adapt to school the less your chances are of later adapting to the actual world. So I figure, the worse you adapt to school, the better you will be able to handle reality when you finally manage to get loose at last from school, if that ever happens. But I guess I have what in the military they call a "poor attitude," which means "shape up or ship out." I always elected to ship out.

Phil's attempt to draw an absolute inverse correlation between academic and real-life skills is strained. His efforts at justification—even glorification—of his school problems gloss over the extreme anxieties he experienced at the time.

The phobias he couldn't fight (as he described them to George Kohler) grew in strength during his ninth-grade stint at Garfield, when he experienced recurrent attacks of vertigo that left him bedridden for days at a time. As a sophomore at Berkeley High, a new friend, Dick Daniels, urged Phil to usher at a performance of the San Francisco Symphony. Phil adored classical music, but the strain of the formal public setting was too great. Anne Dick writes: "Years later, Phil said that he had had [at the symphony concert] a terrible vertigo attack, that something irreversible happened to his psyche when he was ushering. [. . .] His being sank down into itself, it was as if he could only see out into the world with a periscope, as if he were in a submarine. He felt that he had never recovered the ability to perceive the world directly."

What underlay these attacks? In a December 1981 letter to daughter Isa (then fifteen, Phil's age when the attacks began), he outlined the stakes—survival or oblivion:

At about the seventh grade in school the person's own individual identity starts to come into being; [. . . .] And (and this is what I think, although I may be wrong) the person senses the possibility that this new self, this unique identity, may be snuffed out, may be engulfed by the world that confronts him or her, especially by all the other identities coming into existence on all sides. The real fear, then, is that you yourself—which at one time did not exist—*may again not exist*; fear inside you, flooding over you in wave after wave of panic, is what is experienced as an engulfing of that self.

Vertigo as the fear of engulfment, of extinction. In his 1965 essay "Schizophrenia & The Book of Changes," Phil linked those fears with the urge that led him to write within the fantasy and SF genres. In *Martian Time-Slip* (1964), protagonist Jack Bohlen, an "ex-schizophrenic" who hated school and serves as repairman for the Earth colony on Mars, must fix the Public School teaching simulacra. When one unit, "Kindly Dad" (the obverse of the "Father-thing"), begins to rattle off rote assurances, Bohlen lashes out in rage:

"Now here's what I think," Jack said. "I think this Public School and you teaching machines are going to rear another generation of schizophrenics, the descendants of people like me who are making a fine adaptation to this new planet. You're going to split the psyches of these children because you're teaching them to expect an environment which doesn't exist for them. It doesn't even exist back on Earth, now; it's obsolete. [. . .]"

"Yes, Little Jackie, it has to be."

"What you ought to be teaching," Jack said, "is, how do we—"

"Yes, Little Jackie," Kindly Dad interrupted him, "it has to be." [. . .]

"You're stuck," Jack said. "Kindly Dad, you've got a worn gear-tooth."

"Yes, Little Jackie," Kindly Dad said, "it has to be."

The battle lines were already drawn by the time Phil entered Berkeley High: Either engulfment or refuge in the realm of imaginative art. Phil had come to see—could not help but see—that his "unique identity" was not about to be tamed or reasoned away.

3 Forward Into The "Real" World, Or, Phil And The Cosmos Start To Compare Notes Seriously (1944–1950)

This original struggle to break free of my mother (when I left high school) was the moment/situation/act in which and by which I asserted my independence and identity at last, as an adult and as a man; [. . . .] The greater the pain the greater the victory; [. . . .] Those years right after I left my mother were the happiest years of my life.

PHIL, November 1981 journal entry

I had never kissed a girl, I did not shave. I read Astounding Stories for entertainment. At 21, I have been married and divorced, shave every day, and read James Joyce, & Herodotus' "Persian Wars," & the "Anabasis" of Xenophon for entertainment. [. . .] At 15, I thought I knew what I wanted out of life, now I do not. At 15 I was a big psychological mess. I still am, but differently.

PHIL, letter to Herb Hollis (Phil's first and only boss)
on Phil's twenty-first birthday, December 16, 1949

Without knowing it during the years I wrote, my thinking & writing was a long journey toward enlightenment. I first saw the illusory nature of space when I was in high school. In the late forties I saw that causality was an illusion.

Exegesis entry, 1979

IN 1944 Dorothy and Phil moved to a new Berkeley address—1711 Allston Way. It was a narrow, two-story house close to the street, with a pointed roof. Dorothy had the upstairs bedroom, Phil the downstairs. Neither did much housekeeping, and shared meals were not a major affair. Their relationship was so adult in tone that Phil's friends were sometimes taken aback—he spoke his mind more vehemently than they would have dared with their parents. Dorothy, whose brown hair was now flecked by grey, seemed to hold herself aloof. But the tension between them showed. Phil never complained about her to friends—it wasn't something he discussed.

Gerald Ackerman, a high school friend, recalls that the house "had something quaint and temporary about it." His attempts to talk books with Dorothy were rebuffed—"she was either impatient or just inclined to discourage any show-offy precosity, pretentious and awful anyway. Her bedroom was rather stagey: it was shallow, and her bed was against the wall facing the door in which she was centered as I stood talking to her. A rather formidable set up."

Phil entered Berkeley High in February 1944. Dick Daniels, who met Phil in sophomore-year German class, recalls him as "meticulous" in his classroom preparation. "He was permanently in search of a dis-embarrassed state. He didn't like to be put in a situation where he was found wanting, and tried to avoid exposure." Phil acquired a working knowledge of German which would serve him well—his independent research in the Nazi war archives kept at U Cal Berkeley forms a vital backdrop to *The Man in the High Castle*.

Another class Phil enjoyed was advanced English, taught by Mar-garet Wolfson, for whom Phil developed a sizable schoolboy crush. Even as an adult, he retained a considerable respect for Wolfson. In a 1970 journal entry, Phil spoke of his then-current love as being "plenty smart enough to challenge me, as no woman has ever done before with the exception of Margaret Wolfson."

Wolfson confirms that Phil was a highly intelligent student who kept within a "quiet shell" and rarely spoke in class. Phil possessed an "in-tuitive imagination" and was, in his classwork, "never satisfied with an off-handed kind of treatment." Once, instead of the assigned literary analysis, she received an SF story, the contents of which she cannot recall. "I would have preferred that he follow the assignment, but once I read what he had written I knew perfectly well that what I had gotten was exceptional and that I had better not carp about it." She suggested that Phil send it off to one of the SF magazines; if he took up that suggestion, he never spoke of it, and no Phil Dick story was to appear until 1952. One unpublished SF story—"Stability"—does survive from his high school years, however. "Stability" depicts a post–twenty-fifth-century dystopia governed by the stifling principle of "Stabilization," which permits no political or technological change. Similar static dystopias would appear in two of Phil's SF novels of the fifties: *The World According to Jones* and *The Man Who Japed*.

While friends and Wolfson recall Phil as a bright student, Phil would often portray himself, in retrospect, as a tormented rebel who couldn't hack even basic coursework. In a 1974 letter to daughter Laura—written in response to her complaints about school—he tried to cheer her up by painting a portrait of himself as the ultimate fuck-up: "It was super hard for me in high school. I got an F minus on a geometry test. I flunked

Latin and P.E. I hated every minute of it. I learned nothing. Finally I fell behind in my grade and into a Z type group of the previous grade, including English." In truth, Phil never flunked a class. In gym he got mostly B's; in academic subjects it was all A's and B's. He even joined the literary magazine and the chess club. What made high school "super hard" was the vertigo. From May to September 1944 Phil was beset by recurrent attacks and was forced to drop several classes, setting back his progress toward graduation.

That same summer, George Kohler contracted polio. Phil had recovered sufficiently from his attacks to pay his friend frequent visits. Kohler recalls his kindness and also the worry that crossed Phil's mind: "I wonder if *I* have a mild case of polio." He did not, but Phil's bouts with asthma, tachycardia, and now vertigo had instilled what would remain a lifelong consciousness—and dread—of ill health.

But Phil could always offset his dreads with exuberant passions. Gerald Ackerman and Dick Daniels shared his consuming interest in classical music. Phil later wrote: "I began to study and grasp huge areas on the map of music; by fourteen I could recognize virtually any symphony or opera, identify virtually any classical tune hummed or whistled at me." Ackerman recalls marathon talks in front of Phil's Magnavox, with topics including not only music but also Phil's favorite SF stories in the latest pulps. Phil had not yet turned to the mainstream classics, a lack of taste that Ackerman deplored. But Phil was already suspicious of cultural pretensions. He would convince Daniels that a recording was by Tchaikovsky (whom Phil knew Daniels disliked), get him to fulminate about it—then reveal the composer to be Berlioz. "Phil was constantly devising tricks and situations in which his friends could be embarrassed. That was simply part of his style and made life fun." But Phil was not without his own bristling pride. "He had an *amour propre* suitable for a Spanish *hidalgo*."

Daniels, who accompanied Phil to the San Francisco Symphony the night of his terrible attack, did not witness any difficulties on Phil's part. But neither Daniels nor Ackerman could convince Phil to cross the Bay again. Daniels recalls: "He would back out because of a terrible fear of being stuck in the middle of a row, in the middle of an act, having to urinate and not being able to get out without embarrassing himself. He had the same fears when it came to riding the train to and from San Francisco. It was a point of contention: I didn't tend to take his phobic responses seriously, and that would offend him."

Phil's bathroom fears were genuine—they persisted on into his early twenties. But Daniels found himself nonplused not only by Phil's phobias but also by his tendency to take offense easily: "He could have an astounding array of complaints against you. He would also characterize things that happened to him as the responsibility of others, mostly malign. Phil took personal responsibility for himself at an early age—but he had that way of reading the world, deriving motives out of thin air, believing that people intended to do him harm."

If Phil had his fears, he also possessed considerable charms. These did not, however, include a stylish appearance. Phil had lost his baby fat but paid little attention to his clothing ("a walking trash can," Daniels concedes), and often, as a neophyte shaver, missed scraggly whiskers. But he did possess smooth, intelligent features and penetrating blue eyes. And he had a line of gab quick and funny enough to intrigue when he was in the mood. But Phil kept to a small circle of friends. Crushes came and went, but he didn't date much or find anything like a steady girl.

Which left a lingering pain. In "Schizophrenia & The Book of Changes," Phil used the sexual rejections of high school days as a metaphor for the battle between the sheltered individual ("*idios kosmos,*" or personal consciousness) and the external world ("*koinos kosmos,*" or shared social consciousness). The sly *koinos kosmos* tempts the *idios kosmos* out of its lair by tactics that include sexual desire. "This bipolar internal war goes on endlessly; meanwhile the actual girl has no idea you're alive (and guess why: you're not)." Yes, it reads funny, but there's no doubt rejection was hard for a boy with a hungry heart who was just learning to shave.

Phil later accused Dorothy of instilling in him, during high school and immediately after, fears over his manhood due to her persistent concern that he would turn gay. (Edgar's disparaging comments, in earlier years, as to Phil's poor athletic skills also contributed here.) But Dorothy's concerns arose in part from Gerald Ackerman's youthful discovery of his own homosexuality. Ackerman recalls his flirtatious high school days this way:

> I was, at the time, the only one among us who had the idea that he was gay. [. . .] At times I even tested or used their naivete. I touched all of them rather continuously, [. . .] and even, at times, took one of their hands in mine while walking. [. . . .] Once Phil told me that his mother had complained about the practice; [. . .] He told me rather matter of factly about this, without scandal or admonition, as if it had no special import, even in the interpretation his mother might have given to the incident. Even so, [. . .] it happened only this once—it didn't appeal to him, and he submitted only out of friendship, perhaps a little curious and a little flattered as well.

As this incident shows, Phil was neither gay nor a homophobe. But calm as he may have seemed to Ackerman, Phil was intensely fearful of discovering gay tendencies in himself. The acceptance he bestowed on gay friends was taboo in his own case.

Like his classmates, Phil expected to attend U Cal Berkeley someday, though he seemed less enamored of college and career than most. But the pressure of achieving good grades produced a classic case of final-exam anxiety that (in perfect Phildickian fashion) induced an epiphany he cherished all his life.

It was a physics test. Phil was screwing up very badly. He couldn't remember the key principle behind displacement of water, on which eight of the ten exam questions were based. Time was nearly up, and Phil started to pray. Just as all seemed lost, a voice within explained the principle in simple terms—and Phil got an A. In a 1980 *Exegesis* entry, Phil pointed to this incident as a starting point of his spiritual life:

> This shows the hauntingly eerie paradoxical (almost seemingly whimsical or playful) nature of enlightenment: it comes to you only when you cease to pursue it. When you totally & finally give up. [. . .] Yes, emerging from this maze of paradox & mirrored opposites, of seeming, of infinite change, here, finally, is the answer I sought, the goal I sought. & it is where I started from back in high school in my physics final when I prayed to God, the Christian God—who was always there, leading me to him.

Phil did not identify this voice (which spoke to him far more frequently in the seventies) exclusively with the "Christian God." In the *Exegesis* he also termed it the "AI Voice" (for Artificial Intelligence), "Diana," "the Sibyl," "Sophia" (Gnostic goddess of wisdom), the "Shekhinah" (divine feminine principle of the Jewish kabbalah), and many names more.

If Phil was not, in high school, the heroic rebel figure he later invented, he certainly did go through something like hell and come out of it a writer. During his senior year, Phil experienced intense attacks of agoraphobia, claustrophobia, and vertigo. Earlier difficulties with eating in public returned. On one occasion, he developed extreme panic while walking down the aisle of a classroom—the floor seemed to be tilting away from him. These attacks forced Phil, in February 1947, to withdraw from Berkeley High; he graduated in June by working at home with a tutor.

Throughout the 1946–47 school year, Phil received weekly psychotherapy at the Langley Porter Clinic in San Francisco. To acquaintances, he explained these frequents trips as his participation in a special study of high-IQ students. Phil was more frank with friends like George Kohler, who recalls terrible bouts of dizziness that forced Phil to lie in bed, unable even to raise his head. Phil described it at the time as "vertigo." Kohler (now an M.D.) conjectures that the dizziness was caused by labyrinthitis, an inflammation of the inner ear. Kohler further stresses that "at no time was he mentally confused."

For two years, Phil recalled, he kept up weekly sessions with a Jungian analyst who "overworked" Phil's "intuitive processes." Phil's attitude toward therapy included a healthy dose of anger. The phobias had temporarily disabled him, but they hadn't diminished his intellect.

Phil didn't like being told he was crazy. In this 1977 interview, genuine defiance cuts through the add-on story polish:

> I remember I was in my teens and I saw a psychiatrist—I was having trouble in school—and I told him that I had begun to wonder if our value system—what was right and what was wrong—were absolutely true or whether they were not merely culturally relativistic. And he said, "That's a symptom of your neurosis, that you doubt the values of right and wrong." So I got ahold of a copy of the British scientific journal "Nature," which is the most reputable scientific journal in the world. And there was an article in which it said virtually all our values are derived essentially from the Bible and cannot be empirically verified, therefore must fall into the category of the untestable and the unprovable. I showed this to him, and he got very angry and said, "I consider this nothing but horseshit. *Horseshit*, I say!" Here I was, a teenager in the '40's, and here he was, a psychiatrist; now I look back and I see this man was cemented into a simplistic mode. I mean his brain was *dead* as far as I could determine.

A 1970 letter provides this account of a 1946 Rorschach test: "the tester in her report said that the strongest drive in me was to refind my twin sister who died about a month after she and I were born [. . .]" This drive may have contributed to the psychic state that allowed for Phil's awareness of a voice during his exam—yet another of his names for the voice, in the *Exegesis*, was "Jane."

According to Phil, his Jungian therapist pronounced him "agoraphobic." Another diagnosis that Phil himself often employed with respect to that time was "schizophrenia." He confided to third wife, Anne Dick, that he had been so diagnosed in high school—whether this diagnosis was made by his Jungian therapist or another source is unknown. In any event, his use of the term does not necessarily render it accurate; as Anne Dick points out, "Phil was hypochondriacal about his mental condition."

The key factor in Phil's ability to weather these storms was his employment—which had begun at age fifteen, while he was still in high school—as a clerk at University Radio and later at Art Music, two Berkeley shops owned by one Herb Hollis, who became the father figure Phil needed.

It was within the confines of his job as salesclerk for Hollis—the only job, aside from SF writer, that Phil ever held—that he fought his successful rearguard action against the phobias that beset him in academia. Not that selling radios, TVs, and records to the public was without its anxieties, but Phil blossomed under Hollis's tutelage and the daily music debates, soulful revelations, and silly banter with his fellow employees.

The values Hollis and his strange crew embodied—craftsmanship, loyalty, independence of spirit, the little guy over the soulless corporate cartel—formed the social credo Phil held to through all the otherwise shifting realities in his fiction. The Berkeley of Phil's youth was a hotbed of political activity left and right. No one who knew Phil in the late forties regarded him as politically engaged. He was liberal, a Henry Wallace supporter in 1948, an admirer of C. Wright Mills's leftist sociological critiques of capitalism. But at the heart of Phil's thinking on the big issue of how the world ought to be run were lessons under the wing of driven, eccentric, droll, protective, autocratic dreamer and small-time finagler Herb Hollis.

Hollis was originally from McCloud, Oklahoma. His personal identification with his retail operations was extreme. He was a perfectionist who worked six or seven days a week, a hands-on boss who installed fixtures when customer traffic was slow. Recalls Kleo Mini, "Phil always admired anybody who could control the outside world to any extent. That meant picking up a hammer as much as anything else." Customer service, product selection, and employee loyalty were matters of honor as well as mere economics. The epitome of the loyalty ethic was Eldon Nicholls, a dwarfed, hunchbacked accountant who had been with Hollis from the beginning and served as a kindly emotional buffer between the boss and his minions—the young salesclerks and repairmen who worked at the two stores.

University Radio, located at Shattuck and Center, sold radios, appliances, records, and, beginning in the late forties, a new fad called television. There was a basement repair shop. Art Music was located much closer to the campus scene at Channing and Telegraph, just four blocks from Sather Gate, where soapbox oratory was commonplace—and where, in the mid-sixties, the Free Speech movement led by Mario Savio would win national attention. In the late forties and early fifties, Art Music became a Berkeley landmark, offering classical music, jazz, and (Hollis's own favorite genres) folk music and novelty groups.

As a young man Hollis had hankered, in fantasy, for the life of a writer, and he always liked to surround himself with creative types; his employees were often budding artists from the Berkeley scene. He and his wife, Pat, never had children, and perhaps for this reason Hollis was susceptible to strays—faintly distracted, odd-seeming Berkeley idealists—who wandered into his orbit. One such was Homer Thespian, who went barefoot through the streets and was a crack repairman when he wasn't engaging his boss in surly philosophical disputes or disappearing for days at a time. Hollis kept him on the payroll without complaint.

Phil, budding artist *and* stray, was a favorite of Hollis's from the beginning. Phil's first part-time job was breaking apart vacuum tubes and adapters to scavenge the parts (scarce during wartime) for reassembly. Menial as it was, the job may have been—at first—something of a favor to a boy in need of a break. Phil would later say that working for Hollis was his first "positive validation." For a time, Phil had an innocent crush on Pat Hollis. For one of Phil's birthdays, Hollis's gift was a choice of any recording in the catalogue; Phil picked Bach's *St. Matthew's Passion*, featuring his then-favorite vocalist, Gerhard Husch.

In a letter on his twenty-first birthday ("I am writing this on my own time," he states in the first line) Phil recounted how he had joined on in 1944. The letter was a paean (in a painfully self-conscious man-to-man tone) to Hollis's guidance:

> The first words I ever was addressed by you, were, "If you like both albums so much it really doesn't matter which you buy; you'll get them both, sooner or later." You were right, I did, within a week. I thought: what a smart fellow. I was fifteen. Six mo. later I went to work for you at AMC [Art Music] [. . .]
>
> [. . .] You aided and abetted my mental growth, and also frightened me backwards occasionally, because I take everything you say seriously, then and now. [. . .]
>
> At 15, I did everything wrong, at 21 you are at AMC and can't see what I'm doing. [. . .]
>
> I once made a series of pictures of you, which you seemed to like. They are still hanging up at UR&E [University Radio], and when I noticed them I am inclined to think that if I drew them again they would be exactly the same at 21 as I drew them at 16. Maybe you know what I mean. [. . .]
>
> Love,
>
> pkd

As the letter indicates, Phil found it difficult, at first, to cope with the job. But the anxieties and vertigo attacks arose in connection with Berkeley High—not the Hollis stores. Life with salesclerks and repairmen could be fun, especially when you got the news (in 1945) that at long last the war was over:

> [W]e all piled into the store truck, grabbed a carton of professional-size firecrackers, picked up some GIs along the route, and turned on Berkeley by blowing it up. Later, everybody went across to San Francisco and we really tore it down for like ten days, roving about in armed bands menacing everything which walked. It was fun. Later in the year I was promoted from sweeping floors to emptying the ashtrays. All in all it was a good year.

Dick Daniels (who also worked for Hollis for a time) recalls the banter between Phil and his boss:

> Phil was never really loose around Hollis, but was instead in something like the position of the fool who jests in the king's court—but only within understood parameters. Phil played the fool and Hollis responded. The affection

that Hollis had for him was Phil's repayment—that is, that Hollis let him get away with it. Hollis was the first older person with whom Phil had that kind of relationship.

Hollis sponsored and supplied records for a folk-novelty program on local FM station KSMO in San Mateo in the late forties. Phil wrote DJ patter and Hollis shop commercials for the programs. He claimed, in later years, to have hosted a classical music program on KSMO, but no one who knew Phil at the time can recall his having been on the radio. But he must have paid frequent visits to KSMO: The ambience of an FM station is captured in fine detail in his 1956 mainstream novel, *The Broken Bubble of Thisbe Holt,* and the genial manner of a small-time DJ is touchingly embodied in Walt Dangerfield, whose broadcasts from the Earth-orbiting satellite (in which he is trapped until he dies) are of great solace to the postnuclear war survivors in *Dr. Bloodmoney* (1964). A few pages of Phil's writing for KSMO survive. Already he had the ear for American sales shuck that would, in his SF, sound so strangely right coming from the mouths of aliens. Here Phil pitches those newfangled TVs:

University Radio in Berkeley greets you. Yesterday when we came to work we found that our salesman had moved his potted palm to the other side of the store, so that he could see the television screen better. Customers are requested not to bother him with inquiries about buying things. If you wish to purchase a Magnavox, kindly lay the money on the counter with a note describing the set you want. If you are lucky, he may notice your request between television programs.

The years with Hollis provided Phil with a mother lode of writer's capital. Characters based on Hollis can be found in several of Phil's mainstream and SF novels, particularly in the fifties and sixties (see Chronological Survey). The lonely, cranky figure of the "repairman" also recurs as a symbol of integrity and courage in the face of impossible odds. In the *Exegesis,* Phil observed that much of his work was "palpably autobiographical—the little business firm, & the fatherly owner or world leader." The boss-employee relationships between Jim Fergesson and Stuart Hadley (*Voices from the Street,* c. 1952–53), Leo Bulero and Barney Mayerson (*The Three Stigmata of Palmer Eldritch,* 1965), and Glen Runciter and Joe Chip (*Ubik,* 1969) are the most notable portraits of the trust and tension that existed between Hollis and Phil.

In *Voices from the Street,* an apprenticeship mainstream novel, the Hollis figure is Jim Fergesson, owner of "Modern TV Sales and Service"—"a small, muscular man in a blue serge suit, middle-aged, face red with wrinkles and wisdom." As *Voices* was written during and just after Phil's employment with Hollis, vivid memories lingered. How strong a figure was Hollis in Phil's psyche? Fergesson's opening of Modern TV for the day's business is patterned after the creation in *Genesis*:

> Here no life existed. [. . .] He bent down and clicked on the main power; the big neon sign sputtered on, and after a moment the window lights warmed to a faint glow. He fixed the door wide open, caught up some of the sweet outdoor air, and, holding it in his lungs, moved about the dark, damp store [. . .] The dead things came reluctantly back to life. [. . .] He threw the Philco display into whirring excitement and carried it to the back of the store. He illuminated the luxurious Zenith poster. He brought light, being, awareness to the void. Darkness fled; and after the first moment of impatient frenzy he subsided and rested, and took his seventh day—a cup of black coffee.

The ultimate tribute to Hollis is Leo Bulero in *Palmer Eldritch*, the greedy, needling, cigar-chomping, heart-on-sleeve owner of Perky Pat Layouts, Inc., who becomes Earth's only hope of resisting the psychic invasion (conducted through masterful marketing of the drug "Chew-Z": "GOD PROMISES ETERNAL LIFE. WE CAN DELIVER IT.") by Palmer Eldritch, the magisterial embodiment of pure evil. Bulero, whose "Can-D" drug product is being pushed off the market by Eldritch, writes the little memo (Hollis frequently wrote memos to employees) that serves as a frontispiece to the novel—a pure, stuttering affirmation of the human spirit:

> I mean, after all; you have to consider we're only made out of dust. That's admittedly not much to go on and we shouldn't forget that. But even considering, I mean it's a sort of bad beginning, we're not doing too bad. So I personally have faith that even in this lousy situation we're faced with we can make it. You get me?

In a 1977 interview, Phil refuted the notion of an "anti-hero" slant in works such as *Palmer Eldritch*:

> I think very often I'm accused of writing my protagonist as an anti-hero. [. . .] And what I'm doing is just taking the people that I've worked with, that I've had as friends, had as fellow workers and I get a tremendous sense of satisfaction. [. . .]
>
> And I always think, well, the ultimate surrealism [. . .] is to take somebody that you knew, whose life time ambition was to sell the largest television set that the store carried, and put him in a future utopia or dystopia, and pit him against this dystopia, or place him in a position of power. Like I like to take employers that I've had who've owned small stores and make them supreme rulers of entire—
>
> **Uwe Anton [interviewer]:** Galaxies?
>
> **Phil:** Galaxies, yes. That to me is very enjoyable, because I still see this

person as sitting at his desk, looking at a lot of invoices for purchases that have never been made, saying who authorized this?

Phil loved to tell stories of the philosophic realizations he achieved while working in the Hollis shops. Once, while sweeping the floor at age fifteen, Phil got into a debate with a repairman as to whether radio speakers allowed one to hear music (the repairman's view) or a "simulation" of music (Phil's position). Another time, a repairman pointed out to Phil, while they were at a traffic light, that there was no way to prove that they were both seeing the same color, even though they both called it red. Underlying the lessons was the sense of dignity provided by doing one's work well. There was the time they tried to repair a Capard, a complex marvel that automatically stacked records. After much labor it was fixed, but the bumpy ride to the customer's house undid the effort:

And we said there is no bill, we're not charging you. [. . .] And I was very proud [. . .] that we had all admitted to our own defeat, in the face of the situation. [. . .] I was only about fifteen years old—this made a vast impression on me—that this Capard epitomized an inscrutable ultra sophisticated universe which was in the habit of doing unexpected things. [. . .] But the great merit of the human being is that the human being is isomorphic with his malfunctioning universe. I mean, he too is somewhat malfunctioning. [. . .] He goes on trying and this, of course, is what Faulkner said in his marvelous Nobel Prize speech, that Man will not merely endure, he will prevail.

The support and warmth of the Hollis operations, and the steady salary they provided, assisted Phil in an undertaking that he came to regard as one of the most difficult—and ultimately triumphant— challenges of his life: moving out of his mother's house in the fall of 1947:

Parents have a vested interest in keeping their kids little and dumb and in chains, like all oppressed groups. I remember when I told my mother I was moving out. "I'll call the police," she said. "I'll see you in jail first." Naturally I asked why she felt that way. "Because if you move out and leave me," she said, "you'll wind up a homosexual." I had to go and ask why, again. "Because you're weak," she said. "Weak, weak, WEAK."

Dorothy heard out these accusations again and again, but never acknowledged them to be true:

Philip was 19 when he moved out of the house. Here again, his account will differ from mine. It was friendly, in fact it was at my suggestion, and he came back almost every evening for a long talk-fest. I remember the yellow cat we

55

had at the time; he couldn't understand why Philip would come in the front door, stay a couple of hours, and then leave.

But Phil was always adamant: The struggle to break free from his mother's rule was a paradigmatic act of courage that allowed him to enter the dreaded *koinos kosmos* on his own terms. He recognized the erotic overtones of the struggle. To third wife Anne he confided: "When I was a teenager, I had 'the impossible dream.' I dreamt I slept with my mother." His interpretation of the dream: "I won my Oedipal situation." But true victory would not come until he left Dorothy's home. In a 1981 journal entry, Phil theorized that his pattern of impermanent relationships with women was rooted in that event: "I am drawn to women who resemble my mother (proud, intelligent, cruel, judgmental, suspicious, scathing, etc.) in order to re-enact the primordial situation in which I fight my way loose at the end and divide off into autonomy." Later in the same journal entry Phil flip-flopped: "An even more important point could be made: I am searching—not for my mother, the cruel i.e. bad mother—but the good mother, the tender, kind, sympathetic and loving mother I never had but always wanted."

Whether or not Dorothy ever threatened to call the police when Phil moved out, it is fair to assume that she was concerned over Phil's choice of accommodations. His new Berkeley address of 2208 McKinley Street was a warehouse, the upper floor of which had been converted into a rooming house. The rooms were occupied by some of the most notable young gay artists on the Berkeley scene. The leader of the group was Robert Duncan (then twenty-nine), who had just returned from a visit to Ezra Pound at St. Elizabeth's Hospital at Washington, D.C. Others in the shifting house population included poet Jack Spicer, in his early twenties, and Phil's high school friend Gerald Ackerman (a future art historian), who had become lovers with the charismatic Duncan.

Ackerman recalls that Robert Duncan (himself a U Cal Berkeley dropout) and Phil would have long talks: "Being with Duncan was like being in a literature class." Phil also got on well with Spicer, who would come to Phil's room to listen to classical music. Writes Ackerman: "I remember once as they were listening to the Kipnis recording of excerpts from Boris Goudonoff, I waited for the music to end, and knocked on the door, thinking I was not interrupting their music, but I had wrecked, as they loudly lamented, their mood: Boris had just died." The fondness for marijuana by certain of the house residents was not shared, at the time, by Ackerman or Phil. "[T]he giggling and talk Phil and I heard through the door made us think the 'ecstasy' produced by the drug was pretty silly."

Phil's prize possession was a disc recorder, a floor model from University Radio that could produce shellac records. There were "game" sessions in Phil's room, in which Duncan and various visitors would gather to produce strange recordings. Ackerman recalls:

George Haimsohn started out with a slow cut-time "Edna St. Vincent Millay, Millay, Millay," very nancy on the last name. Duncan came in with a deep "W. Somerset Maugham, W. Somerset Maugham, W.W.W.W.W. Somerset Maugham," as in a round. Then I came in with a high, piping "E. E. Cummings. E.E.E.E. Cummings E.E." And while this was all going along someone else started a loud Salute to the Flag. [. . .] Then we all broke down laughing.

Phil's friendships with Duncan and others encouraged him along mainstream literary paths. His interest in SF fell off correspondingly. As for career, Hollis would provide the framework. As Phil recalled in his 1968 "Self Portrait":

I would advance up the ladder, step by step, and eventually I would manage a record store and then at last I would own one. I forgot about sf; in fact I no longer even read it. Like the radio serial, "Jack Armstrong, the All-American Boy!" sf fell into place as an interest of childhood. But I still liked to write, so I wrote little literary bits which I hoped to sell to the New Yorker (I never did). Meanwhile I gorged myself on modern classics of literature: Proust and Pound, Kafka and Dos Passos, Pascal—but now we're getting into the older literature, and my list could go on forever. Let us say simply that I gained a working knowledge of literature from *The Anabasis* to *Ulysses*. I was not educated on sf but on well-recognized serious writing by authors all over the world.

In a 1977 interview, Phil allowed that he had continued to read SF, but that the Berkeley culture of the late forties "required you to have a really thorough grounding in the classics." An SF fandom was emerging, but only "freaks" read SF—who were as ignorant of the classics as the literati were of Robert Heinlein. "I chose the company of those who were reading the great literature because I liked them better as people." The earliest fans were "trolls," and "being stuck with them would have been like something in the first part of Dante's Comedy—up to your ass in shit."

While Phil enjoyed the literary talk at McKinley Street, other aspects of life there—passes made at him by one of his housemates—disturbed him. Ackerman doesn't recall Phil having any affairs—homo or hetero—during his stay. "Phil may have begun to think that since he had similar tastes to the rest of us, he might have similar feelings. I would have told him not to worry."

Meanwhile, a whole new social scene was opening up to Phil due to a new influx of hirings at the Hollis stores.

Vincent Lusby, who joined on in 1947 to manage Art Music, imparted to Phil his enthusiasm for Gregorian chants and Dixieland jazz. In addition, Lusby was serious about writing (producing several well-crafted, unpublished novels of a street-real bent); by the early fifties, he and Phil were exchanging manuscripts and criticism. Lusby also served as the first of many driving teachers for Phil; he recalls Phil as "erratic" behind the wheel. Another newcomer was Alan Rich (now a classical music critic), whose wit and musical erudition provided Phil with a worthy foil for debate. Chuck Bennett, a stylish Irishman from an upper-middle-class family, intrigued Phil as a Lost Generation type (there is something of Bennett—and of Phil himself—in Stuart Hadley in *Voices from the Street*). Jose Flores, a salesclerk with whom Phil developed a particularly close friendship, was gay, a dancer whose skills were failing as he neared forty. When Jose later committed suicide after a failed romance, Phil was desolate.

Among these new faces, Phil was still the youngest of the Hollis crew. At nineteen, Phil had developed a reasonably assured sales manner. His cartoons and graffiti were comic highlights on the walls of the employee bathroom. His typing speed earned him the bill-preparation chores, which he handled flawlessly. But Phil was subject to streaky moods, often starting the day by walking straight to the back of the store without turning his head—"as if on a beam," Lusby recalls. Phil later credited his sales work with providing useful discipline in curbing his temper. He preferred evening shifts, on the theory that passersby would be drawn to the lit-up TVs. In the process, he became a devoted on-duty viewer of *Kukla, Fran and Ollie*.

Phil would sometimes go to hear Dixieland and jazz in local bars like the Steppenwolf, the Blind Lemon, and Hambone Kelly's. The Lu Watters and Turk Murphy bands were the big draws. But by and large he was a hard guy to get out of the house. Vince Lusby recalls him as "agoraphobic." Whatever the label, it was more than an aversion to night life. The Art Music staff habitually lunched at the nearby True Blue Cafeteria. Phil would always choose a balcony table very close to the men's room—both to stay out of sight while he ate and to assure a quick trip if required.

By early 1948, Phil was looking to move out of McKinley Street. He enjoyed Lusby's footloose company and confided in him his worries over being gay. (The irony: Phil had been initially fearful that Lusby was gay and that he would have to do some "ass-kissing" to get in good with the "old auntie" manager.) Lusby first pointed out differences in literary taste between Phil and his gay friends. When that failed, Lusby took more drastic measures:

At that time we had some rather peculiar ideas about homosexuality. Philip, who was a virgin, thought he might be one. I thought it was a curable

58

condition. A good piece of ass and it would be all over. So I availed him of a good piece of ass.

And so came about, at age nineteen, Phil's first marriage—which lasted for six months in 1948, and of which he seldom spoke for the rest of his life.

She was named Jeanette Marlin, a blond-haired regular customer with whom Lusby was acquainted. Edgar Dick, who met her after the wedding, recalls Jeanette as a "short fat little girl." Lusby's physical description is less flattering, and he adds that Jeanette was not particularly artistic or musical. She was no "girl," however, being, in her late twenties, several years Phil's senior. Jeanette was outspoken, with a frank approach to sex. They were introduced one day as she was browsing at University Radio. Phil led her to a listening booth and brought in his favorite classical recordings. Their talk became ever more friendly. There was a seldom-used storage room down in the basement, past the repair shop. Lusby notes that this room—in which Phil first made love with Jeanette—forms an important setting (as shelter, during the nuclear blasts, for the employees of Modern TV Sales & Service) in *Dr. Blood-money*.

As Phil was below the age of majority under California law, Dorothy had to sign the certificate to make their spring 1948 marriage legal. She had her doubts but gave her consent in hopes that marriage would make Phil feel better about himself. At the least, from her point of view, it separated him from the McKinley Street scene. The new couple found a tiny apartment (located behind a drugstore) on Addison Way. Gerald Ackerman recalls the setting:

All was dark, messy, disorderly; the usual painting of the new apartment had not taken place, nor did there seem to be any furniture of charm. I have the feeling that although they had been there some time, the place was full of unpacked boxes. [. . .] And perhaps I was mad that he got married, as if that was a betrayal of our communal life. [. . .] At any rate, the visit was one of discomfort: the apartment was uncomfortable, the circumstances un-comfortable; the wife seemed to fit into no conception of Phil's or my life. I can only see her as either an unfriendly or frightened presence, standing behind a stuffed chair with her hands resting on the back, as if it were a shield. [. . .] I can see now that they were just as bewildered to be there as I was to see them there.

One could speculate that a brief account of a marriage in *Gather Yourselves Together,* written shortly after the divorce from Jeanette, ex-presses some of Phil's own feelings on their home life: "Her treasure was sold dearly; he found himself married, all at once, living in a one-room apartment, watching her string bras and underpants across the bathroom, smelling the starch and iron in the kitchen, and the eternal mechanical presence of pin curls next to him on the pillow. The marriage lasted only a few months."

Phil told his fifth wife, Tessa, that when he and Jeanette had been married less than two months, she told Phil that she had the right to see other men. At this, he moved her things outside the apartment door, changed the locks, and refused to allow her to return. "Looking back," Tessa writes, "Phil realized his mother had been right, that they were too young to get married. At the time, though, it cut him to the quick."

But the crowning blow to their marital bliss was Phil's love for his Magnavox. Jeanette complained that Phil kept her up at night by playing records over and over, records that Jeanette said she hated—the same records with which Phil had wooed her that first day in the listening room. Once she threatened to have her brother come over and break the damn things.

The judge at their autumn 1948 court hearing said he had never heard more silly grounds for divorce than threatened record smashing, but granted it anyway. The one thing Phil liked about Jeanette, he would later say, was that she left him alone while he worked on stories—primarily mainstream—that did not sell. The marriage might not have been a roaring success, but it did wonders for Phil's confidence. Three decades later, in the mid-seventies, Phil called Lusby long distance to thank him again for saving him from homosexuality.

In early 1949 Phil moved to a new place on Bancroft Way. The Magnavox and piles of SF magazines dominated the tiny space. In addition, he and Lusby leased an apartment near Grove and Shattuck, which they time-shared on the basis of who had gotten lucky with Art Music's female customers that day. Phil at twenty had boyish good looks—brown hair that hung lankily over his broad forehead, sensual lips, and the guarded, penetrating blue eyes. He walked slightly stooped and dressed in flannel shirts. But he could turn on a smile and had the gift of gab. Lusby's assessment: "Phil became fairly competent at hustling once he found out what girls were for."

It's doubtful that Phil quite kept pace with Lusby (who would soon remarry). But he did go through a series of brief, intense affairs of the heart. Not all of his loves were reciprocated, of course. He developed a mad crush on Kay Lindy, who worked at University Radio, but she preferred Lusby. There was a Miriam whom Phil adored, but she instead became lovers with Connie Barbour, a future Jungian therapist; Miriam and Connie became Phil's neighbors when he moved (later in 1949) to larger digs at 1931 Dwight Way. Kleo Mini describes Connie as "like an older sister" to Phil; she led him to read virtually all of Jung's work available in translation.

One love whom Phil would recall with deep feeling was Mary, a striking Italian woman who worked in a drugstore and was unhappy in her marriage. Like Jeanette, she was several years older than Phil. Mary soon called off the illicit affair, in part because of guilt, in part because she felt that Phil *needed* her more than he loved her. Also, she felt uncomfortable within Phil's circle of friends, disliked his narrow musical tastes, which excluded popular songs, and distrusted his casual sophistication (newly acquired!) about sex. Phil insisted, in letters pleading with her to see him again, that they had a unique understanding; he contrasted this understanding to his vision of a *koinos kosmos*, rife with pseudo-realities, that resembles the SF novels to come. Adults must protect their "unique center of consciousness" by "a series of false-front personalities which we shine in the faces of the people we meet to try to dazzle them." One longs to find someone with whom all masks can be dropped. "Have you someone in your life that you can feel this freedom with, Mary?"

But the woman whom Phil was to bemoan, in later years, as his great lost love was Betty Jo Rivers. He and Lusby both marveled at her beauty one day in April 1949, as she stood outside the Art Music window. Phil thought that her short brown hair looked like the helmet of a Valkyrie from Wagner. When she entered the shop, looking for a gift for her clean-cut boyfriend (a fellow English major at U Cal), Phil immediately took her by the arm and led her to a listening room. When she mentioned Buxtehude (a composer her boyfriend had requested but whom she'd never heard of), Phil assumed she adored classical music and brought her album after album for approval. When she made her purchase, he walked her home. They talked fervently the whole way, and upon arrival Betty Jo invited Phil in for a sandwich. She recalls that he "turned green" and asked, "Eat with another person in the room?"

A love affair blossomed, and the clean-cut boyfriend was shown the door. "We had an almost exaggerated, movie-type romance." They spent hours discussing books, music, and the big issues. Phil soon felt comfortable eating in Betty Jo's company, but he would not go with her to restaurants. When he tried to attend events that mattered to her, embarrassments abounded. "Phil didn't fit into any circle I had. He was difficult to take anywhere—extremely shy." After one fiasco, Phil gave her inscribed copies of two of his favorite books, William James's *The Varieties of Religious Experience* and James Stephens's *The Crock of Gold:* "To Betty, in exchange for six social errors at once." He could handle people at work, he assured her, though he preferred to be out of sight unpacking records. Phil was seeing a therapist and blamed many of his fears on Jane's death. "He always felt it was like the German myth or legend of the person who has to look for his other half and that he was an incomplete person because he was born one of twins. He used to attribute his food problems to that."

Much of their time together was spent at Phil's Dwight Way attic apartment. His room was crammed with pulps, to which he was trying, as yet unsuccessfully, to market tales that were closer to fantasy than to SF. Some of these found their way into print (in highly revised form) in the early fifties, once Phil started to make it as an SF writer. But his primary efforts were devoted to mainstream stories. Phil wrote dozens of these during this period, all now lost. All that is certain is that their repeated rejection by editors was a heartbreak to Phil, who yearned for mainstream status—then and always.

But if Phil was as yet an unpublished writer, his fervor and commitment were evident enough to Betty Jo: "Phil's attraction was all that talent boiling around, getting ready to explode." But Phil wasn't yet comfortable identifying himself as a writer. Instead, he imagined a blissful future in which Betty Jo was the writer and he would bring in fresh orange juice as she worked. "I think he was fantasizing somebody to share the pressure he was under to get started writing, and that was the last thing I wanted." Betty Jo had won a grant for graduate study in France and was completing her master's thesis, an effort that Phil encouraged despite his own academic discontent. But when he asked her to choose between France and marriage, Betty Jo had no hesitation. Off to France she went.

That autumn, Phil gave academia one last try. From September to November 1949, he attended U Cal Berkeley. He'd been out on his own for two years, and the decision must have required considerable soul-searching in light of the horrific memories of vertigo in high school. Phil was twenty when he registered for courses in history, zoology, and philosophy (his major) along with the mandatory ROTC training. One of his philosophy teachers directed him to David Hume, whose wry, polished skepticism was right up Phil's alley; in particular, he admired Hume's argument against causality: that A precedes B cannot prove that A caused B. Phil also attended lectures on the German Romantics, which deepened his love for the lyrics of Goethe and Heine. But the ROTC courses were distasteful. Phil retained Dorothy's pacifistic outlook and voiced his objection to the policy of widening U.S. military involvement in Korea. Phil would recall his refusal to march with a rifle, instead taking a broom to parade.

But the U Cal transcript reflects that he voluntarily withdrew from the university in November and was granted an honorable dismissal in January; his later claims that he was "expelled" and "told never to come back" because of defiance shown to ROTC training and/or pompous professors seem unlikely. After withdrawing, Phil became subject to the draft, but he was rejected due to high blood pressure.

Iskandar Guy, a Berkeley friend of Phil's in the fifties, would hear of a far less rebellious, far more terrifying university experience. There was a renewed attack of vertigo, in which agoraphobia or high blood pressure could have played a part. Whatever the label, the experience was devastating:

He would mention the horrible experiences he'd had while going to Cal. The whole bloody world collapsed on him psychologically as he was walking down a classroom aisle. It was something of such pain—not hyperbole, but extreme fucking pain we're talking about—like the whole world disappeared in front of him and he was turned into this painful, vulnerable, embattled thing, and where at any moment the floor might open up and he might be canceled out as a living entity. Those were the kinds of statements he would make. Apparently he had been somewhat tenuous about his involvement with formal education before, but that did it. He felt crippled by this experience; he gave me the impression of feeling handicapped by it.

To interviewer Paul Williams—who inquired in 1974 about the self-styled "nervous breakdown" that caused him to leave college—Phil acknowledged the rebellion and the fear:

PKD: [. . .] Well, I mean that at about nineteen, um, I was unable to continue doing what I was doing, because I really unconsciously didn't want to do it. [. . .]

PW: And "it" was going to Berkeley and taking ROTC and all that kind of thing?

PKD: Yeah!

PW: Both, right, not just the ROTC?

PKD: Correct. Yeah, I had a whole bunch of courses that were just so much birdshit. [. . .] I'm standing there looking in the microscope. And there aren't even any paramecia in there at all, 'cause the slide moved. And the instruction is, "Draw what you see," And I realize that there's nothing there, nothing at all. But I can't consciously face the fact that this is a symbol of my whole projected four years there, I'm drawing pictures of things that—

PW: That aren't even there.

PKD: So I began to get terribly frightened and anxious and I didn't know why. Now I know why. I would have screwed up my life forever. [. . .] Fortunately I listened to my unconscious because it was too strong to be denied. [. . .] It drove me out of the cloistered realms where I would have been cut off from the broader, truer world, and drove me into the real world. It drove me into a job, and marriage, and a career in writing, and a more substantial life. [. . .] I'm very defensive about all this still, you see? Because I didn't finish college.

Phil's defensiveness didn't show itself at the time. None of his friends recall any apologetics over dropping out—and this in a markedly academic community. Phil's outward calm was due in part to the respect shown his intelligence even in erudite circles.

His two major writing efforts of the late forties, a fragment of a novel, *The Earthshaker* (c. 1947–48), and a completed novel, *Gather Yourselves*

Together (c. 1949–50), evidence the jarring, passionate impact of Phil's discovery of sex. Only portions of the first two chapters of *The Earthshaker* survive; he did not complete it, but an outline and treatment notes give some indication of what Phil intended for the whole. These notes make reference to gnosis, cabala, and the world-tree Yggdrasill, among other esoteric themes. Major characters are derived from Jungian archetypes: wanderer, miraculous child, silly old wise man, earth woman, serpent. The prose style is unvarnished realism. As for sex, it is (as the treatment notes state) an "act of unreason, of impersonality, of unhumanity, of unbeing." When a woman lures a man into sex, and then later gives birth, her "control over the man is complete." From out of the depths of mother hatred and adolescent sexual despair, Phil was conceiving a most fearful novel. It is hardly a wonder that he could not bring himself to finish it.

Gather Yourselves Together, which remains unpublished (but may find a publisher in the near future) is set in the emergent Maoist China of 1949. Three employees of an American corporate operation that has been nationalized await the Chinese troops who will take control of the grounds. There is a faint political theme (tacked on as an ending) comparing the atheistic Chinese, in their fervor, to the early Christians, while America has become an imperial Rome. But most of the novel explores, through flashbacks, the psyches of the three employees—Verne, Carl, and Barbara—who go through a turbulent ménage à trois during their isolated wait. Verne is a cynical man of the world who some years before took Barbara's virginity (as the novel stresses) and left her embittered. She tries to overcome that hurt by making love with Verne again. Mistake. Her thoughts turn to young Carl, whom she seduces (recapitulating her seduction by Verne). Poor Carl goes through spiritual shock on first espying her body as she swims in the pond of the Edenic company grounds:

> He had lost all the cherished images and illusions, but he understood something now that had eluded him before. Bodies, his body, her body, all were about the same. All were part of the same world. There was nothing outside the world, no great realm of the phantom soul, the region of the sublime. There was only this—what he saw with his eyes [. . .] all the dreams and notions he had held so long had abruptly winked out of existence. Vanished silently, like a soap bubble.

The life of randy bachelorhood to which Lusby had introduced Phil, which he immediately sought to escape by marrying Jeanette Marlin, never did take hold. Since leaving his mother's house Phil had been seeking a home. The domestic fantasy of serving Betty Jo orange juice as *she* wrote was a transposition (as Betty Jo observes) of his own fear of entering the writer's life without a companion to whom to turn when his daily imaginings were done.

Phil needed a wife. He also needed the guidance of an editor sympathetic to SF plots concocted with mainstream style and smarts.

And the sometimes kindly Cosmos, seeing the plight of this young writer and, perhaps, sensing within him the works that would pick It apart, promptly provided both.

4 A Real Writer At Last, Phil Learns The Facts Of Life In The SF Ghetto And Tries To Get The Hell Out—But Writes His Best Stuff Inside It (Hence The Confusion) (1950–1958)

It was like living in La Bohème—*great, extremely romantic. Were we poor? We had a house, though never any money to speak of . . . We had Linden chicken gravy with giblets at ten cents a can once a week—or more. We loved it! With baked or steamed potatoes.*

KLEO MINI

In reading the stories included in this volume, you should bear in mind that most were written when SF was so looked down upon that it virtually was not there, in the eyes of all America. This was not funny, the derision felt toward SF writers. It made our lives wretched. Even in Berkeley—or especially in Berkeley—people would say, "But are you writing anything serious?" We made no money; few publishers published SF (Ace Books was the only regular book publisher of SF); and really cruel abuse was inflicted upon us.

PHIL, "Introduction" to *The Golden Man* (1980)

You knew [as to writing SF in the early fifties] you had the shitty end of the stick, but at least you had your hand on the stick. Terry Carr [SF editor] used to have a line about how if the Holy Bible was printed as an Ace Double it would be cut down to two 20,000-word halves with the Old Testament retitled as Master of Chaos *and the New Testament as* The Thing with Three Souls.

KAREN ANDERSON, wife of SF writer Poul Anderson

AMERICA in the fifties was a strange and wondrous place to set up shop as an SF writer, as Phil would.

It is true enough that SF was disdained by all clean and decent persons with pretensions to culture. But it is also true that a steadily growing number of readers (mostly kids, but also World War II and

Korean War vets who could well believe in the futuristic perils of the new Atomic Age) loved the stuff. Not only did it offer unbridled action and adventure, it also recognized—as mainstream fiction seldom did—that society was heading irrevocably toward major technological changes that would, in turn, redefine the scope of the shit that happens to us all. Long before computers became bureaucratic fixtures, they were consulted by mad scientists in fifties SF.

As a result, the SF pulps enjoyed, in the first half of that decade, an economic boom time. There was a proliferation of soon-to-vanish titles—such as *Dynamic SF, Rocket Stories,* and even, *very* briefly, *Les Adventures Futuristes*—out there on U.S. newsstands. Selling stories to the pulps did not bring fame and fortune, but it did allow young writers serving their apprenticeships to make a living at writing SF.

Phil may have felt déclassé early on as an SF writer, but he *was* honing his talent. And he was fortunate enough to find two persons who guided him through the solitude and uncertainties of a writer's life. The first was Kleo Apostolides, whom Phil married in June 1950 and with whom he spent the most placid (for Phil) eight years of his life. The second was Anthony Boucher, editor of *The Magazine of Fantasy and Science Fiction,* who helped transform Phil into the most prolific young SF writer of his era.

Kleo was eighteen when she first met Phil in Art Music in the winter of 1949. She enjoyed opera, so naturally she and Phil began to talk. Kleo was Greek, dark-haired, with strong features, a rounded figure, and a pleasant laugh that shifted easily into high-pitched giggles. She liked life, knew what she was about, and was intensely curious and intellectual without the least bit of pretension. Kleo noticed that Phil was shy. She invited him over to her place to listen to records. Then they had their first real date.

Yee Jun's, in San Francisco's Chinatown, was Phil's place to take people because of its small size and high-walled private booths. A waiter named Walter knew Phil well. Recalls Kleo: "Walter wound up ordering for us. We didn't eat very much—we were too nervous—and at the end of dinner Walter scolded us, then packed everything up and made us take it home. Very charming."

Kleo became a regular visitor to Phil's Dwight Way attic apartment. He had two roommates at the time: Alex, a tall, blond Pole, and Taufig, of Turkish or Syrian descent. Everyone got on well, and the garretlike atmosphere of slanted ceilings and walls painted in bright primary colors (the prevailing Berkeley style) delighted Kleo. Phil's room was all books and records, along with a Dutch oven and a little gas stove for the simplest of meals. Ultimately Alex and Taufig bowed out and Kleo moved in.

While Phil alternated between Art Music and University Radio, Kleo was attending U Cal and changing her major often, finally settling on a general curriculum major. She read omnivorously and took up sculpture. A variety of university-related part-time jobs allowed her to make do and, ultimately, provide critical economic support for Phil through the first years of his writing career.

Even before meeting Kleo, Phil had begun making payments on an old house at 1126 Francisco in the west Berkeley flatlands. He was due to take occupancy in May 1950. Phil proposed marriage. Says Kleo:

> I didn't care one way or the other but we were in a very romantic period, Phil mentioned it, and so I said okay, but it would have been fine if it hadn't been brought up—if you're living together everyone assumes you're married, so why make a big deal about it? But Phil was a little anxious. For one thing, I was under 21, and he was afraid that his mother might report us to the authorities at one time or another. I don't know, it sounded wacky to me.

Dorothy proved easily amenable to her son's second marriage at age twenty-one. But she never got on with Kleo, who seemed to Dorothy to be withdrawn in her company. Dorothy was quite right: Kleo did not like her, due to Phil's tales of childhood woes and to her own perception that "Dorothy was such a bright woman and made her own way but her relationships with people stemmed from a very bitter view of the world— one I didn't share."

The little opposition to the marriage that arose came from Kleo's side of the family. When Kleo told her mother, Alexandra, the news, she burst into tears—Phil wasn't Greek. Her father, Emmanuel, a San Francisco physician, didn't learn of the wedding until after the fact because it was assumed that he would vehemently disapprove. But Phil soon got on splendidly with them both, talking medicine with Emmanuel and Greek drama and mystery religions with Alexandra, who had a B.A. in classics.

The June 1950 ceremony took place in Oakland City Hall. Kleo recalls:

> The judge was very sweet to us. He took longer than priests usually do in more formal weddings and gave a nice talk reminding us not to get angry and to try to see each other's point of view. On the way home we had to transfer buses, and I was wearing this awful brown coat, and while we were waiting for the second bus a bird on top of a building made droppings right on the coat. And I asked, "What does this portend?" Philip laughed like hell and said his mother had sent the bird.

Phil describes their two-story house just off working-class San Pablo Avenue in *Radio Free Albemuth* (1985): "The house was very old—one of the original Berkeley farmhouses—on a lot only thirty feet wide, with no garage, on a mud sill, the only heat being from the oven in the kitchen.

His monthly payments were $27.50, which is why he stayed there so long."

His determination to be a writer held strong, despite a steady stream of rejections of his mainstream stories. It was still, as the decade began, the mainstream that held him. While his writing time was limited by his Art Music job, Phil was disciplined enough to pursue his craft in the late-night hours. He used the tiny dining room as his writing office; alongside his desk and typewriter were his Magnavox and record collection (he always wrote to classical music) and cats such as Magnificat, who would fall asleep and slide off Phil's file cabinets. Rejection slips were taped to the walls. Kleo swears that once seventeen manuscripts came back on the same day. "We had this little mailbox and they spilled out onto the porch. He just sent them right out again. We both knew Philip had talent. We also knew that didn't have much to do with whether his work would sell."

In the living room was a large TV (Phil believed in the Hollis goods he sold), for which he built a protective plywood case. The roof leaked (they positioned buckets when the rains came), and mice nested in a gap in the kitchen ceiling. Says Kleo:

> We sat at our little kitchen table and looked up at the mouse tails. If you flipped its tail, the mouse would go away. When it got to four tails, we decided to rig up a trap in our little pantry—a coffee can propped up on a matchstick to which we tied a string. We caught thirty-two mice over several weeks, and would take them across to the vacant lots and let them go. Over the weeks the tails kept getting smaller and smaller, and we began to have bad feelings about it all. One of the last small mice was so weird and clever. We thought hard—and we just let him stay.

Phil had been devoting his primary writing energies to mainstream fiction—the massive *Gather Yourselves Together* and at least two dozen stories that have not survived. His return to SF came through his meeting with William Anthony Parker White, a/k/a H. H. Holmes or (as the SF world knew him) Anthony Boucher.

Under his real name of White, Boucher reviewed mystery novels in the *New York Times* and *San Francisco Chronicle*. As Holmes, he wrote mystery novels and scripts for the *Adventures of Gregory Hood* radio show. As Boucher, he published SF and fantasy stories. Boucher's stories never influenced Phil, but his editing skills surely did. At age thirty-eight, in 1949, he had co-founded *The Magazine of Fantasy and Science Fiction* with J. Francis McComas. *F & SF* stressed literary graces over the hard-science angle—usually pseudo-science in execution—favored by most SF editors. If that doesn't seem like revolutionary literary theory, it passed for it in the pulp climate of the early fifties.

Boucher was a record collector and host of *Golden Voices of the Opera* on KPFA. It was at Art Music that Phil met him. Through him, Phil recalled in his 1968 "Self Portrait," "I discovered that a person could be not only mature, but mature and educated, and still enjoy sf." Phil was also struck by the man himself. Boucher was urbane and kindly, Catholic in faith and in intellect as well. Utterly devoted to books, Boucher read even as he walked along the Berkeley streets.

Boucher taught a weekly writing class at his Berkeley home at 2643 Dana Street. Every Thursday night, anyone who paid a nominal one-dollar fee (generally eight to ten students per night) could submit man-uscripts to Boucher's exacting yet gracious scrutiny. He read them aloud in a voice resembling that of Dylan Thomas. A constant smoker, he kept an atomizer near to hand. Writer Ron Goulart, who attended Boucher's classes in 1951, recalls that he stressed this rule for SF and fantasy: "You were allowed *one* initial premise from which everything followed—you could have a person who walked through walls, but not another person in the same story who was invisible. He would quote H. G. Wells that a pig that could fly over hedges was fantasy, but if all animals could fly it became something else."

Among the occasional students was Dorothy, whose efforts at main-stream fiction were having no more luck than Phil's. For all of his anger toward Dorothy, Phil often gave her his manuscripts to read. At her urging, Phil attended a few sessions, but soon felt twinges of the fear that so often marked his classroom experiences. Kleo would go in his stead and note down Boucher's comments on his manuscripts. At last came a breakthrough. The "Self Portrait" continues:

> The literary ones he did not respond to, but to my surprise he seemed quite taken with a short fantasy which I had done; he seemed to be weighing it in almost terms of economic worth. This caused me to begin writing more and more fantasy stories, and then sf. In October, 1951, when I was twenty-one years old, I sold my first story: a tiny fantasy to *F&SF*, the magazine which Tony Boucher edited.

The story was "Roog" (originally titled "Friday Morning"), and Boucher forced Phil to go through several drafts before finally accepting it. In the tale, Boris the dog realizes that the garbagemen who haul away the trash are really alien Roogs who thrive on the food packed in metal "offering urns." Boris barks "Roog!" to alert his owners, but they are annoyed and plan to give him away. This human indifference helps the Roogs' cause:

> "Roog! Roog!" Boris cried, huddled against the bottom of the porch steps. His body shook with horror. The Roogs were lifting up the big metal can, turning it on its side. The contents poured out onto the ground. [. . .]

Then slowly, silently, the Roogs looked up, up the side of the house, along the stucco, to the window, with its brown shade pulled tightly down.

"Roog" was inspired by Snooper, an Australian shepherd next door, who barked every Friday morning during garbage collections. Phil lost sleep, but the story remained a favorite:

So here, in a primitive form, is the basis of much of my twenty-seven years of professional writing: the attempt to get into another person's head, or another creature's head, and see out from his eyes or its eyes, and the more different that person is from the rest of us the better. [. . .] I began to develop the idea that each creature lives in a world somewhat different from all the other creatures and their worlds.

Phil always remembered with pleasure "that day a letter arrived in the mail, instead of a manuscript back with a rejection slip." Boucher had paid him *money* (seventy-five dollars) for a *story* that he could write (or rather type at breakneck speed, with Kleo copy editing) in the magical privacy of his own home!

I began to mail off stories to other sf magazines, and lo and behold, Planet Stories bought a short story of mine. In a blaze of Faust-like fire I abruptly quit my job at the record shop, forgot my career in records, and began to write all the time (how I did it I don't yet know; I worked until four each morning). Within the month after quitting my job I made a sale to Astounding (now called Analog) and Galaxy. They paid very well, and I knew then that I would never give up trying to build my life around a science fiction career.

Did Phil really quit his job on the basis of that first sale? No doubt he considered it, but Kleo recalls that Phil was fired due to his breach of the rigid Hollis loyalty code.

In retrospect, the transgression seems ridiculously petty. Hollis had hired Norman Mini as a salesclerk for University Radio. Mini (who would marry Kleo a decade later, after her divorce from Phil) was a colorful Berkeley character, twenty years older than Phil, who once was a Communist party member. By the early fifties, Mini had renounced all party ties and even testified before the California State House Un-American Activities Committee.

By the early sixties, Phil would speak in worried tones about un-specified "communist" activities on Mini's part that somehow had led to Phil's coming under surveillance. At the time, however, Phil admired Mini, who was one of the few men in Berkeley to wear three-piece suits and was commonly taken to be the owner of the shop. While Hollis could stand being upstaged, he could not tolerate what he regarded as dis-respectful behavior toward female customers. The ax fell when one day

71

Mini punningly responded, after a woman asked for an album by the Kunsthalle Orchestra, "Oh, you mean that *all-girl* orchestra from Germany?"

Despite his agoraphobic fears, Phil (who had in the past made vehement protests against Hollis's autocratic style) testified on Mini's behalf at the unemployment hearing. Some months later, when Mini dropped by Art Music to visit, Phil spoke with him and was spotted by Eldon Nicholls, Hollis's second-in-command. Nicholls and Phil were fond of each other, but Nicholls's first loyalty was to Hollis, and he felt bound to report the unseemly fraternization. Hollis, outraged, fired Phil. The pain was considerable. (Phil later drew from his memories of Nicholls in creating Hoppy Harrington, a genetic freak whose fortunes rise in the aftermath of nuclear holocaust in *Dr. Bloodmoney* [1965].)

SF story sales made Phil's firing seem fated in the long run. He gave the record store business two more brief tries. Shortly after being fired, Phil caught on with Art Music's leading competitor, Tupper & Reed. But he quit almost immediately. Phil later described this time as his second "nervous breakdown" (the first having been his flight from U Cal):

I bought a house, I was married, and I felt like I should be leaving in the morning and going to work like everybody else. My unconscious just saturated me with anxiety when I got there, to the record store, and I couldn't comprehend why. And I started to faint.

Now these are obvious [. . .] hysterical conversion symptoms, to get you out of a situation that you don't want to be in. Later I realized, my God, I would have been back in the retail record business [. . .] But I was forced to go back to writing.

Kleo observes that the formality of Tupper & Reed, after Phil's years of familiarity with Hollis, played a critical part:

A sense of stuffiness was one of his major sensations during times of agoraphobic fear. Those breathing and swallowing problems—Phil would confuse the physical and social realms, or rather the social realm underlay those physical symptoms. During family dinners with his mother, he would have those sorts of physical manifestations and be forced to leave early. He could have casual dinners with three or four people he felt comfortable with. And stand-up parties were OK as long as you were free to come and go. But Tupper & Reed was too tight—it was up on a second floor, carpeted, and catered to a wealthier clientele. Phil couldn't handle it and he wanted to be home writing anyway, so he quit.

There was one more try. In late 1953, Herb Hollis died, and his wife, Pat, asked Phil to help with the business. Phil gave it a try for a few days, but he had already tasted freedom. Again he quit. Phil would later mention an A & R (Artists and Repertoire) job offer made to him at this time by Capitol Records. It may be; Kleo doesn't recall it, and at any rate he turned it down.

Phil could fantasize about cutting a swath in the big wide world. At heart, however, he was happy to let that world go by. Or rather, he imagined he could write in peace and have it to come to him. After all, he could *sell* SF stories.

Which allowed him, with Kleo's help, to just scrape by.

♦

In 1946, in the aftermath of the wartime paper shortage, there were eight SF magazines appearing regularly. By 1950 there were nearly twenty; by 1953, the number had climbed to twenty-seven. They were readily distinguishable—by their bug-eyed-monster covers and pulpy titles like *Thrilling Wonder Stories* and *Fantastic Story Magazine*—from respectable "slicks" like *Collier's* and the *Saturday Evening Post*.

What led to the SF boom? In part, the pulps rode with the economic good times of postwar America. But there was also a growing public fascination with the possibilities, wondrous and dreadful, posed by the threat of atomic destruction. Even before Hiroshima and Nagasaki, this had been a frequent theme of SF writers. The convergence of the SF future and the American present lent a vitality to SF—it could be both glorious escapism and serious prophecy.

Phil moved fast after "Roog." By May 1952 he had sold four more stories on his own. It was time to find an agent. Scott Meredith, who had just founded an agency, drew much of his clientele from regular pulp contributors. Phil first proposed that the agency represent only his mainstream work. Meredith insisted on the SF as well. Phil gave in, and the relationship endured (give or take a few severe bumps) for his entire career.

The Meredith Agency's cozy contacts with New York–based pulp editors, plus Phil's amazing capacity for generating startling possibilities, produced an explosion in a market that was ready for one. SF historian Michael Ashley observes that by mid-1953 "Sf writers had never had it so good: with titles appearing daily, their writings would sell somewhere. New writers had ample opportunity to ply their wares and also to experiment."

In 1952 four Phil Dick stories—fantasy and SF—appeared. In 1953 there were thirty, including seven in June 1953 alone. In 1954 he published twenty-eight more. In 1955 Rich & Cowan, a British publishing house, chose fifteen for hard-cover publication (an honor seldom accorded SF in the U.S. at that time) as *A Handful of Darkness*. A second collection, *The Variable Man*, was issued by Ace in 1957. Phil was prone to deride their quality in comparison to his later work, and it is hard to disagree. They were, at their best, trial runs for far more intricate

Phildickian worlds. But a good many are very good indeed—suspenseful or funny as hell or both. Phil pounded them out at the rate of a story per week. From his "Afterthoughts" to the 1977 *The Best of Philip K. Dick* collection:

> The majority of these stories were written when my life was simpler and made sense. I could tell the difference between the real world and the world I wrote about. I used to dig in the garden, and there is nothing fantastic or ultradimensional about crab grass . . . unless you are an sf writer, in which case pretty soon you are viewing crabgrass with suspicion. [. . .] One day the crab grass suits will fall off and their true identity will be revealed. By then the Pentagon will be full of crab grass and it'll be too late. [. . .] My earlier stories had such premises. Later, when my personal life became complicated and full of unfortunate convolutions, worries about crab grass got lost somewhere. I became educated to the fact that the greatest pain does not come zooming down from a distant planet, but up from the depths of the heart. Of course, both could happen; your wife and child could leave you, and you could be sitting alone in your empty house with nothing to live for, and in addition the Martians could bore through the roof and get you.

The closest Phil ever came to this crab grass story is a brilliant little horror tale in SF clothing called "Colony," which appeared in the June 1953 *Galaxy*, edited by Horace Gold; it was also adapted for the *X Minus One* radio program aired in October 1956. An overpopulated Earth needs worlds to colonize. Commander Morrison (a woman—highly unusual for fifties SF) pushes for approval of a new planet that passes all scientific tests. Then Major Hall's microscope tries to strangle him. Hall is suspected of "psychotic projection." But the attacks continue, carried on by faked objects—the mimickry of the planet's malevolent life force:

> The towel wrapped around his wrist, yanking him against the wall. Rough cloth pressed over his mouth and nose. He fought wildly, pulling away. All at once the towel let go. He fell, sliding to the floor, his head striking the wall. Stars shot around him; then violent pain.
> Sitting in a pool of warm water, Hall looked up at the towel rack. The towel was motionless now, like the others with it. Three towels in a row, all exactly alike, all unmoving. Had he dreamed it?
> [. . .] His belt got him around the waist and tried to crush him. It was strong—it had reinforced metal links to hold his leggings and his gun.

In the end, the entire exploration crew is gobbled up by a fake rescue ship into which they have all climbed naked (no longer being able to trust their clothes). Phil wrote of "Colony": "The ultimate in paranoia is not when everyone is against you but when every*thing* is against you. Instead of 'My boss is plotting against me,' it would be 'My boss's phone is plotting against me.'!"

For a time, Phil enjoyed a happy relationship with *Galaxy* editor Gold. During 1954 they corresponded as to their mutual agoraphobic difficulties, and Phil confided that he felt stuck at the "emotional age" of nine years and six months (when he and Dorothy moved from Washington to Berkeley). But Gold, in typical pulp fashion, felt free to substantially revise stories without consulting the writer. The practice drove many writers (financially dependent, to the tune of three to four cents per word, on Gold's good graces) to despair, Phil among them: "[D]espite the fact that Galaxy was my main source of income I told Gold that I would not sell to him unless he stopped altering my stories—after which [1954] he bought nothing from me at all."

Such was life in the SF subbasement, even with the best editors. But Phil was gracious enough to give Gold credit for improving the ending of Phil's best fantasy story, "The King of the Elves," which appeared in the September 1953 *Beyond Fantasy Fiction* (a sister publication to *Galaxy*). Shadrach Jones, an old man in a desolate small town, offers shelter from the rain to a tattered troup of Elves, whose ailing King dies in Shadrach's bed. The Elves are battered from their fierce war with the Trolls; they badly need a new King and convince Shadrach to lead them. His neighbor, Phineas Judd, tries to persuade Shadrach that he is losing his mind—but Phineas is himself revealed, in a master stroke of paranoia become real, as the evil and ghastly Great Troll. At the end, with Phineas and his Trolls defeated in fierce battle, Shadrach abandons the throne. It was Gold's idea to have Shadrach change his mind and come back to lead the Elves. The ending, as Phil revised it:

> The little circle of Elf torches closed in joyously. In their light, he [Shadrach] saw a platform like the one that had carried the old King of the Elves. But this one was much larger, big enough to hold a man, and dozens of the soldiers waited with proud shoulders under the shafts.
> A soldier gave him a happy bow. "For you, Sire."
> Shadrach climbed aboard. It was less comfortable than walking, but he knew that this was how they wanted to take him to the Kingdom of the Elves.

Efforts have been made to precisely distinguish the SF and fantasy genres; in 1981 Phil declared it "impossible to do": "Fantasy involves that which general opinion regards as impossible, science fiction involves that which general opinion regards as possible under the right circumstances. This is in essence a judgment-call [. . .]" Back in 1954, the difference was clear enough to the young writer. He saw his fantasy characters as projected Jungian archetypes. "I had a term I used. Inner-projection stories. Stories where internal psychological contents were projected onto the outer world and became three-dimensional and real and concrete." In a September 1954 letter, Phil confided that fantasy was his own "private love" but that it was "disappearing from the marketplace." "[A] writer doesn't work in a vacuum; if people don't want or don't like what he's doing, the fire seems to go out of it."

"Impostor" was the only story of Phil's ever purchased for *Astounding* (June 1953) by the then-doyen of SF editors, John W. Campbell, Jr. Earth is at war with the Outspacers, and Spence Olham, a defense researcher, is under suspicion of being an Outspacer "humanoid robot" (Phil would later adopt the term "android") that has killed the real, human Spence. There is a "U-Bomb" implanted in the robot triggered to explode when a certain phrase is spoken. The robot "would become Olham in mind as well as the body. He was given an artificial memory system, false recall. He would look like him, have his memories, his thoughts and interests, perform his job." And so Security is out to kill Spence, who can't convince them that he's really human. And he really *isn't*—and that realization sets off the U-Bomb. The implanted-memory theme remained one of Phil's favorite means of exploring the possibilities of "fake" reality.

In "Impostor," robot Spence wins the reader's sympathy far more than do his calculating human pursuers. In "Human Is" (Winter 1955 *Startling Stories*), an alien also takes over a human form. Lester Herrick was a jerk to his wife, who prefers the gracious and loving alien soul now occupying his body—she saves the alien's life when the authorities track it down. Phil wrote of "Human Is":

> I have not really changed my view since I wrote this story, back in the fifties. It's not what you look like, or what planet you were born on. It's how kind you are. The quality of kindness, to me, distinguishes us from rocks and sticks and metal, and will forever, whatever shape we take, wherever we go, whatever we become. For me, "Human Is" is my credo. May it be yours.

Editor Campbell presided over *Astounding* for the unheard of duration of 1937 to 1971. His "archetypal sf story": "I want the kind of story that could be printed in a magazine of the year two thousand A.D. as a contemporary adventure story. No gee-whiz, just take the technology for granted." Campbell, Phil recalled, "considered my writing not only worthless but, as he put it, 'Nuts.' " Campbell also told Phil that he viewed psionics (e.g., telepathy, telekinesis, and precognition) as a *"necessary* premise for science fiction." While Phil did write stories during this period—notably "A World of Talent" (1954) and "Psi Man" (1955)—that utilized psi powers, his interest in them did not peak until the sixties, when psi powers played key roles (as unexcelled plot devices to multiply realities) in masterworks such as *Martian Time-Slip, The Three Stigmata of Palmer Eldritch,* and *Ubik.*

Before taking leave of Phil's stories, mention must be made of "Beyond Lies the Wub," the very first to appear in print (July 1952 *Planet Stories*). It is a lovely parable about a hoglike Martian creature—the "wub"—a slobbering, ungainly creature with a kind, enlightened soul. An Earth spaceship is short on provisions, and Captain Franco (a dig at Spain's Generalissimo) decides that wub meat would make good eating. The wub, eminently urbane, objects: "Eat me? Rather you should discuss questions with me, philosophy, the arts—" Captain Franco does kill and eat the wub, which emerges triumphant by taking over the Captain's human form. Sixteen years later, in a story called "Not by Its Cover," Phil again employed the services of the unstoppable wub. An Earth publishing firm sells classics bound in "gold-stamped Martian wub-fur." Too late, the firm learns that the wub-furs are still alive, and changing the texts of those classics to proclaim the truth of eternal life.

By 1954 Phil's attention had turned to novel writing—SF and mainstream—on a full-time basis. The great pulp exfoliation was withering away. Its deathblow was strictly business. American News Company, a giant distributor, handled most of the pulps. But ANC was liquidated by a financial raider, who saw that its warehouses were far more valuable as real estate than as overhead against magazine profits. SF writer Frederik Pohl describes the chaotic aftermath:

> The publishers came running to the offices of the various Independents [competing distributors], hats in hands, tears in their eyes. Most of them were turned down flat. There was just so much volume that each Independent was capable of handling, and they picked and chose. *Life* and *Time* they were glad to take. But who wanted to bother with some bimonthly pulp about spaceships and monsters? Especially if the publisher was rather inadequately financed and in the habit of hitting up his distributors for advances to pay the printers?

SF stories, even at the rate at which Phil produced them, didn't bring in much income. With Kleo's part-time jobs, they only just made ends meet. For Kleo, the shortage of cash was no grave concern. Her stories of how they scraped by are whimsical:

> Movies were a little difficult. The Roxy Theater near University and San Pablo was an artsy theater that showed strange, foreign films we wanted to see, but we didn't always have the money. So we would go into the lobby—the manager ran the candy counter but went upstairs to count the money a few minutes into the second feature—and we'd sneak in. But every once in a while our timing was off and Phil would be acutely embarrassed and make a big show of saying good-bye to me and buying my ticket and going home—he didn't think it would look right for me to go home too.

For Phil, poverty was far more difficult. Not that he craved luxuries. Poverty was a humiliation, the stigma of his inability—and un-willingness—to act the part of a wage-earning American male. Phil knew that his vocation was as a writer, but knew also that his writing allowed him to hide from the world. To daughter Laura he wrote, in May 1978, as to why he could not attend her high school graduation:

> I really don't dress very well and am uncomfortable in formal situations. I suppose the roots of this is that I have always been poor, and ashamed of it. At one time my wife [Kleo] [. . .] and I ate dogfood. I did not go to college but worked in a radio and TV store. I have an enormous knowledge along certain lines, such as literature and theology and classical music, but in other respects I am ignorant. [. . .]
>
> I am uncomfortable around power and money, and am happy in what we call the street. [. . .] My only ambition has been fulfilled: my writing, about which I am very proud. I have been successful in the terms by which I define success for myself, but outside of my writing my life has been something of a failure.

This is Phil in the downcast mode he often employed in letters warding off travel. But his shame over his early poverty (by 1978 Phil was no longer in want) was genuine enough. It reappeared in the 1980 "Introduction" to *The Golden Man*. Phil tells of purchasing the "dogfood" referred to above:

> So anyhow there I am at the Lucky Dog Pet Store on San Pablo Avenue, in Berkeley, California in the Fifties, buying a pound of ground horsemeat. The reason why I'm a freelance writer and living in poverty is (and I'm admitting this for the first time) that I am terrified of Authority Figures like bosses and cops and teachers; I want to be a freelance writer so I can be my own boss. [. . .]—and all of a sudden, as I hand over the 35¢ to the Lucky Dog Pet Store man, I find myself once more facing my personal nemesis. Out of the blue, I am once again confronted by an Authority Figure. There is no escape from your nemesis; I had forgotten that.
>
> The man says, "You're buying this horsemeat and you are eating it yourselves."

Kleo points out that the pet shop sold horsemeat to humans with no questions asked, and that broiled horsemeat is very nice. As to Phil's sense of humiliation: "All I can do is tell you that *at that time* he was not humiliated. We had worked out a modus vivendi which, after all, continued for almost *eight years*. So much of this 'Oh how terrible it was to be so poor' is latter-day reconstruction."

Phil had his wife, his house, his cat, his Magnavox, and his writing stints on into the night (usually to 2:00 A.M.). In the earlier part of the day he read voraciously—Flaubert and Balzac, Turgenev and Dostoevsky, metaphysics and Gnosticism, the latest SF by Bradbury and Van Vogt. He could manage his way through German verse and was (from his Ojai days) a reasonable Latinist. Phil admired, above all other prose models, the plain style and intensity of Xenophon's *Anabasis*. And he was enamored of Joyce's *Finnegans Wake*, for which he devised numerous interpretations, such as the text's being Earwicker's dream from which he is, at novel's end, awakening. Says Kleo, "In symbolic terms, Philip would have liked to be James Joyce—and not blind."

To interviewer Gregg Rickman, Phil recalled the time he told Kleo about his latest reading discovery, Moses Maimonides's *Guide for the Perplexed* (a medieval Jewish treatise probing the limits of reason in matters of faith): "She [Kleo] says, I talked to one of my professors and he says there's probably not another human being in the United States who's reading Moses Maimonides at this moment."

Kleo does not remember this episode. Her explanation of Phil's way of telling it is one that many of his friends (in different words but very similar substance) offer:

I shouldn't say it's not true. If we're talking about Philip, essentially it's true—it just didn't happen. This is a Philip construct of a situation that existed and it's a little way to describe that situation without strictly adhering to specifically real life data. But then, that's what he *did*.

Or, as Phil might have said just now, that's what reality *does*.

Kleo describes Phil as without formal religion but possessing a "strong sense of mystical unity with the universe." They shared an "animism" that made them watchful of, and easily delighted by, small daily events. Phil several times had the sense of leaving his body. In a 1977 interview he recalled one such instance: "Back at the time that I was starting to write science fiction, one night I was asleep and I woke up and there was a figure standing at the edge of the bed looking down at me and I grunted in amazement and all of a sudden my wife woke up and started screaming—she could see it too—and I recognized it and I reassured her by saying it was just me that was there, not to be afraid." Adds Kleo (in 1987): "And then I realized it was the reflection of the moon shining through the window over the stairs and onto the multipaned glass door to the bedroom." In the interview, Phil continued:

That was, say, 1951, and within the last two years I've dreamed almost every night that I was back in that house and I have a strange feeling that back then in 1951–52 I saw my future self who had somehow in some way that we don't understand—I wouldn't call it occult, I would just say it was some way you don't understand—that I crashed backwards as my future self through one of my dreams now of that house, going back there and seeing myself again. That would be the kind of stuff I would write as a fantasy in the early Fifties.

During his marriage to Kleo, Phil kept up his family ties—not only with Dorothy, but with Meemaw and his aunt Marion, who had married Joseph Hudner, a gifted sculptor who supported his family through work at the Oakland Ship Yards. Marion had demonstrated talent as an actress and a painter. In 1944, she gave birth to fraternal twins, Lynne and Neil, and was a warm and loving mother. In the late forties, Marion began to suffer disturbing episodes and was, at one point, admitted to Napa State Hospital, where she was diagnosed as a catatonic schizophrenic. By 1952, Marion's episodes had increased in intensity and duration.

Dorothy recommended a somewhat unorthodox female physician, who, with Joseph and Marion's assent, took Marion into her home. Shortly thereafter, Dorothy told Phil and Kleo that Marion was having wonderful visions that compensated for the painful circumstances of her life. As with Jane's death, the seriousness of Marion's condition was not recognized. She would stand for hours on end and, when questioned, was fearful of being unable to breathe—a complaint Dorothy regarded as a symptom of her mental state. Lynne Cecil recalls: "At the time of her death Dorothy was with her. Marion said she couldn't breathe and Dorothy tried to calm her down and didn't realize until too late that for real she couldn't. Dorothy told me that. When she did realize what was happening, a doctor was called."

Marion died on November 11, 1952. Phil was furious with Dorothy for her handling of the matter. He had long regarded his mother as a health-cult fanatic (her interests had included Reichian orgone box theory and Dianetics). The tragedy of Marion's death fueled the flames. It is by no means clear that Phil was correct in his accusations; both Marion and her husband had approved the course of treatment, and prior stays in hospitals had done her little permanent good. Dorothy attempted—in a journal entry written a week after Marion's death—to explain what had happened. Her focus on the "two worlds" of the psyche parallels Phil's fascination with the *idios* and *koinos kosmos*. Mother and son, perhaps despite themselves, were spiritual kin:

[. . .] I do not believe we shall ever know what happened to her physically, and we already know what happened psychically: she decided not to live. [. . .] The attraction of that other world of hers, which contained all that we recognize as the creative one and much more besides, was so strong; [. . .] she meant to keep it at any cost, but she thought she could do that and keep the actual, physical world around her too. [. . .] But the more I learn of other people's thoughts the more universally true it seems that each person has another world in him and that no one really belongs to the world as it is. In other words, we are all aliens. None of us belong to this world; it does not belong to us. The answer is to fulfill one's other world through this one; [. . .]

Dorothy soon received a unique opportunity to achieve just such fulfillment. Before Marion's death, relations between Dorothy and Joseph Hudner had been cool. But Hudner, who was conscious of possessing unusual psychic gifts, received a message from Marion after her death instructing him, to his surprise, to marry Dorothy. Dorothy turned him down flat several times and then, in a sudden strange experience of her own, saw how it could be—her reservations melted away. They were married in April 1953 and spent eighteen happy years together. And Dorothy was at last the mother of twins, devoting herself to Neil and Lynne's upbringing.

Again, Phil's reaction was one of pain and anger. Phil saw Hudner as an interloper who had at last displaced Edgar and (through the twins) Phil himself. According to Phil's friend Iskandar Guy, a black writer and artist who with his wife rented a small cottage in the backyard of Joe and Dorothy's Berkeley house, "Joe was trying to find a place where he would be allowed by Phil to relate to him. Phil would give him no place to do that." Phil would pay visits to Dorothy (paying little attention to Hudner if he was there) that were difficult on both mother and son: Phil would depart grumbling, and Dorothy would be worn and ashen for hours.

There was no solace in Phil's relations with his father. Edgar had moved to Palo Alto, where Phil and Kleo paid him a visit. Aside from acrimonious debate—Edgar's staunch conservatism versus Phil and Kleo's Berkeley liberalism—their talk was lifeless. Recalls Kleo: "With Edgar, you wondered if he had any emotions. With Dorothy, you felt that she had them and that they were repressed." As the visit proceeded "there just didn't seem to be any contact points." Edgar never invited them back.

But Phil had succeeded, with Kleo, in constructing his own world. He took walks down San Pablo Avenue, peeking into the cafés and shops and kicking the tires in the used-car lots. That small-time commercial strip (along with the Shattuck Avenue locale of Hollis's University Radio) forms the backdrop to several of the fifties mainstream novels. Phil also enjoyed sitting on the front steps watching the children at play across the street—until he became afraid of what his neighbors might think. (A similar fear arose during the early seventies, when Phil helped a neighborhood girl carry newspapers; whether or not he was abused in his own youth, Phil carried considerable guilt and anxiety on the subject.)

As a published SF writer, he had no problems with celebrity. In 1953 Phil noted wryly: "Have finally arrived as a writer. Droves of small boys, all aficionados of science fiction, greet me on the street. Ah, Fame!" The Elves, Gnomes, Little Men's Science Fiction, Chowder and Marching

Society was the most active Berkeley SF fan group. Phil would have none of it. He refused to dwell in the genre ghetto, though his saleable work was written for it. "The early fans were just trolls and wackos. They were terribly ignorant and weird people." But Phil did occasionally write for fanzines. His essay "Pessimism in Science Fiction" appeared in the December 1955 *Oblique*; in it Phil declared, with respect to the "dour tone" of post–nuclear holocaust SF: "In science fiction, a writer is not merely inclined to act out the Cassandra role; he is absolutely obliged to—unless, of course, he honestly thinks he will wake up and find that the high-minded Martians have sneaked off with all our bombs and armaments, for our own good."

Despite his objection to "trolls and wackos," he did attend the 1954 Science Fiction Worldcon, where he met a young fan named Harlan Ellison; he and Phil would later become close friends. He also met A. E. Van Vogt, an introduction that struck him deeply at the time; *The World of Null-A* (1948) was one of Phil's favorite SF novels, laden with ideas on superior mutant intelligences, general semantics, and (one of Phil's favorite themes) implanted false memories. In his 1964 story "Waterspider," Phil incorporated Van Vogt's response—back at the 1954 Worldcon—to Phil's question about plotting novels: "Well, I'll tell you a secret. I start out with a plot and then the plot sort of folds up. So then I have to have another plot to finish the rest of the story." Phil made this method his own. What Kleo recalls is that Van Vogt was wearing the first polyester suit they had ever seen. "The suit *glowed*. We were both impressed."

One fellow Berkeley SF writer with whom Phil formed a close bond was Poul Anderson (for a time they considered collaborating on an SF novel). Together, they could talk over the facts of SF life: editors chopping stories, lousy royalties, no recognition outside of fandom. Recalls Anderson:

> I bitched, and so did everyone else. You have to remember that in those days a science fiction writer—unless he was Robert Heinlein—was really at the bottom of the totempole. If you wanted to work in the field you had to make the best of what there was. But we didn't feel put upon. I don't recall that we ever went into self-pity, the most contemptible emotion there is. We were young then, and there was always tomorrow. Okay, you get shafted this time, but there was always more where that had come from.

When the talk was on books, Phil championed Nathanael West and admired Tolkien's *The Hobbit*. His sense of humor showed itself by deadpan assertions that left listeners wondering whether he was joking or revealing a strange new truth—Phil's favorite effect.

Of all the old Art Music crowd, Phil remained closest to Vince Lusby, who, by a recent marriage, had an autistic son. Phil and Kleo baby-sat for the boy, and he strongly influenced the character of Manfred (an autistic boy trapped in a schizophrenic "tomb world") in *Martian Time-Slip*. Phil tended to avoid parties but felt comfortable at the loose bohemian gatherings held at the Lusbys' house. Virginia Lusby, who married Vince in 1954, remembers: "Phil analyzed everything, and he was good at it. He didn't resent interruptions, but once he got started he was rarely interrupted—you just sat and listened. I think he was brilliant, really brilliant." But one Lusby party proved disastrous. Allan Temko, an architecture critic, confronted Phil with a drunken song-and-dance parody of the kinds of people who wrote SF. Says Vince Lusby: "It was a horrible experience even if you weren't Philip Dick." At another party, Phil met mainstream writer Herb Gold; Phil later recalled that Gold "autographed a file card to me this way: 'To a colleague, Philip K. Dick.' I kept the card until the ink faded and was gone, and I still feel grateful to him for this charity. (Yes, that's what it was, then, to treat an SF writer with courtesy.)"

One of Phil's neighbors was Jacquin Sanders, a mainstream novelist who came over to watch the McCarthy hearings with Phil and Kleo. When Sanders returned to New York, he bequeathed them his 1952 Studebaker, with a unique wraparound window design that made it hard to tell front from back. Phil loved it and decided to learn to drive, taking lessons from several volunteers—including an FBI agent investigating his and Kleo's possible Communist ties.

FBI surveillance and questioning were not unusual in McCarthy-era Berkeley. Sather Gate was the usual site for political speech of all persuasions—more often than not, to the left. FBI agents up on the rooftops would photograph the crowds, just as they did during the Free Speech Movement a decade later and just as they do to the present day. Kleo, who enjoyed taking in all sorts of viewpoints, was a Sather Gate regular. Phil never joined her and seldom attended political meetings of any kind.

Nonetheless, one day in 1953 or 1954 FBI agents George Smith and George Scruggs knocked on the door. "They were dressed," Kleo recalls, "in gray suits and Stetson hats—like nothing in our world." Politely they asked the couple to identify faces in Sather Gate surveillance photographs; Kleo pointed out some obvious Berkeley political luminaries and then herself. Then Phil and Kleo asked questions of their own, fascinated by the agents' knowledge of splinter parties. There were more visits; Kleo describes Phil and herself as "nervous, not threatened—they were obviously just fishing." Scruggs became friendly and took Phil for driving lessons. Says Kleo: "We would have socialized with Scruggs but he was quite a bit older. Really, they could see [Kleo bursts out laughing] that we were a couple of dips and didn't want much to do with us." But there *was* something the agents wanted. They offered Phil and Kleo the opportunity to study at the University of Mexico, all expenses paid, if they would spy upon student activists there. Phil and Kleo found the offer attractive except for the spying, and refused. The visits petered out after that.

For Phil, the lasting importance of these visits is unquestionable. From 1964 on, he frequently believed himself to be under FBI or other agency surveillance; the Berkeley "Red Squad" (as he came to call Scruggs and Smith) provided a vivid foundation for that belief, which caused him great anxiety and was central to the events of 2-3-74. Phil later claimed that the agents had asked him to spy on Kleo. Kleo regards this claim as highly unlikely.

At least Phil had finally learned to drive. They swapped the Studebaker for a Plymouth and, in typical fifties fashion, set out to see the U.S.A. In 1956–57, they took two separate driving tours—Phil's only time off from writing during their marriage—which included a return visit to Ojai (Phil hated the school but loved the mountains) and wanderings through the Rocky Mountains (Cheyenne, Wyoming, is a vital capital in many of the SF novels because Phil loved driving through it) and as far east as Searcy, Arkansas, where the women still wore poke bonnets. They disdained "sights" like the Grand Canyon. "We weren't interested in anomalies," Kleo explains. "We wanted to see the country." For the first time, they considered moving from Berkeley.

Phil's old love from his pre-Kleo days, Betty Jo Rivers, returned to the Bay Area in 1956 and found him a far more assured person than she had known in 1949. He could walk down the street comfortably, and his sense of humor was more developed. Kleo was protective of Phil and tried to keep the house as a studio for him. Phil had become fascinated with sports cars and swapped the Plymouth for a Renault.

But Phil still found public settings difficult. When Kleo purchased tickets to Beckett's new play, *Waiting for Godot*, Phil could not bring himself to go. Even dinner guests in their home had to be carefully chosen. These frustrations fueled the blasts of anger he leveled so often at Dorothy. Iskandar Guy recalls Phil's telling him that "to the extent that he was in any way crippled or enfeebled psychologically, it was because of his mother and father. It was as if he'd been treated like a feral child."

It was standard medical practice in the fifties to provide amphetamine analogues such as Semoxydrine for patients who complained of anxiety or depression. The extent to which Phil used amphetamines while in Berkeley just isn't clear. On at least one occasion, Phil obtained Semoxydrine samples from Kleo's physician father. Iskandar Guy recalls that Phil took it regularly in low, commonly prescribed 5 mg doses and possessed a sophisticated pharmaceutical knowledge. But Kleo insists that, other than the Semoxydrine sample from her father, Phil took no drugs but Serpasil (a muscle relaxant) for tachycardia and an aspirin and a teaspoon of soda every night before bed.

There came, at last, a buffeting of the tranquil marriage. In 1957, after seven years of marriage, Phil had his first affair. The woman was a friend of Lusby's who was unhappily married and had children. She was dark-haired and sensual, and possessed a sunny disposition and an unashamed directness. When Kleo learned of the affair, she took a bus trip to Salt Lake City to let Phil think things out. "We both had to know if he wanted to do something else, and if he did . . . I didn't think ahead." When Kleo returned a few days later, Phil was confused—his relations with the woman had declined, and Kleo's calm frustrated him. "He'd hoped I'd make the big traditional scene." Instead, Kleo had dinner with the woman, who confided to her: "I never feel like I know a man unless I go to bed with him."

The affair was never a serious threat to the marriage, but it was intensely gratifying for Phil. In the early sixties, during his marriage to Anne, this woman paid several visits to their Point Reyes home. Phil would be proud, Anne recalls, that "his ex-mistress was on the way." Most importantly, she served as inspiration for the seductive Liz Bonner in his finest mainstream novel of the Berkeley fifties, *Puttering About in a Small Land* (written in 1957, published in 1985).

Oh yes. While all this was going on, Phil wrote, from 1951 through 1958, eighty-odd stories and thirteen novels—six SF, seven mainstream. The six SF novels were all promptly published, but the seven mainstream novels languished.

It was an anguish to him. And out of that anguish, his best work would come.

♦

Phil never gave up writing stories; in truth, his finest achievements in that form were to come in the sixties and after. Nor did he ever abstain from writing novels; even in 1952 and 1953, while producing SF stories at white heat, Phil finished two novels, a massive mainstream work, *Voices from the Street*, and a fantasy, *The Cosmic Puppets*, and started a third, the mainstream *Mary and the Giant*. (See Chronological Survey.)

But from 1954 on, there was a distinct shift: From this point, Phil would devote his main energies to writing novels. In his 1968 "Self Portrait" he confessed:

With only a few exceptions, my magazine-length stories were second-rate. Standards were low in the early '50s. I did not know many technical skills in writing which are essential . . . the viewpoint problem, for example. Yet, I was selling; I was making a good living, and at the 1954 Science Fiction World Convention I was very readily recognized and singled out . . . I recall someone taking a photograph of A. E. Van Vogt and me and someone saying, "The old and the new." But what a miserable excuse for "the new"! [. . .] Van Vogt in such works as THE WORLD OF NULL A, wrote novels; I did not. Maybe that was it; maybe I should try an sf novel.

For months I prepared carefully. I assembled characters and plots, several plots all woven together, and then wrote everything into the book that I could think up. It was bought by Don Wollheim at Ace Books and titled SOLAR LOTTERY [1955]. Tony Boucher reviewed it well in the N.Y. *Herald Tribune*; the review in *Analog* was favorable, and in *Infinity*, Damon Knight devoted his entire column to it—and all in praise.

Standing there at that point I did some deep thinking. It seemed to me that magazine-length writing was going downhill—and not paying very much. You might get $20 for a story and $4,000 for a novel. So I decided to bet everything on the novel; I wrote THE WORLD JONES MADE [1956], and later on, THE MAN WHO JAPED [1956]. And then a novel which seemed to be a genuine breakthrough for me: EYE IN THE SKY [1957]. Tony gave it the Best Novel of the Year rating, and in another magazine, *Venture*, Ted Sturgeon called it "the kind of small trickle of good sf which justifies reading all the worthless stuff." Well, I had been right. I was a better novel-writer than a short-story-writer. Money had nothing to do with it; I liked writing novels and they went over well.

So Phil Dick the SF writer became Phil Dick the SF novelist. The above account includes the usual Phildickian inaccuracies and omissions: The Meredith Agency had received the manuscript of *Solar Lottery* in March, before the 1954 Worldcon and Phil's meeting with Van Vogt. But the essence is true. From 1954 on it was novels that he wrote and as a novelist that he identified himself.

SF novels were not his first love, however. His mainstream efforts were so important to him that in 1956–57 he abandoned SF altogether. Says Kleo:

Publishing a mainstream novel would have been his dearest dream. Not mainstream, necessarily, but just *non*-science fiction. He didn't really expect it—it would have been the gift of the gods. He knew that his unpublished serious novels were in no way popular fiction and that they didn't fit into any particular category. But some of the stuff out of New York then was wonderful. Styron—Phil loved *Lie Down in Darkness*—Malamud, Sigrid DeLima. It gave us a hope that someone would pick up on his work.

Iskandar Guy recalls Phil's struggle to balance mainstream ambition and a sense of dignity as to his SF work:

I got the impression at that time that he was writing science fiction because that's what was *happening*—but he just hoped to Christ he could get some serious work published. Science fiction was what he did. It was a format in which a few ideas were presentable, but he didn't think of it as the format for serious intellectual inquiry—no way. Who the fuck ever paid attention to paperbacks?

86

When he finally accepted that he could write about society and the denigration of men's minds in science fiction, he felt free to do that. He would tell what was going on—good, bad or indifferent. Sometimes it was so *bad* . . . it's hard to hold on to clarity and vision when it gets that painful and kicks up everything you remember. But you can try.

Phil would talk about the Vedas. The world was what you create with your mind. Mind pretty much sets up reality as it exists. And he made no bones about that, especially when he said screw it, I'm not sure I can make it as a straight writer so I'm going to put everything I know in science fiction.

If Phil felt ashamed of his genre, he was by no means uncertain of his talent. Throughout his life, Phil displayed remarkably little ego when it came to awards or critical acclaim. He seldom suffered from professional jealousy of his fellow SF writers, even when they pulled in considerably higher advances than he did. At the same time, Phil showed a certain cockiness about his own talent. Fellow writer Lusby (with whom Phil exchanged manuscripts) states that Phil "had this complex feeling about perfection—he thought the books were perfect. There were certainly flaws and defects, but he never discovered them."

John Gildersleeve, a copy editor at the University of California Press, served as a volunteer reader for some of the mainstream novels. The logical plot holes distressed him: "His so-called serious writing would go on beautifully, and then he'd fall back on one of the tricks he'd learned in writing science fiction." Phil could be prickly; Gildersleeve recalls a threat to make him a character in one of the novels, "and I wouldn't like it one bit." There was a protean aspect to Phil's talent that Gildersleeve recognized: "My God, the way he could type! He would compose at eighty to a hundred words per minute—making up his story as he typed it out, and he typed so fast he had to keep one jump ahead of himself on one side or the other."

Just how boastful or bashful Phil was about his SF career depended, in part, on just whom he was around. When *The Man Who Japed* came out in 1956, Phil proudly made a special visit to display a copy to Dorothy. But Chuck Bennett, a crony from the Art Music days, recalls a surprise visit by Phil in which he made his entry by flipping a paperback across the floor:

And I looked at him, at this strange behavior, and he came on in and he ignored the book that he'd thrown away. And I walked over and picked it up and saw it was a science fiction novel by Philip Dick. . . . "What *is* this?" "Oh yeah," he said, "I had that published, I got that published." You know, as though that were the last thing in the world, that this elaborate, almost grotesque ploy, you know, of throwing this book—with this total indifference—halfway across the room and then walking on past it.

Bennett remembers it as being Phil's first published book, which would make it *Solar Lottery*. If so, the story fits. Kleo recalls that when copies of the Ace paperback first arrived, Phil told her: "Isn't it a hell of a thing that this is the one they picked up first?" Now, *Solar Lottery* is a pretty good SF adventure in the Van Vogtian tradition, written when Phil was twenty-five. It didn't deserve the abuse Phil gave it, but the hurt of the mainstream works gathering dust was too great.

Since Phil saw his SF and mainstream writing as, in essence, two separate careers, it may be wise to follow separately his progress in each.

As to SF novels, the major influence within the genre was Van Vogt, as opposed to the "hard"-science approach favored by Asimov, Heinlein, and Clarke. To Phil, a focus on scientific probability—as opposed to plot possibilities—meant that the writer wasn't doing his job. Phil's approach to technology was, simply, to make up whatever gizmo he needed to keep his characters' realities in suitably extreme states. Science aside, the shift from stories to novels involved a definite change in narrative strategy. For Phil, the startling "What If?" premise lay at the heart of SF. Stories could develop such premises without detailed characterization; but novels required sympathetic protagonists. In 1969 Phil wrote:

> It is in sf stories that sf action occurs; it is in sf novels that worlds occur. [. . .] As a writer builds up a novel-length piece it slowly begins to imprison him, to take away his freedom; his own characters are taking over and doing what they want to do—not what he would like them to do. This is on the one hand the strength of the novel and on the other, its weakness.

Because SF stories are preeminently SF "action," Phil was often able to cannibalize parts from old stories for his novel plot engines. (The Chronological Survey traces these genealogies.)

During the fifties there were only two real players in the (strictly paperback) SF novel market: Ace and Ballantine. But Ballantine didn't put out as many SF titles as Ace's two a month (in *one* "Ace Double"), overseen by Don Wollheim. Ballantine paid slightly better, but it wasn't until 1964 that Ballantine finally purchased one of Phil's novels, *Martian Time-Slip*. All told, twenty of Phil's SF novels and story collections were first published by Wollheim—at Ace and then DAW (Wollheim's initials) Books. It's a fact: Phil's bread and butter for the first two decades of his writing life was Wollheim's love for his work.

There could be no more dyed-in-the-wool veteran of the pulp SF wars than Wollheim. He sold his first SF story to *Wonder Stories* in 1934 at age nineteen. In 1936 he organized the first World SF Convention (nine guys attended) in Philadelphia. He was also a charter member of the Futurians, a New York–based fan club whose members included future SF writers Frederik Pohl, Cyril Kornbluth, and Isaac Asimov. The first SF magazine Phil ever bought, *Stirring Science Stories*, was edited by

Wollheim, as was the first-ever paperback SF anthology, *The Pocket Book of Science Fiction* (1943). Wollheim recalls: "That was the first book to carry the words *science fiction* on the cover. They wanted to call it *The Pocket Book of Scientific Romances*, which would have been death." In 1952 pulp magnate A. A. Wyn installed Wollheim as editor in chief of Ace Books and revealed to the young editor the esoteric art of blurbing. "The secrets Wyn taught me still work. I can't tell everything. Part of the secret is—you don't summarize a story or novel, you give a bit of a tease, let them guess."

Wollheim recognized Phil's talent from the first:

> I am a science fiction fan, I know what Phil was doing and I love his work. Other editors don't. They look at it like any writing, not science fiction. Phil was always unusual. He had a great technique. In the first two or three chapters, you meet two or three people who apparently have no connection with each other. By the time the book is finished, they all become entangled with each other—I love that technique. And of course his viewpoint of the future world was always so different from the stock science fiction viewpoint. It was marvelous stuff—I loved his work. He was one of those I was really happy to publish. Phil and [Andre] Norton and [Samuel] Delany were my favorites.

The first and only time Phil and Wollheim met was in 1969, by which time their professional relationship had spanned fourteen years. "Gee, I thought you'd be seven feet tall," Phil said to the slight-framed Wollheim, who was one of those "Authority Figures." As with Hollis, Phil's dominant feeling was admiration—Wollheim was a scrappy businessman whose love for SF redeemed the rough edges (such as nasty letters demanding editorial changes).

Life with Ace Books was tough, even with Wollheim's backing. Wollheim recalls that "Wyn was not a generous man. That was always my handicap at Ace—he never quite got over his pulp mentality." Wyn, who died a multimillionaire in 1969, utilized one key tactic when dealing with writers: They *always* need money, and you can earn their pathetic loyalty by paying them a piddling advance promptly. Royalties might or might not show up later, but that only served to keep writers writing. Wollheim recounts the standard Ace deal:

> We'd buy your novel as part of an Ace Double, pay you maybe $750 or maybe $500, and you'd get a royalty of 3 to 4 percent. It wasn't a good deal, but it was the only game in the business. Later, when we got into singles, you got more—about $1,200 or $1,500, a royalty of maybe 5 percent. [. . .] I think I can remember instances where books came within $2 of earning royalties— and then nothing. It's ridiculous. [. . .] In one case we had a double book in which one title sold more [according to Ace's royalty statement figures] than the title on the other side.

89

Ace Doubles, now cherished by collectors, were two twenty-thousand-word novels smacked together cheeseburger-style into one book with title covers on *both* sides. The cover art kept to classic pulp themes: bug-eyed aliens, rocket ships, strong men and screaming women. Wollheim routinely changed Phil's titles: *Quizmaster Take All* to *Solar Lottery* (1955), *Womb for Another* to *The World Jones Made* (1956), *With Opened Mind* to *Eye in the Sky* (1957), and *A Glass of Darkness* to *The Cosmic Puppets* (1957). Of the early novels, only *The Man Who Japed* (1956) came out as Phil named it.

Wollheim insists that he did not meddle with Phil's plots:

> The editing was done by me, or my secretary. Just spelling and punctuation. I don't believe we ever changed any plots of his—just the titles. I wouldn't have dreamed of telling him what to write. He was what he was. He had such an unusual mind—I think it would have turned him into another hack—it couldn't be done.

In fact, Wollheim called for substantial changes in *Solar Lottery*, *The World Jones Made*, and *Vulcan's Hammer* (1960). Phil paid attention, though he did not always accede to Wollheim's demands. Sometimes the changes were insisted upon by Wyn. It was Wyn who raised objections to *Eye in the Sky*, Phil's self-termed "breakthrough" novel, to which Wollheim paid the ultimate tribute—publication as a "Double-Size" book all its own.

Eye is Phil's first novel to pose successfully the "What is Real?" theme that obsessed him. His approach to this theme, by the time he wrote *Eye* in a blistering two weeks in early 1955, was philosophically sophisticated in the extreme. He had absorbed Hume's argument that we cannot verify causality (that B follows A does not prove that A *caused* B), Bishop Berkeley's demonstration that physical reality cannot be objectively established (all we have are sensory impressions that *seem* to be real), and Kant's distinction between noumena (unknowable ultimate reality) and phenomena (*a priori* categories, such as space and time, imposed upon reality by the workings of the human brain). From Jung he adopted the theory of projection: The contents of our psyches strongly color our perceptions. As a *coup de grâce*, Phil's study of Vedic and Buddhist philosophy led to a fascination with maya: True reality is veiled from unenlightened human consciousness. We create illusory realms in accordance with our fears and desires. Small wonder that Phil's original title for *Eye*, which set out to delineate the structure of those realms, was *With Opened Mind*.

There are strong political themes in *Eye* as well, drawn from Phil's firsthand experience of FBI surveillance. The novel begins with Jack Hamilton's being fired from his defense job because of the alleged Communist leanings of his wife, Marsha. McFeyffe, the McCarthyesque agent who has investigated Marsha, is also Hamilton's friend. At novel's end, Marsha is proved innocent while McFeyffe proves to be a closet Communist, whose slogan truths are as despicable as the Senator's witch hunts. Hamilton abandons weapons research to start up a hi-fi assembly company with a black co-worker, Bill Laws. The closing scene—in which Laws shouts out: "What are we waiting for? Let's get to work!"—was an *idée fixe* for Phil at the time. One or more characters deciding to put their shoulders to the wheel to set society right (or better) is an ending employed in *Gather Yourselves Together*, *Voices from the Street*, *Solar Lottery*, *The World Jones Made*, and *The Man Who Japed*.

Underlying the need for change is this danger: Things are not as they seem, but those in power are anxious to dispense with questions. Phil was both nervous and proud of his reputation as a radical within the confines of fifties SF. In the privacy of his *Exegesis* (c. 1979) he defined the stance of his fifties work: "I may not have been/am CP [Communist Party], but the basic Marxist sociological view of capitalism—negative—is there. Good."

But shelves are filled with dusty tomes that pose just such issues. What Phil could do was to whip them all up into an SF alternate-universe thriller. Blurb master Wollheim had little difficulty hyping *Eye*: "Worlds Within Worlds!" "Trapped in a madman's universe!" And the blurbs were true.

There is an explosion at the Belmont Bevatron. Eight people (including Jack, Marsha, and McFeyffe) plunge through the Proton Beam Deflector to the floor. One by one they begin to ascend from their unconscious haze—passing through worlds of religious fanaticism, sexless prudishness, psychotic paranoia, and Communist party-line prattlings. These worlds spring from their own psyches: As each one revives, he or she is able to project realities binding upon the rest. (Just how does this happen? That's the little pseudo-science leap allowed in SF.) In an unpublished "Prologue," Phil had all eight characters in *Eye* review the novel differently, to underscore the subjectivity of even the reading experience.

When war veteran Arthur Silvester's universe of religious fanaticism takes over, Hamilton and McFeyffe seek out a priest who sprinkles holy water onto an umbrella that gives them a flying tour of a Ptolemaic solar system. The forges of Hell come into sight, and then the vast blue expanse of Heaven:

It wasn't a lake. It was an eye. And the eye was looking at him and McFeyffe!

He didn't have to be told Whose eye it was.

McFeyffe screeched. His face turned black; his wind rattled in his throat. [. . .]

The eye focused on the umbrella. With an acrid pop the umbrella burst into flame. Instantly, the burning fragments, the handle and the two shrieking men dropped like stones.

91

What did A. A. Wyn object to in all this? Silvester's fanatical universe, in which engineers work on the problem of "maintaining a constant supply of untainted grace for all major population centers," was just the sort of thing that could piss off the American Legion and fundamentalist Christians. And so Wyn insisted that Silvester's God be called "(Tetragrammaton)" and that his "Babiist" cult be designated Moslem in origin—how many outraged Islamic SF readers could there be?

In retrospect, Phil saw *Eye* as a parable like unto Plato's shadows on the walls of the cave: pointing us away from maya toward a recognition, if not of truth, then of the fact of our ignorance:

> My writing deals with hallucinated worlds, intoxicating & deluding drugs, & psychosis. But my writing acts as an *antidote*—a detoxifying—not intoxicating—antidote. [. . .]
>
> [. . .] It's like "Eye" when actual rescue is right at hand but they can't wake up. Yes, we are asleep like they are in "Eye" & we must wake up & see past (through) the dream—the spurious world with its own time—to the rescue *outside*—outside *now*, not later.

Eye established Phil, at age twenty-eight, as one of the very best young SF writers. As a practical matter, however, Ace paid only a flat rate of one thousand dollars for Phil's SF novels—with future royalties very much in doubt. There were other avenues to bolster his SF income. Phil recalled being offered, around 1957, a job writing radio scripts for the *Captain Video* program. The pay was five hundred dollars per week, but the job meant moving to New York, a horror that Phil would not even consider. (Kleo says, "Nonsense!"—there was no job offer; Phil was asked to do a single script.) In 1958 Phil sold at least one radio script to the *Exploring Tomorrow* show on the Mutual Broadcast System.

But beyond economics, Phil wanted to break through into the mainstream so badly he could taste it. And so, in 1957, just as the glowing reviews of *Eye* were pouring in, Phil informed Wollheim and Boucher—the two editors most responsible for encouraging his rise in the SF ranks—that he was giving the field up to devote himself fulltime to mainstream novels.

It wasn't as if Phil hadn't been trying up until that time. From 1952 through 1958 Phil wrote eight mainstream novels: *Voices from the Street* (1952–53), *Mary and the Giant* (1953–55, published in 1987), *A Time for George Stavros* (1955; manuscript lost), *Pilgrim on the Hill* (1956; manuscript lost), *The Broken Bubble of Thisbe Holt* (1956, published in 1987), *Puttering About in a Small Land* (1957, published in 1985), *Nicholas and the Higs* (1957; manuscript lost), and *In Milton Lumky Territory* (1958, published in 1985). (See the Chronological Survey for plot summaries.) The Meredith Agency marketed them with zeal, and there were awfully close calls. Crown and Julian Messner were extremely interested in *Mary and the Giant* (for Messner, Phil performed an extensive rewrite); Harcourt Brace was tempted by *A Time for George Stavros*. Always there was encouragement: Submit again, young man, you are gifted and on the verge.

Small wonder, then, that in 1957 he gave SF the brush. That same year Phil informed Boucher that he had broken with the Meredith Agency. If so, the rift was very brief. Perhaps the agency's attempts to dissuade him from strictly mainstream efforts had wounded Phil's pride. But he also received strong support for the shift. Boucher and Wollheim wrote letters cheering him on. But when Wollheim read *Mary and the Giant* and *Nicholas and the Higs* he turned them down flat and urged Phil to stick to SF: "I felt his science fiction was exceptional and his mainstream was not."

Since Phil's death, most of the mainstream novels from the Berkeley fifties have found publishers. Those that survive are, without exception, dark visions of working-class life in which ideals are thwarted, love is a rarity, and sex leads to remorseful self-confrontation. Phil used humor to brilliant effect in his SF, but there is scarcely the trace of a smile in these novels—aiming for the mainstream seemed to freeze him up just a bit. And, of course, he had to devise plots based on common reality preconceptions. No Bevatron explosions allowed in mainstream.

Each of the mainstream novels has its remarkable characters—raw, striving souls such as Stuart Hadley, the young TV shop clerk in *Voices from the Street*, for whom reality is painfully fragile, and Mary Anne Reynolds, the young woman trying desperately to launch herself in the world in *Mary and the Giant*. The finest of the group—the one that deserved to be published at the time—is *Puttering About in a Small Land*, which Phil was writing just as *Eye* hit the SF market in 1957.

Roger and Virginia Lindahl, unhappily married, move to a Los Angeles suburb after first meeting in the Washington, D.C., of Phil's childhood. They send their asthmatic son, Gregg, to a boarding school in Ojai, California. Virginia has a good deal of Dorothy in her, and Roger seems an amalgam of Edgar and of Phil himself—young Gregg all but disappears as the novel proceeds. Roger, a repairman, starts up Modern TV Sales & Service (a shop that reappears in *Voices from the Street* and *Dr. Bloodmoney*) but is frequently "on the edge" due to vague yearnings for freedom that threaten his business and family stability.

Roger commences an affair with Liz Bonner, the mother of one of Gregg's classmates. Liz is a simple soul without Virginia's intellect or maddening scruples, and so she basks in the warmth of her new love for Roger. Immersed in the pleasures of lovemaking, Liz is as purely the Eternal Feminine as Molly Bloom:

> I love you, she said. I've got you. Out in the world the people grow old. She felt them age; she heard them creak; she heard their bones snap. In the different houses dust filled the bowls and covered the floors. The dog did not

recognize him; he had been gone too long. Nobody knew him. He had left the world.

[. . .] She made him open his mouth; she put her open mouth near his, her teeth to his, holding him there as he moved inside her, and then she pressed her mouth to his mouth as she felt it happen again inside her, for the third time. Did you ever do it so many times before? With her? She kept his mouth against hers. You are inside me and I am inside you, she said, putting her tongue into his mouth, as far as it would go. I am as far into you as I can be: we are exchanged. Am which am I? Maybe I'm the one who must go back to her, all worn-out and empty. No, I'm the one who will never wear out. I am here forever, lying here on the ground, holding you down where I can reach you and get at you and inside you.

Leave it to Phil to include, even in a thought-flow of towering passion, confusion as to which lover is which.

Virginia, in exposing the affair, permanently wounds her husband. One of his ideals, vaguer yet than the yearnings for freedom, has been shattered. Call it the sense of honor inherent in marriage. Virginia has him dead to rights, and he cannot bear it. And so Roger takes to the road—funding his escape with TVs stolen from the shop he once owned.

Phil had come of age as a stylist. And in 1958 he decided, without in the least forsaking his mainstream ambitions, to put that style to work in an SF novel. He called it *Biography in Time*, but Lippincott ultimately published it (Phil's first U.S. hard-cover) as *Time Out of Joint* in 1959. It was marketed not as SF but as a "novel of menace." Phil kept watch in *Time* and the *New York Times Book Review*, hoping for the first officially serious reviews of his career. They didn't happen. Sales were poor. The next edition, six years later, was a Belmont paperback with an SF cover depicting spacemen and the moon falling out of the sky.

No matter. Phil's achievement in *Time Out of Joint* was to write a novel that met the future-world requirement of SF while focusing on a 1958 present reality in which he could put his mainstream talents to use. The tension of the story—and *Time* is a page-turner—comes from watching that perfectly realized 1958 world transformed into something *other*.

Ragle Gumm uses his psychic talents to solve the daily "Where-Will-The-Little-Green-Man-Be-Next?" contest in the newspaper. Ragle works at home, and people with real jobs think he's a little odd. (Ragle and SF writers have a lot in common.) It turns out his contest picks are being relied upon by the 1998 Earth military to defend against Luna's missiles. In that 1998 reality the strain of the war had driven Ragle to a nervous breakdown. So the military built a fake 1958 small town from his childhood (similar to the "Wash-35" babyland of *Now Wait For Last Year*) to keep him working at defense while ensconced in delusion. At the end of the novel Ragle learns the truth. Well and good, except that this neat SF ending in no way explains the happenings that give the novel its uniquely cerebral surreality. In this scene, for example, Ragle's 1958 reality decomposes in a manner unforeseen by the military:

"Got any beer?" he [Ragle] said. His voice sounded funny. Thin and remote. The counter man in white apron and cap stared at him, stared and did not move. Nothing happened. No sound, anywhere. Kids, cars, the wind; it all shut off.

The fifty-cent piece fell away, down through the wood, sinking. It vanished.

I'm dying, Ragle thought. Or something.

Fright seized him. He tried to speak, but his lips did not move for him. Caught up in the silence.

Not again, he thought.

Not again!

It's happening to me again.

The soft-drink stand fell into bits. Molecules. He saw the molecules, colorless, without qualities, that made it up. Then he saw through, into the space beyond it, he saw the hill behind, the trees and sky. He saw the soft-drink stand go out of existence, along with the counter man, the cash register, the big dispenser of orange drink, the taps for Coke and root beer, the ice-chests of bottles, the hot dog broiler, the jars of mustard, the shelves of cones, the row of heavy round metal lids under which were the different ice creams.

In its place was a slip of paper. He reached out his hand and took hold of the slip of paper. On it was printing, block letters.

SOFT-DRINK STAND

Turning away, he unsteadily walked back, past children playing, past the benches and the old people. As he walked he put his hand into his coat pocket and found the metal box he kept there.

He halted, opened the box, looked down at the slips of paper already in it. Then he added the new one.

Six in all. Six times.

Phil came up with the idea for *Time* when one day in his Francisco Street bathroom he reached for a light cord that wasn't there and never had been there—the light was operated by a wall switch. The impulse could be explained as merely freakish, or as a subliminal awareness of alternative worlds. Phil the fiction writer naturally chose the latter. As he was aware, the themes of *Eye* and *Time* resemble each other: We humans may be deceived as to the reality in which we dwell. In the *Exegesis* he wrote:

"EYE," "Joint," "3 Stigmata," "Ubik" & "Maze" are the same novel written over and over again. The characters are all out cold & lying around together

95

on the floor.* (*Mass hallucinating a world.) Why have I written this up at least five times?

[. . .] What's got to be gotten over is the false idea that an hallucination is a *private* matter. Not hallucination but *joint* hallucination is my topic, inc[luding] false memories.

If the mainstream failures rankled, life with Kleo on Francisco Street provided solace. They were poor but happy, the perfect Berkeley bohemian-libertarian couple with limitless intellectual curiosity. In February 1958 Phil wrote to Alexander Topchiev of the Soviet Academy of Sciences, concerning Soviet research that had allegedly discredited Einstein's theory of relativity: "I have no particular desire to see this Theory stand. In fact, I'd very much like to see elaborated indications that major parts of the Theory do not fit reality." The letter was intercepted by the CIA, as Phil learned after putting in a Freedom of Information Act request in May 1975. Yes, sometimes they really were watching him.

The urge to move on from Berkeley grew persistent in them both. In the mid-fifties, as an experiment, they rented an apartment across the bay in Sausalito, but stayed only one night. The second-floor apartment looked out on the Bay, and when Phil woke up and saw nothing but water his response, as a good Jungian, was to see in the vast Bay a sign of his own overwhelming unconscious forces. Back to Berkeley they went.

Then, in late summer 1958, came the sadness of Meemaw's death. With her passing, the ties that held Phil to Berkeley were further diminished. In September of that year they uprooted for real. Their new home was a little house with a real caboose in the backyard (perfect for a writing studio) on the corner of Mañana and Lorraine in Point Reyes Station, a remote little dairy town set just south of Point Reyes, a granitic finger thrust by the San Andreas fault into the Pacific.

It seemed to them like an idyllic escape from the Berkeley scene. "Phil liked feeling comfortable enough to walk down into the town," Kleo recalls.

They had a short happy life together in Point Reyes Station. And then everything turned upside down—starting with their marriage.

5 Phil Falls In Love, Becomes A Country Squire, Starts Writing Great Books, & Has "Nervous Breakdown" #3 (Love Can Be A Very Deep Hole To Fall Into) (1958-1963)

My Phil was like the man who wrote The Man in the High Castle. *Modest, sensitive, funny, wonderful talker and listener too—he was fascinated with every word you said. He was telling me how brilliant I was, how fun I was, what a wonderful mother I was. He was a wonderful lover, wonderful around the house, very giving, very agreeable. We talked for hours about every subject under the sun.*

ANNE DICK in interview

Here's how you can represent me to your rustic but well-placed family & friends: "He's well known in Russia and England . . . in fact, in Germany & Italy and France—also in South Africa and in Argentina (in translation, of course) . . . and he's beginning to become known here in the U.S. Lippincott is bringing out a novel of his next spring." And you can refer vaguely to "some very favorable reviews in the New York Herald *Tribune." And you can mention that "Harper's took notice of him several years ago, in an editorial . . . had to do with a story of his in an anthology of short stories." And you can mention that "his agent is also the agent for that fellow Traven—you know, the fellow who wrote* The Treasure of the Sierra Madre, *which won an academy award." (Notice that in desperation I'm name-dropping. But what the hell.) Give my love to the children also.*

PHIL, December 1958 letter to Anne

But then, at that point, my private life began to become violent and mixed up. My marriage of eight years broke up; I moved out into the country, met an artistically inclined woman who had just lost her husband.

PHIL, 1968 "Self Portrait"

NEWS of the Berkeley writer and his wife spread rapidly through Point Reyes Station. They were soon invited to attend a meeting of a little local group that believed that when the world ended—on April 22, 1959—they would be saved by extraterrestrials who would transform their Inverness meetinghouse into a flying saucer. Phil, amused yet frightened by the group's beautiful dark-haired female leader, declined the invitation and hid the next time she came to call.

Anne Williams Rubenstein, who lived on nearby Mesa Road, also became curious to meet them. Her husband, Richard, a well-educated poet from a wealthy background who had helped to edit a little magazine called *Neurotica*, had died that summer while in the Yale Psychiatric Institute, a victim of a severe allergic reaction to tranquilizers prescribed for him. Anne now suddenly found herself raising three young girls alone. Getting to know a neighboring writer seemed a welcome diversion.

Anne was thirty-one, of medium build and height, with shoulder-length blond hair and blue eyes, a WASP intellectual with energy and assertiveness to burn. Her New England father traced ancestors to the *Mayflower* and was a successful Wall Street broker. He adored Anne but had died when she was four. Her mother's family raised her through the Depression years in St. Louis. Anne majored in psychology at Washington University and there met Richard. Their marriage was happy enough, but somehow Anne hadn't lost her heart.

When she came by to introduce herself, the Dicks responded warmly. Phil was twenty-nine, slender, with thick brown hair, a high forehead, and those piercing blue eyes. His standard attire: flannel shirt, work pants, and army boots. Phil was impressed by Anne's connection with the officially literary *Neurotica* and, when listing his own accomplishments, stressed the mainstream novels. "I am only a very minor science fiction writer," he insisted.

Phil and Kleo paid visits to Anne together, and then Phil started paying visits on his own. Kleo was commuting three times a week to a part-time secretarial job in Berkeley and Phil wrote mostly at night, leaving his days open. Anne's "swanky modern San Francisco type of house" (as Phil described it in his mainstream novel *Confessions of a Crap Artist*) included a glass-walled kitchen and living room that faced out onto rolling hills and meadows; a circular open fireplace; hi-fi speakers built into the wall—Phil could not but be dazzled by this first hands-on exposure to the American Dream. The underbelly of the Dream did set him to thinking: The house, built on a concrete slab, had to be expensive as hell to heat. But everything about Anne seemed expensive to Phil after eight years of the Lucky Dog Pet Shop.

Anne called him a "Berkeley beatnik," and Phil loved it. Raptly they told each other the stories of their lives. In her unpublished memoir, *Search for Philip K. Dick*, Anne recalls:

> I found him to be the most enchanting conversationalist I had ever met! He was the first person I ever stopped talking long enough to listen to.

We found that we had endless ideas, attitudes, and interests in common. [. . .] Both of us were shy, though each of us covered our shyness up. Both of us were trusting to the point of gullibility, and terribly romantic. [. . .] Phil told me about his twin sister who had died three weeks after birth—how he still felt guilty about this. He felt that somehow he carried his twin sister inside of him.

"And she's a Lesbian," he told me very seriously.

As to Jane-as-lesbian, Kleo recalls: "Philip would say things straight-faced often, and after a while people started to take him seriously, which was too bad. Once in a while he'd say, 'Well, I've decided my whole problem is that I'm a lesbian and it's all because of the identification with the sister,' and he'd talk about it for a bit and go on to something else." Was Phil serious? Anne thought so. Of course, one of Phil's favorite effects was to blur the funny/serious distinction that most people take too seriously (leaving reality free to conceal itself in funny forms). In Phil's 1974 novel *Flow My Tears, The Policeman Said*, character Alys Buckman is a somewhat campy leather-queen lesbian whose death rends the soul of her surviving twin-brother, a policeman.

Two weeks after he and Anne met, Phil declared his love and their course was set:

We sat at either end of the couch talking. Suddenly Phil grabbed my hand and said in a low and intense voice, "You represent everything I've ever dreamed of."

I was so surprised I almost fell off the couch! I stared at the floor like some Victorian maiden. I didn't know what to say.

Phil drew me towards him and kissed me. After a moment I returned his embrace and kissed him back. We kissed and talked and talked and kissed. [. . .] I felt like one of those mythical heroines who has been awakened out of her enchanted slumber by the hero leaping over a ring of flames.

The affair became a minor scandal in little Point Reyes Station. Anne turned to a psychiatrist to help her cope with her feelings of guilt; the psychiatrist (hereafter known as Dr. X—he was to treat Phil, sporadically, through 1971) was quite taken with Phil when they met, a reaction that Anne attributes to Phil's incredible "charisma." But by December 1958, despite her rapture and Dr. X's advice to her not to worry, Anne decided to break things off. Phil begged her to reconsider. To assuage Anne's guilt, he argued that Kleo refused to bear children—grounds for annulment under Roman Catholic doctrine. (Kleo denies any such refusal; within a few years, she had children with Norman Mini.)

Anne's stance forced Phil to break the news of the affair to Kleo. He set forth reasons for ending their marriage as solicitously as he could, even hinting that he was bound by necessity due to Anne's having become pregnant. But Kleo was unconvinced by this shamming and infuriated that Phil seemed so completely under Anne's dominion: "In this situation Phil had turned into a namby-pamby shit." At one point, Phil demanded that Kleo return all photographs of him in her possession, claiming that Anne insisted upon it (which Anne denies). But Kleo was more than kind in the formal divorce proceeding, conceding ownership of their Mañana Street house and waiving all royalty claims on works written during their marriage. It did annoy her that the legal "fault" Phil alleged was a supposedly faithless trip by Kleo to Salt Lake City—the one she'd taken to give Phil time to think through his 1957 affair. In *Crap Artist*, Phil drew from his own experience to describe protagonist Nathan Anteil's day in court: "Was there any truth to what I said? Nathan wondered. Some truth. Part truth, part made up. Strange to lose sight, blend it together. [. . .] Aloud, he said, 'Like the Moscow Trials. Confessing to whatever they want.' "

At last Kleo resolved to leave Point Reyes Station, and asked only for their '55 Chevy. Phil was supposed to bring by the registration slip one day but forgot. It was "one thing too much," Kleo says. She yelled, Phil started to whine, and she slapped him. "We were both pretty surprised."

Phil paid further visits to Dr. X, who informed him that if Anne wanted a husband, she would go out and select the best one—like choosing a bar of soap. Phil found that observation hilarious. Anne was less amused, but it seemed a minor matter. They made plans for Anne and her daughters to return to St. Louis to try to reach a child-support arrangement with the family of her deceased husband, Richard. While she was gone Phil wrote her impassioned letters. In the first (December 21, 1958), Phil recounted how he got "the shakes"—induced by Anne's absence—while driving home after taking them to the airport. In the second (December 27), written just after Anne had called long-distance, Phil's love was expressed in a manner he retained for the rest of his life: The Woman, the Loved One, is the ground-source of the Real—without Her, it fades away:

You have no idea how much your phone call affected me. For an hour (more like two) afterward I was in a state of what I would in all honesty call bliss—unlike anything I've ever felt before. Actually, the walls of the house seemed to melt away, and I felt as if I were seeing out into time and space for an unlimited distance. It was a physical sense, not a mere intellectual thought. A genuine state of existence new to me. Evidently my not having heard from you for a couple of days had had the effect of starting into motion a sense of separation from you [. . .] Then when you called, this distance was abolished, and the return of you as a physical reality caused a genuine transformation in me, as if I had stepped from one world to another. [. . .] This is no doubt similar to the religious experience of conversion, and in a sense, I did undergo conversion upon hearing from you. There is a direct relationship between my

100

hearing you, and the religious person who, after the traditional isolation and fasting and meditation, "hears" the voice of "god." The difference is that you exist, and I have some deep doubts about that fellow god.

Phil went on to "introspect" as to his own character. He conceded to a strong streak of "intolerance":

I'm violently partisan and sectarian, and I have the word of god with me—or haven't you noticed? [. . .] It's not that I'm holier than thou, but that I'm filled with the moral wrath of the godly—admittedly a dreadful thing, and a cause of much human suffering. My image of myself is this gentle saint-like sage, full of bookish wisdom—and in actuality I'm more like some minor Communist official getting up and attacking the "slug-like blood-swilling depraved homosexual lice of the whiskey-infested West." In theory I'm a relativist, but in many situations I'm an absolutist, and unfortunately your circles and your views bring out the latter as often as not. [. . .] There is some virtue in this moral wrath, too, in that it permits me to act out, carry out, certain strong convictions that run contrary to practical gain—it gives me the psychic energy necessary to actually being an idealist, rather than merely thinking idealistic thoughts. Beethoven was the same way.

Three days later, in a letter to a high school friend, Phil saw fit to paint a guarded picture of life as usual with Kleo. He added that, as to the highly publicized San Francisco Renaissance, ". . . I'm favorably inclined toward *On the Road*, but not the poetry & jazz. . . ." Phil felt little attraction for the Beat social scene, though he later recalled meeting Gary Snyder and Robert Duncan (his McKinley Street housemate in 1947) during this period.

Anne returned from St. Louis with a financial settlement, and all continued to fare well. Phil got on splendidly with Anne's three daughters—Hatte, age eight; Jayne, six; and Tandy, three. They called him "Daddy" (Rubenstein was their "first father"). Phil cooked breakfast for them, played "monster" and baseball with them in the pasture-sized backyard, gave scary nighttime readings of Lovecraft stories, and quoted by heart from *Winnie the Pooh* and *When We Were Young*. (Phil refrained from adopting them so as not to create a barrier to payments from the Rubenstein estate.) The newly formed family played typical American games: In "Life," Phil never took the path through college; in "Monopoly," his marker was always the old shoe.

When Phil at last moved into Anne's "swank" house, his possessions (aside from cherished pet cat Tumpy) were relatively few: a Royal Electric typewriter, the faithful Magnavox, an enormous quantity of records and books, and complete collections of *Astounding*, *Amazing*, *F & SF*, *Mad*, and *Mandrake the Magician* comic books. While Phil shared with the girls his love of pulps, he was also concerned that they read good books. "He'd say, 'Don't read crap,' " Jayne recalls. "He'd make jokes about his books—he'd say, 'This one I wrote in a week—it's crap, too.' " The girls received daily lessons in music appreciation by way of the Magnavox: Wagner, Bach, Beethoven, Handel, and Gilbert and Sullivan filled the house. One of his obsessions was the Fischer-Dieskau recordings of Schubert's songs (quotations from these songs occur often in the SF novels of the sixties).

Phil did have one additional collection when he moved in: a wide variety of pills and medicines, which he kept in a large closet and prescribed from when the girls had colds. Phil was taking two Semoxy-drines a day (they'd been prescribed years ago, he told Anne), as well as quinidine for his recurrent tachycardia (he warned her that he could "drop dead" from taking quinidine). Phil was fearful of germs and fretted intensely when any of the girls fell ill. Jayne recalls: "He'd tell me adults don't feel well very often. He'd tell me about life in a roundabout way—being an adult wasn't too great, kids have a better time of it."

In late March of 1959 Phil and Anne drove down to Ensenada, Mexico, and found a judge; they were married on April Fools' Day. On the drive back, Phil confessed to Anne—fearful that she would cease to love him when she knew—that he had a hernia. Anne suggested medical treatment, but Phil couldn't face the idea of a hospital. At the border, Phil decided not to declare the gallon of tequila they'd purchased for the equivalent of thirty cents and hidden under their luggage. Twenty miles on into the U.S. they heard a siren and Phil went pale, recovering only when the cops passed on.

The marriage prospered. Phil was grateful when Anne made no objections to his growing a beard. He helped with the cooking and cleaning and knew how to make excellent martinis—two each night for Anne, while Phil sipped wine (he loved Buena Vista's Zinfandel). They raised ducks, guinea fowls, and banty chickens. Phil was a bit afraid of Anne's quarter horse and yearned for an owl as a pet (the title of Phil's last projected novel, which he did not live to write, was *The Owl in Daylight*). They had their first real fight over Phil's continuing to tend his old Mañana Street house. Anne wanted *their* home to be his primary concern. Phil sold the house. Afterward, he felt guilty about not giving Kleo half the proceeds.

Later that year, while eating lunch with Anne after their marriage, he suddenly told her: "I had a perfectly good wife I traded in for you." Within a short time, Phil and Kleo had resumed amicable relations. As Kleo says: "You don't throw away good friends, and Phil and I were best friends." But nearly two decades later, in the *Exegesis*, Phil retained a sense of guilt: "I am punished for the way I treated Kleo."

Anne and Phil made plans for how to make their money last while Phil pursued his mainstream ambitions. He still dabbled in SF, expanding two mediocre novelettes of the fifties into *Dr. Futurity* (1960) and

Vulcan's Hammer (1960), each appearing as half of an Ace Double. Ace was "the lowest of the low pulp publishers in New York," he told Anne. Once, when her dinner guests asked what he wrote, Phil refused to answer, later insulting them so that they never returned. If a genre label was required, he preferred "fantasy writer."

But the mainstream was what he wanted. And if the young couple utilized carefully Phil's house-sale proceeds and his annual SF earnings (roughly $2,000), plus Anne's $20,000 from the Rubenstein estate, maybe they could make it for a while—Phil computed it, based on his Berkeley-days budget, at twenty years. Anne recalls: " 'You know,' said Phil, 'it takes twenty to thirty years to succeed as a literary writer.' He was willing to make this long term effort! I thought this attitude was great! However the word 'budget' wasn't a part of my vocabulary."

Anne was no raging spendthrift—her standards of the "good life" were no different from those of her Marin County neighbors—but there were three daughters, a house, a horse, banty chickens, and black-faced sheep, and, yes, an occasional luxury. Enchanted as she was by Phil, confident as she was of his talent, Anne worried about money. And that struck fear in Phil, who knew damn well what the chances were of his talent bringing in the big bucks.

Still, it was a lovely life for a time. At Anne's request, Phil changed over his late-night writing hours into a nine-to-five labor, in order to be with the family in the evening. Come lunchtime, he would emerge from the study, light up a Corina Lark, and he and Anne would talk. She writes:

> We got so involved with our conversations that I often burnt the first two cheese sandwiches that were in the broiler. We talked about Schopenhauer, Leibnitz, monads, and the nature of reality—or Kant's theories as applied by Durkheim to the culture of the Australian aborigines—or Phil would hold forth on the Thirty Years War and Wallenstein. Light topics like these. Germanic culture had had a great influence on Phil. Phil told me he was one-quarter German and a *sturm und drang* romantic.

His lineage was English and Scotch-Irish, but that's love. These lunch talks were warm-ups for the novels to come. The Kant-Durkheim theory, for example, shaped Phil's depiction of the Martian aboriginal tribe of Bleekmen in *Martian Time-Slip* (1964).

Phil began a correspondence with Eleanor Dimoff, an editor at Harcourt, Brace. Harcourt had turned down *Crap Artist* but on the basis of that novel's promise offered Phil a contract: $500 down, $500 more upon acceptance of a new novel he was to write. He could smell the mainstream. In his February 1960 letter, Phil was suitably suave:

We're forty miles from San Francisco and we get in now and then, to eat in Chinatown or have coffee out around Broadway and Grant or visit friends on Potrero Hill. I nearly always manage to drop by the City Lights Bookshop and pick up thirty dollars worth of paperback books. My wife buys oriental rugs with holes in them from a rug dealer she knows, and if we can make it out to the Fillmore District we pick up a good supply of Japanese dishes from a little Japanese hardware store, there. If there's time to spare I stop along Van Ness and drive various new foreign cars, which is my favorite pasttime. And of course I pick up a supply of Egyptian cigarettes, if I have the money. If you think all this types me, consider that—before they tore down Seals Stadium—I went to S.F. primarily to see baseball.

It wasn't only Anne who enjoyed the good life. They were flush, and Phil was out and about and having some fun. Anne wasn't even aware that he had suffered from agoraphobia in the past. Except for one thing: Harcourt wanted Phil to come out to New York to confer with Dimoff on the new novel. No way. Not for *Captain Video* in the fifties—not even for the mainstream now.

There was one gaping omission in his self-portrait for Dimoff (did he fear she would think his mind couldn't be on his work?): Anne was pregnant. Within the month, on February 25, 1960, Laura Archer Dick—Phil's first daughter, Anne's fourth—was born.

Phil was nervous as hell in the months before the birth, urging Anne to eat Adelle Davis recipes and devising a vitamin-intake plan for himself that turned his tongue black. (A physician diagnosed the cause as an overdose of vitamin A; Phil mistrusted health food "nuts" ever after.) Before picking Laura up at the hospital, Phil scrubbed the old Ford station wagon for six hours—"I mean, even the *lights*," says Jayne.

Anne recalls that when Phil first looked into Laura's face he said: "Now my sister is made up for." And when, on their first day home, Dorothy and Joseph Hudner came out to see their grandchild, Phil allowed them a single minute and then rushed them out of the room.

♦

The Harcourt contract didn't pan out. Phil submitted *The Man Whose Teeth Were All Exactly Alike* (w. 1960, p. 1984) and *Humpty Dumpty in Oakland* (p. 1987), a 1960 rewrite of his 1956 work, *A Time for George Stavros*. Harcourt rejected them both; they are discussed in the Chronological Survey, and they have their moments.

But the best mainstream novel Phil ever wrote is *Confessions of a Crap Artist*, written in the summer of 1959, in the flush heat of his romance with Anne—a time she regards as their "honeymoon." Knopf almost bought it in 1960, but asked for a rewrite instead. The Meredith Agency told him it was his big chance. "I can't rewrite this book!" Phil explained to Anne. "It's not that I don't want to, it's that I'm not able to."

Crap Artist was published, at last, by Entwhistle Books in 1975, which eased the pain.

Just maybe the reason Phil couldn't rewrite *Crap Artist* is that it didn't need rewriting. *Crap Artist* is Phil's first novel to put multiple narrative viewpoints to wild work. He had described his earlier mainstream novels to Anne as "borderline surrealism." But there is nothing truly resembling surrealism until *Crap Artist*. What Raymond Chandler did for the neon-lit Los Angeles of the forties, Phil did for the Bay Area teetering on the brink of the sixties. Instead of the whiskey poet Philip Marlowe, we see through the eyes of Jack Isidore—"a schizoid person, a loner" and "one of God's favored fools," as Phil later described him.

Crap Artist is, beneath the shifting narrative realities, a hell of a novel about the male psyche at war with its demons. Isidore is named after Isidore of Seville, Spain (560?–636), whose *Etymologiae* was regarded as a universal compendium of knowledge during the Middle Ages. But the modern-day Isidore is drawn to pulps like *Thrilling Wonder Stories*—reading tastes shared by young Phil. Fay Hume, Isidore's sister, is a wiry, aggressive, seductive woman unhappily married to Charley Hume, a fall-guy American businessman who pays the bills, suffers a heart attack, and is driven to killing the household animals—and himself—by his wife's demands and betrayals. Nat Anteil is a passive, college-educated intellectual whose low-rent life with loving wife Gwen is swept aside by his passion for Fay, which he starts to regret as soon as it happens. But it's too late for regrets when you've found what you always thought you wanted.

In a copy of *Crap Artist* inscribed for friend Chris Arena in September 1980, Phil made a series of notes on the novel's narrative techniques and autobiographical sources. Like Charley, Phil feared falling victim to a heart attack. More fundamentally, Phil acknowledged the link between himself and both Jack Isidore and Nat Anteil: "Jack is a parody on myself as a teen-ager; his instincts and thoughts are based on my own when I was about 16 years old." He added: "Nat is based on me but as an adult, whereas Jack is my stunted adolescent side. Nat is mature, but he is psychologically weak, and falls under Fay's control."

And Fay was based on Anne. Phil told her so when he gave her the manuscript to read during their "honeymoon" period.

In Chapter 3, Charley hauls off and sucker punches Fay because he is humiliated by her having sent him to buy—*publicly* ask for—Tampax at the local store. In "real" life, Phil bought Tampax for Anne without comment. When Anne read the novel, she asked Phil why he hadn't said if he minded buying them for her? In the seventies, Phil would tell male friends about the time he hauled off and slugged Anne after having to buy her Tampax. By 1963, four years after *Crap Artist* was written, there was occasional, minor physical violence on both Phil and Anne's part. *Crap*

Artist had known it was coming. Precognition—Phil claimed, in the seventies, to have displayed it in some of his novels. Listen to Nat:

> I wonder if I'll wind up hitting her, he thought. He had never in his life hit a woman; and yet, he already sensed that Fay was the kind of woman who forced a man into hitting her. Who left him no alternative. No doubt she failed to see this; it would not be to her advantage to see this.

Chapter 11 begins with Nat wondering if Fay had "gotten herself involved with him because her husband was dying and she wanted to be sure that, when he did die, she would have another man to take his place." Nat recognizes intellectually that Fay picks out husbands as she would soap—Dr. X's joke—but is incapable of acting on his insight. By 1963 Phil was telling friends that Anne had killed her first husband and was trying to kill him.

Fay is not only Nat's lover-wife but also Isidore's sister. And Nat/Isidore "laminated together" (to borrow a phrase Phil used in the *Exegesis* when conjoining characters or ideas) are the man-child confronting a wife who arouses their worst childhood fears:

> I went to so much trouble, he [Nat] thought, to break away from my family—in particular my mother—and get off on my own, to be economically independent, to establish my own family. And now I'm mixed up with a powerful, demanding, calculating woman who wouldn't bat an eye at putting me back in that old situation again. In fact it would seem perfectly natural to her.

How would the "old situation" be reinstated? Maybe by Fay/Anne telling Isidore/Nat/Phil to chuck *Thrilling Wonder Stories* and get a real job. Charley Hume says of Fay: "The sharp contempt in her voice made him shiver. It was her most effective tone, full of the weight of authority; it recalled to him his teachers in school, his mother, the whole pack of them." In 1980, Phil noted that "Fay's speech patterns are authentic—based on those of an actual person."

In her *Search for Philip K. Dick*, Anne says of Fay:

> I was blunt and direct; but not that crude, and not devious like Fay. If Fay was a portrait of me it wasn't one of warts and all, but all warts. Phil portrayed Fay as needing a husband for herself and a father for her children, so she acquired Nat. It seemed never to occur to Nat that Fay loved him.

One can imagine Phil smiling now: the proof of his subjective truths borne out by placing side by side his novel and Anne's memoirs. The nature of their love—and their differences—is exemplified in their feeling for Isidore. In a January 1975 letter Phil wrote: ". . . Jack Isidore of

Seville, California: more selfless than I am, more kind, and in a deep deep way a better man." Writes Anne, in response to that letter: "Jack Isidore that weird, provincial, sexless fellow with a head filled with garbagy science-fantasy! Phil was about as much like Jack Isidore as a bird of paradise is like a bat. Phil was Nat!"

◆

Phil tried to blend strict writing discipline with the new demands of family life. He worked during the day and spent evenings with Anne and the kids. As a good provider, he would keep to a pace of two novels per year—each novel taking six weeks for the first draft and another six weeks for the second (retyping and minor copy editing). Between each novel would be six months devoted to thinking out the next plot. He warned Anne never to interrupt him when it seemed that he was only sitting quietly. "Beware," he would say, "of the person from Porlock"—the stranger who, knocking to ask the way to Porlock, shattered the composition of Coleridge's dream vision "Kubla Khan."

Once a novel was under way it moved swiftly. Phil still had his awesome typing speed. He told Anne: "The words come out of my hands not my brain, I write with my hands." Phil might make preliminary notebook entries, but the novel took true shape only in actual composition:

> The intuitive—I might say, gestalting—method by which I operate has a tendency to cause me to "see" the whole thing at once. Evidently there is a certain historical validation to this method; Mozart, to name one particular craftsman, operated this way. The problem for him was simply to get it down. If he lived long enough he did so; if not, then not. [. . .] The idea is there in the first jotting-down; it never changes—it only emerges by stages and degrees. If I believed that the first jotting-down actually carried the whole idea, I would be a poet, not a novelist; I believe that it takes 60,000 words for me to put down my original idea in its absolute entirety.

The intense writing bouts had their physical cost. Some weeks after Laura was born, Phil was hospitalized by chest pains (shades of Charley Hume). He remained cheerful: "I'm either going to die or else I'm going to have a baby," he told Anne. The diagnosis was pyloric spasms; the doctor told Phil to reduce his coffee intake and to meditate. Did the subject of Semoxydrine ever come up? By now it was a steady fuel for the writing.

For Phil, one of the great joys of his new "good life" was sports cars. They bought a used Peugeot, then traded it for a '53 white Jaguar Mark VII saloon with a mahogany dashboard, gray leather upholstery, and a sun roof. Phil cranked it out to 96 mph on the freeway. But it broke down, and in the autumn rains the sun roof leaked and the blue carpet

to induce fugue states. During these, Louis lives out multiple fantasy lives with Pris. At last, in one fugue, they have a child together, and Louis is ecstatic: "Across from them I sat, in a state of almost total bliss, as if all my tensions, all my anxieties and woes, had at last deserted me." But in his normal consciousness, Louis realizes that Pris is "both life itself—and anti-life, the dead, the cruel, the cutting and rending, and yet also the spirit of existence itself."

In a February 1960 letter to Harcourt, Brace editor Eleanor Dimoff, Phil had acknowledged—even prior to *Build*—his difficulties with female characters in his mainstream novels: "I tend to take it for granted in a novel that a man's wife is not going to help him; she's going to be giving him a bad time, working against him. And the smarter she is, the more likely she's up to something." The "evil woman problem" (as Phil termed it) preceded his marriage to Anne. The source of his rage was mother Dorothy. But despite Phil's apparent awareness of the problem, evil women continued to proliferate in the SF novels of the sixties. Many resembled Anne in life details and speech patterns. The high-water mark of the "problem" came in Phil's 1974 short story "The Pre-Persons," which reflects Phil's deeply felt antiabortion stand. The vehemence of its woman-hate is extraordinary. Father explains to son about aborting women: "They used to call them 'castrating females.' Maybe that was once the right term, except that these women, these hard cold women, didn't just want to—well, they want to do in the whole boy or man, make all of them dead, not just the part that makes him a man." It is as if female fetuses did not exist.

Phil later regretted the vehemence. In a 1980 "Afterword" he wrote: "In 'The Pre-Persons' it is love for the children that I feel, not anger toward those who would destroy them. My anger is generated out of love; it is love baffled." Precisely this anger that springs from "love baffled" was aroused by Anne's abortion.

Somehow, things settled back to something like normal. Which is to say that a strange new force entered Phil's life, a book to contend with: the *I Ching*, Book of Changes, with roots three thousand years old if they're a day. Truths consonant with the reader's ability to apprehend them. Maybe not truths at all—maybe the Oracle is a malevolent crock. Spiraling yin-yang forces, impossible to nail down. Perfect vehicle for Phil. By summer 1961 he was consulting it at least once a day and had even dreamed of Chinese sages superimposed upon each other, whom he believed to be the many authors who had contributed to the *I Ching* over the centuries.

But during a 1961 visit, Iskandar Guy heard Phil complain that the Oracle could speak with forked tongue. Guy recalls: "I told him, 'It goes back to at least 1165 B.C. Who are we to question an entity functioning at that level all this time?' He said, 'Fuck it, I'll fix it—I'll write a novel based on it.'" The novel, *The Man in the High Castle*, written in 1961 with the help of plot queries posed to the Oracle, is one of Phil's best and will be discussed shortly.

When he was not wrestling with yin and yang, Phil loved being outright silly. On April Fools' Day 1962 (Phil and Anne's third anniversary) Phil and the girls, for their trick on Anne, ran into the house exclaiming about a flying saucer that had just landed. Phil enjoyed the trick enough to pull it again some months later. (What did Phil really think of flying saucer sightings? He had parodied the little local UFO group that had invited him to join its ranks in *Crap Artist*, but in 1980 he noted that the group's belief in superior beings leading us to destruction for the sake of our salvation "doesn't seem as crazy to me now as it did when I wrote it.")

If there were no saucers in the sky, there were hints—sometimes—of something far stranger. One night Phil thought he saw a meteor. The family spent the next day looking for fragments, finding none. And then, on Good Friday 1962, Phil saw something far different. He had just finished listening to Handel's *Messiah* and was outside gardening, with baby Laura in tow, when he saw what he described to Anne as "a great streak of black sweeping across the sky. For a moment there was utter nothingness dividing the sky in half." Her response: "There was no doubt in my mind but that he had seen *something*." This vision of "nothingness" would linger with Phil as a confirmation, however frightening, of his capacity to see into the spiritual underpinnings of reality. As will be seen, the "nothingness" would be superseded, within a year, by a vision of still more stark dimensions.

A strictly terrestrial incident from this time concerns the death of a rat. Its lasting emotional impact on Phil recalls his third-grade "satori" while tormenting a beetle. It all started when rats began to eat their organic garden compost. One rat—Phil praises its courage and will to live in the *Exegesis*—went on to eat holes in their walls. Phil set out poison, on which this rat thrived. He then set out traps, which the rat eluded several times before it was finally caught—neck broken but still alive. Phil tried to drown it in a laundry tub. The rat swam frantically, dragging the trap. At last it died. Phil dug it a grave, in which he placed his Saint Christopher's medal.

That same summer of 1962, there was a hue and cry in Point Reyes Station over roaming dogs that were killing sheep. Phil purchased a rifle to protect their own small flock, as did other neighbors. According to Anne, Phil began to use the rifle recklessly, shooting without carefully aiming when dogs walked by on the road; eventually she gave the rifle away, without protest on Phil's part. Phil's love for his flock was pronounced—he would develop sympathetic wrist paralysis when the time came to butcher the sheep.

Throughout their marriage, Phil and Anne paid regular visits to Dorothy and Joseph Hudner in Berkeley. After Phil sold his Mañana

Street house, the Hudners gave him title to a cabin they owned in nearby Inverness. This graciousness may have contributed to the smoothest relations Phil and his mother had enjoyed in some time. Anne recalls: "Phil never had a good word to say about his mother to me, but sometimes, when they were together, I could see such a closeness between them it was as if one nervous system were working both bodies. Dorothy doted on Philip and was very proud of his writing." When, in 1962, Dorothy and Joseph considered moving to Mexico, Phil complained to Anne that his mother was "abandoning" him. The move never took place. Soon afterward Dorothy, whose chronic Bright's disease was worsening, nearly died. Phil was distraught and planned to offer Joseph a home if the worst occurred.

The greatest crisis Phil faced at this time arose from a cottage-scale jewelry business Anne had started up with a neighbor. Phil at first encouraged their efforts, even making their first sale by paying a call on a posh Berkeley store. As a game, he tried his own hand at making jewelry. Anne liked using randomly formed molten shapes, and Phil avidly took up the technique. One treasured piece, a triangular shape, he gave to neighbor Jerry Kresy, who recalls nailing it to his door as a coat hook, prompting fierce "voodoo stares" from Phil. It was no wonder. Phil loved the piece so much that he made it the touchstone of Mr. Tagomi's redemptive reality change in the *The Man in the High Castle*: "a small silver triangle ornamented with hollow drops. Black beneath, bright and light-filled above." The random-shape technique bestows *wu* (wisdom, tao), as opposed to *wabi* (intelligence, craft), both terms Phil picked up from a book on Japanese gardening.

But the threat Phil saw in the jewelry business—the possible economic eclipse of his writing career—brought about Phil's self-termed third "nervous breakdown," at age thirty-three, in 1962. Phil and Anne have highly contrasting versions of the key events. Anne relates that Phil's enthusiasm became so great that she had to insist that jewelry was *her* business while writing was *his*:

> I think he saw it as a way for him to have a normal business. He found himself trapped in writing at the time because he couldn't really make enough money to raise a family on it—I think he was real sensitive about that. He was a great jewelry maker, he had talent. I think he was so mad I pushed him out—that's why he talked so badly about it.

Cut to Phil on the couch in 1974 with interviewer Paul Williams on the third nervous breakdown that wasn't really:

PW: What specific event did you have in mind when you called that a nervous breakdown?

111

PKD: [pause] Ummm . . . the most profound kind of all. I was ceasing to, quote, cope adequately with my responsibilities—

PW: As defined by your wife.

PKD: As defined by my wife. And it was easier to imagine I was having a nervous breakdown than to face the truth about the situation. It wasn't until [a year later] that my psychiatrist [Dr. X] told me what the real situation was—which was her psychiatrist, too—that there was nothing wrong with me, that in point of fact the situation was hopeless . . . with her.

PW: For you.

PKD: In other words there was no way I could cope with it because it was uncopable. [. . .] But you could say that I didn't face reality, in that I did not face the fact that it was my fault. [. . .] But at that time I didn't realize it, I thought I was having a nervous breakdown. As a matter of fact I was not, in a peculiar way. I was showing the result of terrible pressures on me. . . .

"What "terrible pressures"? Consider: Anne's fledgling business was quickly threatening to outearn Phil's ten-year writing career.

Time for the first masterwork of his career. Phil wrote *The Man in the High Castle*, and its hard-cover publication by Putnam in 1962 helped him endure the storms of self-doubt. In a 1976 interview, Phil recounted:

I had actually decided to give up writing, and was helping my wife in her jewelry business. And I wasn't happy. She was giving me all the shit part to do, and I decided to pretend I was writing a book. And I said, "Well, I'm writing a very important book." And to make the fabrication convincing, I actually had to start typing. And I had no notes, I had nothing in mind, except for years I had wanted to write that idea, about Germany and Japan actually having beaten the United States. And without any notes, I simply sat down and began to write, simply to get out of the jewelry business. And that's why the jewelry business plays such a large role in the novel. Without any notes I had no preconception of how the book would develop, and I used the *I Ching* to plot the book.

To make the getaway complete, Phil had a hideout prepared. Ironically, it was by Anne's doing that Phil first came to rent the "Hovel," a small hut up the road on the property of local sheriff Bill Christensen. Phil had developed the habit of coming out of his study to read new passages to Anne. It wore her out, and she suggested that he find a work space away from the house.

Phil moved the Royal, the Magnavox, books and desk into the Hovel and kept a supply of candy bars on hand for when the girls dropped by. Anne regretted his absence at once, but Phil would not change his mind, though he too suffered from the separation. Dorothy had taught him to accept the consequences of his actions—"I never chew my cud twice," he explained. And he pointedly dedicated *The Man in the High Castle* "To my wife Anne, without whose silence this book would never have been written."

It was a drastic break. But in the isolated Hovel, Phil the writer was not merely reborn, but transformed.

◆

Phil often spoke of his two themes: "What is Human?" and "What is Real?" Within the span of eighteen months, in the Hovel, he wrote two novels that constitute his first great explorations of these themes: *The Man in the High Castle* and *Martian Time-Slip*. *High Castle* remains Phil's finest treatment of his "What is Human?" concerns—a subtle tale of moral frailty and courage in a world in which Nazi Germany and Imperial Japan have prevailed.

The United States has been divided (like Germany in our world) into separate political regions: The east is governed by the Nazis, while the more humane Japanese (who have no racist mythologies and draw from the *I Ching* as a kind of Bible) govern the west, with the Rocky Mountain states as a buffer zone with a modicum of self-rule. *High Castle* holds the distinction of being the first American novel to refer to the *I Ching* and employ it as a plot device (and deviser). Many who, in the sixties, elevated the *I Ching* to cult status first learned of it in *High Castle*.

There is, however, another text that exceeds even the *I Ching* in plot prominence—*The Grasshopper Lies Heavy*, a novel-within-a-novel in *High Castle*. *Grasshopper* (the title is from Ecclesiastes) poses a world in which the Allies, not the Axis, have prevailed. (In this twist, Phil was influenced by Ward Moore's novel *Bring the Jubilee* [1953], in which the South has won the Civil War.) The alternative world of *Grasshopper* does not match perfectly with our "real" world—for example, Rexford Tugwell, not Roosevelt, is the President who led America through the War. *Grasshopper* author Hawthorne Abendsen uses the *I Ching* to plot his novel, and the results are impressive: despite the novel's banned status, it circulates widely, read by everyone from Nazi leaders to fugitive Jews. *Grasshopper* points to a startling possibility: The world as we see it may not be real. We are in bondage only so long as we close our eyes.

So threatening is its premise that *Grasshopper* is banned and author Abendsen must hide in a "High Castle" in Cheyenne, Wyoming. Abendsen, who appears only in the last chapter, is drawn from Phil's memories of A. E. Van Vogt. The key inspiration for the "High Castle" symbol was Vysehrad, a Czech castle used by Protestants in their revolt against the Catholic dominion of the Holy Roman Empire. Research into Nazi policies (in the fifties, anticipating their use in a novel, Phil read, in the original German, SS files kept at U Cal Berkeley) revealed further castle metaphors:

113

Various lofty and beautiful castles from the old days of the kings and emperors were taken over by the SS and used as places to train young SS men into an elite body cut off from the "ordinary" world. These were to be bases from which the Ubermenschen would emerge to rule the Third Reich. [. . .] the two castles are bipolarized in the book: the legendary High Castle of Protestant freedom and resistance in the Thirty Years War versus the evil castle system of the elite youth corps of the SS.

Phil's knowledge of Nazi tactics lent *High Castle* a chilling dimension. Without hyperbole, he created a world in which evil is as palpable as death.

Unlike the novels to come, however, the grail-like quest for true reality does not take center stage in *High Castle*. Instead, the focus is on individuals whose lives are bonded by coincidence, conscience, and yearning. The third-person voice is used throughout, but in an intimate, hovering manner, with characters shifted quickly into and out of prominence. In a July 1978 letter, Phil commented on his "multiple narrative viewpoint" technique:

In the forties I got into novels written around that time by students at the French Department of Tokyo University; these students had studied the French realistic novels (which I, too, had read) and the Japanese students redesigned the slice-of-life structure to produce a compact, more integrated form [. . .] When I went to write MAN IN THE HIGH CASTLE I asked myself, How would this novel have been written—with what structure—if Japan had won the war? Obviously, using the multiple viewpoint structure of these students; [. . .]

These multiple viewpoints provide *High Castle* with a richness of texture that encompasses even the most subtle emotional shifts of its characters. The novel demonstrates convincingly that our smallest circumstantial acts can affect our fellow humans—for good or ill—more than we can ever likely know. By way of example, there is Robert Childan, a San Francisco dealer in antiques, who clings to Nazi dreams of white supremacy while kowtowing to the Japanese victors who govern his life. But Childan experiences a redemption of sorts because he can recognize the intrinsic meaning and value *(wu)* of a piece of jewelry crafted (unbeknown to Childan) by a despised Jew, Frank Frink. Then there is Nobusuke Tagomi, a customer of Childan's, who slays three Nazi killers with a purportedly antique Colt .44 (illegally counterfeited by Frink) in order to halt Nazi plans to incite a new war between Germany and Japan. Through Tagomi's courage, Frink's dishonesty is transformed into a contribution toward a better world.

Karma, as Phil depicts it in *High Castle*, is nothing like simple cause and effect. Goodness cannot assure peace of mind. Tagomi is anguished by his acts of murder, though it would seem that the Nazi killers left him no choice. In an effort to calm himself through aesthetic contemplation, Tagomi purchases from Childan a piece of Frink's jewelry (the same piece nailed to the door, in real life, by Phil's Point Reyes Station neighbor). But while Frink's craftsmanship opened the way to inner harmony for Childan, it transports Tagomi into a world of personal horror—the *Grasshopper* world in which the Allies have prevailed. His confrontation with that world recalls to Tagomi his ethical responsibilities in his own realm. He refuses to sign the extradition papers that would allow the Nazis to kill Frink.

Tagomi is one of the finest character portrayals of Phil's career. A middle-level trade official, he bears within his proper bureaucratic self a reverence for life and the tao. That very reverence causes Tagomi exquisite pain—the price of empathy. During a briefing on the German leadership (Bormann, who succeeded Hitler, has died, and Goebbels will succeed), Tagomi undergoes an anguish resembling those endured by Phil in school classrooms:

Mr. Tagomi thought, I think I am going mad.

I have to get out of here; I am having an attack. My body is throwing up things or spurting them out—I am dying. He scrambled to his feet, pushed down the aisle past other chairs and people. He could hardly see. Get to lavatory. He ran up the aisle.

Several heads turned. Saw him. Humiliation. Sick at important meeting. Lost place. He ran on, through the open door held by embassy employee.

At once the panic ceased. His gaze ceased to swim; he saw objects once more. Stable floor, walls.

Attack of vertigo. Middle-ear malfunction, no doubt.

He thought, Diencephalon, ancient brainstem, acting up.

Some organic momentary breakdown.

Think along reassuring lines. Recall order of world. [. . .]

There is evil! It's actual, like cement. [. . .]

It's an ingredient in us. In the world. Poured over us, filtering into our bodies, minds, hearts, into the pavement itself.

Why?

We're blind moles. Creeping through the soil, feeling with our snouts. We know nothing. I perceived this . . . now I don't know where to go. Screech with fear, only. Run away.

Pitiful.

Tagomi is not alone in recoiling from evil. The Swiss Mr. Baynes (name borrowed from Cary Baynes, the English translator of the *I Ching*), is really Rudolf Wegener, a German double agent seeking to avert war with Japan. While talking to a Nazi fellow passenger during a rocket flight, he undergoes his own horror:

115

They [Nazis] want to be the agents, not the victims, of history. They identify with God's power and believe they are godlike. That is their basic madness. They are overcome by some archetype; their egos have expanded psychotically so that they cannot tell where they begin and the godhead leaves off. It is not hubris, not pride; it is inflation of the ego to its ultimate—confusion between him who worships and that which is worshipped. Man has not eaten God; God has eaten man.

There is a second double agent in *High Castle*. Frank Frink's ex-wife, Juliana, commences an affair with Joe Cinnadella, who proves to be a German assassin seeking to utilize Juliana's charms (Abendsen, like Phil, is partial to "a certain type of dark, libidinous girl") to get into the "High Castle" and do away with the loathsome author, whom Joe cannot resist reading. When she learns of the plot, Juliana first attempts suicide and then cuts Joe's throat. On the advice of the *I Ching*, she proceeds to Cheyenne on her own. To her alone is granted the privilege of reaching the "High Castle"—which she finds is an ordinary suburban house. Abendsen abandoned his fortress years before; he recognizes that there is no refuge from the world's horrors.

But Juliana seeks no refuge, only the truth. Face to face with Abendsen, they consult the Oracle to determine what truth there is in *Grasshopper*. As in all cases where characters in *High Castle* use the *I Ching*, Phil first tossed the coins offstage and let his characters deal with the outcome. In the final chapter, Juliana and Abendsen confront the *Chung Fu* (Inner Truth) hexagram:

> Raising his head, Hawthorne scrutinized her. He had now an almost savage expression. "It means, does it, that my book is true?"
> "Yes," she said.
> With anger he said, "Germany and Japan lost the war?"
> "Yes."
> Hawthorne, then, closed the two volumes and rose to his feet; he said nothing.
> "Even you don't face it," Juliana said.
> For a time he considered. [. . .]
> "I'm not sure of anything," he said.
> "Believe," Juliana said.
> He shook his head no.

In a 1976 interview, Phil accused the *I Ching* of being a "malicious spirit" largely because it "copped out completely" as to the "unresolved" ending chapter of *High Castle*: "It is a liar. It speaks with forked tongue." (Notwithstanding such pronouncements, Phil consulted the *I Ching* regularly up to the time of his death, with peak use in the sixties and early seventies.) What frustrated Phil (as well as numerous critics who otherwise admired the novel unreservedly) was that the revelation of the truth—that the Allies prevailed in World War II—does nothing to dispel the characters' foreboding. Juliana remains isolated; Abendsen continues to live in fear. The sense of Nazi oppression remains. Truth alone, it seems, is not enough to liberate the soul. In an August 1978 letter, Phil tried to make the *High Castle* ending cohere:

> Juliana tells Hawthorne Abendsen that his book is true and it makes him angry. [. . .] Simply because he knows that if this woman, this stranger, this ordinary person knows, *then the Fascist authorities must know,* and his life is in danger. Abendsen feels two opposite ways about his novel; on one level he would like the truth of it to be palpable, but it scares him that he knows the truth and has publicly stated that truth: he is a Geheimnistrager: a carrier (knower I mean) of a secret, and it is a secret which frightens him.

Phil's sense of being a frightened "knower" of a "secret" appears throughout the *Exegesis,* begun in 1974. That same year he returned briefly to the idea of writing a sequel to *High Castle.* Back in 1964 he made a start at it (two chapters, twenty-two pages total, survive; see *High Castle* in the Chronological Survey) but could not face further research on hideous Nazi tactics. Dictated cassette notes of 1974 describe one scene in which Abendsen would be brutally interrogated by Nazis who seek (like Juliana) the truth as to the alternate Allied universe ("Nebenwelt"), which Abendsen cannot provide—*he does not know.* The secret is forever elusive.

◆

Of *Martian Time-Slip,* written in 1962 and published by Ballantine in 1964, mention has been made in Chapter 2 with regard to the parallels between Phil and *Time-Slip* protagonist Jack Bohlen: their shared hatred of schools and their horrific visions of reality coming apart at the seams. But *Time-Slip* does more than cast light on Phil's development. It is a brilliant novel of ideas and a humane and hilarious look at life on Earth's struggling colonies on Mars (which bears little resemblance to the Red Planet of pulp dreams). The central themes: the nature of schizophrenia, and of what by tenuous common consent we term the "real."

The appearance of *Time-Slip* as an SF paperback was a letdown for Phil. In 1974 he recalled:

> With *High Castle* and *Martian Time-Slip,* I thought I had bridged the gap between the experimental mainstream novel and science fiction. Suddenly I'd found a way to do everything I wanted to do as a writer. I had in mind a whole series of books, a vision of a new kind of science fiction progressing from those two novels. Then *Time-Slip* was rejected by Putnam, and every other hardcover publisher we sent it to.

As Paul Williams has noted in *Only Apparently Real*, a biographical sketch and collection of interviews with Phil, Phil's memories of *Time-Slip*'s fate are not entirely accurate. The novel that was submitted to, and rejected by, mainstream publishers was *We Can Build You*, ultimately published in 1972 by Don Wollheim's DAW Books. Phil's original title for *Time-Slip* was *Goodmember Arnie Kott of Mars*, and the Meredith Agency treated it as SF all the way, first serializing it (as *All We Marsmen*, a title even worse than Phil's, in *Worlds of Tomorrow*) and then selling it to Ballantine.

But if Phil misremembered the details, his sense of defeat by the reception of *Time-Slip* as SF was very real. Even its reception as SF was troubled: Wollheim at Ace—who in 1960 had purchased Phil's two worst-ever SF novels, *Vulcan's Hammer* and *Dr. Futurity*—turned down one of his best in *Time-Slip*. Why? The novel was set in 1994. "It offended my science fiction sense," says Wollheim. "There couldn't have been a Mars colony when he put it—if he'd thrown it ahead a hundred years, I would have liked it." Live by the SF sword, die by the SF sword.

◆

Reviewers treated *High Castle* as a political thriller on the order of *Fail-Safe* ("Scarifying," pronounced the *New York Times*), but sales were poor. And with *Time-Slip* Phil was back in the SF ghetto. But something strange happened. In late 1962 Putnam sold the rights to *High Castle* to the Science Fiction Book Club. And the SF fans saved Phil's ass, talking up *High Castle* so much that in September 1963 it received the highest SF honor: the Hugo Award.

If Phil was in the ghetto, at least he was its king. A local reporter took his picture standing beside the rocket-shaped trophy.

Meanwhile, the Meredith Agency, weary at last, had returned all of Phil's unsold mainstream novels in one big package that was dumped on his doorstep in January 1963. Those rejections, coupled with the ray of hope of the Hugo, made it official. After seven years, Phil's mainstream breakthrough effort was formally at an end.

So be it. Phil would move right on to work on an SF novel (the mainstream be damned!) that for sheer hairpin plotting and metaphysical weirdness soared far beyond anything in *High Castle* or *Time-Slip*.

For he would now see a vision of absolute evil in the sky.

And his marriage would come to seem, at times, even worse.

6 Phil's Marriage Mimics "Reality" By Coming Apart At The Seams, A Vision In The Sky Inspires The Most Brilliant Invasion Of Earth Story Ever Written, And, Country Squire No More, Phil Moves To East (Gak!) Oakland, Gets Weird, And Finds A New Wife (1963–1965)

And I wrote at a fantastic speed; I produced twelve novels in two years . . . which must be a record of some sort. I could never do this again—the physical stress was enormous—but the Hugo was there to tell me that what I wanted to write was what a good number of readers wanted to read. Amazing as it seems!

PHIL, 1968 "Self Portrait"

I was supporting, at one time, four children and a wife with very expensive tastes. Like she bought a Jaguar and so forth. I just had to write and that is the only way I could do it. And, you know, I'd like to be able to say I could have done it without the amphetamines, but I'm not sure I could have done it without the amphetamines, to turn out that volume of writing.

PHIL, 1977 interview with Uwe Anton

Well, I have an East Oakland care quotation, which is the brochure from the pills I've been taking for seven years (or is it nine? My mind seems oddly fuzzy, somehow), semoxydrine hydrochloride, which I now learn is methamphetamine hydrochloride (i.e. another name for methedrine), because, see, this last refill time—I am up to six 7.5 mg of them a day, and 7.5 is their strongest dose—the druggist forgot to snatch loose the accompanying brochure, so after all these years I got to read about the side-effects, etc. of the pill. One sentence under the subtitle HUMAN TOXICITY particularly made my decade. It reads like this, gang: Overdoses, may, in addition, cause hallucinations, delirium, peripheral vascular collapse and death. (Eeg, gak, wach, fug, gugh, whuh!)

PHIL, October 1964 letter to Terry and Carol Carr

IN 1963 and 1964, Phil wrote a mere eleven (not twelve) SF novels, which include three of his best (*Dr. Bloodmoney, The Simulacra, Clans of the*

Alphane Moon), one of his worst *(The Crack in Space)*, and, for good measure, an outright masterpiece *(The Three Stigmata of Palmer Eldritch)*. He also produced eleven stories, two essays, and two extended plot treatments that served as the bases for subsequent collaborations with Ray Nelson *(The Ganymede Takeover*, 1967) and Roger Zelazny *(Deus Irae*, 1976). Not to mention hundreds of letters and God knows what all else that may have been lost or destroyed along the way.

All this is worth stating at the outset because, in light of the tumultuous tales of these two years—told variously by Phil, Anne, friends, and rivals—it would be easy to overlook one central fact: Phil was not only a gifted writer, but a highly disciplined one. Swirling chaos never kept him from the trusty Royal for long. Indeed, it can be said that Phil thrived on the chaos, drawing from it the sustenance for his novels and stories.

There *were* times of peace and happiness between Phil and Anne. Of course. It's just that they became lost amidst the anger and accusations. Anne concedes that they possessed "hair-trigger tempers." She can't recall what it was they fought over so frequently, or rather, it was any and all things, most seemingly minor. Simple talks accelerated into verbal sparring and then into outright rage. In interview Anne says:

> He was powerfully brilliant, much smarter than me—putting out eighty different things simultaneously. It was very difficult to relate to him. You couldn't help loving him. He was scary. You never knew what bizarre thing he would do next. He made me angry too. Also, he was this charming lover, but the other Phil was just dreadful. You couldn't make out what was happening. I was very competitive with Phil, I had the college degree, and I was very, you know, "Now I've got you, you son of a bitch." I'm sure I gave Phil a lot of problems with that in the old days. I'm sure I did.

Never mind who started what when or why. They both were in love up to their ears, and it brought out the demons in them. Both Phil and Anne spoke freely to friends about the anger and violence that went on between them. Anne recalls: "I had a bitchy tongue back then. Who hit who on what occasion isn't so important. I know I participated spiritually in the violence." She acknowledges that each struck the other on more than one occasion. And Phil, though he more than held his own, grew ever more terrified by the escalating tensions. Several times he claimed to their friends that she was trying to kill him.

Anne denies any such thing, and no one who knew them at the time considers it plausible. But there's no question that Phil had reached the point where Anne scared the hell out of him. The jewelry experience had left him humiliated both as writer and as practical breadwinner. Phil would bemoan the double bind of facing complaints both about how little money he made and about the long writing stints that kept him away from his family.

And yes, by 1963 he did fear that Anne was out to kill him. Daughter Hatte recalls that during their arguments Phil would scream: "You killed [first husband] Richard and now you're trying to kill me." Anne recalls that one day, as Phil was opening a gate for her to drive through, she revved the motor and started forward slowly. In a panic, Phil bolted. "I thought disgustedly, 'What is he doing, now?' After I had driven out on the road he came back and got into the car. I didn't even ask him what he thought he'd been doing." What he thought—and accused Anne of for years to come—was that she had intended to run him down.

Phil had long been threatened by Richard Rubenstein due both to his mainstream literary status and to his wealth. When he was not falsely accusing Anne of plotting Rubenstein's murder, he worried that he himself was no more than an emergency replacement. Anne writes:

> But I do remember Phil saying on a number of occasions, "You don't love me, you just wanted a husband and a father for your children."
> No answer I gave would carry any weight with him. I tried an indignant, "I do too love you!" but when I couldn't get him to acknowledge this avowal I finally replied, "Well, of course I just wanted a husband and a father for my children. Why else would I marry you?"

Phil found two important allies who helped him to do what he knew he must: separate from the wife he could not help loving. Dr. X, to whom he and Anne paid alternate weekly visits, was the first. The second was his Hovel landlord, local sheriff Bill Christensen ("Sheriff Christen" in *The Man Whose Teeth Were All Exactly Alike*). Anne recalls one argument in which they both threw furniture, culminating in Phil's striking her. Their daughters looked on, frightened. Anne called Sheriff Christensen. When he arrived in his squad car, Phil went out to him while Anne glowered on the porch. Whatever he said satisfied the sheriff, who was sympathetic to Phil due to prior accounts Phil had given him of Anne's allegedly severe mood swings.

Anne's jewelry business was going well, but that wasn't totally good news to Phil, who was still selling his SF novels for a lousy $1,500 a shot to Ace. (He would enjoy a post-Hugo economic boomlet of sorts that saw him earn $12,000 in 1964, but it didn't last long and came too late to matter to this marriage.) During 1963, either Phil or Anne (each claimed it was the other) decided to sell the Inverness cabin, which Dorothy and Joseph Hudner had deeded to Phil. The understanding had been that the cabin would someday be reconveyed to them; Dorothy was furious at them both.

During this time, Anne recalls, Phil told her he was tired of being a writer; he suggested that they finance a record store by mortgaging their home. Anne states that Phil told both Dorothy and Dr. X that the mortgaging plan was Anne's idea. Dorothy promptly expressed her disapproval, while Dr. X informed Anne that she suffered from delusions of grandeur. Both accused her of trying to end Phil's writing career.

During summer 1963, Phil backed out on a planned family vacation to Yosemite National Park at the last moment. It seemed to Anne that he was suffering, for the first time in their marriage, from agoraphobia. By contrast, Harlan Ellison recalls that during this period Phil visited him in Los Angeles several times. They'd first met at the 1954 Worldcon—Ellison as a punk SF fan, Phil as the young pro. Now their friendship as fellow writers grew. They even went hunting together:

> I told him once about hunting for javelina pig, which is something I used to do. [. . .] We talked about it and I said, "Let's go."
> I suppose that was when I first got an insight into the way he looked at the world. Which was a very peculiar way indeed. His stories already had a strange slant: the feeling that a shadow world existed beside our own. I didn't realize it was paranoia until a great many years later; I wasn't that smart. Anyway, Phil found it an interesting experience. We didn't find anything. We had rifles along, rode out in the jeep to Nevada; he was fascinated by the guns.

Ellison's perception of "paranoia" in Phil during this period is not an isolated one. Old Berkeley friend Iskandar Guy recalls:

> Phil was talking stuff so outrageous it made no bloody sense. What he *was* experiencing, what *was* going down—I couldn't make sense of it. He was going through extreme vacillations between depression and almost manic things. He would say, "Anne hooked up the stereo to the Jaguar and dragged it down the street." It could have happened, I don't know—but that's pretty *far* out. He said Anne tried to kill him. I would see her and, my God, Anne's pretty mellow. Nice lady. Talking about her Phil had gone from she's the greatest thing that ever happened to me to she's a pseudo-demonic creature, the destructive feminine principle of the world.
> There was a general paranoid cosmology—faces in the clouds, government, FBI. You name it. It was like he was holding the fort against the forces of evil.

Phil came to rely upon Dorothy as a refuge from his wife. Whatever Dorothy's faults, she had never failed to rally behind Phil's writing career, and now she came to sympathize with his view of Anne as a threat to it. Phil was often in despair during his visits: shutting down, sitting and staring. If he did talk, it was in flat tones. Dorothy knew to allow for a degree of elaboration in his tales. Recalls Lynne Cecil, who was still living with her aunt/stepmother Dorothy at this time: "Phil exaggerated and dramatized. Mom used to say about him, if he didn't have a book going, he made one. I don't think he ever knew he was doing it, and his imagination was so rich that it was difficult to sort out."

Dorothy was alarmed by the increasing amounts of amphetamines her son took to bolster his moods and his writing production. She'd known of his prescription Semoxydrine use in the fifties. But now she found herself in the position of a passive supplier. Lynne Cecil recalls: "Mom would say she wished she could put a lock on her medicine chest because he'd come to the house, open it up—Mom had everything because she had so many physical problems. He preferred speed, but I think he'd try anything to see what it felt like. He was like a little kid in some ways."

Dorothy's medicine cabinet was not Phil's only source of drugs—he continued to obtain prescriptions for antidepressants. While he could seem childlike in his trust in the efficacy of uppers and downers, he was by no means as naïve as he sometimes liked to pretend. Phil knew drugs, and by the early sixties the deleterious side effects of amphetamines were widely discussed. But he found it difficult to acknowledge his own responsibility here. To the end of his life he blamed Anne for his increased amphetamine usage during this time. Likewise Dorothy. After one visit to his mother, Phil told Anne: "I'm afraid that I'm going to kill myself with the drugs in Dorothy's medicine cabinet. She's going to kill me the way she leaves those drugs around."

By the end of summer 1963, Phil had decided that things with Anne had gotten totally out of hand. Dr. X helped him realize that his marital problems were due largely to Anne's mental condition; Dr. X's diagnosis, Anne recalls, was "manic-depressive." Sheriff Christensen, who'd witnessed Anne in a fury the one time he had come out in response to her call, was not inclined to disagree. Phil told them both that her spending had gotten out of hand, that she had tried to run him down with the car and had threatened him with a knife.

And so one night, during dinner, Sheriff Christensen came to the door with involuntary commitment papers signed by Dr. X. While the girls watched, Anne was hauled off for seventy-two hours of observation at Ross Psychiatric Hospital.

Phil had made a rather definite decision as to what was real.

Anne explains why she never stopped loving Phil during the ordeal to come: "I was rooted in my marriage. We had four children. I felt that, no matter what, you just had to try to work things out. Loyalty was a very strong value to me."

The shrink at Ross believed Anne when she explained that marital fights were one thing and craziness another. But having come this far, she had only two options: a full-scale legal hearing on her sanity or two weeks of further evaluation at Langley-Porter Clinic. She chose the second, residing in a locked ward. Phil and the kids came to visit every day. Daughter Hatte (then thirteen) recalls that during one such drive Phil said: " 'I'm going to talk to the doctors today. I'm sure they're going to tell me that I'm the one who should be in there, not your mother.' On the way home he said: 'That's what they told me. I already thought that, myself.' Well, maybe it's true and maybe not—that's the kind of thing he'd say."

The clinic records of her stay include (according to Anne's transcription) the following comments: Mr. Dick "was very unhappy—he says that he has never seen his wife looking worse. Mr. Dick feels that he is the mentally ill partner and should be hospitalized. He feels he may be schizophrenic." The recording male physician stated that Mr. Dick's problem was that he was "unable to control his wife."

Anne was released after the two weeks. On the way home, Phil insisted that they pay a visit to Dr. X, who informed Anne that, Langley-Porter notwithstanding, she was manic-depressive. While in the clinic, Anne had spit out the daily Stelazine pill; her first day in, she had swallowed it obediently and been left logy. According to Anne, Dr. X now insisted that she keep taking them at home; Phil threatened to leave her if she refused. Phil's faith in Stelazine (a phenothiazine downer used to manage certain psychotic disorders and high anxiety) was sincere; he took it himself on occasion and found it beneficial. Anne's experience with a regular dosage: "They turned me into a zombie. Once I had taken them I didn't have sense enough not to take any more." Anne stayed on Stelazine for two or three months, suffering some impairment of memory. She and Phil began seeing a female marriage counselor who made little dent in what was happening. Anne, after her Stelazine haze, was furious but still determined to save the marriage. Phil had his doubts.

In later years, Phil never alluded publicly to the commitment, though he continued to maintain that Anne was "schizoid," lacking in human kindness. Surely his lingering anger over the 1960 abortion played a part in these comments. But his reticence on the subject of Anne's commitment (as opposed to frequent and vehement accounts, in interviews, of the jewelry fiasco) does indicate a degree of discomfort. But while Phil kept a public silence on the real-life events, he drew heavily on his memories of the commitment in his SF novels. Phil made no secret of the fact that many of his sixties female protagonists were inspired at least in part by Anne. Three examples that cast some light here are Emily Hnatt in *The Three Stigmata of Palmer Eldritch* (w. 1964, p. 1965), Mary Rittersdorf in *Clans of the Alphane Moon* (w. 1963–64, p. 1964), and Kathy Sweetscent in *Now Wait for Last Year* (w. 1963, rewritten, p. 1966).

Emily, in *Palmer Eldritch*, undergoes E (for Evolution) Therapy along with her second husband, Richard (a name likely drawn from Anne's first husband). E Therapy is risky business. Subjects either evolve—with larger brains creating a "bubblehead" look—or regress to become husks of their former selves. As it turns out, Richard evolves and

Emily regresses. Anne speculates that this was Phil's way of comparing their differing responses to Stelazine. Richard's higher vision affords a benign, enlightened view of the wife he loves. Emily's decline is an unavoidable sorrow. It should be added that the character of Emily was also likely influenced by second wife, Kleo. In particular, the regret felt by Emily's first husband, Barry Mayerson, over the end of their marriage parallels Phil's own sense that in Kleo he had lost a "perfectly good wife."

But in the latter two examples, the figure of Anne clearly dominates. In *Clans*, hapless Chuck Rittersdorf and his brilliant psychiatrist wife, Mary, both undergo psychiatric-profile testing. The result: Mary is forced to admit that Chuck is "without a trace of mental disturbance" while she is a depressive type. She admits: "My continual pressing of you regarding your income—that was certainly due to my depression, my delusional sense that everything had gone wrong, that something *had* to be done or we were doomed."

In *Now Wait*, love is put to the test. Dr. Eric Sweetscent is a confused but kindly artiforg (artificial organ) surgeon; his wife, Kathy, a consultant, is a brilliant, driven harridan, whose salary exceeds Eric's. Kathy loves Eric and tries to keep him even as he struggles to get out of the marriage. She becomes addicted to JJ-180, a hallucinogen with toxic side effects and looping time-travel properties. Kathy tricks Eric into taking JJ-180 to motivate him to discover an antidote. Despite Eric's loyal efforts, which Kathy hardly deserves, the truth is—as Eric's future self tells him during a JJ-180 trip—that Kathy suffers from Korsakow's syndrome ("pathological destruction of cortical brain tissue due to long periods of intoxication") due to narcotics use prior to JJ-180. The situation is hopeless; but, as the future Eric notes: "Under phenothiazine sedation she's quiet, anyhow."

At the end of *Now Wait*, Eric has a talk with a flying cab on the meaning of *caritas*. As is often the case in Phil's SF, the machine speaks with soul:

> To the cab he said suddenly, "If your wife were sick—"
> "I have no wife, sir," the cab said. "Automatic Mechanisms never marry; everyone knows that."
> "All right," Eric agreed. "If you were me, and your wife were sick, desperately so, with no hope of recovery, would you leave her? Or would you stay with her, even if you had traveled ten years into the future and knew for an absolute certainty that the damage to her brain could never be reversed? And staying with her would mean—"
> "I can see what you mean, sir," the cab broke in. "It would mean no other life for you beyond caring for her."
> "That's right," Eric said.
> "I'd stay with her," the cab decided.

"Why?"

"Because," the cab said, "life is composed of reality configurations so constituted. To abandon her would be to say, I can't endure reality as such. I have to have uniquely special easier conditions."

"I think I agree," Eric said after a time. "I think I will stay with her."

"God bless you, sir," the cab said. "I can see that you're a good man."

"Thank you," Eric said.

The cab soared on toward Tijuana Fur & Dye Corporation.

The worth of these novels does not depend upon the correctness of Phil's evaluation of Anne's mental state. He was a *fiction* writer, imagining and elaborating even the events of his life. But this cluster of husband-wife sanity bouts fairly indicates that, in committing Anne, Phil took action that he felt was necessary and, ultimately, loving. For the record, Anne does not suffer from insanity or brain damage, and after Phil left the marriage she built up a successful jewelry business while raising and educating four daughters.

After the commitment, even after the Stelazine, the fights continued. In autumn 1963 Phil and Anne attended a party at a house on Mount Vision in Inverness. Anne recalls that, quite atypically, Phil downed several martinis. On the way home he swerved the car off the steep road—the front wheels hanging in air. Anne writes that as they waited for help, "Phil took my arm and tried to forcibly lead me into the driver's seat. He said, 'Get in and I'll push.' If he had pushed the car, it would have gone over the side of the mountain. Of course, there were trees to stop it from going very far."

Late in 1963 tensions came to a head and Phil left, moving in with Dorothy in Berkeley. Before long Anne came to take him back, and Phil returned docilely, seeming flattered by this demonstration of her love. But there was no return to happy times. President Kennedy's assassination in November shocked Phil so severely that he dropped to the floor when he learned of it, then remained depressed for days. When Phil's beloved cat Tumpy disappeared they purchased twin Siamese cats, who died of distemper. Phil, who had lived with cats all his adult life, refused to consider finding replacements just then.

Anne suggested that church attendance might help. They joined St. Columba's, an Episcopal church in Inverness, and attended "religiously" (as Phil liked to say) every Sunday. He would sometimes claim that this was due solely to Anne's social climbing: "She says, If we're going to know judges and district attorneys and important people, we have to be Episcopalian."

But the primary force that led Phil to his brief involvement with the Episcopal Church was not Anne, but a horrific vision in the second half of 1963 that brought him to the point of spiritual crisis. In the late seventies, Phil recalled:

There I went, one day, walking down the country road to my shack, looking forward to eight hours of writing, in total isolation from all other humans, and I looked up in the sky and saw a face. I didn't really see it, but the face was there, and it was not a human face; it was a vast visage of perfect evil. I realize now (and I think I dimly realized at the time) what caused me to see it: the months of isolation, of deprivation of human contact, in fact sensory deprivation as such . . . but anyhow the visage could not be denied. It was immense; it filled a quarter of the sky. It had empty slots for eyes—it was metal and cruel and, worst of all, it was God.

I drove over to my church [. . .] and talked to my priest. He came to the conclusion that I had had a glimpse of Satan and gave me unction—not supreme unction; just healing unction. It didn't do any good; the metal face in the sky remained. I had to walk along every day as it gazed down at me.

The vision—not "really" seen but decisively encountered—endured for several days. Isolation and the anguish of his failing marriage were not the only causal factors. Phil had also been taking what he described alternately as "certain chemicals" and "psychedelic drugs." What drugs these were is unknown; Phil did indicate, in a 1967 letter, that LSD was not among them; amphetamines alone, in sufficiently high doses, could account for such a vision. By the seventies, his accounts of the vision no longer included mention of drugs, likely because his attitude toward drug experimentation had changed.

However, at the heart of the vision lay not drugs, or even isolation, but rather memories of father Edgar putting on a gas mask as he told four-year-old Phil stories of World War I: "[T]he sight of him wearing his gasmask, blending as it did with his accounts of men with their guts hanging from them, men destroyed by shrapnel—decades later, in 1963, as I walked alone day after day along that country road with no one to talk to, no one to be with, that metal, blind, inhuman visage appeared to me again, but now transcendent and vast, and absolutely evil."

The visage—which became Palmer Eldritch—was a psychic implosion on the order of Phil's classroom horrors. The difference was that now, as a writer, Phil possessed a means of response, of integration. Even so, the challenge was severe. Phil later said: "[W]e must have our *idios kosmoses* to stay sane; reality [the *koinos kosmos*] has to filter through, carefully controlled by the mechanisms by which our brains operate. We can't handle it directly, and I think that this was what was occurring when I saw Palmer Eldritch lingering, day after day, over the horizon."

Phil did not tell Anne of the experience. She writes, "If he had I might have said to him, 'You probably ate something that didn't agree with you.' "

For Christmas 1963, Phil and Anne gave their daughters Barbie and Ken dolls. That very month, Phil had published (in *Amazing*) "The Days of Perky Pat," a strange, hilarious story of life on a bleak, defeated Earth whose survivors are kept alive through the relief efforts of the Martian victors. To keep their sanity, the survivors play with dolls and models in elaborate "Perky Pat layouts" styled after Barbie and Ken wardrobes and accessories. Daughter Hatte recalls that Phil measured the proportions of Barbie dolls to confirm that they could not exist in the real world—their heads were too small for their bodies.

A vision in the sky, Barbie dolls, memories of Edgar and the teachings of the Episcopal Church—all forming into a novel that Phil would start just after Christmas, in early 1964.

The final touch was provided by the world-toppling theories of Gnosticism, a body of religious thought that has persisted through the centuries despite vehement persecution by the Catholic Church. Phil and Anne were taking confirmation classes at this time, and Phil grew fascinated with the doctrines of the Episcopal Mass and, most especially, of the transubstantiation of the Eucharist. This fascination led him to read, quite independently, Jung's essay on "Transformation Symbolism in the Mass." In it, Jung speculates that underlying the Christian view of Christ dying for our sins lies a Gnostic sense of the punishment fitting the crime—a divine being rightly punished for creating a flawed world. Jung concludes: "For reasons that can be readily understood, a satisfactory answer is not to be expected from orthodox Christianity. [. . .] And from certain Gnostic systems it is clear that the *auctor rerum* [world creator] was a lower archon who falsely imagined that he had created a perfect world, whereas in fact it was woefully imperfect."

For Phil, the Gnostic view that our world is an illusory reality created by an evil, lesser deity was utterly compelling. It could account for the suffering of humankind, as well as for startling phenomena such as a vision of "absolute evil" (the Gnostic god's true visage!) in the sky. Not that Phil would have labeled himself with conviction as a Gnostic. But as a fiction writer, Phil naturally gravitated to theories that spurred his imagination and provided a useful framework for his experiences—and Gnosticism fit the bill most excellently.

Phil, Anne, and the kids were all duly baptized together in January 1964. But Anne recalls: "As we drove home Phil told me cheerfully, 'At the moment of my baptism I saw, slinking out of the baptistry, his tail between his legs, a small red devil, the classic type, with horns and a spiked tail.'"

◆

Palmer Eldritch, which Phil mailed off to the Meredith Agency in March 1964, came in the middle of an amphetamine-fueled writing streak that was torrid even by Phil's standards. In the twelve months that preceded *Palmer Eldritch*, Phil had written six SF novels: *Dr. Bloodmoney, The Game-Players of Titan, The Simulacra, Now Wait for Last Year, Clans of the Alphane Moon, The Crack in Space*. In the five months that followed it, he wrote three more: *The Zap Gun, The*

Penultimate Truth, and the novelette-length *The Unteleported Man.* (See Chronological Survey.)

Sure, he felt under the gun to provide for the family and wrote at the warp speed required of writers who sought a living from SF back then. But Phil was also at the height of his powers. Never again would he produce at this white-hot pace, even though the pitifully low advances for his novels—and the amphetamines—continued through the early seventies. Hell, the low advances never really changed.

But with *Palmer Eldritch* the dam burst. Phil was through with playing to the mainstream. *High Castle* had won the Hugo. There were SF readers who gave a damn. And they let you have fun so long as you astonished them. Nothing easier than that.

Phil's plots didn't require much in the way of fancy space-exploration gear. For the most part he plops his characters on the nearby Martian colonies or a post–nuclear holocaust Earth. His future technology consists largely of flying "flapples" and other talking homeostatic devices that try futilely to straighten out their hapless human owners' lives. When Phil really wants to shake things up, he introduces psi talents such as telepaths ("teeps") and precognitives ("precogs"), or aliens of sinister and saintly persuasion, or brand-new drugs that, regardless of what they promise, *always* make things ever so much weirder and worse. The characters confronting all this tend to be—as who wouldn't?—frantic, confused, fierce, broken, and sometimes even full of faith in human goodness. *Voilà!* The Phildickian world.

Palmer Eldritch is Phil's first SF novel to take the genre, shake it by the throat, and make it work *his* way. John Lennon read it, admired it, and expressed interest in making a film of it. It was the book that, Phil said more than once, had the best chance of enduring out of all of his work. *Valis* (1981) is its superior in metaphysical and psychological brilliance; *Ubik* (1969) outdoes it in sheer pataphysical slapstick; *A Scanner Darkly* (1977) explores more convincingly hell's domains. But if you want to read a breathtaking page-turner about Earth being secretly invaded by alien forces beyond our comprehension while Barney Mayerson passes through numberless alternate realities trying to win back his ex-wife in one of them, just one, and desperate Martian colonists yearn for the bright, shiny world of Perky Pat, and Leo Bulero turns to the highly suspect Dr. Smile to help him escape the giant rat, and Palmer Eldritch proves to be *everyone*, at least for a while, and have it all add up—while you're not paying attention—into a moving parable on the nature of reality and the struggle for our eternal souls, then you'll have to read *Palmer Eldritch.*

The novel takes place in the early twenty-first century. Earth is parched—the temperature in New York in May is 180 degrees Fahrenheit. Precog Barney Mayerson wakes up in a strange bed with a woman he doesn't recognize and immediately switches on his suitcase psychiatrist—Dr. Smile—that Barney hopes will help drive him crazy, thereby precluding his being drafted by the world government to live in the Martian colonies, where things are even worse. Dr. Smile explains to Barney that the woman is Rondinella Fugate, Barney's new assistant at Perky Pat Layouts, and that she wants his job.

Perky Pat Layouts (PPL) is officially in the business of producing ideal miniaturized ("minned") "layouts"—penthouse apartments, sleek convertibles, glorious resorts—to which Martian colonist users of the illegal drug "Can-D" are "translated," during their all-too-brief intoxication, into the perfect bodies of Walt (for the guys) and Perky Pat (for the gals). When three couples sit together in a "hovel"—Phil named their bleak living quarters after his own writing "Hovel"—all three guys can be in Walt at once, and all three gals in Perky Pat. It's a mystery as unyielding as that of the triune God who is One. Here's a day at the beach Can-D layout style:

> The waves of the ocean lapped at the two of them [Walt and Perky Pat] as they silently reclined together. [. . .]
> Rising to her feet Perky Pat said, "Well, I can see I might just as well go for a swim; nothing's doing here." She padded into the water, splashed away from them as they sat in their body, watching her go.
> "We missed our chance," Tod Morris thought wryly.
> "My fault," Sam admitted. By joining, he and Tod managed to stand; they walked a few steps after the girl and then, ankle-deep in the water, halted.
> Already Sam Regan could feel the power of the drug wearing off; he felt weak and afraid and bitterly sickened at the realization. So goddam soon, he said to himself. [. . .]
> And, by the layout, a plain brown wrapper that had contained Can-D; the five of them had chewed it out of existence, and even now as he looked—against his will—he saw a thin trickle of shiny brown syrup emerge from each of their slack, will-less mouths.

Barney Mayerson's precog powers enable him to predict—at least most of the time—which "minned" fashions will go over with the fantasy-craving colonists. Mayerson's boss, the owner of PPL, is Leo Bulero, who is not your standard hero. He's the big-time Can-D pusher, and while the colonists treat the "translation" experience as a religion, Bulero knows better even as he justifies himself by the solace Can-D brings to their wretched lives. But it's Leo Bulero who winds up saving Earth and us all.

The threat is posed by the return of Palmer Eldritch, a renegade industrialist who has been away in the Prox solar system for ten years and mysteriously crash-landed on Pluto on the way back. Eldritch has survived, though in just what form no one knows, as Eldritch is keeping himself in seclusion. But he has brought back with him a new drug—Chew-Z—which threatens to drive Can-D off the market. As any Mar-

ᴜonist will tell you, Can-D dumps you back in yoᴜ
ᴜickly, and it requires expensive "minned" accessories to sᴜ
Chew-Z lasts and lasts and leaves you with no doubts whatsoᴇ
reality of what you experience in its domain. The Chew-Z
slogan: "GOD PROMISES ETERNAL LIFE. WE CAN Dᴜ
IT."

Eldritch doses Bulero with Chew-Z, which proves to be horrifᴜ
escape, Bulero builds a staircase that ascends through a luminous hooᴜ
the sky and descends into New York, the home of PPL. Having madᴇ
back to his office, he tries, as a good leader should, to reassure Barney anᴅ
Roni Fugate:

> "I've now got an idea of what this new Chew-Z substance is like. It's
> definitely inferior to Can-D. I have no qualms in saying that emphatically.
> You can tell without doubt that it's merely a hallucinogenic experience you're
> undergoing. Now let's get down to business. Eldritch has sold Chew-Z to the
> UN by claiming that it induces genuine reincarnation [. . .] It's a fraud,
> because Chew-Z doesn't do that. But the worst aspect of Chew-Z is the
> solipsistic quality. With Can-D you undergo a valid interpersonal experience,
> in that the others in your hovel are—" He paused irritably. "What is it, Miss
> Fugate? What are you staring at?"
>
> Roni Fugate murmured, "I'm sorry, Mr. Bulero, but there's a creature
> under your desk."
>
> Bending, Leo peered under the desk.
>
> A thing had squeezed itself between the base of the desk and the floor; its
> eyes regarded him greenly, unwinking. [. . .]
>
> Leo said, "Well, that's that. I'm sorry, Miss Fugate, but you might as well
> return to your office; there's no point in our discussing what actions to take
> toward the imminent appearance of Chew-Z on the market. Because I'm not
> talking to anyone; I'm sitting here blabbing away to myself."

Slowly but surely everyone (whether or not they themselves have
taken Chew-Z, and who are "they" anyway?) takes on the Palmer Eldritch
"stigmata," based upon Phil's vision in the West Marin sky: stainless-steel
teeth, slotted artificial eyes, and a black mechanical arm. In the novel,
these are explained as prosthetics supplied to the wealthy Eldritch after
his crash on Pluto. But they become the signs of a pervasive hallucinatory
reality controlled by Eldritch. Mayerson sees the truth behind the evil
visage:

> . . . it's all the same, it's all him, the creator. That's who and what he is, he
> realized. The owner of these worlds. The rest of us just inhabit them and
> when he wants to he can inhabit them, too. Can kick over the scenery,
> manifest himself, push things in any direction he chooses. Even be any of us
> he cares to. All of us, in fact, if he desires. Eternal, outside of time and

r segments of all other dimensions . . . *he can even*
ch he's dead.

ldritch had gone to Prox a man and returned a god.

 dritch is a god, he is a mirthless one. However many realms he
, Eldritch remains alone. To Mayerson, who wonders how he
ear the eternities of Chew-Z, Eldritch suggests (with something as
to kindness as a figure of absolute evil can get) that he turn himself
o a rock.

But the novel ends—or rather, begins—with a business-memo epigram that assures the reader that Leo Bulero, grasping entrepreneur and ultimate human hero, will win the day. Dated after the hellish events of the narrative to come, the memo acknowledges that humankind is "only made out of dust," which is "a sort of bad beginning," but concludes brusquely: "So I personally have faith that even in this lousy situation we're faced with we can make it. You get me?" Bulero's resemblance to Phil's first boss, Herb Hollis, is discussed in Chapter 3. But there is a deeper influence here, one that first showed itself in the fifties story "The Father-thing":

> In the novel my father appears as both Palmer Eldritch (the evil father, the diabolic mask-father) and as Leo Bulero, the tender, gruff, warm, human, loving man. [. . .] the horror and fear expressed in the novel are not fictional sentiments ground out to interest the reader; they come from the deepest part of me: yearning for the good father and fear of the evil father, the father who left me.

Palmer Eldritch was Phil's first SF novel sale to Doubleday, which published this book (and seven more) in hard-cover in the sixties and seventies. For the first time, Phil had found a steady market for his books alongside Ace, which continued to publish the majority of his titles through the end of the sixties. While Doubleday didn't pay much more than Ace—an advance of $2,000, on average—they did provide the dignity of dust jackets. And so, in a market sense, *Palmer Eldritch* was a breakthrough novel for Phil.

More important, it was the confirmation of what he could do with SF. *Palmer Eldritch* terrified him—Phil claimed that when the galleys arrived he couldn't bring himself to read them. Anne calls it a "black mass" and laughs, in retrospect, at Phil's having written it in the midst of confirmation classes. In a 1974 interview, Phil termed the Chew-Z realm "not a dream or even a hallucination. It is a state entered into by the characters . . . and their attempts to find their way back to 'sanity.' "

Certainly the novel lends itself to intriguing interpretations. Consider Palmer Eldritch. A palm branch, in Christian symbolism, suggests the martyr's triumph over death. A palmer is a pilgrim who, as a sign of having been to the Holy Land (or the Prox solar system?), carries a palm branch (or the Chew-Z lichen?). *Eldritch*, of course, is a favorite adjective of Lovecraft and other writers of the *Weird Tales* pulp era of the twenties and thirties. As for Leo Bulero, the lion appears in the prophecies of Ezekiel and, as a symbol of Christ the Lord of Life, is associated with the Resurrection. And the Chew-Z realm may be seen as the hellish Gnostic parallel to the Christian Eucharist, which, as described by Jung, "contains, as its essential core, the mystery and miracle of God's transformation taking place in the human sphere, his becoming Man, and his return to his absolute existence in and for himself."

In the *Exegesis*, Phil frequently turns to Gnostic doctrines in an attempt to explain *Palmer Eldritch* to himself. For example, Eldritch is "the arrogant one, the Blind God (i.e. the artifact) which supposes itself to be the one true God." The true God—the true Father—has abandoned this world. Most fundamental, however, is this 1978 entry: "Leo Bulero defeating Palmer Eldritch is the savior/messenger (Son of Man) defeating the demiurge creator of this prison (& illusory) world. Breaking his power over man."

All that and a great invasion-of-Earth tale too. God bless SF.

♦

By early 1964 the marriage was nearing its end. Phil's stays with Dorothy in Berkeley grew more frequent. On March 9, Phil filed for divorce (the decree became final in October of the following year). Phil did circle back to Point Reyes Station for several brief efforts at reconciliation, staying as little as an hour and as long as a day or two, always leaving with a renewed sense of the marriage's failure.

The worst of it was leaving Laura and his three stepdaughters behind. Phil had been, through all the turmoil, a devoted father, accepting Hatte, Jayne, and Tandy as his own. But fundamentally, Phil was ready for a change. He was markedly ill-suited for the confines of middle-class family life. And his love for the children could not compensate for his bitter restiveness with Anne. Like most men of this era, Phil scarcely considered sharing custody after the marriage ended. Child raising was a woman's task. Phil would come to resent Anne's reluctance, in later years, to have Laura visit him. But he never objected to Anne's taking on the primary duties of care, including economic support—Phil resolutely dodged child support payments to Anne over the next decade. Even as he separated from Anne in March 1964, his primary energies were focused on starting up life anew.

In particular, Phil was happy to return to city life and decidedly on the prowl. Moreover, he became, for the first and only time, a mainstay of the Bay Area SF social scene. At first Phil moved in with the Hudners in Berkeley. Then a serendipitous correspondence arose—and Phil had a new romantic interest.

Grania Davidson (now Grania Davis, with three published SF novels to her credit) was twenty and living in Mexico. Her marriage to SF writer Avram Davidson, a friend of Phil's, was coming to an amicable end. She wrote to Phil in praise of *High Castle* and the *I Ching*, which Grania was consulting regularly. This led to an epistolatory courtship. When Grania and her son came to the Bay Area in June 1964, she and Phil hit it off and decided to share quarters at 3919 Lyon Avenue in East "Gakville," a/k/a Oakland. It was a small old house in a less than fashionable neighborhood. Officially, to avert embarrassment during the divorce, Phil rented the house while Grania occupied the backyard cottage.

Their relationship, which lasted until Halloween, provided Phil with a striking change from life with Anne. Grania was a free-spirited lover who admired his writing and made no difficult demands. Grania recalls that Phil was affectionate and considerate both to her and to her son, for whom he built a sandbox in the backyard. His gifts to her were on the practical side: an old Chevy and a salad bowl. But his declarations of love were breathtaking. Says Grania: "Phil had this marvelous ability to love-blast people, to turn on this incredibly intense affection—I think that was his main attraction to women and also to his friends. When he loved you, he really loved you."

She describes Phil as beset by "inner demons" during that summer. He would awaken in anguish in the middle of the night. One fear was that Anne was spying on him for information to use in court. He confided to friends that Anne had somehow planted a bug in his Magnavox. Anne did saw off the lock of the Hovel to obtain Phil's financial records for her lawyer. Outraged, Phil obtained a court restraining order; he also purchased a .22 Colt derringer to protect himself against potential violence on Anne's part. Grania recalls that he "became rather overly fond of it, waving it around at people," including once at Anne when she came to the Lyon Avenue house with Laura. Grania doesn't know if it was loaded on those occasions. She observes: "Phil was interested in violence, attracted to it. It was part of the whole pattern of his life at that time—with fears of the CIA and Nazis being around."

Phil did make numerous allusions to his friends of Nazis, CIA and FBI bugging of his house, and of Anne's alleged spying efforts (which she denies). Phil being Phil, when he told these stories he was often hilarious—deadpan accusations that the CIA had bugged his cat box. And while Phil talked a gruff act toward Anne and toward those who he felt threatened people he loved (and, as Grania emphasizes, Phil loved many people—including platonic adoration of several women—at this time), he avoided violent confrontations and would often flip-flop into a jolly mood just when it seemed a crisis was at hand. For example, shortly after obtaining his restraining order against Anne, Phil gave her his unlisted phone number. When Anne then came by to visit, Phil asked Grania to hide in the closet. He then proceeded to have a friendly tea with Anne while Grania was kept secluded, as she recalls, "longer than the capacity of any human bladder."

Grania speaks of Phil's having "angels and devils. That he kept as together as he did, as grounded, is interesting." Laughing, she adds: "Of course he was crazy—as a hoot owl. But Phil was also so far beyond that—a rich and complex person. Crazy is merely one facet of this incredibly complex man—brilliant, a genuine mystic, very human." She recalls that Phil was fond of "implying that everyone around him was crazy—and they *were* [laughing again] or they wouldn't be closely involved with Philip K. Dick." He would often administer the James Benjamin Proverb Test (a psychological diagnostic tool featured in *We Can Build You*) to new acquaintances to measure their human qualities, but Grania recalls that Phil interpreted answers largely in accordance with whether or not he liked the person to begin with.

Phil's changeable moods were exacerbated by injuries he sustained in a July 1964 accident. While driving with Grania, he flipped their VW bug on a curve; Grania emerged without serious injury, but Phil wore a body cast and arm sling for two months. While his writing pace had already slowed since leaving Anne, the accident put an end to all sustained effort. Phil's wretched life in a body cast, intensified by his fears of ending a marriage and starting a new life, led him to entertain thoughts of suicide. His desperate mood was described by Grania in an anxious July 1964 letter. Immediately, Grania regretted its tone and threw it away; Phil fished it out of the trash and saved it. Here is an excerpt:

[H]e is separated from his children. . . . He is in constant pain from his shoulder . . . and helpless in many ways, cant drive, cant write, cant wash, tye his shoes, [. . .]. . . . It is not all in his mind, you see . . . he has reasons . . . good, mundane reasons for feeling as he does . . . except that there are the other things TOO . . . the things which ARE IN HIS MIND . . . which are added to his daily problems . . .[. . .] until the dear, delightful, intelligent and interesting Philip turns [. . .] unrecognizeable. . . .

She also wrote of "rages" alternating with gloomy moods in which Phil would choke on his food—a recurrence of the childhood swallowing difficulties.

But their relationship had its many happy times as well, and Phil was adept at writing what Grania calls "beautiful, ardent, apologetic letters" to atone for his bad moods. In a subsequent October letter, Grania regretted that her fears over Phil's moods, confided to friends, had "been fed into the Bay Area loud speaker and blown up into [. . .] unbelievable proportions." But Grania wasn't the only source of rumors—Phil himself had the knack of acting out and blowing up the events of his life. Many who knew him found it difficult to sort out how much was Phil being deadpan funny and how much was Phil frightened for his life. He had earned the reputation (as he complained in one letter) "of an advanced schizophrenic paranoid who believed everyone was plotting against him and so for whom anyone might become the enemy at any moment. (The very fact that all this bewildered me, that I could not imagine who would circulate such an image and for what reasons demonstrates its falsity. [. . .]"

Their East Oakland house was, in fact, a peaceable SF social hub. Phil's long isolation in Marin County made him relish contact with writers. On Sunday afternoons, a group that variously included Ray Nelson, Marion Zimmer Bradley, Jack Newkom, Poul and Karen Anderson, Avram Davidson, and others met at Phil and Grania's place to brainstorm plot ideas. The collaborative novel by Phil and Ray Nelson, *The Ganymede Takeover* (p. 1967), was inspired by one such session. There was a proposed novel, *The Whalemouth Colony*, ideas from which Phil worked into *The Unteleported Man* (p. 1966).

But the most important fantasized project was *Ring of Fire*, which Phil conceived as a sequel to *High Castle*. Nelson writes that the title "refers to the ring of volcanoes and earthquake faults around the edge of the North Pacific Ocean which corresponds to the Japanese Empire." In the story, "a remarkably creative society called Amerasia came into being, produced a few immortal works of art combining Eastern and Western influences, then was destroyed along with all but one of its artists, writers and musicians on the first day of World War III, which ends *Ring*." There was also discussion of a third volume: *Fuji in Winter*. Nelson recalls that it "described the brief and apocalyptic war that almost exterminated humanity, but ended in a note of hope as a new religion, uniting the best elements of all the previous religions, arises in the ruins." The whole was to be called the "Amerasian Trilogy."

Ideas abounded, but for the first time Phil was suffering from writer's block. He feared it would be permanent. Combining forces with other writers seemed the most likely way out. The only two collaborations of Phil's career—*The Ganymede Takeover* and *Deus Irae* (first with Ted White, ultimately with Roger Zelazny; p. 1975)—were commenced during this period.

Another SF writer whom Phil befriended was Ron Goulart. And to Goulart, during summer 1964, Phil sent a long letter that comes as close to a definite blueprint on novel construction as Phil ever wrote. Which is not to say that any of the novels fits precisely the blueprint proposed in the letter—Phil could outswerve any plan in the course of his white-hot typing stints. But the letter is revelatory as to the strategies that went into creating the multiple-viewpoint Phildickian worlds. It's also a striking letter to have written during a writer's block—maybe it helped Phil reassure himself that he could do it again.

In the first three chapters, says Phil, you introduce three key characters. In Chapter One comes:

First character, not protagonist but "subhuman," that is, less than life, a sort of everyman who exists throughout book but is, well, passive; we learn the entire world or background as we see it acting on him; he is "the guy who has to pick up the tab," the "Mr. Taxpayer," etc. Okay. Dramatically we get little him, but, more important, we see the world we are going to be inhabiting, and here the novel differs from the short story: it is not a dramatic progression culminating in a Scene or Crisis but, as I say, an entire world . . . "with all the holes plugged up," as Jose Ortega y Gasset says.

In Chapter Two comes the "protag," who gets a two-syllable name such as "Tom Stonecypher," as opposed to the monosyllabic "Al Glunch" tag for the Chapter One "subman." The protag

works for—and here comes the Institute or organization or business or—well, almost anything just so long as it supplies these: it tells us what Mr. S. does, and what *it* does: its function. We also learn this: the personal (or private or domestic) life of Mr. S. His marital problems or sex problems or whatever it is that worries him uniquely and not the big corp for which he works . . . so we no longer have background or mass or abstraction, here; we have the immediate, the now, this not that; the problem is urgent and involves someone else, such as a wife, a brother, etc. See?

In Chapter Three comes a figure who soars beyond the prior two in stature, and the scope of the novel is transformed:

We switch tracks, and here we begin to develop in a manner forbidden to a short piece. We continue with both Mr. S. and the subhuman Mr. Glunch . . . in a sense. But in another sense, although technically we carry on with Mr. S., we are in another dimension; that of the super human. This is the huge They problem, for instance, an invasion of Earth, another sentient race, etc., and, through Mr. S.'s eyes and ears, we glimpse for the first time this superhuman reality—and the human being, shall we call him Mr. Ubermensch? who inhabits this realm; [. . .] just as Mr. G. is the taxpayer and Mr. S. is the "I," the median person, Mr. U. is Mr. God, Mr. Big. [. . .] He is Atlas, carrying the weight of the world, so to speak, however evil—and he may well be the heavy—or good; in any case, power has brought responsibility, and it hurts; it weighs, ages him . . . yet he is big enough to fill this high office; he can endure it; he is sufficient.

Phil stresses that "the entire dramatic line of the book hinges on the impact between Mr. U. and Mr. S." A first glimpse of this impact is given in Chapter Three. "We are deep in a book, not a mere story, now [. . .]" because of the interplay between the three characters. It is the fate of Mr. S. to "dramatically evolve along a pathway which carries him into a direct confrontation with Mr. U.—and hence the option to decide which way

Things—i.e. Mr. U.—will jump ultimately, in the crisis section, fall on Mr. S."

And now comes the great fusion of worlds toward which the narrative has pointed:

> Mr. S., in ch ii, thought he had problems (he did: personal ones). But now look at him here in ch iv. He's got a bit of the Atlas weight on him: quite a jump problem wise. And: the original, personal problem has not gone away; in fact it's gotten worse. So we have true counterpoint, two problems, the earlier personal along side the later world-wide, each inflicting harm or injury or increment on the other.
>
> And, the great dramatic moment comes at last when Mr. U., now deeply involved with Mr. S., enters the personal problem area originally stated for Mr. S. And so in a sense at the latter part of the book the two worlds or problems or dramatic lines fuse.

The drama is heightened by total entanglement:

> So the terminal structural mechanism is revealed: THE PERSONAL PROB-LEM OF MR. S. IS THE PUBLIC SOLUTION FOR MR. U. And this can occur whether Mr. S. is with or pitted against Mr. U.; see what deep-cut varieties already present themselves structurally? (For instance, what if Mr. S., after a period of "working for" Mr. U. has dramatically quit—has turned against him to rejoin PPI ["Phenotype Products, Inc." or whatever company "of dubious moral value" has been invented] in its fight to survive—has gone back to his old boss again?

Phil suggested one possible "final dramatic development" in the form of a clash of some kind between Mr. S. and Mr. U., with the latter perishing despite his great power. But "Mr. S. survives, and all is well . . . except for some very deliberately left-untied loose ends: Mr. S. has perhaps solved his personal problems or the world's problem—but whichever it is that has, in this book, been solved—the other is worse now, ironically . . . and here we bow out." Earth has been saved from "the Demolishing Green Pea Giants from Betelgeuse IV after all . . . so we can relax, world-wise, and leisurely take time out to feel along with Mr. S."

The "coda" is a final glimpse of Mr. G.—"how goes it with him . . . he who is almost forgot, in all the turmoil?" Pretty much the same, though he may have a slightly better job. It's a wrap:

> Anyhow, dearly beloved, this is how PKD gets 55,000 words (the adequate mileage) out of his typewriter: by hav[ing] 3 persons, 3 levels, 2 themes (one outer or world-sized, the other inner or individual sized), with a melding of all, then, at last, a humane final note. This is, so to speak, my structure. 'Nuf said.

The letter to Goulart is a wonderful gallery of Phil's male character types (surprisingly, given their key roles, women are here only incidentally alluded to as plot pawns). In practice, the range of those male characters exceeds the apparent simplicity of G, S, and U. In *Palmer Eldritch*, for example, the G in the first chapter is Barney Mayerson, who fits the S type far better. Palmer Eldritch is clearly enough a U of the evil variety, but Leo Bulero is a cross between S and U: very human, and at the same time an "Atlas" who confronts Eldritch. There are no consistently accurate schema for the novels, not even those of Phil's devising.

Goulart recalls Phil's preference for letters over phone calls. Visits to Goulart in Pacific Heights were out of the question. "Phil would say, 'My car only works to and from my house and my psychiatrist's office—it breaks down if I cross the bridge.' " When they did speak by phone "Phil would make asides like 'Are you guys getting this?' and 'Do you want me to spell that name?' He said that the FBI was tapping his phone." Goulart didn't know what to believe, but Phil's unpredictability scared him and his wife. At the same time, he thought that Phil was "a terrific comedian." With his beard he could look "Dickensian" while dissolving a crowd in laughter.

By a strange quirk of fate, the September 1964 SF Worldcon was due to be held in Oakland, not far from Phil and Grania's house. Gossip led some incoming SF writers and fans to expect the worst upon meeting Phil. At the Con one well-known writer (later to become a great admirer of both Phil and his work) remarked: "Just by glancing at him, I think he's certifiable."

Phil and Grania decided to throw a convention-eve party. It was a success, unless you count the cats getting into the party dip. Just in from New York were Ace editor Terry Carr, who worked under Don Wollheim, and his wife, Carol, with whom Phil immediately fell in love. Now, everyone flirted at Cons; Phil enjoyed flirting and was good at it: intense blue eyes, deadpan humor, rapt listener. But once in a while he really fell head over heels, and with Carol, a warm, attractive, and funny woman, it was one of those times. Phil didn't pursue an actual affair with her—that wasn't the point for him (or for Carol, who enjoyed Phil's attentions but was happily married). Phil *loved* her.

Love for Phil was urgent business: He loved ardently, hilariously. At that time he was living with Grania and had invited Anne (in one more brief effort at reconciliation) to attend the Con with him the following night. But at the party, Phil, true courtly lover, ignored the difficulties and flirted madly with Carol throughout.

It was a tribute to the late Terry Carr's patience and to Phil's comedic talents that the flirtation went on as smoothly as it did. Terry and Carol stayed over at Phil's East Oakville house their first night in town. The next morning, Carol recalls, "Phil gets up and calls the Dial-A-Prayer of one county, doesn't like it, hangs up and calls the Dial-A-Prayer of another county." All through the day, according to Terry, Phil "kept offering to buy or trade something for Carol. I finally said, just to get rid of him, 'Go, Phil, go away, I'm the jealous type.' " At four the next morning, he and Carol were awakened by a phone call from Phil, who excoriated Terry (his editor at Ace!) for his unseemly jealousy. Phil apologized later that day but was back in action that night, locking Terry out of his own party.

Dick Ellington, a knowledgeable SF fan, first met Phil at the Con and recalls:

"My belief system at *that* time"—that's the way Phil operated. He changed his ideas often, but he made no bones about it; he wasn't embarrassed by it. "Oh yeah, I was heavily into that for a while." Like the dope. Phil dabbled in a lot of dope, but I never saw him befuddled by it. He used to talk sometimes about some kind of acid, but I never saw him wasted. At times he would allow as he'd had a few of this and a few of that kind of pill, but it didn't seem to affect him. He was one of the most completely normal people to talk to—erudite, intelligent, witty, nice person. But very run-of-the-mill. There was nothing whatsoever in Phil that a shrink would describe as inappropriate behavior.

Lots of folks had fun with chemicals at the '64 Con. Ellington threw a party to which one of the invitees brought a friendly off-duty Berkeley cop:

Phil showed up in this three-piece suit with lots of vest pockets, and this cop was standing around. And I swear to God Phil had enough foreign and exotic substances in those pockets to stock a large drugstore, with enough left over for a voodoo shop. And Phil was really going into the lore of different drugs, their effects and backgrounds. Finally the cop left—I'd assumed someone told Phil, but no one had! Then someone said, "Thank God that cop is gone." And Phil went: "Jesus Christ!" I told him it was cool. "I don't give a damn!" He was really pissed off at the guy who brought him along.

Terry and Carol returned to New York after the Con, which provided the perfect context for Phil's strange brand of love letters. Through late 1964 and early 1965, Phil sent off a flurry of missives—a blend of confessions of the heart and pure wordplay. There are stories of Phil's severe bouts of depression and visits to the shrink, collaboration with Ray Nelson and deep platonic love for Ray's wife, Kirsten, all-night talk-and-write sessions with close pal Jack Newkom, pulling a .38 on a "creature" who threatened the life of a friend. As to spiritual solace, Phil was lost in doubt and pissed off to boot:

When I took communion the last time I refused to say the general confession: "We do earnestly repent, and are heartily sorry for these our misdoings; the remembrance of them is grievous unto us; the burden of them is intolerable. Have mercy upon us, have mercy upon us, most merciful Father." I can never go to the rail, now. *Non credo.*

Around Halloween, Grania moved out and took new lodgings in an apartment in the Berkeley home of SF writer Marion Zimmer Bradley. It was a blow for Phil, who hated to live alone and had made it clear to Grania that marriage was fine with him. Grania recalls: "Phil believed in serial monogamy. His idea was when you made love, you then got married." She didn't want to leave off seeing Phil altogether, but she was weary of his mood swings.

In December, to fill the void, Jack Newkom and his wife, Margo, moved in with Phil. This awkward living arrangement endured roughly a month; Phil wound up asking Jack to leave, after Margo had already departed on her own. But their blood-brother friendship endured. After all, Phil had given Jack the manuscript of *High Castle* as an "insurance policy" (on the correct assumption that it would one day be a valuable collector's item), and Jack swore he'd hold on to it as long as Phil lived, which he did. And while they were housemates they had fun—like hooting the Calcutta taxi horn on Phil's '56 Buick while roaring past Grania's new home. Was it Phil who stole the diaper-service delivery off the porch, infuriating Marion Zimmer Bradley? Street pranks, two guys out on the town. Newkom says that he gave Phil his first hit of acid sometime in 1964.

Phil never much liked LSD. He took it only a very few times, despite wild rumors that he often wrote on acid—rumors Phil resented but himself helped get started. In 1964 he dropped acid on at least two occasions, with Newkom and with Ray Nelson. Nelson recalled that during his trip Phil was sweating, feeling isolated, reliving the life of a Roman gladiator, speaking in Latin and experiencing a spear thrust through his body. In a July 1974 letter Phil confirmed that *A Maze of Death* (1970) included "my own LSD vision from 1964 which is depicted with exact accuracy." Here's the quote in Phil's edited version in that letter:

"*Agnus Dei,*" she said, "*qui tollis peccata mundi.*" She had to look away from the throbbing vortex; she looked down and back . . . and saw, far below her, a vast frozen landscape of snow and boulders. A furious wind blew across it; as she watched, more snow piled up around the rocks. A new period of glaciation, she thought . . . A chasm opened before her feet. She began to fall; below her the frozen landscape of the hell-world grew closer. Again she cried out, "*Libera me, Domine, de morte aeterna.*" But still she fell; she had almost reached the hell-world, and nothing meant to lift her up.

Phil further detailed this acid vision in an August 1967 letter:

141

. . . I perceived Him as a pulsing, furious, throbbing mass of vengeance-seeking authority, demanding an audit (like a sort of metaphysical IRS agent). Fortunately I was able to utter the right words [the *"Libera me, Domine"* quoted above], and hence got through it. I also saw Christ rise to heaven from the cross, and that was very interesting, too (the cross took the form of a crossbow, with Christ as the arrow; the crossbow launched him at terrific velocity—it happened very fast, once he had been placed in position).

During the autumn, Phil contributed to Terry Carr's fanzine *Lighthouse* an essay entitled "Drugs, Hallucinations, and the Quest for Reality," which appeared in November 1964. In it, Phil proposed, quite shrewdly, that "hallucinations, whether induced by psychosis, hypnosis, drugs, toxins, etc., may be merely quantitatively different from what we see, not qualitatively so." He reasoned that hallucinations may simply be aspects of genuine reality that are, in daily life, filtered out by our Kantian a priori neural organizing categories (such as space and time). When hallucinations, however triggered, arise to confront the human psyche, there is an override of those categories—new perceptions come flooding in despite our best efforts to hold to our standard reality convictions. This override leaves us isolated and terrified. "No-name entities or aspects begin to appear, and, since the person does not know what they are—that is, what they're called or what they mean—he cannot communicate with other persons about them." Isolation, for Phil, was always too high a price to pay for any revelation (though he would wind up paying it again and again):

> Real or unreal, originating within the percept-system because, say, of some chemical agent not normally present and active in the brain's metabolism, the unshared world which we call "hallucinatory" is destructive: alienation, isolation, a sense of everything being strange, of things altering and bonding—all this is the logical result, until the individual, formerly a part of human culture, becomes an organic "windowless monad." [. . .]
> One doesn't have to depend on hallucinations; one can unhinge oneself by many other roads.

Ever since leaving Anne, Phil had been warding off solitude with might and main. Falling in love was the best method he had found. That December, in letters to Kirsten Nelson, he typed out (as he had for Carol Carr) pages of his favorite poems, including Yeats's "The Song of the Happy Shepherd" and verses from Lucretius, Euripides, Spenser and the libretto for Schubert's *Die Winterreise*. He even wrote a long poem of his own for her.

They talked so often on the phone that Phil bought an extra-long cord to allow Kirsten to sit more comfortably during their sessions. Having just emigrated from Norway, Kirsten was often lonely and uncomfortable in social situations. She recalls: "I don't know that he exactly fell in love with me so much as he kind of adopted me. I think he cast me in the role of his dead sister. He felt he had to watch out for me." Phil was a most attentive caretaker: "One time I had a kidney infection and I was very ill. Phil called and I was home alone—Ray was busy. That got Phil very upset—he cooked me some clam chowder, came in a cab with the chowder from Oakland, took care of my kid, gave him a bath, put him to bed."

But, as Phil well knew, there was no future for him with the married Kirsten. And Phil yearned not only to adore from a distance, but to have a wife by his side.

In early 1964 Phil had become acquainted with Maren Hackett, a brilliant woman who also attended St. Columba's Episcopal Church in Inverness. During one visit to Phil and Anne's home, Maren had brought along her stepdaughter, Nancy Hackett, a shy, attractive young woman with long dark hair. Now, late in the year, Phil again met Nancy, as well as her sister Ann, at a dinner at Maren's home. Phil was strongly attracted to both Nancy and Ann. To complicate matters further, Maren was attracted to Phil. But Phil soon focused his courtship exclusively on Nancy, who still felt attached to a boyfriend she had met in France during a year of study at the Sorbonne. During that year, Nancy had been hospitalized due to a nervous breakdown and had been forced to return to the States and the care of her family.

Nancy worried (as did Maren) that, at twenty-one, she was too young for Phil, who had just turned thirty-six. But Phil, drawn powerfully to this kind, beautiful woman, spared no efforts to allay their fears. During this time he composed a poem, "To Nancy," which began: "High flower, thin with / Instabilities of youth:" and ended with a Lucretian vision: "We are your atoms / You the friendly total world." On his birthday, December 16, Phil sent Nancy a letter in which he tried to play it cool: "Realize, I love you for what you are now, what you can give me and have already given me, not what you might or will give me—in other words, don't think about the future in your relationship with me; don't worry about some form of external ultimate commitment."

But by December 19, Phil was begging her to move in with him. Nancy wanted to pursue painting and poetry; living with Phil would provide her the peace and quiet and economic support to do that, as well as the companionship of "Jack [Newkom] and I, plus about one dozen fellas and their girls [. . .] who are always in the back house." And then Phil had the guts to lay it right on the line:

But mainly, as I said, I want you to move in here for my sake, because otherwise I will go clean out of my balmy wits, take more and more pills, get less and less sleep, eat worse, sleep not at all, be all hung up—and do no real writing. Since I left my wife I have done nothing of importance; I want to get going, and I need you as a sort of incentive and muse . . . someone to write *for*, because of . . . see? I want you to read my stuff as I write it and tell me if it's any good; if you like it, then it's good, if not, then not; I need someone Out There to whistle back into the dark chamber. If you don't move in, I'm afraid I'll have to search for something else to keep me going. But what or where— god only knows . . . it seems unlikely that it even exists. But one must try.

Phil, with three marriages behind him, knew he was facing a long shot. In a Christmas Day letter to Carol Carr he confessed: "Someday she [Nancy] will break me. I love her too much."

But braving the perils of love sure beats turning into a "windowless monad." By March 1965, Nancy had moved into the back cottage of East Gakville. In July 1966, they made it official.

Smack dab in the middle of the sixties.

7 A New Start, A Quiet Life, Then Everything Falls Apart Again—And Phil Can't Find The Handy Spray Can Of Ubik That Could Make It All Cohere (1965–1970)

Philip K. Dick [. . .] lives now in San Rafael and is interested in hallucinogens and snuff. [. . .] Married, has two daughters and young, pretty, nervous wife Nancy who is afraid of the telephone. [. . .] Spends most of his time listening to first Scarlatti and then the Jefferson Airplane, then "Gotterdammerung," in an attempt to fit them all together. Has many phobias and seldom goes anywhere, but loves to have people come over to his small, nice place on the water. Owes creditors a fortune, which he does not have. Warning: don't lend him any money. In addition he will steal your pills.

PHIL, "Biographical Material" typed up in early 1968,
presumably in response to a publisher's request

What matters to me is the writing, the act of manufacturing the novel, because while I am doing it, at that particular moment, I am in the world I'm writing about. It is real to me, completely and utterly. Then, when I'm finished, and have to stop, withdraw from that world forever—*that destroys me. [. . .]*

I promise myself: I will never write another novel. I will never again imagine people from whom I will eventually be cut off. I tell myself this . . . and, secretly and cautiously, I begin another book.

PHIL, "Notes Made Late at Night by a Weary SF Writer" (1968)

Taken as directed, Ubik provides uninterrupted sleep without morning-after grogginess. You awaken fresh, ready to tackle all those annoying problems facing you. Do not exceed recommended dosage.

Ubik commercial in *Ubik* (1969)

THE sixties was a decade that made a lot of big promises to those who lived through it with an open heart. Peace and love were everyone's birthright. Drugs could expand consciousness without the fuss and muss of spiritual sprouted mushrooms. When Phil refused to help build a garage, Anne traded the Jaguar for a new Volvo. Phil was furious.

Petty quarrels like this arose frequently. Sometimes it was mere sparring—spirited competitions to establish who had authority. But more often the fights were heated. Growing up under Dorothy, Phil had never known loud arguments, and life with Kleo had been peaceful. Shouting and profanities were new territory for Phil, and he enjoyed it at first: "We're just like a Mediterranean family, everyone waving their hands and yelling." Then Anne upped the ante one day, flinging half the dishes they owned. Repentant, she suggested a peacemaking family trip to Disneyland.

Phil Dick in Disneyland . . . He was fascinated by the Abraham Lincoln "simulacrum," as he termed it in *We Can Build You*, a novel written in 1961–62 that combined SF and mainstream elements. And the trip did the family good. A new era of peace began. They purchased a spinet, on which Phil played classical pieces. He also had occasional out-of-body experiences (as in the Berkeley days): seeing himself in the living room, or at his own bedside. He also saw the ghost of an elderly Italian man who he suspected had lived on the site of their wonder house.

In autumn 1960, Anne became pregnant again. Convinced that they could not take on a fifth child, Anne told Phil that she wanted an abortion. In interview she recalled:

> I felt it was the only way to go. The doctor thought it might be bad for Phil—maybe Phil had told the doctor he didn't want me to have the abortion—but I persisted because I wanted it. It must have been extremely disturbing to him, looking back now and realizing that *We Can Build You* was about that experience and look at the woman [Pris Frauenzimmer, a "schizoid personality"] in that novel. Demonic, right?
>
> We couldn't cope as it was with four children. Financially, I think he knew he couldn't stand the responsibility of being father to this complicated middle-class family. That was my instinct.
>
> Phil would certainly state his viewpoint strongly if it came to some theoretical intellectual topic—he could be adamant even when he was wrong, so he wasn't any milquetoast. He finally did think it was for the best—he said, "I agree"—and then we went up to Seattle, went to this nice restaurant—it's all in *We Can Build You*—in the novel Pris kills a little robot with her high heel.
>
> I think the abortion may have brought back his awful birth experience with his sister [Jane] dying. One of my daughters says, "He takes this stand against abortion when he didn't raise his own children."

As Anne points out, *We Can Build You*, written in the year following the abortion, includes a naked psychological account of Phil's enduring love—and poisonous hatred—for his wife. In *Build*, protagonist Louis Rosen undergoes psychiatric treatments that employ hallucinogens

108

discipline. Politics was a domain of evil only because those in power had been raised to act out of greed and fear. If you taught your children well, a future generation would arise that would rule benignly. It was only a matter of time.

It is easy, in retrospect, to deride the naïve ideals of the sixties. More painful by far it is to contemplate what we have since become.

One of William Blake's "Proverbs of Hell" goes: "The road to excess leads to the palace of wisdom." For some, sixties excess did just that. For others, as Blake foresaw in his irony, it led straight to Hell.

For a very slim few, it led to both—to Hell and back.

Phil was of this number. And confusing times these were.

For sometimes Hell seemed like Heaven.

And sometimes it seemed like he'd never get back.

◆

Phil and Nancy, a loving new couple, each took joy in caring for the other. After all, they had both come through hard times in childhood.

Nancy's father was an alcoholic who could be very charming or very abusive. Her mother ended the marriage and took custody of the three children, including older brother Michael and older sister Ann. Nancy was her mother's special favorite—the youngest whom she loved to spoil. Briefly, through a second marriage, there was a stepfather on the scene— also an alcoholic and abusive. Then, in 1955, when Nancy was twelve, her mother developed a brain tumor. Tragically, she remained in a coma until her death in 1961.

These events dictated that Nancy's father resume custody. Fortunately, he had in the interim married Maren Hackett, who possessed great warmth and intelligence and took the children under her wing. But the marriage ended in divorce. Nancy, a good student but shy and withdrawn, was sent to a boarding school in San Francisco. She then attended San Jose State College. In her junior year she went abroad to study at the Sorbonne, where her classroom ordeals and those experienced by Phil at U Cal Berkeley seem to converge. Nancy recalls that, during that year, she experimented (as did most students in the sixties) with marijuana and other drugs:

> It was enough to make me more and more out of it. I quit school . . . I couldn't sit in a class. All of a sudden, you feel like you'll die or go mad or something, like a gripping scare for no reason at all. You just feel like you have to get out of there. The classes were so big, I didn't feel I existed—like I was melting. I remember taking a picture of myself to make sure I was there.

Nancy was briefly hospitalized before returning to the States and moving in with Maren in her San Rafael home. (It should be emphasized that Nancy is today a successful career woman and loving mother. She no longer suffers from the difficulties that beset her before and during her time with Phil.)

When Nancy first met Phil, in early 1964, her impression was "that he was just a really sad person. His head was hanging down like he was very depressed. But he looked distinguished with his long grey beard. I thought, he looks like a writer." It was at Maren's, late that year, that her acquaintance with Phil was renewed. And it was a far livelier Phil who pursued the courtship. Around Christmastime, Phil and Jack Newkom had Maren, Nancy, and Ann over for dinner. Nancy recalls:

This time Phil was completely hyper—I think he had been taking a lot of amphetamines. The thing that struck me so much about him was he knew so much about psychology. I was so alienated from everything. It seemed like he understood—he had all these phobias too. We both had a lot in common with that so we got to be friends. I started staying there.

In a Christmas 1964 letter to Carol Carr, Phil rhapsodized:

She has an incredibly lovely body. I think she must be Celtic, a sort of miracle, something from the days of the lithe, tall hunters reborn into our world—she's five eight, and she stands with her firm, smooth legs always slightly bent, as if she's going to spring into the chase or fierce flight, out somewhere, out where it's wild and unknown; she will go anywhere; she has no fear of anything, even death, even absolute isolation and pain; she is sublime.

There was a glee to their early months together. It wasn't only the two of them coming together, but also a brand-new family of sorts that included Nancy's sister Ann, brother Mike, and stepmother Maren. By February 1965 Phil's account to Carol of the latest doings was positively giddy:

Tomorrow night Nancy's sister Ann is coming over to stay. Wowie! It's true! (Fun and games year here in East Gakville.) One night Nancy and her sister [. . .] wrapped me up in pink toilet paper and squirted me with Rise [shaving cream]. Then Nancy climbed the tree out front and got stuck. Then she [. . .] fell in a mud puddle. Ann and I had a pillow fight and I won [. . .] Everyone remembers things strange. But funishly.

In March 1965 Nancy moved into the cottage which Phil had decorated for her, even supplying paints (Nancy was attending Oakland Art College) and bookcases that he built himself. That spring, during a visit to Anne and the girls, he described himself proudly to his ex-wife as "Nancy's consort," and it seemed to Anne that the Phil she knew had "dissolved into a feckless 19 year old."

The writing began to revive. Phil was working on the expansion into full novel length of *The Unteleported Man*, and the material he added was markedly influenced by his painful LSD trips. (For the story of the ensuing flap and the 1967 publication of a truncated version without the "trip" material, see Chronological Survey.) But Phil didn't need acid to write like Phil. As Nancy observes:

> He'd have experiences without LSD that were just as strange. He was always afraid of the Day of Judgment. I didn't believe in it. But he would be so terrified and talk about how terrible it was going to be—there was nothing I could do to calm him.

When Judgment Day was not at hand, Phil and Nancy were enjoying something like domestic bliss. Ask Nancy if Phil was religious and she replies: "No, only humorous. He was only religious when he was scared." He called her "Snug" and she called him "Fuzzy." They doted on each other. Says Nancy: "We talked about psychology, how we saw things, what we wanted to do. We did a lot of joking and being silly. It wasn't as much of a romantic relationship . . . it was almost, I can't say like a father, but he was family or a strong hope for me . . . I depended a lot on him, and he depended on me too, in a different way."

They seldom went out. Phil's agoraphobia had begun to return in full force. After months of running with the Bay Area SF crowd, Phil was back in a steady relationship—mission accomplished—and well content to stay at home. Having flipped over the VW the previous summer, he tended to avoid driving. Eating in public was an ordeal. He declined, at the last minute, to take Nancy out for her birthday, sending sister Ann in his place. Even when company was to come to their house, Phil would often grow fearful and cancel out. The one social situation he most enjoyed was a perfect laboratory for Phil the writer: having over a few close friends for free talk on ideas, with lots of outright silliness thrown in.

Anxiety did not prevent Phil from frequent trips to record stores. Though money was short again after his brief post-Hugo sales boom, Phil did not stint on classical albums. Back home he played them *loud*, listening raptly while seated in his armchair with assorted cans of Dean Swift snuff in easy reach (snuff, which Phil had taken up while with Anne, had now become a dominant passion) and his two cats, Horace Gold and John Campbell, on his lap. In such a posture, undisturbed by Nancy, Phil sat silently conceiving the novels to come, seldom reading or taking notes.

He continued to consult the *I Ching* on a near daily basis—more frequently if he perceived a crisis at hand, which was fairly often. Miriam Lloyd, with whom Phil commenced an enduring friendship during this period, observes, "Phil was a crisis junkie anyway—he loved a crisis." The *I Ching* was a valued touchstone at such times, though Phil no longer consulted it for plot construction. It was during 1965 that Phil wrote the essay "Schizophrenia & The Book Of Changes," in which he argues that the Oracle can't predict the future—fortunately, since total knowledge would immobilize us (as a schizophrenic, whose *idios kosmos* is overwhelmed by the *koinos kosmos*, is immobilized). But it can reveal the gestalt from which the future will emerge. Part of the personal gestalt hinted at in the essay is the qualms Phil felt in living unmarried with Nancy:

> If you're totally schizophrenic now, by all means use the I CHING for everything, including telling you when to take a bath and when to open a can of cat-tuna for your cat Rover. If you're partially schizophrenic (no names, please), then use it for some situations—but sparingly; don't rely on it inordinately: save it for Big Questions, such as, "Should I marry her or merely keep on living with her in sin?" etc.

Late in 1965 Phil and Nancy moved across the Bay to San Rafael. They rented a tiny, charming house at 57 Meadow Drive, alongside a canal. In a November 1965 letter, Phil wrote of Nancy's new post office job, which, at $2.57 an hour, paid more than he was making. He also told of talking down a friend during an acid trip: "[H]e suspected that I was trying to 'prevent him from breaking free' or some such thing. I guess I am a party pooper at that." Phil dropped 75 mg, hoping for a trip with "more of a sense of reality." He succeeded: "I saw all manner of joyous coloration, especially pinks and reds, very luminous and exciting, and I had several great insights into myself (e.g. that I had had two attacks of schizophrenia, one when I was six, the other when I was eighteen, and that my basic fear was a return of this)." But Phil soon gave up LSD; memories of frozen hells prevailed.

In the midst of Phil's social seclusion, one new friend of great importance emerged: James A. Pike, the Episcopal Bishop of California. In 1964 Maren Hackett had asked Phil to compose a dazzling letter to persuade Pike to address her American Civil Liberties Union group. The letter succeeded, and as an unexpected aftereffect, Pike (a married man) and Maren became lovers, with a secret apartment in San Francisco's Tenderloin district; for public purposes, Maren was his secretary. As Phil and Pike met at Hackett family gatherings, they drew ever closer—each admiring the other's capacity for startling theories on the true nature of Christianity.

Both Phil and Pike were rapid-fire talkers who relished the scope and beauty of theological speculation. One subject that came up frequently was Pike's efforts, in 1966 and after, to contact his son Jim, who had committed suicide in February 1966, through séances and other psychic means. In Pike's "Foreword" to *The Other Side* (1968) (an account of these efforts—successful ones, Pike believed), he thanked Phil and Nancy for their assistance. Phil's involvement included careful transcription notes of a October 1966 séance held for the purpose of contacting Jim. Present were Phil, Nancy, Maren, and a medium, George Daisley, whose powers Pike respected. Phil was also impressed by Daisley's insights, including: "N. [Nancy] and P. [Phil] are passing through a phase of not being blessed by material things; this will change . . . spirits are taking care of P. and N. materially and spiritually. Spirits will use rebellious aspects of P.'s character." Phil's notes include experiences outside of the séance. The most striking: "While playing one of the lp's from J.'s [Jim's] collection, P. had a distinct impression of J. standing directly across the room from the phonograph, his head slightly to one side, listening to the music. He was wearing a soft brown unpressed wool suit. The presence was very substantial, rather than ghostly. (Later M. [Maren] verified that he had had such a suit.)"

Phil was skeptical of psychic phenomena throughout his life. However broadly he theorized, he disliked "occult" explanations that eschewed rigorous analysis. Phil's stance toward the afterlife during this period is reflected in his February 1966 letter (which went through two careful drafts) to Pike and Maren after Jim's suicide. The following passage is included in both drafts:

I have a feeling that in the instant after death everything real will become apparent; all the cards will be turned face-up, the game will be over, and we will see clearly what we have suspected only . . . and unfounded suspicions will be erased. [. . .] Now it is a mystery to me, a black glass. [. . .] Behold, Paul says. I tell you a mystery. We shall not all sleep. Or something like that. I believe that; in fact it is virtually all I believe. But even that, unproved, will have to wait for its test, like everything else. But even if I'm wrong and Lucretius is right ["We shall not feel because we shall not be"], I'll be content; I'll have no choice.

Turning the cards face up, seeing reality whole—Phil had no deeper yearning than this.

In July 1966 Phil and Nancy were married. Pike attended the ceremony even though it violated Episcopal canon law, since the marriage of Phil and Anne had never been annulled. But after the civil ceremony was completed, Pike pronounced a blessing over the marriage. Years later, in the *Exegesis*, Phil would confess to some pain that, though he was faithfully married to Nancy while Pike carried on an affair with Maren, Pike "was giving the very communion I could not receive!"

Pike had a profound influence upon Phil. The most obvious evidence of this is the inspiration Pike and the events of his life—including his relationship with Maren and the suicide of his son—provided for Phil's 1982 novel *The Transmigration of Timothy Archer*. But the influence went still deeper. Phil acknowledges in his "Author's Foreword" to A *Maze of Death* (1968) the "wealth of theological material" he learned of through talks with Pike.

What was this "theological material"? The precise details are unknown. But Pike, who was making repeated trips to Israel to investigate the historical Jesus, was undergoing a crisis of doctrinal adherence. In a July 1974 letter Phil recalled:

> Jim was tried for heresy shortly before his death [the charge was ultimately dismissed], and later resigned as bishop. Whether it reached the newspaper pages or not, the basic issue, the basic fear about him, was not merely that he had denied the Trinity but that he had picked up Zoroastrian doctrines, probably while going over the Dead Sea Scrolls discoveries.
>
> "If I were not a Christian," I heard him preach in December of 1964 in Grace Cathedral, "I would be a Jew. And if I were not a Jew I would be a Zoroastrian." And then he delivered to the congregation what I know to be a Zoroastrian exhortation: "Come into the Light." (He extended his arms and open hands to them all.) "Come into the Light." And so forth. This is the doctrine of Ormazd (Mazda), the Persian God of Light, identified with the Sun.

Speculations like these spurred Phil, in the *Exegesis*, to consider the possibility that the events of 2-3-74 may have included a cross-bonding of the spirit of Pike (who died in 1969) and his own.

◆

Phil was now emerging from the writer's slump that had plagued him ever since he had left Anne in 1964. If there is a dominant mood to his novels of the late sixties, it is that of a dark night of the soul. Not that any of the novels lacked humor—Phil was a black humorist par excellence, and besides, he couldn't help but laugh now and then at the loopy plots SF allowed him. Where the darkness lies is in Phil's despair at ever knowing what it all meant. The exhilaration of the "What is Real?" quest had begun to pall. In novel after novel he had posed ultimate questions on God and Truth. Where the hell were the ultimate answers? Hadn't he worked at them long enough? As he later wrote in the *Exegesis*, recalling this time: "I had nothing to say, nothing to offer because I knew nothing. Oh, & how I sensed this lack of knowledge!"

But at least the flow of the writing had returned. And even in the midst of his doubts, Phil could write brilliantly.

During the latter part of 1965, Phil was at work on two novels—*The Ganymede Takeover*, in collaboration with Nelson, and *Counter-Clock World* (p. 1967). Through 1966 he completed his work on *Ganymede* and wrote *Do Androids Dream of Electric Sheep?* (p. 1968) and a children's SF novel, *The Glimmung of Plowman's Planet* (p. 1988), a preliminary foray into material also utilized in the excellent *Galactic Pot-Healer* (p. 1969).

But above and beyond all these soars *Ubik* (w. 1966, p. 1969). This is the novel that propelled Phil's election, in France, as an honorary member of the College du Pataphysique, a society established in loving memory of Alfred Jarry's predilection for turning solemn ideas on their heads in strange and nasty plays like *Ubu Roi*.

There's precious little nastiness in *Ubik*, however. Phil, far more humbly, chips away at tiny chinks in time and space until society—and reality itself—falls apart. Pratfalls, that is (the one spaceship in the book is named *Pratfall II*). As with *Dr. Bloodmoney* and other of his SF novels, Phil set the *Ubik* future in what should have been his lifetime: 1992. Perhaps it was his way of forcing recalcitrant readers to see that his SF partook as fully of the present as the latest official mainstream "masterpiece."

The plot set out in the opening chapters is a grand red herring, but we meet a gratifying range of characters. Glen Runciter is the vibrant, heart-of-gold owner of Runciter Associates, which employs "inertials" (gifted psychics who can neutralize the psychic talents of others) to combat the "teeps" (telepaths) and "precogs" (precognitives) employed by scumbag Ray Hollis (named, as a twist, after the Art Music boss Phil adored). For business advice in tough times, Runciter consults with his dead wife, Ella, who is kept in a "cold-pac" casket to sustain a "half-life" existence (patterned on the Bardo Thodol post-death realm described in the Tibetan Book of the Dead) in the Beloved Brethren Moratorium of Herbert Schoenheit von Vogelsang. But Ella is fading. Her cold-pac neighbor, a kid named Jory, is tapping her dwindling life force.

Joe Chip is the little guy, a loyal Runciter employee who tests inertials. The latest applicant is a beautiful dark-haired girl named Pat Conley who has a brand-new talent—she can change the past so that Hollis's precogs will see a different future (or never even get around to looking). Could be a breakthrough for Runciter Associates. But will Joe Chip ever be able to open the door of his conapt to let her in for testing? You see, he's a little behind on his Magic Credit Keys payments. But Joe dons suitable business attire—a "sporty maroon wrapper, twinkle-toes turned-up shoes and a felt cap with a tassel"—and meets the challenge:

The door refused to open. It said, "Five cents, please."

He searched his pockets. No more coins; nothing. "I'll pay you tomorrow," he told the door. Again he tried the knob. Again it remained locked tight. "What I pay you," he informed it, "is in the nature of a gratuity; I don't *have* to pay you."

"I think otherwise," the door said. "Look in the purchase contract you signed when you bought this conapt."

152

In his desk drawer he found the contract; since signing it he had found it necessary to refer to the document many times. Sure enough; payment to his door for opening and closing constituted a mandatory fee. Not a tip.

"You discover I'm right," the door said. It sounded smug.

From the drawer beside the sink Joe Chip got a stainless steel knife; with it he began systematically to unscrew the bolt assembly of his apt's money-gulping door.

"I'll sue you," the door said as the first screw fell out.

Joe Chip said, "I've never been sued by a door. But I guess I can live through it."

Plot devices ransacked from Phil's fifties SF set up the real fun and games. Bad guy Hollis lures Runciter, Joe Chip, and the staff of inertials to a death trap on Luna (lifted from *Solar Lottery*), and the resultant explosion casts them into a radically transformed reality that may or may not be controlled by Pat Conley or Runciter or Hollis or someone or something else (a situation lifted from *Eye in the Sky*). But in *Eye* the pseudo-science rational solution allows the straight-arrow characters to get back to liberal action. In *Ubik* there are no answers. Is Runciter half dead in cold-pac? Or is it Joe Chip and the inertials who lie hallucinating in caskets? Runciter thinks he knows and composes a graffito to let Joe in on it: "Jump In The Urinal And Stand On Your Head. / I'm The One That's Alive. You're All Dead." But how can Runciter be so sure, especially when the face of Joe Chip shows up on a coin in his pocket?

A student once asked William Burroughs if he believed in life after death. Burroughs asked back: How do you know you're not dead already? *Ubik* offers no solutions to Burroughs's question, because there are none. But there is the mysterious Ubik (Latin *ubique*: everywhere; ubiquity), which might just be enough for all us half-lifers to get by. But despite its tantalizing name, Ubik isn't easy to come by. It requires hard work (as *Eye* said it would), and it also takes a kind of religious faith (that *Eye* mocked). Runciter, the "coming-into-existence" force, is trying to get some to Joe Chip, but "going-out-of-existence" entropy has Joe in its grasp: Milk sours, cigarettes go stale, and death looms.

Runciter resorts to unique stratagems to get his message across— showing up on bathroom walls, matchbook covers, and tacky TV commercials:

"Yes," Runciter's dark voice resumed, "by making use of the most advanced techniques of present-day science, the reversion of matter to earlier forms can be reversed, and at a price any conapt owner can afford. Ubik is sold by leading home-art stores throughout Earth. Do not take internally. Keep away from open flame. Do not deviate from printed procedural approaches as expressed on label. So look for it, Joe. Don't just sit there; go out and buy a can of Ubik and spray it all around you night and day."

Standing up, Joe said loudly, "You know I'm here. Does that mean you can hear and see me?"

"Of course I can't hear you and see you. This commercial message is on videotape [. . .]"

What is Ubik? It declares itself in the final chapter:

I am Ubik. Before the universe was, I am. I made the suns. I made the worlds. I created the lives and the places they inhabit; I move them here, I put them there. They go as I say, they do as I tell them. I am the word and my name is never spoken, the name which no one knows. I am called Ubik, but that is not my name. I am. I shall always be.

Critic Peter Fitting has noted the resemblance to the opening of the Book of John. But jumping to doctrinal conclusions would be unwise. In a November 1977 *Exegesis* entry, Phil linked *Ubik* and *Palmer Eldritch*: "So Runciter and Ubik equals Palmer Eldritch and Chew-Z. We have a human being transformed into a deity which is ubiquitous (no one seems to have noticed that Palmer Eldritch is ubiquitous as is Ubik, that the same themes dominate both novels)." Phil went on to describe the theme of *Ubik*: "Salvific information penetrating through the 'walls' of our world by an entity with personality representing a life- and reality-supporting quasi-living force."

What remains constant in Phil's novels is a sense of apparent reality as false or untrustworthy. In one 1978 *Exegesis* entry, Phil stated: "I don't write beautifully—I just write reports about our condition to go to those outside of cold-pak. I am an analyzer." These reports must take trashy SF forms for the same reasons that Runciter found it necessary to employ TV commercials—the delusional world has no use for gnosis (direct experience of divine wisdom), so camouflage is necessary. In another 1978 entry, Phil focused upon this strategy. In its utter candor, it is as revelatory a statement on method as Phil ever made:

[. . .] I do seem attracted to trash, as if the clue—*the clue*—lies there. I'm always ferreting out elliptical points, odd angles. What I write doesn't make a whole lot of sense. There is fun & religion & psychotic horror strewn about like a bunch of hats. Also, there is a social or sociological drift—rather than toward the hard sciences. The overall impression is childish but interesting. This is not a sophisticated person writing. Everything is equally real, like junk jewels in the alley. A fertile, creative mind seeing constantly shifting sets, the serious made funny, the funny sad, the horrific exactly that: utterly horrific as it is the touchstone of what is real: horror is real because it can injure. [. . .] I certainly see the randomness in my work, & I also see how this fast shuffling of possibility after possibility might eventually, given enough time, juxtapose & disclose something important & automatically overlooked in more orderly thinking. [. . .] Since nothing absolutely nothing is excluded (as not *worth* being included) I proffer a vast mixed bag—out of it I shake coin-operated doors & God. It's a fucking circus. I'm like a sharp-eyed crow, spying anything that twinkles & grabbing it up to add to my heap.

Anyone with my attitude just might stumble onto, by sheer chance & luck—in his actual life, which is to say, the life of his *mind*—the authentic camouflaged God, the deus absconditus, by trying odd combinations of things & places, like a high speed (sic) computer processing everything, he might outdazzle even a wary God, might catch him by surprise by poking somewhere unexpectedly. If it is true that the real answers (& authentic absolute vs the merely seeming) are where we would least expect them, this "try it all" technique might—might take at face value as true the most wornout, most worked over & long ago discarded obvious "staring us in the face all the time" as the crux of the mystery. [. . .]

This kind of fascinated, credulous, inventive person might be granted the greatest gift of all. To see the toymaker who has generated—& is with or within—all his toys. That the Godhead is a toymaker at all—who could seriously (sic) believe this? [. . .]

Too dumb to know you don't look for God in the trash of the gutter instead of Heaven.

Phil longed for a revelation. As the sixties progressed and his novel production stayed steady (prolific for anyone but Phil), he was anguished that the "the greatest gift of all" had been denied him. Not that the novels lacked force and subtlety: *Do Androids Dream of Electric Sheep?* (w. 1966, p. 1968), *Galactic Pot-Healer* (w. 1968, p. 1969), and *A Maze of Death* (w. 1968, p. 1970) belie the mask of unsophistication donned above. But in his sixties SF novels that posed the reality theme again and again, Phil came to feel that—at critical junctures—he was outright faking it. From a 1981 *Exegesis* entry on *Galactic Pot-Healer*:

[. . .] thus in writing "Pot" that exactly was where I reached the end—wore out & died as a writer; scraped the bottom of the barrel & died creatively & spiritually. What misery that was!

[. . .] if "Pot" shows signs of psychosis, & it does—it is not because I experienced & knew God but precisely because I did not. [. . .] Thus in a very real sense my sanity depended on my experiencing God, because my creative life logically demanded it—& as [name of a therapist] said, my sanity depended on my writing.

And as the writing began to fail him, so, it seemed, did everything else. Gradually at first, then in a rush.

♦

Phil and Nancy got married primarily because Nancy had become pregnant. Their daughter, Isolde Freya, Nancy's first, Phil's second, was born on March 15, 1967, a little over eight months after the ceremony. Nancy recalls: "I didn't really believe in marriage but we decided we wanted a little baby to keep us company—we were like children ourselves. I thought it would be okay to have children and not be married, but Phil thought we should be married. Later I was glad we did."

In the weeks just prior to the birth, Phil and Nancy attended a confrontation-oriented therapy group for "well" people, which Phil felt made them stronger. He also completed a treatment for *The Invaders*, a TV show whose premise was that aliens were secretly taking over Earth, with only the lonely protagonist aware that it is happening. Small wonder that Phil was drawn to the program, but the treatment didn't sell. During this time *Counter-Clock World* appeared as a Berkely paperback, with a cover featuring a dark-haired girl who resembled Nancy (upon whom the novel's character Lotta is based), a serendipity that delighted Phil.

As if by instinct, in anticipation of dramatic change, Phil purchased an expensive four-drawer fireproof case in which to house his treasured collections of *Unknown Worlds* and *Astounding*, as well as letters, photographs, his stamp collection, rare tapes, volumes of poetry, and copies of his own books and stories. It was an adult version of the secret desk drawer of his adolescence. In a February 1967 letter Phil wrote:

Without the drawers, the file-case weighs 700 pounds, and it took four men to hoist it up, on a dolly, three steps. I was one of the four men, and I got a hernia for my trouble, which annoys me, because it's as if God is saying, "You can't do it, Phil; you can't save any of the treasures of this world." Anyhow, I am wrapped up in a cloak of pain; I know that much of it is hysterical and psychosomatic, due to fear about the baby and the responsibility it'll mean . . . I'm getting all sorts of physical stress-symptoms, despite the tranquilizers and codein[e] I'm taking.

As the March 1967 delivery due date neared, Phil's anxieties grew, as they had prior to Laura's birth in 1960. Since his 1964 accident, driving had loomed ever more threateningly to Phil, and the prospect of being at the wheel for Nancy's trip to the hospital appalled him. He asked Mike Hackett to stay with them during the final days and to be available as a driver. Mike recalls:

I believe Phil got her to the hospital by himself, but I went and joined him in the waiting room. Anyway, a couple of months later he showed me something he had written describing his beautiful daughter Isa, and he said, "My brother-in-law quit his job to sit with us and wait for Isa." I had quit my job, but it was over anyway. But that's like Phil to say I quit my job for Isa.

Isa's birth transformed their life as a couple. In the early years of their relationship, Phil had seen himself as Nancy's older and wiser protector. There was, of course, some basis for this: He loved her deeply and had provided a stable home after her tumultuous time in Europe. Nancy, in turn, had fallen in love with "this sensitive, protective, playful kind of person. He accepted me the way I was. I didn't have to know a great deal or be articulate or slim or whatever. He never put me down."

But the relationship included, even in the early days, a decidedly two-way dependence. "Phil was a real rescuer," Nancy recalls. Was he good at it? "Well, not completely, because he wasn't superstrong. Nobody can really rescue you, but he had so many problems of the same nature. So that eventually, even though it's a great comfort to have someone understand, you kind of drag each other down." At first, when Nancy took jobs at the post office and as a volunteer at a neighborhood kindergarten, Phil would have dinner waiting when she returned. But as time went on, and especially after Isa was born, his tolerance of her outside activities diminished. "He never wanted me away from there— like out to breakfast or anything. There wasn't a lot of freedom."

Lynne Cecil, who was close to both Phil and Nancy during this time, observes that "Nancy was somebody that Phil could focus upon totally. The urge to care for her comes from not being very good at taking care of yourself." Lynne recalls that the marriage had a "childlike" quality: "They just weren't mature adults together. Isa was somewhat threatening to him when she was little. Phil had a hard time sharing Nancy." Mike Hackett has similar memories: "Their relationship changed after Isa was born. Nancy became more independent and also changed her focus to Isa, and, well, Phil liked taking care of people but he also needed a lot of taking care of himself. Nancy didn't have as much time to do that with Isa."

Despite his anxieties, Phil was a most loving father. He seldom saw his first daughter Laura during this period. Phil's animosity toward Anne, and Anne's animosity toward Phil's lifestyle, combined to make visits a rarity. With Isa, Phil could resume the paternal doting that he had relished in the Point Reyes Station days. But the strain of sharing Nancy with a new baby showed itself in a strange sort of feeding contest. Recalls Nancy: "I was breast-feeding her at first and we started having competition about how much milk she would drink, and Phil wanted to feed her [with a bottle] twice a day. So Isa stopped eating all at once and the doctor said, 'There's too much tension in your house.' " It is difficult not to see a connection here to twin sister Jane's inadequate nourishment. Another, more surprising parallel came in the form of Phil's insistence that holding Isa every time she cried would spoil her—a child-rearing philosophy that had been employed (much to Phil's retrospective contempt) by his mother.

Phil's feelings toward Dorothy, which had softened somewhat during the desperate months following his breakup with Anne in early 1964, reverted to pronounced antipathy during his marriage to Nancy. Dorothy was still greatly concerned—and with good reason—over Phil's considerable intake of both uppers and downers. But her warnings were met with rage. It was a sensitive nerve due to Phil's own fears, which escalated along with his intake.

Nonetheless, it was Dorothy and Joseph Hudner who made the down payment for a bigger house for Phil and family to move into in June 1968. Located in the Santa Venetia district of San Rafael, at 707 Hacienda Way, it was a suburban tract house with a lawn and garden that did not thrive under new ownership. Grania Davis, who visited with her husband in 1969, received a Phildickian tour of the garden: "He took us around saying, 'This is the dead lemon tree, this is the dead rose bush, this is the dead lawn. The Unwelcome Wagon is coming to pick me up next week.' "

The house was registered in the Hudners' names because of Phil's poor credit rating. But despite the strained relationship between mother and son, Nancy emphasizes that she and Isa were treated with the greatest kindness by Dorothy, and adds:

> There was a lot of misunderstanding between Phil and Dorothy. He would take things she would say and twist them around. One time she was over, and Phil and I used to wrestle and fool around, and she wrote to say she was afraid he'd hurt me. Not in a mean way—she had trouble communicating in a straightforward way; she had to write him a letter. He got so mad.

Phil and Dorothy's battles over drugs grew ever more heated. Before going into the details, it would be wise to recall that the sixties *Zeitgeist* lent to drugs a patina of glory and adventure lacking today even among avid users. When Phil took and talked drugs he thought he was being hip and was taken as such (Dr. Timothy Leary made a telephone fan call in spring 1969). Acid, pot, and hash held no special fascination. But pills . . . ah, pills. He could mix, match, and fine-tune effects with Stelazine; muscle and stomach relaxants; Librium, Valium, and other tranks; Dexamil and all manner of speed—prescription quality preferred, white crosses (amphetamine pills) and street batches accepted. "It was," says Nancy, "like he was medicating himself—trying to get to a certain place."

One place he often tried to get to, with considerable success, was the state of inner focus required to write the way Phil nearly always wrote his novels—in streaks of two to three weeks. Says Nancy: "When we needed money, like when Isa was born and we were broke, he could just sit down and write a book and get money." Phil wrote nine full novels, parts of three others, and numerous stories and essays during his years with Nancy. It wasn't quite the rate of 1964, but at its heights it was awesome.

During the composition of *Flow My Tears, The Policeman Said* in 1970, Phil poured out 140 pages in a forty-eight-hour session. Speed enabled him to work on little sleep and lifted him out of his searing depressions. Recalls Nancy: "His depressions just stopped him. He could go maybe three, four days without saying a word." Once he started a book, Phil's identification with his characters was extreme. During the writing of *Androids*, says Nancy, "Phil was working all night, and when he came to bed he was talking like a different person. He'd had some kind of experience while writing and thought he was someone else or somewhere else."

Phil's primary source for pills were multiple prescriptions from a revolving group of doctors to whom he'd recite the requisite symptoms. This routine was and is a favorite method of users. Miriam Lloyd points out: "You could go to any meeting of Narcotics Anonymous and find out dope fiends are the cleverest people imaginable. Phil was way cleverer than most. In the world of drug abuse, prescription drugs are the most common." But Phil had further motivations for consulting psychiatrists. Recalls Nancy:

> It seemed like he had this terrible fear of being crazy, so the psychiatrist would say you're not crazy. All the doctors would always tell him he was okay. He needed to hear that—he had a lot of anxiety. But he wasn't crazy. Even though he had crazy ideas sometimes, he knew what was going on all the time. He was never out of touch with reality.

Phil's fondness for speed led him to street dealers as well. These dealers tended to be in their teens and early twenties. They were a ubiquitous presence by 1967; Phil's stepdaughter Hatte, who attended San Rafael High School that year, heard through school friends that her father's house was a known locale for selling drugs.

From 1967 through the end of the decade, Phil and Nancy's life together became ever more difficult and desperate. Drugs were part of the problem, but only part. Entropic forces were shaking the once-placid household. First came the difficult adjustments that all parents face in caring for a new baby. Then Phil's two cats died. The ill tidings took on tragic proportions with the suicide of Maren Hackett in June 1967. In the next two years would come two more deaths—Anthony Boucher and Bishop James Pike, the two men who served most clearly as mentors to Phil, passed on. Now add in an IRS audit, economic instability, marital infidelity, the standard twisted weirdness of the California sixties, and the hairpin psychic risks of plotting SF novels that sought to mirror these realities. Loving couple though they were, Phil and Nancy were brought to their knees.

Weaving in and out of these crises were the mood pills—uppers, downers, and downright outers. Phil's pill consumption was marked by a near-blind confidence in the benefits the right drug at the right time could bestow. A typical example was his self-prescribed treatment of a "nervous breakdown" he suffered in July 1967. The primary catalyst here was Maren Hackett's suicide in June. Maren's woes had stemmed in part from the painful end of her affair with Bishop Pike; Phil and Nancy, who had seen it coming, were nonetheless shattered by her death. Maren had been a trusted source of encouragement to the younger couple.

In the weeks just prior to his "breakdown" Phil had been "mildly paranoid and very hostile," and then "what my psychiatrist called 'border-line psychotic symptoms' became the full and overt thing." The full breakdown lasted half a day and consisted "of vast distortions in perception"—horrible tastes, loss of memory and time sense, physical helplessness, acute terror while feeding Isa, suicidal urges. In addition, Phil misplaced "important IRS documents." So vivid were the distortions that Phil asked Nancy to hide his .22 pistol. But he battled through—"I took a good big dose of phenothiazines (sp) and made it over to see the Dr." (Stelazine, a phenothiazine, was the depressant Phil had urged on Anne in 1963.) Phil emerged "feeling active and vigorous and even elated—because I reasoned, I had met it head-on and licked it (however temporarily)." Now comes the paradoxical twist that marks so many of Phil's accounts of crisis:

> The interesting thing, now that I look back on that day, is the amount I got done. At nine a.m. a T-man (i.e. a cop from the Treasury Department) showed up and demanded the back taxes I owe. I reached a settlement with him. [. . .] The Dr. thought it was remarkable that in such a state I could deal with the T-man, since I fear them above all other life forms Terran or otherwise.

Phil had good reason to fear the IRS. Whatever settlement he thought he had worked out soon fell apart. Continued audits of Phil's 1964 and 1965 returns (in which he reported twelve thousand and five thousand, respectively) led to ever-greater penalty demands. In a September 1967 letter Phil pleaded: "How can it go on and on? I have almost no money left." But Phil moved courageously from the frying pan into the fire when he signed (along with five hundred others) a "Writers and Editors War Tax Protest" petition that appeared in the February 1968 *Ramparts* magazine. The signatories, in oposition to the Vietnam War, pledged: "1) None of us voluntarily will pay the proposed 10% income tax surcharge or any war-designated tax increase. 2) Many of us will not pay that 23% of our current income tax which is being used to finance the war in Vietnam." Phil's stance, which enabled him to influence public opinion without facing the psychological ordeal of leaving the house, nonetheless exacted high personal costs—an IRS seizure of his car in 1969, as well as an intense, lingering fear. In a 1979 *Exegesis* entry, Phil reflected: "Looking all this over I realize that the 'Ramparts' petition & then my failure to file until the war ended was not just an anti-war act, a dissenting, or even civil disobedience but an outright sacrifice of my freedom and career: the punishment was inevitable, as was Jesus' when he entered Jerusalem. & *I knew it.* By '74 I lived in terror of them arresting me [. . .]"

The *Ramparts* petition was not Phil's only source of anxiety. He would speculate that somehow, by accident, he had depicted a vital, classified secret in his SF—and had aroused the government's suspicion. The two works Phil most often suspected, in this regard, were *The Penultimate Truth* (1964) (see Chronological Survey) and "Faith of Our Fathers," a story written for Harlan Ellison's SF anthology *Dangerous Visions* (1967), which portrays a Chairman Mao–like totalitarian leader who conceals his true form by dosing the water supply with hallucinogens. Phil would later charge that Ellison's "Introduction" to "Faith of" contained misstatements that had threatened his reputation and security. Ellison's piece included the following:

> Philip K. Dick has been lighting up his own landscape for years, casting illumination by the klieg lights of his imagination on a terra incognita of staggering dimensions. I asked for Phil Dick and I got him. A story to be written about, and under the influence of (if possible), LSD. What follows, like his excellent offbeat novel, *The Three Stigmata of Palmer Eldritch*, is the result of such a hallucinogenic journey.

Ellison recalls that Phil assured him that both "Faith of" and *Palmer Eldritch* were LSD-inspired; further, letters from that time by Doubleday editor Lawrence Ashmead—who supervised the *Dangerous Visions* project—confirm that Phil made no changes to the "Introduction" galleys. Phil's 1967 "Afterword" to the story itself stresses the LSD theme (though he did not say he had written under its influence). But in all editions of *Dangerous Visions* from 1975 on, there is an expanded "Afterword" in which Phil rebuts the acid-inspiration claim. It seems likely that Phil's 1975 denial is truthful and that the 1967 version sounded fun at the time.

Despite the later furor, Phil's friendship with Ellison, fueled by phone calls and occasional parties at Cons, continued. Ellison, who was at this time one of the most dominant figures in SF, saw Phil as one of the few writers in the field whose fervor and talent exceeded his own:

> Phil, it seemed to me, was an outsider who was on one of those holy missions. Held by the madness and the demon. That's what drew me to him. I knew how painful it was for me, but I'm a tough little fucker and I knew how to handle it—I know how to fight back. Phil, I thought, was a flounderer in that area. He didn't know how to handle the business or life side of it. When he sat at the typewriter he was pure and clean and could do it, motivated by his

madness that inspired his work. Beyond that, he kept getting shit upon. Mostly because of his own social ineptitudes. It was a strange feeling on my part in that he was more than my equal, probably a superior writer . . . the sort of writer I wanted to know. In that way I was parallel to Salieri looking to Mozart.

With fellow writers such as Ellison, Phil more than held his own as a dedicated professional. But in his strictly private life, the drugs were taking hold to the point where he looked to them for both solace and inspiration. Phil would go so far as to plan little festive occasions around pills. For example, Phil had managed to obtain a prescription for Ritalin, an upper intended for the relief of mild depression. (Its major side effects: high and low blood pressure, mood changes, heart irregularities.) Ritalin is contraindicated for persons with marked anxiety. Phil would save up a month's worth and down it all while close friends were over; the energy burst would fuel blue streak ideas and wild humor. The paradoxical truth is that drugs both estranged Phil from the world and intensified his sociability among fellow drug users.

One day in 1968, when Miriam Lloyd decided to throw away her pill stash, Phil rushed over to help (and salvage what he wanted):

So he helped me flush them. The last bottle, I said, "I don't even know what these are." Phil said, "Oh, these pills—you don't ever want to take these pills. I took these once and I ended up in Union City, which is a place you never want to be, especially on these pills." He hung out awhile, took some pills, drank some beer. He was a funny man.

Miriam points out that the sixties drug culture had an accepting, sharing ethic that contributed to Phil's fascination with it:

One of the things about the drug scene is that it creates instant intimacy. You have a gang, you have all this communal thing because, you know, joints are passed, trays of lines are passed, someone wants wine and we don't have any—quick, go get wine. Everyone's needs are taken care of.

Phil was really into being gracious—he loved it. He was incredibly egalitarian. Everything he liked, he just loved. He wasn't naïve—he was very sophisticated and egalitarian. His politics were good, very humanistic. He really cared about people.

Phil seemed to be in his glory while attending the September 1968 SF Baycon, referred to as the "Drug Con" by many who attended. Several conventioneers, including Phil, ingested what they thought was THC (the active ingredient in marijuana) but proved to be PCP, a horse tranquilizer later known as angel dust. Nonetheless, Phil kept up active social rounds, socializing with Ray Bradbury, Robert Silverberg, Fritz Leiber, Philip Jose Farmer, Norman Spinrad, and—for the first time—

162

Roger Zelazny, with whom Phil had agreed, the previous October, to collaborate on *Deus Irae*.

At the Con there was considerable debate swirling around the SF "New Wave" that had been masterfully hyped by Ellison in conjunction with *Dangerous Visions*. Phil had his doubts about the substance of much "New Wave" writing. Still, he'd feared—as a fifties SF veteran—being regarded as passé (even though he had recently sold his first film option, on *Do Androids Dream of Electric Sheep?*). It was with relief that he wrote to his editor at Doubleday, Larry Ashmead, that his status had climbed since the '64 Con, due to the popularity of *Palmer Eldritch*.

Phil seems, at this time, to have been wracked by greater insecurities as to the worth of his writing than at any point since his Berkeley neophyte days. He would systematically underrate the novels he had produced since *Palmer Eldritch*. To stepdaughter Tandy he wrote in May 1969: "I haven't been able to do an *important* book since 1964, and I feel very unhappy about it." Phil later came to regard *Ubik* as a highly significant work, as has been discussed. As to "important" writing, mention should also be made of "The Electric Ant," a late-1968 story that is the finest of Phil's career. Protagonist Garson Poole thinks that he is a human being. But inadvertently he learns that he is really an "electric ant" (organic robot). Within him, a plastic punched tape roll serves as a "reality-supply construct." What happens, Poole asks, "if no tape passes under the scanner? No tape—nothing at all. The photocell shining upward without impedance?" Technicians inform him that he will merely "short out." But Poole is undeterred. "What I want, he realized, is ultimate and absolute reality, for one microsecond. After that it doesn't matter, because all will be known; nothing will be left to understand or see." Poole opens himself up with a microtool and gets his wish. Read the story to learn the ending, which Phil said always frightened him.

But 1969 was a year of wheel-spinning by Phil's standards; the only novel he completed that year was a potboiler, *Our Friends from Frolix 8*, for Don Wollheim at Ace. In a March 1969 letter he explained his slump this way: "I have a theory: I can't sit and write one novel following another; between each I have to emerge from my shell and be with people; otherwise my novels resemble each other too much." But Phil was reading everything he could find concerning the Dead Sea Scrolls; the theological concerns fueled by his encounters with Pike were burning brightly.

In another March 1969 letter, Phil emphasized the slow gestation of a novel idea within him. His early holographic notes would include minor details on the technology and culture of the SF future world. He would then type up and revise these notes in the order in which they had occurred to him. Character creation was the most difficult step. The male protagonist would be a "composite" of actual persons. Female characters were to be "expertly developed, with many complications, contradictions—in other words, real women." Plot comes last:

> I would go so far as to say that I plot in advance only the first chapter or so of the novel, and the further I go into it the more I tend to depend on the inspiration of the moment (which sometimes never arrives, or arrives too late, say after the novel is in print). [. . .] For me, knowing the characters comes only when I am actually writing the novel; I need to hear them actually speak, actually do things, react, etc. [. . .] Thus I frequently find myself arriving at a point in the novel where, for example, the notes (and if there is an outline, then the outline) calls for the protagonist to say "Yes," where in fact he, being what he is, would say "No," so "No" he says, and I must go on from there, stuck with the fact that that is the way he is . . . which fouls up the plot-line terribly. But I think a better novel comes out of this. Other writers would not only disagree with me; they would be horrified.

Phil's "inspiration of the moment" approach required a fervor that just wasn't there at this time. Too many people dear to him were dying.

In April 1968, longtime mentor Anthony Boucher died of cancer. Phil would write two essays in tribute to Boucher, and also dedicated *Ubik* to him. To the end of Phil's life, memories of Boucher lingered. For it was Boucher who had tapped young Phil on the shoulder and told him that he could be a writer. And Boucher's urbanity and intelligence had bolstered Phil at those times in the bleak fifties when it seemed that the SF field was populated exclusively by "trolls and wackos." Then, in September 1969, Bishop Pike died in the Judean desert while in quest of the truth as to the historical Jesus. The Bishop's influence upon Phil had been immense—Pike exemplified the passionate, no-holds-barred quest for ultimate knowledge that fueled Phil's best work. In a later interview, Phil recalled this dual loss: "It was terrible, man, they were croaking like—they were falling around me like World War One, you know, just like in the end of 'All Quiet on the Western Front.' "

These deaths added to the strain of a marriage in which both Nancy and Phil had begun to bristle in their caretaking roles. Nancy was experiencing a recurrence of the nervous difficulties that had beset her in 1964, and, in addition, Phil's mounting speed intake frightened her. Some nastily cut street speed led to Phil's hospitalization, in August 1969, for pancreatitis and acute kidney failure. Severely weakened, Phil couldn't return to novel writing until well into the following year. The prospect of renewed pancreatitis attacks was a torment to Nancy. "I was so afraid he'd die. I used to be that way about my parents—and then my mother died. Then I just felt like I can't handle this." Despite the risks, Phil continued to purchase street speed. Occasionally he'd try to quit, to no avail. Nancy recalls: "I tried to hide the amphetamines. Then he'd go through this horrible bit. I couldn't stand it. Then I ended up in the hospital, and I realized I couldn't go back and live that stuff again. I couldn't get above his depressions and stuff." Nancy did go back, briefly, but she could not remain.

Phil's account of their final year is equally painful. In a later interview he explained that speed was a necessary means of escape:

> [T]he taking of amphetamines at that point, I think, was masking why my memory was faulty and my behavior was erratic and my perceptions were disturbed. They were disturbed because of traumatic shock, and because of deeper mechanisms, like amnesia. But if I didn't take the dope, I would have to face it myself, and other people would have to face it, and it was easier to just pass it off in a simple way, "Well, he's spaced, he's spaced from the amphetamines."

But Phil was being evasive here. As he well knew, the speed did more than conceal his problems. It *heightened* them. The bouts of fear, panic, and anguish that constantly plagued him were amphetamine-fueled. These side effects of the massive dosages he downed were ineluctable, however much he tried to explain them away.

The writing well had been too long dry. Phil applied for welfare and food stamps for July–August 1970, a step that wounded his pride. But by that time he was at work on a novel again.

To understand how Phil lived through the pain of again losing his family, it helps to understand the genesis of *Flow My Tears, The Policeman Said*, a novel that Phil wrote and rewrote furiously between March and August 1970.

In May 1970 Phil took a mescaline trip. He never seems to have used mescaline again, but this particular trip wowed him:

> With acid I never had any genuine insights, but on the mescalin[e] I was overwhelmed by terribly powerful feelings—emotions, I guess. I felt an overpowering love for other people, and this is what I put into the novel [*Flow*]: it studies different kinds of love and at last ends with the appearance of an ultimate kind of love which I had never known of. I am saying, "In answer to the question, 'What is real?' the answer is: this kind of overpowering love.["]

The basic tale is of TV star Jason Taverner—rich, famous, brilliant, and incredibly handsome—losing all status when transported into an alternate world in which, according to the police state of General Felix Buckman, he does not officially exist.

With its *noir* atmosphere of dread, *Flow* is the culmination of a series of post-1964 novels—*Counter-Clock World, Do Androids Dream of Electric Sheep?, Galactic Pot-Healer,* and *Our Friends from Frolix 8*—in which the terror of living in a "betrayal state" of police spies and surveillance dominates the characters' lives. But only *Flow* can boast a character of the subtlety of Felix Buckman, into whom Phil poured all his intense fear and hatred of authority, as well as his love for his fellow lost and lonely humans.

It is Buckman who lives out the novel's title, when his twin sister and incestuous wife, Alys Buckman—a bisexual leather queen who abuses drugs and binges on direct brain-stimulus at orgies—dies of an overdose of the mysterious time-binding drug KR-3. The parallel, in Alys's death, to Phil's loss of Jane is confirmed by the *Exegesis*. Phil often imagined Jane as a lesbian, and always he thought of her as strong and courageous. In the razor-tongued Alys, who hates the aloof efficiency of her brother, the sister within finds fictional form.

Felix and Alys do love each other, and exploration of the various forms of love is the grand theme of *Flow*. In 1969 Phil had written that the greatest weakness of SF was its "inability to explore the subtle, intricate relationships which exist between the sexes." Phil intended *Flow* to rectify this situation. Protagonist Taverner encounters many women in his hellish new world—lovers old and new, a dark-haired girl, and even a friend—and *Flow* is a portrait gallery of sexual styles. But Taverner begins as a crass TV crooner and ends as little more. The heart of *Flow*, as Phil himself confirmed, lies in the scene in which General Buckman cries.

It is the middle of the night, and Buckman is flying home in his quibble, trying to cope with the loss of Alys—his twin, his sister, his wife. He cannot. Stopping the quibble at an all-night gas station, he meets a black man, Montgomery L. Hopkins. Buckman cannot speak, but hands him a piece of paper on which he has drawn "a heart pierced by an arrow." At last Hopkins understands that it is sheer grief that has silenced this white stranger. And they hug. As simple as that.

Phil realized, in August 1970, that *Flow* needed one final run-through, but he was tired. Then, in September, Nancy and Isa left him. Their years of efforts at happiness were at last at an end. It was Phil's fourth failure at marriage and second sundered family. He was forty-two, poor, portly, and woefully weary of losing love. Sustained writing would remain out of the question for the next two years. (In 1971, in the midst of his sorrows, Phil entrusted the *Flow* manuscript to his attorney, and it was not until 1973 that he typed the final draft for Doubleday.)

But the May 1970 mescaline trip had given him not only the plot for *Flow*, but also the vision he needed to get by. In a September 1970 letter he wrote of "a kind of mystical love of strangers that I previously never thought existed. It is all new to me, this divine love; it fills me up and I hate no one, even Mr. Jackson, Nancy's paramour."

Nancy had an affair with Honor Jackson, a black neighbor who lived across the street, but it was not love for another man that finally prompted her departure. But Phil later referred to Jackson in letters and interviews as a "Black Panther" who stole Nancy away.

Jackson, who still lives across the street, bursts into laughter when asked about Black Panther ties back then, and Nancy confirms that there were none. Back then Jackson and Phil got on well; after Nancy left Phil even bought a used car from Jackson—a red '63 Pontiac. Jackson remembers Phil as a "nice guy" who also seemed "a little loony" because "he had trouble thinking straight from day to day" and tended, when outside the house, to hunch, stalk, and peer. Jackson never spent time in Phil's house, but heard about the drug deals and would see cars come and people go in and stay two or three days. Nancy left, Jackson says, because there were too many drugs.

Why accord Black Panther status to a man who held an ordinary, peaceful job? A number of Phil's friends suggest the obvious: Given the sixties scene, it was just the detail to lend drama to a sad, drawn-out parting. Mike Hackett moved in with them in the final weeks to help with driving and other chores, but his presence only eased the break.

Isa, then three, recalls the day in early September: "We were in the car leaving, and my dad came running out of the house after us. And we were driving away."

8 Dark Night Of The Soul, Dark-Haired Girls, A Scanner Darkly—It's Always Darkest Before The Dawn, Of Course, But Try Remembering That When The Shit Has Finally Hit The Fan Like It Does In Those Weird Phil Dick Novels (1970–1972)

But, um—there really was no point in writing. As a matter of fact, when you conceive of how you write—one writes by going off into privacy, alone—one hour of solitude would have meant my demise, after Nancy left with my little girl, it was too risky. I had to be with people. I flooded the house with people. Anybody was welcome. Because the sound of their voices, the sound of their activity, the din in the hall, anything, it kept me alive. I literally was unable to kill myself then, 'cause there was too much going on.

PHIL, 1974 interview (in *Only Apparently Real*)

This has been a novel about some people who were punished entirely too much for what they did. They wanted to have a good time, but they were like children playing in the street; they could see one after another of them being killed—run over, maimed, destroyed—but they continued to play anyhow. We really all were happy for a while, sitting around not toiling but just bullshitting and playing, but it was for such a terribly brief time, and then the punishment was beyond belief: even when we could see it, we could not believe it.

"Author's Note," *A Scanner Darkly* (1977)

PHIL was a bachelor again—of the middle-aged variety, with greying hair and beard, expanding gut, and a litany of lost loves and bitter memories. Yet he remained an imposing figure. His blue eyes flashed beneath his broad, writerly brow. He could set a roomful of people aglow with his brilliance, or awash with laughter at his straight-faced absurdities.

These gifts served him well just now, because, above all else, Phil needed to hold a crowd.

To do so, he would consent to any terms. He opened his Santa Venetia house first to friends, then to all comers. He offered them drugs, beer, music; his mind, wit, kindness, and broken heart.

He craved affection. And embraced chaos.

♦

The same week Nancy left Phil, Nancy's sister Anne left her husband, Bernie Montbriand. And Nancy's brother Mike, already living in the Santa Venetia house, was served with divorce papers. So Phil invited Bernie to join them. Bachelors three.

And amiable companions they proved to be. Late-night giggling, dazzling raps fueled by white crosses. Music going always—Mozart to the Grateful Dead. Young drifters and dealers passing through free and easy, which was fine since Phil was generous with his drugs and money. He felt safer with strangers around; trusting strangers, he believed, was very antischizophrenic. But he didn't much like to leave the house. Mike handled errands. Bernie recalls: "There was a lot of fear in Phil. He was living in that one world—in that house. Things would come to that house, things would leave that house. He never dealt in real-world things . . . he talked about pills a lot, oh, good shit, bad shit, where can we get some more of this?"

The fear seldom took the form of overt anger. Phil was gentle, almost withdrawn, when he wasn't in animated monologue mode. He could not easily be aroused, even by classic roommate irritations. Bernie tells of dropping the needle of Phil's expensive stereo right into the middle of a treasured record with the volume cranked to the max. "He'd just come out of his room and nicely say not to play it so loud. Polite and kind, a gentleman."

But threats from *without*—real or imagined—weren't as easy to handle. Recalls Mike: "He was fearful about the police, the drug thing. I think it also gave him a sense of adventure—you know, we have to watch out or they'll bust us." Tom Schmidt, who in October 1970 replaced Bernie Montbriand as the third housemate, acknowledges that Phil worried over communists, Nazis, the FBI, and the CIA. But keep in mind that there were, on Phil's premises daily, various weird and dangerous casualties of the drug scene who owned guns and were subject to mood swings of their own. It wasn't unreasonable to keep an eye open for rip-offs or bust setups.

It's also not unreasonable to point out that bouts of intense paranoia are a known common side effect of amphetamine abuse, and that Phil was abusing amphetamines—Dexedrine, Benzedrine, and god knows what awful street shit thrown in—to the hilt. In the refrigerator he kept cartons of protein-fortified milkshakes side by side with large jars of white crosses—$100 for a jar of a thousand, which Phil consumed by downing unmeasured handfuls with the milkshakes (damn smart to avoid speeding on an empty stomach). Phil and others in the house would stay up three or four days or even a week straight without sleep and then would crash out into forty-eight hours of bed immobility. And when you're speeding that long on large doses, a sense of high energy and utter awareness can—and usually does—turn into watchfulness, suspicion, fear. You look through the blinds to see who's out there. Phil would often say he saw someone lurking in the yard, or even beside his bed, during the night. His housemates never knew whether to believe him (mostly they didn't), but they knew what it felt like. Says Bernie: "In my personal experience—you've been up three days, your mind is screaming up there, you need relaxation; all vitamins, anything that gives stability to your body and mind, are depleted. That's when the paranoia hits."

Phil was aware of the side effects of speed. In notepad journals of the time, Phil speculated now and then as to whether a fear of the moment was the product of the pills. Once, late at night, he documented the struggle: "12:30. I am going to bed. I hate the bedroom—an empty bed—but I hate even worse sitting out here in the cold living room at night with the music muted [. . .] The happiness pills are turning out to be nightmare pills." A few paragraphs later, a fortunate upturn: "The happiness pills have been helping me—putting a warm glow of possession in my stomach."

Speed gives for a time—a good, glorious, roaring time—and it can take away forever. Phil understood the dialectic and didn't give a damn. He was playing, the grasshopper mocking the ants of the "real" world, and imagining a masterwork—*A Scanner Darkly*—without knowing it. In a November 1970 letter he gave a portrait of life in what had come to be nicknamed "Hermit House":

> We all take speed and we are all going to die, but we will have a few more years and we will be happy. We don't want to live more than a few more years, and while we live we will live it as we are: stupid, blind, loving, talking, being together, kidding, propping one another up and ratifying the good things in one another. [. . .]
> [. . .] No group of people can be this happy. We knew we were ignoring some fundamental aspect of reality, such for example as money, or in my case sleep. Soon it will catch up with us. [. . .] That's all one can really hope for, I think, to be happy awhile and then remember it.

Phil's detachment from economic pressures was no mean feat. Since May he had been having trouble with house payments. The credit company was on his ass, and he borrowed often from the Hudners. But the emptiness left by Nancy's departure made holing up alone to produce a novel unthinkable. And so he turned his intense range of feeling on his housemates. Tom Schmidt recalls that moving in with Phil was like changing worlds:

> There was something about him that made you feel involved. Phil had this softness. But depth. He was like a director. Almost like he'd bring certain

170

people in to see how they'd react. And sit back and watch and create science fiction.

I think he lived in a fantasy overall. He seldom left the house. His whole existence was like he could create everything there. [. . .]

Phil told me he thinks in paragraphs. When he'd carry on a conversation, the whole thing is already there. He could talk about anything. There would be a variety of people coming in, dumb people. I'm not saying he brought himself down to their level, but he could deal with them like on any level.

Of the people I've known, if I had to spend eternity with one, it would be Phil.

But Tom, who abstained from drugs, could not choose to spend eternity in "Hermit House" and moved out after a few months. The open-door policy was too much to bear. Word of mouth had Phil's place a safe bet for selling or scoring drugs. By spring 1971 Mike also had decided to move on: "What made Phil fun in a way, and difficult in other ways, was that he'd create his own reality. It took a large supporting cast to accommodate his phobias. On the other hand, he had a lot to offer on his own, so it isn't a parasitic thing. Just as time wears on, there are other things you have to do."

Even while living with Mike and Tom, Phil had been intently searching for a woman to replace Nancy. As he had in 1964, between Anne and Nancy, Phil fell in love again and again, and absolutely sincerely each time. But there were differences this time around. Phil was now in his early forties. Pale from an indoor nocturnal life, his features ranged from youthful innocence during manic raps to deep-lined weariness when he crashed. He slouched and packed a gut from too many frozen chicken pot pies and chocolate chip cookies (for all his speed use, Phil never fit the archetypal strung-out mode). And he dressed badly, even by the tattered standards of the sixties—a haphazard look that included a never-pressed Nehru jacket.

Phil's intensity and disheveled-genius aura could easily override his physical shortcomings. What stacked the game against him, causing him to undergo a bruising series of heartbreaks during this period, were two critical factors: He usually pursued women half his age or a little less; and he wanted, wanted, WANTED so much.

Also, there were the personal problems that sometimes marked the women he pursued. Tom recalls: "Phil always had relationships with women who were troubled. I don't think he was capable of having a relationship with a straight woman. Because he wouldn't have control. Not that he really had control—it was a sort of uncontrollable control."

Phil would fantasize—quickly, vividly, and in ideal terms—ardent futures with women he'd just met and scarcely knew. It maddened even the madness of ardent courtship. One of the women whom Phil courted in late 1970 was J'Ann Forgue, dark-haired, attractive, and in her mid-twenties when she first befriended Phil, during his marriage with Nancy. (J'Ann served as a model for Sally Jo Berm in A *Maze of Death*, w. 1968.) After Nancy left, Phil tried to deepen the relationship. J'Ann recalls:

> I know I was frustrating to Phil, because as much as I respected him as a writer, I wasn't interested in a romantic attachment. I had such an intense feeling that he didn't know who I was—that he was in love with some internal image of his that he had pinned on to me. I went over to see him because he would beg me to, basically. He didn't come down too hard in telling me that he loved me—what he did say was that he needed me and that I could save him.
>
> The J'Ann he thought he loved had remarkably little to do with me. He would make grandiose and quite abstract statements about how I was so bright and how I could cope with things. It's true I'm a strong woman, but that time in my life was an extremely bad one—I wasn't coping with *anything*. So for him to say how strong I was really struck me as bizarre.

By November 1970, J'Ann felt compelled to break off her visits. Phil's journal entries on their failed romance parallel J'Ann's account. Early on, Phil wrote that J'Ann "stepped in and saved me." How? By filling in for bitch-mother Dorothy:

> In contrast, consider my mother who has not visited me since Nancy left, although she visited [stepsister] Lynne and in fact came right to the door of this house—but wouldn't come in. Well it was she 42 years ago [at the time of Phil and Jane's birth] who set into action the security drive that finally at long last someone satisfied. [. . .] So in a sense J'Ann has been the mother I never had [. . .]

And now J'Ann was gone. "I don't merely love her; I require her to live." But within a month, Phil (demonstrating the recuperative powers that fortunately accompanied his head-over-heels approach) was able to see J'Ann more clearly: "Maybe the reason I turned so bitterly on her did not have to do with her flat point out blank refusing to go in my room but rather her detailing how realistically she had failed to cope—in contrast to my idealistic, romantic picture of her coping to beat hell."

By December Phil had fallen in love again—with both members of a lesbian couple in their early twenties. Again the relationship was rather intense, especially since Phil identified one of the couple with Jane and fantasized about bringing both of them to confront his mother. From his journal:

> I would be saying, "Look, Dorothy; I know two girls who are stronger than you. You are old and will soon die, but these girls are strong and young and

capable. They will survive long after either of us." [. . .] A lifetime ambition fulfilled. One-upmanship on my sainted, aged mother who, when I was nineteen, told me I was so weak that I would become homosexual once I left her.

Whether the visit—Phil presenting a living Jane to Dorothy—ever took place is not known. But Phil's journals indicate that by January 1971, the relationship had come apart. The young girl who had reminded Phil of his sister had looked to him to "ease the pain," but instead he brought only more pain. "She was like Jane—and she was killed—neglected—allowed to die—all over again. Can I bear it? Has she the courage to face the life ahead of her without me?" Further on, Phil realized that she would survive. Still further on, his concern for her (and others) turned to fear:

I hate them because they let me hurt them because their love for me depends on me trusting me. I'm terribly afraid of them and of what I might further do to hurt them—I just want to get away. [. . .] Maybe they were all weak, fragile, delicately balanced people and my intensity was too much for them. What I wanted from them and to see happen—I was imposing myself on them and their reality the way I do in a book. Maybe I tried to write their lives. I wouldn't let the people around me live; I had to mastermind everything.

In his next entry Phil could absolve himself: "I'm very angry and I can't sleep—I also know I'm tired—nuts to their protective drives; in the final upshot no one can protect anybody. It doesn't matter whether you're well or sick, you still have to do it."

With this girl, Phil reenacted the trauma of Jane's death, including both his desperate desire to bring Jane back to life (through the fantasized visit to Dorothy) and his guilty identification with Dorothy (through failing the girl). Jane's survival as a defiant lesbian (like Alys Buckman in *Flow*) would be a slap in Dorothy's face; her taunts over Phil's "weak" "homosexual" tendencies would be refuted in an ultimate manner: by the sight of a strong child who had survived her neglect (which Phil, the guilt-filled surviving twin, had in fact done but could not *believe* he had done). It was, to Phil, an agony that at forty-two he still yearned for Dorothy to visit, to love him, to affirm his manhood.

In fact, Phil was in close contact with Dorothy—through lengthy, frequent phone calls—all through the misery of 1970–71. Vituperative contact it was, but it persisted. Son and mother remained bound, even as Phil's search for a woman to eclipse her intensified.

Joseph Hudner, Phil's stepfather, kept a diary for the first half of 1971, some entries of which reveal the painful relations between Phil and Dorothy, as well as Phil's utter unreliability, during this period. The entries summarized here provide a valuable record of Phil's doings and of

Dorothy's (and Joseph's) view of him. Early 1971, as seen through a diary darkly:

January 13: Phil calls Dorothy twice. He has taken on the care of a seventeen-year-old girl whom Phil describes as "psychotic." Phil's psychiatrist says he functions best in crises—and so must have them one after another. Dorothy believes "Philip cannot function in the dull daylight." He handles emotional crises on four-to five-year-old level—his age when she and Edgar divorced.

January 18: Phil phones, excited over new use of I *Ching*.

January 31: Phil's house full of "oddball characters," whom Phil terms a "family."

February 4: Joseph unhappy that Hacienda Way house is in their name. "We love him. Let it go."

February 26: The loan company begins foreclosure. Phil late with payments but never told the Hudners. Joseph fears his credit is shot.

February 27: Phil phones to say he'll repay fifty dollars he just borrowed. Dorothy tells him they know about the foreclosure. Phil shocked to learn of possible effect on their credit, assures Dorothy that Doubleday has agreed to give him enough per year to live on [not true] and that he'll pay up the back loans.

March 31: Phil phones, depressed about house and relationship with seventeen-year-old girl living with him. Says he attempted suicide.

April 4: Phil phones, is living with a new woman—"Jennifer." [Here and throughout the rest of this book, false names are used in every case where someone is introduced by first name in quotes.] Joseph tells him he wants no more responsibility for the house; Phil agrees to figure out a way to accomplish this. Problem: If Phil files the deed of gift Dorothy and Joseph gave him two years ago, the IRS will foreclose on the house for back taxes.

April 9: Phil phones. He and Jennifer will try a life together. He's into something so bad he can't tell Dorothy what it is. Jennifer opposed, so he's already half out of it. Joseph appalled.

April 13: Phil phones. He's staying at Jennifer's place, can't cope with his house and wants to sell it.

April 19: Phil phones. Wants to sell house in June, use half the profits to go down to Mexico with Jennifer.

April 22: Phil phones. Has no money. Joseph sent in late payment to loan company.

April 23: Phil phones. Has some money but not enough for house payment, wants a loan. Dorothy doesn't tell him they've already sent in payment. Phil claims his money tied up in bank accounts in Jennifer's name—she won't let him at it. Joseph concludes: "Can't believe anything he says."

April 26 and 27: Phil phones. Convinced he can help Jennifer. Joseph sees it as part of Phil's pattern of believing he can "save" women. "He can't help himself; so he can help her."

April 30: Phil phones, tells Dorothy he's a drug addict, takes a thousand amphetamine tablets a week. Jennifer helping him quit. "We knew Philip was taking drugs but didn't know he was hooked that bad. [. . .] Philip says it's either quit or die. [. . .] Shock of Philip being a dope addict is great to both Dorothy and me."

May 2: Phil phones. Always talks to Dorothy and not Joseph. Says good-bye to Dorothy, he's going to kill himself. Dorothy tries to keep the conversation going, but Phil hangs up. Calls back a few minutes later to say Dorothy is right—he has a responsibility to his daughters and his pets. Keeps saying that no one has ever really cared for him, that he has wanted to die ever since he was five—when Edgar left. He's been on Benzedrine and other drugs since 1951, when Kleo's physician father gave him a prescription. Can't write if he's off drugs. While with Nancy was off them two months, didn't write, went back on them when she said he could. "Dorothy badly shaken up." Joseph (concerned over suicide threat) phones Jennifer, who finds Phil at her place, listening to music.

May 3: "Dorothy feels there is no hope for Philip because of his bent and distorted personality." "He told Dorothy last night that he could make more off his drug deals than his writing." [Note: Those who knew Phil well during this time recall that he *gave* pills away freely. His statement, if made, was likely intended to shock and impress.] Jennifer phones, says she and her doctor have taken Phil to the psych ward of Stanford University Hospital (Hoover Pavilion).

The idea of a stay in the psych ward did not appeal to Phil initially. But he felt he had no choice—as he was staying at Jennifer's place in Palo

175

Alto, without money or car, it was hitchhike back to San Rafael or deal with her insistence that he was a drug addict.

He was admitted on May 3 and checked out on May 6 with the approval of the examining psychiatrist, Dr. Harry Bryan. Dr. Bryan's records state that Phil said he was taking one thousand Methedrine tabs per week, costing him three hundred dollars per month. He was also taking 10 mg of Stelazine four times a day, as well as other tranquilizers. There was a past threat of suicide. Phil's mental-status exam showed an "astute" intellect with no evidence of delusions. Physical exams showed sustained recovery from the pancreatitis—and no physical drug addiction or internal organic damage. Phil was in remarkable shape for someone downing a thousand beans a week. Even his blood pressure was normal. In their discussions, Dr. Bryan found Phil optimistic with respect to the hippie movement. Dr. Bryan recalls: "In all of his behavior he was so people-oriented, so friendly and compassionate, that any paranoia would have been temporary and a spin-off from stopping the speed or taking the speed." While Phil was in Hoover Pavilion, Joseph's diary shows that he spoke often by phone with Dorothy. After he was discharged on May 6, Phil continued to pay visits to Dr. X (whose diagnosis of Phil then was schizophrenic reaction), as well as to two other psychiatrists (who posited paranoia and malingering, respectively).

Lynne Cecil confirms that during 1971 Phil was often "very dramatic"—everything became exaggerated in his presence. This year stood out as one of Phil's worst times:

> He was paranoid—I know it was from the effect of the drugs. At one point he knocked on my door in the middle of the night. I was also living in San Rafael, and he had gotten a friend to drive him over at 4:00 A.M. I was really upset and angry about it—I didn't want him in my living room and there he was. He was talking about some kind of plot with the CIA. It was very involved—he had written something in one of his books that corresponded with something true and the CIA was interested. It was full-blown—he was looking over his shoulder all the time.

Phil's crises, financial calamities, and paranoia worsened to the point where, in June, he accused Dorothy and Joseph of conspiring to take his house away from him. On June 15 Joseph remarked that "Dorothy feels that Philip will have a psychotic break if he doesn't have this continuous string of crises he gets into. (And often invents.)" Later that month Joseph wrote of the house accusations: "So ends things for me with Philip. If and since he can construct and believe a lie like that, there is no reason to believe anything he tells us about his doings, life, and other people. I have a feeling of sadness about this."

Joseph's diary ends in July 1971. He died shortly thereafter. In the course of a most difficult relationship with Phil, Joseph extended contin-

◆ Phil at age eleven months.

◆ Phil and his father, Joseph Edgar Dick.

◆ Phil and his mother,
Dorothy Kindred.

◆ Dorothy, circa 1927,
just prior to becoming a
mother.

◆ Phil at approximately age six,
the time of his parents' divorce.

◆ Cowboy Phil.

◆ Phil (in foreground) with grandmother Edna Matilda Archer Kindred ("Meemaw"), aunt Marion Kindred, and grandfather Earl Kindred.

◆ Phil, with cat, outside the Francisco Street house in Berkeley.
Photo by Kleo Mini

◆ Kleo Mini (then Aposto-
lides) in 1948 high-school
graduation photo.

◆ Phil and Anne Dick; Phil was pleased that Anne let him grow a beard.

◆ Phil with his cat, circa 1960.

◆ Kleo with Norman Mini, early sixties. Kleo terms this a "fair representation" of her look through the fifties.

◆ Phil with sheep, but no beard, at his Point Reyes Station home, early sixties. *Photo by Anne Dick*

◆ Phil, Nancy, and Isa Dick, San Rafael, California, September 1968. *Photo by William Sarill*

◆ Phil in 1979. *Photo by Doris Sauter*

♦ Phil and Tessa Dick, 1973. *Photo by Linda Hartinian*

♦ Phil and Isa, circa 1977.

◆ Phil with cat in February 1982, just three days before the first of the fatal strokes. *Photo by Gwen Lee*

◆ The gravesite, in Fort Morgan, Colorado, of Phil and Jane.

ual financial and emotional support. And love. The diary, for all its horrors, confirms that as well.

The chasm between Phil and the Hudners lent urgency to Phil's desire to create a new family in Santa Venetia. Phil's obsession—which put fiction writing on hold—was to reassemble what had been shattered by Nancy's departure. Lots of young folk passed through these last months of 1971. Bikers and boppers, diagnosed schizos and violent crazies, even a few sweet souls. They came to listen to the good stereo, to score, or just to get to a place where they were welcome. A few moved in rent-free when Phil asked them to. To visitor Paul Williams, Phil seemed to be "playing a kind of guru role. It was a weird scene." Indeed, there were those toward whom Phil played the role of wise rescuer. And in this role, Phil had his successes. He provided food and shelter, listened intently, cared deeply.

But Phil did not aspire—and was quite unfit—to play the role of a full-fledged commune leader. However much he yearned to rescue his friends, he needed their love back quite as much. To need is to become equal: poor strategy for a guru. The boppers were never in awe of Philip K. Dick the writer. They liked this strange older guy Phil, who always had beans to share and swung from mad raps to kindness to fear to three-days-straight crashing in his bedroom, door closed. Sometimes they teased him, sometimes they ripped him off outright. They sensed the loneliness, the need.

Two men who came to live with Phil in June 1971 were "Rick" and "Daniel," two speed freaks who were both dead by the time A Scanner Darkly was published in 1977. Rick, in his mid-thirties, had spent time in a mental hospital. He was thin, with scary eyes, and kept several loaded rifles under his bed. Both Phil and Rick feared that the FBI or CIA was watching the house, but Phil hid Rick's ammunition and removed the firing pins from the rifles. Daniel, a talented musician in his early twenties, was dark-skinned with blue-black hair. In Scanner, burnout Jerry Fabin believes that aphids are crawling all over him. Daniel suffered from the same mental agony. Like Fabin, he sprayed Raid on himself. At times (as in Scanner) Daniel's obsession struck his housemates as funny. Head-tripping was common sixties drug fun: How far can you get someone to go with your/their fantasy? Rick flicked imaginary bugs at Daniel from across the room. Phil kept a shoebox supposedly full of captured aphids.

Other Santa Venetia regulars included two brothers, "Mike" and "Lonnie," both of junior high age. When the jack holding up the car he was working on started to give, Mike was saved by the courage and quick action of a drug burnout—an incident Phil included in Scanner, as it expressed for him the human kindness preserved even within the husk of addiction.

"Gene" and "Sandy" were a teenage couple whom Phil befriended.

Both Gene and Phil owned guns and played around with them; Phil once shot a hole in a window. Phil was off and on in love with Sandy, an attractive young Japanese woman who was studying nursing and could lend an air of calm to Phil's confusions. In his worst fits of jealousy over her love for Gene, Phil would ask Sandy to leave, then shortly afterward plead for her to return.

Then there was "Don," a fifteen-year-old veteran of juvenile court, who would hide when Phil's SF friends—Terry and Carol Carr, Ray and Kirsten Nelson, Grania and Steve Davis—came by to visit. Don recalls that Phil would act totally straight with these older friends and would keep his writing office an oasis of neatness in the house. But as the year went on, Phil grew subject to fits of rage, during which he would fling books off the shelves and even knock over his own speakers. Once Don insisted that Phil *sell*—not give him a hundred bennies. Phil asked for two dollars, well below street price. Don gave him four. The next day Phil burned the bills.

Phil had a sunnier friendship with Loren Cavit, a fifteen-year-old who heard about Phil's house through a friend. Loren succeeded in coaxing Phil out of the house for a question-and-answer session with her high school class, which had read "Roog," his first story sale back in 1951. (The delightful exchange between Phil and the kids was published in *Reflections of the Future*, a 1975 SF anthology.) Loren recalls that Phil was nervous on the way to the talk—and ecstatic afterward:

> Phil didn't consider himself old. He's the only person I know of who can transcend levels. He can rap with a two-year-old and then turn around, at a dinner, and talk with intellectuals. Maybe he played with people; I do believe he did. But he would never put you down. He was in conflict with himself, but he wouldn't share that except in little bits once in a while—the confusion he felt.

During their talks, the perpetually lovelorn Phil sought advice from Loren. "He always fantasized about every woman he knew—maybe it was more fun to fantasize than to act on it. He'd want feedback on chicks— 'Do you think she'd go out with me?' He'd get crushes like a sixteen-year-old."

But the young woman who meant the most to Phil first rode up to the house, in late 1970, on the back of her boyfriend's Harley Davidson. She helped inspire Donna Hawthorne in *Scanner*, Gloria in *Valis* (p. 1981), and Angel Archer in *The Transmigration of Timothy Archer* (p. 1982). It is as "Donna" that she'll be referred to here.

They were friends, never lovers. Phil would have wanted things differently, but it didn't matter—he cherished Donna's street-smart courage, the beauty and warmth of her dark hair and dark eyes. Household members suspected that Donna was setting Phil up for a rip-off. Phil himself came to share these suspicions—and still he loved her, didn't care if they were true or not. He even wrote up a document giving her the right to use all his possessions and to be on the premises at any time—to preclude her being busted, should she become implicated in any of the burglaries that Phil feared would occur. And ultimately did.

In a letter, Phil described Donna this way:

> She was just a bibbity-boppity gutter-type, [. . .] virtually illiterate, just out of high school, a brooding dark girl of French peasant background whose ambition it was [. . .] to be a checker at Safeway. Nobody paid any attention to what she said except me. I believed everything she said. [. . .] Without her wise and dispassionate guidance during the year after Nancy left me, I would have gone even nutsier than I did.

Donna saw Phil through a time when he constantly doubted the worth of it all. In a 1972 essay, "The Evolution of a Vital Love," Phil wrote: " '[Donna],' I said one time when I had been lying in bed for almost eight days without eating, 'I'm going to die.' 'No you're not,' [Donna] said, and patted me. 'You're a great man. Get up so you can lend me two dollars.' I did so, and am here now." During these long-term depression bedrests, there were inklings of strange visions to come, including a "taco stand experience"—eight hours in duration—in which he felt himself in Mexico.

But Phil's feelings of isolation and loss—the aftermath of Nancy and Isa's departure—continued to undermine him. Phil was admitted to both Marin General Psychiatric Hospital and Ross Psychiatric Clinic in August 1971. Anne Dick writes that Phil consulted with Dr. X that August, telling him that he believed "the FBI or the CIA were tapping his phone, breaking into his house when he was out and stealing his papers." Phil wished to be hospitalized for his own protection. According to Anne, while Phil insisted to Dr. X that he was a drug addict, Dr. X believed that Phil was being hypochondriacal. In Marin General, Dr. X observed no withdrawal symptoms in Phil. Attorney William Wolfson recalls that Phil seemed "all right" during Wolfson's visit to Ross, at which time Phil (who was doing no new writing then) gave him the rough draft of *Flow* for safekeeping.

By September 1971, Phil had returned to Santa Venetia and welcomed in a new arrival. "Sheila" had just graduated from high school and was going out with Phil's friend Daniel. Phil invited her to move in. At first—with all bedrooms full—Sheila slept in his writing office. But the live-in situation was constantly changing, and by November Sheila was the only stable housemate Phil had. At first she was delighted by Phil, who could talk on virtually any subject. They went out often to nearby restaurants. Phil took Sheila for drives in the country and bought her new clothes at the mall. She recalls that Phil hated the IRS for hounding him on back taxes, and would go on spending sprees as soon as royalty checks arrived. Afterward, he would fall into a gloom.

"Phil was like three or four different people," says Sheila. "There was the educated Phil who would talk history and philosophy, and the paranoid Phil who was popping pills and ranting and raving about the CIA. And then there was the Phil who wanted to hug me and marry me and would cry when I refused." The educated Phil seemed to come and go in direct correspondence to his speed binges. "He used to do a handful at a time, several times a day, for a week or two, and then he'd sleep for two or three days. I used to wonder why he was getting crazy, and then I caught on that after a few days on a binge he'd get real crazy, then he'd need to sleep, and then he'd be okay for a while again."

Sheila was drawn into Phil's fears concerning former housemate Rick, he of the loaded rifles. In late summer Phil had forced Rick to move out. Phil was convinced Rick bore a grudge and would kill him. One night the phone rang; Phil answered, and the caller hung up. Sheila recalls that Phil was sure it was Rick:

> So he grabbed a hammer and a hatchet and said let's go in the back room and wait for him. So Rick never shows up. We didn't sleep that night, so we took bennies. The next day Phil decided we needed some contract killers to protect ourselves. I don't know how, but he got two black guys who lived around the corner to be on call twenty-four hours a day. These guys were just out of high school; I'm sure they just wanted the money. One time Phil called and they weren't there, so he decided to fire them. Then he decided to get real contract killers. We drove down to San Rafael and saw a man and wife. I sat in the living room while Phil and they went into a bedroom to talk. Later Phil comes out and says let's go. He told me they were contract killers and would kill Rick if he showed up. I wasn't sure if it was real or not. We get home and these three grown men show up. They had guns with them—they called it going hunting. So they sat lined up on the couch and just waited. Phil and I had been taking bennies for two days and hadn't slept, so we were nervous wrecks. Nothing happened all night, and they left in the morning.

To Paul Williams in 1974, Phil stated that during this time he had hired two "militant blacks" to protect a girl that "a junkie pusher was trying to kill." The fee was $750, and "they did their job beautifully." The girl was trying to break away from the pusher and asked Phil to take her to the hospital, which he did. Sheila doesn't recall any threats against her—but Phil's version has the threat made to him while Sheila was in the hospital. As for her request to be taken there, Sheila's version goes like this:

> Phil decided I was crazy. So he said I'm taking you to a psychiatrist because you're crazy. So I say okay. I wanted to talk to somebody because things were really weird. So we drove to somebody's house, he knocked on the door,

180

nobody answered, and I say, "Who was that?" and Phil says, "I don't know." So then he took me to Dr. [X], his psychiatrist. So I told him all the weird things. I was starting to wonder if these things really were happening or if I was crazy. The doctor wouldn't really discuss Phil's problems with me, but he did say Phil was paranoid and there was nothing wrong with me. I don't think Phil and I discussed the meeting. But he was reassured—he didn't think I was crazy anymore.

It was getting to the point that I had to get out of there. I didn't know how or when. Then Phil decided I was a junkie. I've never had anything to do with heroin—never even seen it. But I decided to go along with it, thinking I could go someplace and get, you know, rehabilitated. Phil only allowed me to take a few days' worth of clothes. He wanted to make sure I'd come back. I guess he thought I was acting weird. So I went to Marin Open House.

There Sheila arranged for two adults to pose as her parents and return with her to Phil's house to get her things. "Phil was so depressed he looked like he was going to cry." He wasn't taken in by the fake parents, but what did it matter? Sheila was gone.

Part of the weirdness that so frightened Sheila was the intense anticipation, on Phil's part, that there would be a hit of some kind on the Santa Venetia house. There were a number of ominous portents. Phil was experiencing repeated mechanical difficulties with his car, including a brake failure that almost cost Phil and friends their lives on Mount Tamalpais. (Bob Arctor and friends nearly perish due to a car-tampering incident—the accelerator, not the brakes—in *Scanner*.) Then there was the time Phil and Sheila returned to find all doorknobs on exterior doors of the house removed. The stereo was gone, the refrigerator was open, and there was food scattered in the backyard. Says Sheila: "Phil used to call the cops all the time—Rick was going to kill him, the doorknobs, the car. After a while they wouldn't show up anymore."

Perfect time for a major break-in. In a later journal entry, Phil described the horror:

[. . .] in the early part of November 1971 I had reason to believe that some sort of violent hit against my house in San Rafael was about to take place, and because of this I bought a gun. During the mandatory 5-day waiting period before I could obtain possession of the gun, on November 17 or so, my house was hit. I came home (I had to abandon my car because of peculiar damage to it, stranding me miles away) to find windows smashed in, doors broken, locks smashed, most of my possessions gone; my fireproof files had been blown up evidently by plastic explosives [. . .] all business papers, cancelled checks, letters, documents, papers of every sort gone. The floor a chaos of debris, wet asbestos from the files, combatboot footprints, broken drill bits, rugs and towels soaked in water which had been thrown over the files to muffle the explosion.

181

Immediately after the break-in Phil began to theorize about who and why. The many and contrasting fruits of his speculations (set forth in a November 1975 *Rolling Stone* feature by Paul Williams that made the break-in a hip *cause célèbre*/mind twister) will be reviewed in a moment. It may be said, at the outset, that Phil never did find out who or why. There is only one real certainty with respect to the break-in: It scared the shit out of Phil, and made further life in Santa Venetia impossible.

Williams writes: "The night after the break-in, Phil stayed at the house of another science-fiction writer, Avram Davidson. Avram said Phil professed himself to be 'absolutely baffled' at who could have done it; at the same time he seemed 'intrinsically undisturbed, marveling at the efficiency of the job.' " A number of eyewitnesses who saw the Santa Venetia study after the break-in recall a mess much like Phil's description above. These include Tom Schmidt, Donna, and Sheila. Sheila recounts the scene this way:

> The file cabinet had been blown up—Phil said by plastic explosives. There was this powder on the floor that Phil said had lined the files [presumably asbestos] and footprints like army boot prints in the dust. One of the drawers looked exploded—just enough to break the lock, not a big bomb. Phil said some manuscripts were stolen. He seemed to think it was some plot, like the CIA. I don't know if somebody did it or if maybe Phil did it or what.

While eyewitnesses corroborate that the files were broken into, there is some cause to wonder why that would have been necessary. After his hospitalization in August, Phil had noted in his journal that during his absence housemate Daniel had "[s]ystematically and thoroughly damaged beyond repair" the file locking mechanisms.

Tom Schmidt conjectures that "I've always thought maybe Phil did it himself. But there *was* a break-in. The file cabinet—it was forced open. I'm not sure on the explosion. Phil said they were going after his manuscripts." Certainly Phil had been fearful enough over the possibility of the *Flow* manuscript's being stolen to entrust it to his lawyer, William Wolfson, back in August. But other than his mainstream novels of the fifties, there do not seem to have been further unpublished manuscripts of significance in Phil's possession at the time. The SF he wrote was always quickly sold and published. And Phil never spoke, at this point or in later years, of any of his works having been lost by virtue of the break-in. What manuscripts might the perpetrators have been after? Phil never specified.

The investigation was handled by the Marin County Sheriff's Office. In an October 1972 journal entry, Phil recounted:

> A police sergeant in Marin County warned me that if I didn't leave "I'd probably get a bullet in my back some night or worse." He further said, "This

county doesn't need a crusader," referring to me. I feel that the authorities in Marin County did little or nothing to investigate the hit on my house or even to prevent it; I had informed them several times during the week before Nov 17 that I believed my house would be hit; they told me to buy [a] gun and defend myself [. . .] When I did call them [. . .] they objected to sending out a police car and didn't appear for almost an hour. The next day when I came to the County Sheriff's Dept with my list of what had been stolen, they had no report of a robbery having occurred [. . .] I feel I was driven out of Marin County by violence, the threat of future violence, and the authorities were passive, even telling me I ought to leave.

Despite diligent efforts over the next three years—letters to the Sheriff's Office, the FBI, the American Civil Liberties Union, and to congressmen—Phil never learned what, if anything, the police investigation uncovered. The Sheriff's Office report (to which I was denied access) was orally summarized to Williams (who also was not permitted to see it) in 1974:

There was a metal cabinet, the police report said, that had been drilled or pried—the homeowner said it had been blown open but it looked to the reporting officer like it had been pried. A gun was taken. A stereo system was reported missing. The file indicated that there had been a previous burglary "not reported, but heard about indirectly." There was no information on further developments: "We didn't have any suspects."

Confusions, contradictions, and obfuscations . . .

Here are Phil's primary theories of the break-in, summarized from his 1974 interview with Williams and from essays, journals, and letters:

1. Religious fanatics. Phil's association with Bishop Pike led fanatics to ransack Phil's files for info on Pike's heresies.

2. Black militants. Phil's Santa Venetia turf was predominantly black. Certain neighbors with Black Panther sympathies may have wished to drive him out.

3. Minutemen or other right-wing group. Phil believed that "Peter," a sinister house hanger-on, belonged to such a group. Peter (who inspired the diabolical Jim Barris in *Scanner*) tried to persuade Phil to insert "secret coded information" in his novels about a virulent new strain of syphilis being used against the U.S. Peter threatened Phil's life if he refused to cooperate.

4. Local police or narcs. Motive: Check up on drug deals in the house and Phil's influence on the kids who hung out there.

5. Federal Watergate-type agents, including FBI and CIA. Phil stated in a June 1973 letter to the *Alien Critic* fanzine:

An article in the June 11th [1973] Newsweek let the American public in on what may be the most dismal and horrifying aspect of all this: that in the years 1970, 1971 and 1972 (and possibly now) a secret national police, operating outside the law, existed in this country, probably under the jurisdiction of the Internal Security Division of the Justice Department; it acted against the so-called "radicals," that is, the left, the anti-war people; it struck them again and again, covertly, everywhere, in a variety of ugly ways: break-ins, wire-tapping, entrapment . . . all with the idea of getting or forging evidence which would send these anti-war radicals to prison.

Consider the testimony of fellow SF writer Norman Spinrad, who was close to Phil throughout the seventies:

Everything Phil thought about the government always turned out to be true. Anybody who really saw what was going on in the early Seventies would be regarded as paranoid and crazy until Watergate broke.

Phil told me another "paranoid" story. He said, "These guys called me up from a Stanford University radio station, came down and asked me all these weird questions. Then when I called Stanford I found out the radio station didn't exist." Sounds like more Phil paranoia, *except* the two guys had done the same thing to me. Got a call from a Stanford radio station and two guys showed up and took me to dinner, asked me things like is Chip Delany [Samuel R. Delany, a black SF writer active in the antiwar effort] the illegitimate son of Philip K. Dick, a rumor I'd never heard but they'd gotten from God knows where, and about drug habits . . . all this shit. I'm sure they were agents for some agency.

Consider too that Phil later confided to friend Doris Sauter that he *emphasized* the government break-in theory in order to fend off the IRS—after all, his checks and financial records had been stolen. Phil told Doris he'd deny this if she told it to anyone else.

6. Drug-crazed rip-off artists. To Williams, Phil speculated: "There were so many feuds going on in my circle that my friends who looked at it thought it was other friends of mine who had done it."

7. The police theory that Phil did it himself. Phil vehemently denied this on many occasions: He had no insurance, why rip himself off? One possible motive: to destroy financial records of use to the IRS. To fifth wife Tessa, Phil conceded that he *might* have done it himself, either in a fit of craziness or as a result of *Manchurian Candidate*–style hypnotic suggestion. In A Scanner Darkly, Fred the narc unknowingly narcs on himself.

8. Military intelligence. Had certain ideas in his SF come too close to the truth, eliciting interest in his files? Also, a disorientation drug (code name "mello jello") had been stolen from the army, which was looking for leads to recover it. Peter (see theory 3) might have been an intelligence agent.

Granted, the who and why of the break-in remain a mystery. But certain of the above theories do suffer from serious gaps in credibility and logic. The CIA and/or the FBI and/or right-wingers and/or military intelligence would all have been willing and capable of committing the burglary *if* they believed that they would find something of value. Phil's failure to ever pose a reasonable conjecture (traces of "mello jello"? believe it if you will) as to what this might have been casts serious doubt on all of these theories. As for religious fanatics hoping to learn of Bishop Pike's researches, their motive is somewhat more credible, but why would they carry off Phil's canceled checks? The black militants theory seems dubious, given Phil's false attribution of Black Panther status to his neighbor Honor Jackson. One might wonder if there were any black militants in the vicinity who knew or cared about Phil's existence. If they wished to drive him out of the neighborhood, why focus on the particular destruction of his files?

The theory that Phil did it himself is hands down the most intriguing, but Phil certainly never knew it if he did—his letters and journals, as well as the very private *Exegesis*, are filled with fearful speculations as to who it might have been, and he was not one of his own prime suspects. Phil was many things, but very seldom a hypocrite, especially not to himself. Readers of A *Scanner Darkly* (see Chapter 9) can find, in the Fred/Bob mind split, a dramatic exploration of this theory. At one point, Fred/Bob reasons: "One of the most effective forms of industrial or military sabotage limits itself to damage that can never be thoroughly proven. [. . .] the person begins to assume he's paranoid and has no enemy; he doubts himself."

By this tally, the "local police" and "drug-crazed rip-off artist" theories are the most plausible (and, alas, the most mundane). Police have been known to search for drugs—or tips leading to drug dealers—without warrants, and drug users have been known to ransack without reason. Then again, the FBI and the CIA have been known to search for "incriminating" or "dangerous" materials that do not really exist.

Or perhaps the true solution is "none of the above."

In any event, a bare recitation of these theories does little justice to the fervor with which Phil recounted them. Tim Powers, who met Phil in 1972, writes that "Phil had recently bought the Stones' album *Sticky Fingers* [. . .] and I still can't hear 'Sister Morphine' or 'Moonlight Mile' without instantly being back in that living room, me pouched in an old brown-vinyl beanbag chair and Phil on the couch, the bottle on the table between us, Phil frowning as he decided how much of some awful story he dared reveal to me ('and if I told you the rest of it, Powers, you'd go crazy')."

Whatever high drama the break-in provided in years to come, life was grim enough in the days and weeks after it. In his journals, Phil managed to find *one* silver lining: "The No[vember] 17 hit didn't *cause* me to think someone was after me. It *confirmed* it: I thought when I saw it, 'At least I'm not paranoid.' " But overall, the journal traces a chronology of woe.

Shortly after the event, Sheila came back to visit. Phil pleaded with her to sleep with him; he wanted only to be hugged. After their one night together, she left. The next day was: "Entropy day. Disorientation. End of world." Later: "Day after day, alone, I know someone, at night, is going to get me. Isolation. No one comes by or calls." Sandy, Donna, Sheila . . . none was there for Phil in the aftermath. But he continued to love them, despite their refusal to play mother:

> When you lose someone you love, like when a mother animal, a cat, loses her kittens, she runs out into the forest & grabs some first small other living helpless dependent thing to give her milk to—that's what I was doing after Nancy & Isa left. But I craved it for myself, with growing intensity. I had lost my love—I wanted to give, & hug something else to me & protect it. [Donna and Sheila and Sandy] felt this, & got this from me. But a reversal of the roles was intolerable, totally threatening, to all three [. . .]

Fate, at once cruel and kind, intervened. Phil was invited to attend the Vancouver SF Con in February 1972 as guest of honor. Normally travel wouldn't have held much appeal. But with nights filled with fear, a get-the-hell-out all-expenses-paid trip to Vancouver had its charms. Phil bought a ticket for Donna, who promised to accompany him. He then set to work on a speech, "The Android and the Human"—his first sustained writing since Nancy had left. He dedicated it to Donna, and planned to kiss her upon delivering it to the Con audience. But at the last minute Donna traded in her ticket for cash; she hadn't traveled much, and she was afraid.

Just before the trip, there was a brief respite, all the more welcome for being unexpected. Phil paid a visit to Anne at Point Reyes Station for the purpose of seeing Laura and his three stepdaughters. During the visit Phil broke down into tears and Anne comforted him. For the first time since 1964, kind feelings passed between them. This was, in truth, an isolated instance; Phil could never bring himself to forgive Anne for the failings he saw in her. But her kindness at this point was a balm for which he was intensely grateful.

Phil flew up to Canada alone, carrying a battered suitcase, a rumpled trench coat, and a Bible. The Santa Venetia house with broken back windows for easy illicit entry went into foreclosure. Soon after, Phil's remaining possessions were ripped off.

Hard, strange times. And no Donna to set reality straight.

In Canada, alone, Phil tried his hardest to die.

9 Contemplating Suicide In A Foreign Land, Phil Decides Instead To Commence A New Life From The Bottom Up, Kicks The Amphetamine Urge, Finds A New Wife In Orange County, Writes A Tragic Classic On The Drug Culture, And Concludes That Reality Is "Amazingly Simple" Just As His Life Is Turned Upside Down Once More (1972-1974)

They think I'm weird, Carol. That probably surprises you. Weird sexy Phil, they call me. There are no psychiatrists here, so I can't go see anybody; I just bop around getting weirder all the time. Gradually everybody is beginning to realize that despite my fame and my great books I am a distinct liability to know or have anything at all to do with.

PHIL, in black humor mode, in March 1972 letter from Vancouver to
Carol Carr

I live a straight life now; no one here [in Orange County] knows that I was once a hippie doper (as they would put it) . . . and yet I grieve for the loss of my former wife and the child of that marriage, whom I would very much like to see but can't. Anyhow Tessa and I will soon have a new baby [. . .] and it is my hope that the solution to the death of the old life-pattern and elements (if there is one) lies mainly in the forming of new.

PHIL, July 1973 letter

I have already said a great deal about him, and can only add that we had a mad, romantic love affair that nearly killed us both. Phil was no saint, and he could be very cruel at times, but he loved me more than Dante loved Beatrice, and I fear that is something I will never find again.

TESSA DICK, letter to the author

PHIL arrived in Vancouver on February 16, 1972, and found himself, to his evident delight, a feted Con guest of honor.

Within two hours of his arrival, Phil had settled into his hotel room and gone out to visit a cabaret. The next day, the University of British Columbia held a posh Faculty Club luncheon in his honor, at which his speech "The Android and the Human" was received enthusiastically— as it would be by the Con audience two days later. Mike Bailey, the Con organizer who accompanied Phil on his rounds, was surprised by Phil's energy, as Phil had confided to him, during a low moment the first night in, that he didn't expect to live long or ever to write another book.

At the Con the next day, Phil mingled madly, focusing on the women. All vied to make the acquaintance of the SF legend of whom strange tales were told. By the end of day one, Phil was telling folks that he'd decided to stay on. The *Vancouver Provence* ran this proud headline: "Canada Gains a Noted Science Fiction Writer."

"Android," Phil's full-house speech, was his conscious effort "to sum up an entire life-time of developing thought." At the time he thought it was his most important work; then again, he said the same of *Flow*, *Scanner*, and *Valis* just after completing them. "Android" evokes the sixties' impatient transformative *Zeitgeist*, and it's a vital document for anyone seeking to understand Phil. But "Android" is also a roller coaster taking the reader from brilliant heights of insight to vertiginous depths of naïveté.

The speech began with a fine turnabout of the basic cybernetics premise that useful comparisons can be made between human and machine behavior: "[S]uppose a study of ourselves, our own nature, enables us to gain insight into the now extraordinary complex functioning and malfunctioning of mechanical and electronic constructs?" This brought Phil to a question always at the heart of his fiction: "what is it, in our behavior, that we can call specifically human?" Distinguishing the "android" and the "human" was difficult because "inauthentic human activity has become a science of government and such-like agencies, now." In opposition to such Orwellian manipulation, Phil set his hope in the youth. He even prophesied *Scanner:* "These kids, that I have known, lived with, still know, in California, are my science fiction stories of tomorrow [. . .]" What Phil valued in them was not the street protest of the sixties: "[P]olitically active youth, those who organize into distinct societies with banners and slogans—to me, that is a reduction into the past, however revolutionary these slogans may be. I refer to the intrinsic entities, the kids each of whom is on his own, doing what we call 'his thing.' " They rebelled "out of what might be called pure selfishness."

If androidization meant predictability and obedience, the "sheer perverse malice" of youth was the paradoxical guarantor of ultimate values. "If, as it seems, we are in the process of becoming a totalitarian society [. . .] the ethics most important for the survival of the true, human individual would be: cheat, lie, evade, fake it, be elsewhere, forge documents, build improved electronic gadgets in your garage that'll outwit the gadgets used by the authorities." Phil conceded that his faith in youth might be wishful thinking, and he spoke out against the menace of street drugs; while he hadn't yet given up amphetamines (inhaling, during Con rounds, speed mixed into menthol nose drops), he had abandoned all romanticism as to drug explorations.

But the speech concluded with the story of how Donna stole cases of Coke from a truck, drank them down with her friends, then returned the empties for deposit refunds. Phil allowed that this was "ethically question- able," but defended it as "truly human: in that it shows, to me, a spirit of merry defiance, of spirited, although not spiritual, bravery and unique- ness." This was less political oratory than it was an impassioned love letter to Donna. And, like most love letters, it translates badly into sound general advice. One person's righteous rip-off is another person's tragic loss, and Coke trucks are driven by people with families and bills to pay.

On the final day of the Con, Phil met "Andrea," a college student in her early twenties who was the same physical type as Nancy and Don- na. An account of Phil's falling in love with Andrea is included in *The Dark-Haired Girl*, a manuscript he assembled in late 1972 and described, on its title page, as "A collection of personal letters and dreams which undertake the worthy artistic task of depicting what is fine and noble in humanity, found sometimes in the worst possible places, but still real, still shining." *The Dark-Haired Girl* (p. 1988) in- cludes breathtaking love letters, the sentiments of sonnets rendered in on- rushing prose as Phil falls in and out of love with Donna, Andrea, and others. Years later, upon rereading the manuscript, Phil observed in the *Exegesis:* "In 'TDHG' it is evident that I am desperately trying to find a center (omphalos) for/to my life, but that I was failing; I was still 'stateless.' "

Phil was serious about staying in Vancouver. Back in California, his home was being foreclosed on and his friends were scattered. He was truly stateless. Here at least he had adoring fans and a new woman to himself adore.

The account in *The Dark-Haired Girl* of his time with Andrea bears out the intensity of his search for new roots. At first, Phil was enchanted by the look that had drawn him to so many women: "[S]he's so pretty, with her long black hair and her jeans and her fur coat—and so self- conscious. So at bay. So fragile and brittle, but so full of life and ambition and guts." Andrea was from the sparsely populated coastland north of Vancouver; she confided to Phil that she yearned to leave the city and go back home, though her family life was troubled. One night they went out dancing and had an "ecstatic time," losing themselves utterly in the music. Phil saw her to her door, went home, and had a dream that obsessed him for years to come:

I was back in West Marin, in the big glass-walled living room [of the house he and Anne shared], with friends and animals and children. Suddenly I looked up and saw, through the glass side of the house, a horse coming at me, head on, driven by a rider [a policeman]; it was virtually on me, about to shatter the glass. I've never seen or dreamed such an animal before: its thin body, elongated, pumping legs, goggling eyes—like a racehorse, swift and furious and silent it came at me, and then it leaped up to hurdle the house . . . I crouched down, waiting for it to crash onto the roof above me and collapse the house. Impossible for it to clear. But it did. [. . .] I ran out front, knowing it must have hit dirt cataclysmically. There it was, thrashing in the mud and foliage, broken and mutilated, horrible. [. . .]

Phil pondered the dream. As a well-versed Jungian, he likely knew that the horse often symbolizes the "life force" and is linked to the "masculine solar deities" and heroes (in Greek mythology, Apollo, Bellerophon, Perseus). Phil's early interpretation was that the rider-policeman referred to his past misunderstandings with the law, while the leaping horse symbolized Andrea's unhappy state and Phil's inability to help her harness the "life force." Then Andrea told Phil that she was leaving Vancouver, returning to her backcountry home *immediately*. Like Donna, Andrea was scared: of Vancouver, of college, of Phil. And Phil, heartbroken, revised his interpretation: "Andrea has left. Goodbye, Andrea. I am that broken horse."

In the days after the Con, with his expenses no longer reimbursed, Phil needed an interim place to stay while looking for his own apartment. Michael and Susan Walsh agreed to put him up on their living-room couch. Michael was a reporter from the *Vancouver Provence* who had favorably covered the "Android" speech; Susan, an SF fan, found Phil "weird but fascinating." Both welcomed the chance to get to know him better. He was a constant improviser. "Everything was put on," Susan recalls. "Phil was always onstage, even with people he could be sure were with him." In his beard and rumpled trench coat, he grunted: "Me Sam Spade." His tour de force performance came during a sales call by a Kirby vacuum cleaner salesman named (yes) Frank Noseworthy. Says Susan:

Phil set up the scenario. He would be my brother—a writer who was sponging off us—and Michael was my husband—too cheap to buy this expensive vacuum cleaner. When Frank Noseworthy arrived, he started to pleasantly explain the virtues of the Kirby. Then he made a reference to the cleanliness of the house—"if you want to continue living in these conditions"—and that set Phil off.

There was this escalating family argument, with asides by Phil like "Isn't it wonderful to realize that in hundreds of years we'll be dust, but this Kirby will live on?" Frank Noseworthy did not crack a smile. His complete lack of affect delighted and appalled Phil, who had studied these kinds of sales techniques and knew how best to disrupt them. And so he would wander in and out of the room during his pitch and start side conversations about the price of tomatoes.

Phil and Susan developed a flirtation and, briefly, she fell in love with him, though there was no infidelity. Why the attraction to Phil? "I still haven't figured it out. He was intellectually fascinating, cynical, entertaining, and bizarre—a puzzle." But during Phil's two-week stay, Susan came to see a darker side: manipulative, controlling, probing the weak spots of others' psyches. His mood swings were pronounced, and he described himself as manic-depressive. To friends of Michael and Susan's Phil complained of wrongdoing on their part, which, when relayed back to them, bore no relation to events they could recall. He flirted with virtually every woman who came his way, trying all approaches from flattery to piteous declarations of need. Phil finally decided that Michael wasn't good enough for Susan and pledged to take better care of her—which Susan resented. And Michael, who had handled Phil's flirtations with good grace, now grew weary: "Phil lived at a higher level of intensity than anyone I had ever met. He insisted that you be a participant in his world, rather than merely tolerate its existence. I didn't want to."

The hallmark of Phil's intensity during this period was his capacity to fall in and out of love at a vertiginous rate. The strain he placed upon others—in this case, Michael and Susan Walsh—was relatively mild compared to the sufferings he heaped upon himself. In asking for love at every turn, he was living out his sense of being "stateless" by posing impossible emotional demands that, when duly refused, would cause him heartbreak. Phil's statelessness had less to do with being in Canada than with being without a wife. Since losing Nancy he had never stopped falling in love. That the pace should accelerate in a foreign land is hardly surprising.

Phil found new digs. But within a short time he became disenchanted with his new Canadian acquaintances. They were mostly in their thirties, "career-oriented." The Vietnam conflict that had polarized political consciousness in the U.S. hardly mattered in Vancouver. In early March Phil wrote to inquire if he could live at Center Point, an open clinic in the Bay Area he'd dropped by during the final months in Santa Venetia; the Center Point recommendation was that he should not. Phil also wrote to Professor Willis McNelly at Cal State Fullerton, who had interviewed Phil shortly after the break-in, to inquire if Fullerton would be a good place to relocate. On March 14 he canceled plane reservations for San Francisco, then wrote to Ursula Le Guin (with whom he had struck up a correspondence, though they had never met) to

191

suggest that he visit her in Portland. Phil suspected—accurately, Le Guin confirms—that outlandish tales had preceded him, and tried to reassure her: "In spite of the trauma of my move here to Vancouver, my head is really in a pretty good place; I'm not nearly so spaced as I was back in December. I swear I can conduct a civilized, rational conversation, without breaking anybody's favorite lamp. In fact, I would say I've got it all together pretty good, everything considered; my identity crisis seems to be ending."

Sadly, it wasn't. After the loss of Andrea, Donna, Sheila, Nancy, of his entire Bay Area world, Phil fell into the tomb world. Later, to fifth wife Tessa, Phil told of Mafia types in black suits who put him in the back of a limousine and drove him around for hours asking questions he couldn't remember. In all: a two-week gap in memory. As he emerged, he was committing suicide.

The scene was his newly rented, nearly empty Vancouver apartment on March 23. Phil took 700 mg of potassium bromide, a sedative. On a piece of cardboard he had written the emergency number of a suicide-prevention center in case—at the last moment—he changed his mind. "Fortunately the last number was a one," he said later, "and I could just barely dial it."

Before that final digit, Phil had already phoned Susan Walsh to inform her that he planned to "turn out the lights." Susan was unfamiliar with this slang and had no idea that Phil was thinking suicide; meanwhile, Phil was infuriated by her lack of sympathy. In an interview for Vertex, Phil omitted this prior call but told of talking by phone to a counselor for "an hour and a half" (typical of Phil's frequent interview hyperbole—ninety minutes of talk on 700 mg of potassium bromide? No ambulance called by a trained counselor in all that time?). "[The counselor] finally said, 'Here is what is the matter. You have nothing to do; you have no purpose; you came up here and you gave your speeches and now you're sitting in your apartment. You don't need psychotherapy. You need purposeful work.' " And so Phil was taken to X-Kalay, a live-in drug and alcohol rehabilitation center run along the same strict community-within-a-community/hard-work/cold-turkey rules as the onetime Synanon drug treatment center in Los Angeles. Phil told Vertex that to get into X-Kalay ("The hidden path"), he had to pretend he was a heroin addict. "I did a lot of method acting, like almost attacking the staff member interviewing me, so they never doubted that I was an addict." Trained experts taking Phil for a junkie? Heroin was one drug Phil never did mess with. A late-March letter gives a far more somber account:

[. . .] I was really down. The next day or so I had a total freakout, breakdown, identity crisis, psychotic break, convulsion of misery and just general bad time. Now I'm part of X-Kalay; they came in and scooped up the puddle of ooze from the floor of my apartment that was me, or what remained of me, carted me to their house where they—and now I—live, put me to work, put my head back together enough so I didn't try to snuff myself every half hour, kept someone with me night and day . . . and finally, a week later, I'm again beginning to function. For one week I cleaned bathrooms, washed pots and pans, fed the children—there're chicks, dudes and children living together, here—and now I have my own office, typewriter, back at work for the first time in a long while, at writing [PR material for X-Kalay]. [. . .] As you recall, the friends I had that last year in San Rafael led me down and down into the gutter with them; I got started up here in Vancouver with the same kind of bumtrippers, and went the same way fast. X-Kalay cut me off from those people: no phone calls, no visitors, nada. Complete break with my past, the outside world, my alleged friends. There are only two rules here at X-Kalay: No intoxicants and no violence. Those were the two evil verities of my former life; right? Right. I at last have a home, a real home, a family, a real family, and am beginning to develop a meaningful, goal-oriented life.

In the discussion group "attack-therapy games," X-Kalay residents and staff confronted each other no holds barred. In Phil's case, aside from the obvious drug problem, one issue raised repeatedly was his tropism for dark-haired girls. "It's a moving, incredible experience to feel and see the people here [. . .] insert themselves between me and the reality I seek out that kills me. They forcibly stop me from doing what I've been doing. 'You fucking asshole,' they yell at me. 'You dingbat. You like incest? You enjoy screwing your daughter?' "

Phil knew that a "self-destructive drive" lay within him, and was capable, for a time, of enduring extreme abuse (as did all residents) for the sake of coming to grips with it. In the meantime, he developed close friendships within the X-Kalay community. The agony of the young heroin addicts—who seemed to have aged by decades, with bleak pallors and glazed eyes—lingered nightmarishly in Phil's memory.

But Phil's X-Kalay stay lasted only three weeks; its demands began to grate on him as he recovered from the lost weeks in Vancouver. In an April letter, Phil—who, after all, was not a heroin addict—focused on the limitations of X-Kalay life:

The problem here, I think, is that there is so much aggression, so much hostility, sadism and general anti-social violence in these people—most of them have served term after term in Canadian federal prisons—that all emotional and physical expressions must be rigidly disciplined out of them during the normal course of the day, and then released verbally in the game [. . .] And, in the game, accusations really pathological in intensity and nature, are unleashed. [. . .] They guess every possibility, scent out every twist imaginable. They can only score when you respond with the sort of sniv[e]ling freakout "You've got me" look. [. . .] They have not guessed what you are; they have guessed what you *fear*. [. . .] He [the X-Kalay resident] is not broken

193

down into nothing and then rebuilt; the new personality is erected on his fantasy worst self.

Similar criticisms were leveled at Synanon during its heyday in the early seventies. To give X-Kalay (which went out of existence in 1976) its due, it succeeded in making Phil realize the deadly folly of his amphetamine usage. Never again did Phil take speed on a regular basis—this after nearly twenty years of steadily increasing doses.

During Phil's X-Kalay stay, Professor McNelly at Cal State Fullerton read aloud to his class Phil's letters detailing his desire for a new home. This prompted two female students to write, offering to take Phil in as a roommate; a third, Linda Levy, wrote to offer her friendship. In addition, Professor McNelly suggested that the university library might serve as a repository for those of Phil's papers and SF pulp collections that had survived the break-in.

Phil was on his way. In mid-April he flew from Canada to Fullerton, near Los Angeles, in the heart of Orange County, California—one of the most stolidly conservative areas in all of America. The airport greeting committee consisted of his two new roommates plus Linda Levy, a dark-haired-girl type, with whom Phil promptly fell in love, and Tim Powers, then a neophyte SF writer in his early twenties, who would remain one of Phil's closest friends. Phil arrived in Sam Spade trench coat with Bible in hand (in hopes of placating the ominous customs officials) and a suitcase tied shut with an extension cord. That first night, as Phil stared at Linda rapturously, they drove to Norman Spinrad's place in the Hollywood Hills and talked over his stay at X-Kalay.

Phil spent only a short time with his initial two roommates. Life on a living-room couch and high-pitched squabbles over money and household chores led Phil to find a more conventional living arrangement, sharing an apartment with a young man named Joel Stein, with whom Phil enjoyed peaceful relations. Not that melodrama was lacking—Phil carried on wildly over a number of women he had just met, especially Linda. There were no street drugs in the apartment, but there was Dean Swift snuff aplenty. The household ran on a careful budget. They joked, when the money ran low, that they'd have to eat poor old Fred, the rat that lived under the sink (a joke Phil included in *Scanner*). But in Phil's more somber moods, as Tim Powers writes:

[. . .] he was rootless, scared and in hiding. He was kept awake by the quiet sound of cars with ominously powerful engines prowling very slowly down his street in the middle of the night, he noticed two-way radios in parked cars and became alarmed if there was a greater-than-average number of them near his apartment, and he had to buy a fresh copy of the *I Ching* because his old copy was falling to bits under the stress of all the late nights when he'd be up shaking and throwing the three pennies, asking frightened questions and getting unreassuring answers; something big, something mysterious, had passed by close enough to put him in its shade, and he couldn't stop thinking about it, couldn't stop trying to figure out exactly what had happened.

For his first few months in Fullerton, Phil kept his new address—3028 Quartz Lane—secret from even close Bay Area friends.

Their apartment-building neighbors included two young women, Mary Wilson and Merry Lou Malone, with whom Phil struck up close friendships. Mary Wilson, like Powers, remained close to Phil for the rest of his life. This social whirl was just the thing for Phil, despite the twenty-year difference between himself and his new friends. He wasn't writing during this period. Simple rest and recuperation was what he needed, and contact with the young was always Phil's preferred mode of casting sorrows and worries aside.

Not that his age didn't show itself in some respects. Phil was overweight and subject to coughing fits, and he wasn't always up to the pace of college kids. But, broke as he was at the time, Phil's economics did mesh with theirs nicely. Gas was cheap, and they could all go to the beach or for coffee and pie on Hollywood Boulevard.

Merry Lou, then in her late teens, recalls that Phil "had a lost-puppy quality. But he was also very protective of me, and he was always looking for something new—the answer." Phil seemed always infatuated: "He loved being miserable about women. He was my mother's age, but he seemed younger than me in some ways."

Phil was attracted to Mary Wilson and even asked her to marry him, but their relationship remained platonic. Phil could turn to her in the midst of days-long depressions. Mary recalls:

> Phil had depressed times, but I would say he was basically happy. He was a moody person, but I wouldn't put up with it. I'd say, "Knock this off or I'm going home," and he would. He fell in and out of love with women a lot. He was on the rebound from any one of us—pick one.

Phil's one-sided love for Linda Levy was the strongest of all his infatuations during his early months in Fullerton. Her resemblance to Linda Ronstadt, whose looks and singing voice Phil adored (the singer Linda Fox in *The Divine Invasion* is in part a tribute to Ronstadt), must have contributed to her sway over him. Linda could never reciprocate his serious feelings, and they did not become lovers. Linda saw in Phil a strangely moody man old enough to be her father. But she was also fascinated by Phil's brilliant talk and relished the opportunity to mingle in his SF circles. And she recalls: "I was addicted to Phil's flattery. He was the first person who reinforced the things I hoped were true about myself."

A glance at Phil's first love letter to Linda, preserved in *The Dark-*

Haired Girl, makes her addiction understandable. What rapturous flights! Phil's loved one becomes the Ubik that holds it all together. If something bad happened to Linda,

> My books would become more weird, more tired, more empty. [. . .] I'd walk through the side of a building and it'd collapse into dust. Wheels would fall off cars, like in an old W. C. Fields movie. Finally my foot would sink through the sidewalk. Do you see what you mean to us, Linda? Can you dig it? Because if you can't, then I just don't the hell know what I'm going to do. I just can't stand the thought of you sitting somewhere alone with the notion that nobody cares about you. We LOVE you.

The letter concludes with a proposal of marriage. Phil, who had known Linda only a few days, handed it to her as she was driving them to meet Harlan Ellison and his date for dinner. Linda didn't read it until they were in the restaurant. On the one hand, it was glorious praise. On the other: "It freaked me out—I did not know what to do with myself." Ellison sensed the tension and baited them. An argument ensued. Linda recalls: "Phil scared the shit out of me—he was so intense. He thought I wasn't taking his proposal seriously. Later he said he didn't really want to marry me, he just asked because I'd told him nobody ever had before."

Phil and Linda's relationship continued on its difficult course for some weeks. Linda enjoyed going out on the town with Phil, who delighted in the company of a beautiful young woman. But Linda's flirtatiousness frustrated Phil, and she teased him by finding things in his beard. In late April the SF Nebula Awards were held in Los Angeles. Phil and Linda decided to visit Linda's family prior to the banquet. Phil fell silent with her mother, then played catch outdoors with her younger sister. In trying to demonstrate a major-league pitching style, he fell to the ground in howling pain, having dislocated the shoulder he had injured in his 1964 auto accident. With his arm in a sling for weeks thereafter, Phil worried over the figure he cut in her company. The couples counseling sessions Phil convinced Linda to attend with him helped little.

Finally, one night as they were driving, Linda informed Phil that she had made a date with Norman Spinrad. Phil never bore any animosity toward Spinrad, who was unaware of the depth of Phil's feelings. But the news, that night, devastated him. Recalls Linda: "He went into a physical withdrawal, shoulders up, head down in crotch, knees up, didn't speak. I'd never seen anybody do that before—I was ill-equipped to deal with that." To make matters worse, they pulled into a gas station where the attendant was a guy with whom Linda also had an upcoming date. As they drove off, Phil grabbed the wheel with his good arm, swerving them into oncoming traffic. Linda regained control, pulled over, and ordered Phil out. In the shouting match, Phil employed what Linda remembers as "incredibly creative" invective and then began punching her in the face. The blows caused no great physical harm, but they ended the relationship.

The bitterness lingered. When Tim Powers began dating Linda, Phil's implacable hostility led to a temporary breach of that friendship. Phil and Linda did at last reestablish relations, albeit guardedly. Some weeks later, Phil introduced Linda to a friend (possibly his fifth wife, Tessa) as "the girl I was in love with until she beat me up."

Phil had always required a woman's love to make the world truly real. His courtship tactic of the past two years—a relentless romantic search-and-self-destroy mission—had left him frustrated and humiliated often enough, but it may also have kept him sane and whole. For the alternative, solitude, was literally unbearable to him. After four failed marriages, Phil had learned lessons aplenty, but none that could dissuade him from trying matrimony again, if only he was given the chance.

Phil met Tessa Busby at a party in mid-July of 1972. Tessa was eighteen and planned to attend junior college in the fall to study electronics. Shy but intelligent, Tessa had her own writerly ambitions. And, like Phil, she had survived a difficult childhood, which included physical abuse.

At the party, Tessa accepted a dare (issued by Phil's disinterested date of the evening) to sit on Phil's lap. Tessa writes that Phil "seemed more withdrawn than I was. He had sad, puppy-dog eyes, and seemed to have his tail tucked between his legs, like a dog after a scolding." Each was powerfully drawn to the other, though Phil later confided to Tessa that he had feared she was an agent for the organization behind the November 1971 break-in. His fears could not have been too great, however, for within a week, Phil had rented the apartment next door to serve as their new home.

Tessa was delighted by the range and sparkle of Phil's talk. "In his own circle, his light shone like the sun." There were no ideas his imagination could not enliven. "Phil entertained me, so long as I kept the coffee and sandwiches coming." Their Quartz Lane apartment became Phil's first true home since Nancy's departure two years earlier. As the arm healed, as domesticity took hold, the writing would flow again.

There came an early crisis—where else but at Disneyland? They were on a date, accompanied by friends. Phil ran out of money and asked Tessa for a loan. Low on funds herself, Tessa gave him two of her seven dollars. Phil was humiliated when, later that evening, he couldn't afford to buy a hot chocolate for her. Tessa writes:

> He blamed me for not giving him the five. As soon as I finished my drink, Phil got up and trotted out to the parking lot. I followed him, with the rest of our group close behind.
>
> When I found Phil, he was sitting on the hood of the car (not his; he had no car). He looked dark. He refused to talk, and glared at me. I sat down beside

him. The rest came up and started asking Phil what was wrong. Although I didn't fully understand, I knew enough to tell them to leave him alone. I took his hand and sat there quietly till he stood up.

That brief, puzzling crisis provided the moment in which we bonded. [. . .] Instinctively, without any idea what was coming down, I had done the right thing.

Phil's joy in the relationship is evident in this passage from *The Dark-Haired Girl*:

Tess is a little black-haired chick, exactly like I'm not supposed to get involved with (according to X-Kalay), eighteen, who writes (she's sold an article already), pretty and bright, very tomboyish but sexy, small, talks weird, sort of straight, politically uncommitted, rides horses, has never traveled, wants to see Canada. [. . .] My friends call me "Mr. Domestic." It's cool. The thing that's so great about Tess is that she doesn't lay any trips on me that aren't my own. And yet we're quite close. She's the most empathic person I've ever encountered: wise and gentle, but independent. And tactful.

But, as Tessa says, "Life with Phil was a roller coaster." There were, for example, the ongoing revelations: Phil was in his forties, not his late thirties; Nancy had been his fourth, not first, wife; a twin sister had died in infancy (this revelation prompted by Phil's shock upon learning that Tessa had almost been named Jane). And on November 17, 1972 (the first anniversary of the break-in), "Phil went bonkers, and made *sure* every door and window was locked, and would *not* leave the house, or let me leave."

There were also Phil's moods. Tessa notes: "One moment he was calm, happy, the next he was frantic. [. . .] His mood swings were more like a child's temper tantrums than the wild ravings of a lunatic. He became childlike during manic episodes, and he needed motherly nursing when he was depressed." Phil's agoraphobia often confined him to the house, and even to the bedroom. Comforted by the security of marriage, Phil did manage to resume regular writing efforts. But his daily schedule challenged them both. "He slept very little. He stayed up well past midnight, and insisted that I serve breakfast no later than 7:30 A.M. I had to be asleep by 11:00 in order to get up that early, while Phil would stay up till 2:00 A.M. and even longer. He usually woke up before 6:00 A.M." Tessa was supportive but did not lack an assertive nature of her own:

Phil, when he could not convince me by argument, would sometimes stamp his feet, tear open his shirt—buttons flying everywhere—or stomp off and throw himself on the bed. Sometimes he needed to be held, even rocked, and talked to soothingly. He often demanded all his meals in bed. He had to show me everything he wrote, and I had to read it NOW, not a minute from now.

He had no patience. Often, he would snap his fingers to get my attention; this infuriated me. NOBODY snaps his fingers at *me*.

Unfortunately, Phil did more, at times, than snap his fingers. There were episodes of physical violence that left Tessa bruised and emotionally shaken. Linda Levy, herself the victim of an assault by Phil, writes that, early on in the relationship, "Tessa showed up at my apartment one day, covered with bruises, crying and very upset. She described a situation in which, she said, Phil locked the front door, turned up the stereo, turned on the air conditioning, and beat her. She managed to get out after I don't know what period of time, and came to us, she said for help." Linda recommended that Tessa "get out," but this advice was not taken. "Instead," Linda continues, "according to Phil because I never heard anything about this from Tessa, she came home and told him that she had visited us and shared with us her love for him, and we had spontaneously, for some reason, decided to try and turn her against him. Of course, no mention of her obvious physical condition."

Now and then Phil and Tessa went out into the world. Together they attended the Los Angeles Worldcon in September 1972; Phil took part in panel discussions on the state of SF. In October, a former girlfriend brought her new boyfriend by—an honest-to-God narc! Phil, already conceiving the plot of *Scanner*, was both thrilled and terrified by the meeting. The narc, camouflaged by long hair and a flowered shirt, took the four of them for a wild drive and warned that he could bust any of them anytime he wanted. At evening's end he gave Phil his card.

That same October, Phil and Tessa flew to San Francisco for four days to finalize his divorce from Nancy. Custody of Isa was awarded to Nancy, and, given the geographical distance, Isa's young age, and recurrent tensions between the former spouses, Phil saw little of Isa until the late seventies, a situation that anguished him. Unlike in his dealings with Anne, Phil did make regular child-support payments to Nancy, at the $100-per-month rate specified by the court.

Despite two years of writing inactivity, Phil's career wasn't doing badly. Good news came in the form of a visit from his Paris-based editor, Patrice Duvic, whose Editions Opta had published most of Phil's work. (Steady foreign sales, particularly in France, England, and Germany, had supported Phil despite his failure to sell a new novel since 1970.) Duvic spoke of the possibility of a screenplay based on *Ubik*, which several French critics saw as a masterwork of pataphysique. Soon after, Phil was interviewed (along with Spinrad) on Los Angeles's KPFK FM. And there would be glowing mention of his work in Thomas Disch's anthology *The Ruins of Earth* and in Brian Aldiss's study of the SF genre, *Billion Year Spree*—both published in 1973.

Tessa and Phil discussed moving to Vancouver or to the Bay Area, but Fullerton continued its hold on them. As Phil deadpanned in a

December letter to Roger Zelazny: "There is nothing more reassuring to someone who's gone through an acute identity crisis than clean plastic apartments, streets, restaurants and furniture. Nothing gets old or worn or dirty here because if it does the police come in and kill it. I'm not sure if I have an identity again, or if I do if it's the same one (I suppose not to both questions)."

Then, in November, Phil learned that Stanislaw Lem had succeeded, after much struggle, in arranging for the publication in Poland of a translation of *Ubik*. The news thrilled Phil, who speculated that he might travel to Warsaw to make use of any captive royalties. The trip never materialized, but there was a brief correspondence between Phil and Lem. One topic was Lem's 1972 essay "Science Fiction: A Hopeless Case—With Exceptions," the exceptions being solely the works of Philip K. Dick. Phil explained the "trash" elements Lem had noted in his work:

> But you see, Mr. Lem, there is no culture here in California, only trash. And we who grew up here and live here and write here have nothing else to include as elements in our work; you can see this in ON THE ROAD [Phil had, earlier in the letter, stressed his literary affinity to the Beats]. I mean it. The West Coast has no tradition, no dignity, no ethics—this is where that monster Richard Nixon grew up. How can one create novels based on this reality which do not contain trash, because the alternative is to go into dreadful fantasies of what it *ought* to be like; one must work with the trash, pit it against itself, as you so aptly put it in your article. [. . .] Hence the elements in such books of mine as UBIK. If God manifested Himself to us here He would do so in the form of a spraycan advertised on TV.

(When *Ubik* was published in Poland in 1975, Phil was angered at what he saw as broken promises concerning royalties, and (unjustly) blamed Lem. Tit for tat, Phil lobbied for Lem's expulsion from the American-based Science Fiction Writers Association, on the grounds that Lem's honorary, nonpaying membership violated SFWA rules prohibiting honorary membership when a writer was eligible for a regular paying membership. Lem, by virtue of having published in the U.S., was so eligible. Phil was not alone in raising this objection—Lem had raised the ire of several SFWA members by his critical comments on American SF writers—and Lem's honorary membership was ultimately revoked.)

Now that he was settled in with Tessa, Phil's writing energies had returned, in late 1972, in full force for the first time in over two years. In November 1972, he wrote to Disch: "If [Tessa] didn't exist I would have had eventually to invent her, in order to survive; [. . .] My motive for once more writing is so that I can have something to dedicate to her."

His first project was the completion of *Flow My Tears, The Policeman Said*, which had lain unfinished since August 1970. After *Flow*, Phil wrote his first short story since 1969, "A Little Something for Us

Tempunanuts." Then it was on to *Scanner*—with just a brief time out for a brush with extinction. In late 1972 Phil contracted double pneumonia. Things looked so bad that "Death" thought to pay Phil a bedside visit:

> He wore a single-breasted plastic suit, a tie, and carried a sort of samplecase, which he opened to show me. In it he had several psychological tests, and he indicated to me that these tests showed that I was completely nuts and therefore ought to give up and go with him. I felt relief that he would take me somewhere else, because if I was completely nuts there was no point in my trying any more and wearing myself out, and I was really so damn tired. Death pointed to a rising road, up a long twisting hillside, and indicated to me that there was a mental hospital at the top of the hill there where I could go and be and take it easy and not have to try any more. He led me up the winding road toward it, higher and higher. And then all at once Tessa came back into the bedroom to see how I was, and instantly I was back in bed sitting up against my pillow, same as always. But I had really gone a long way before she came in and it ended. Later I realized that Death had lied to me. He told me what would cause me to go voluntarily with him. Another person, he would tell something else, whatever would do it. I didn't see him again, but now I know that Death lies to make his job easier. It's a lot easier for him if you go of your own free will. I still remember, though, what relief I felt to know I could give up. Nothing but relief. How willing I was. But, then, I believed him.

Death did indeed lie. Phil proceeded to write *A Scanner Darkly*, the definitive portrait of the sixties drug endgame. The addictive, brain-toxic drug Phil invented for *Scanner* is called "Substance D" or "Death." The overcoming of Death, the triumph of the spirit over lies that drain life of meaning, is the tale told.

◆

In music, you can form a perfect sixties syzygy with the Beatles and the Rolling Stones, the Beatles embodying the joyous dream that seemed not only possible but more *real* than reality, the Rolling Stones flashing the edge that the dream risk entailed.

In literature, you can fashion an equally telling sixties syzygy with Richard Brautigan's *Trout Fishing in America* and *A Scanner Darkly*. *Trout Fishing* catches the feel of the magic that people could pull, for a time, from the hat of daily life. The sixties provided the wildly colored backdrop, the spacy patter, and the spiritual suspense to make the magic work.

And *Scanner* lets you see and hear how cravings for drug-based special effects maimed and killed many who, as Phil wrote in his "Author's Note," were "like children playing in the street." He added: "I myself, I am not a character in the novel; I am the novel. So, though, was our entire nation at this time." Included in Phil's "Note" is a list of friends who died or suffered permanent injury through drug abuse; included is Phil himself, with "permanent pancreatic damage." Not all of his diagnoses of "permanent psychosis" are accurate, but there is death enough to make the point that "We were forced to stop by things dreadful."

Phil produced a first draft of *Scanner* from February to April of 1973, then revised intensively (with the valued assistance of editor Judy-Lynn Rey) in summer 1975. Phil then wrote to editor Lawrence Ashmead (whom he naïvely addressed as "Editor-in-Chief" when Ashmead worked only on Doubleday SF) *pleading* for the house to treat *Scanner* as mainstream. Indeed, *Scanner* has few SF trappings, and its 1994 Los Angeles is recognizably our own, down to 7-11s and freeway hassles. Not since *High Castle* had Phil's mainstream ambitions shown so fiercely. Ashmead recalls:

> Science fiction is very gutterized as pulp. I can remember trying to get people at Doubleday to read Philip K. Dick, and they'd say, "I don't read science fiction."
>
> I have always thought Phil's books will still be selling in forty years, which is probably not true for most of his contemporaries. I tried to get him out of science fiction, but there was just no way. They just didn't take the genre seriously, and they thought of it strictly as a library sale. It just wasn't a commercial reality.

The basic plot of *Scanner* is the decline into something near total brain death of Fred, an undercover narc who poses as Bob Arctor, a small-time dealer, to track down the ultimate suppliers of Death. There is one standout bit of SF tech: the "scramble suit" Fred wears for anonymity when reporting on Arctor and friends. As the dealers have their own antinarc undercover operatives in the police department, Fred must keep both his real Fred and alias Bob identities secret from both sides. The "scramble suit" (inspired by Phil's phosphene vision experiences of 2-3-74—see Chapter 10) is "a multifaceted quartz lens hooked to a miniaturized computer whose memory banks held up to a million and a half physiognomic fraction-representations of various people"; these rapid-fire images are projected onto a "shroudlike membrane" in human form, in which Fred is enclosed.

What drives a man to go into a line of work in which identity splitting is inevitable? In Fred's case, disgust with suburban life. Fred, a loyal cop, prefers the company of Death addicts to that of the Orange County Lions Club members whom he addresses on the evils of drugs. In this, Phil and Fred are one. Phil wrote in a September 1973 letter:

> During each marriage I was the bourgeois wage-earner, and when the marriage failed I dropped (gratefully) into the gutter of near-illegal life: narcotics and guns and knives and oh so many crimes . . . not so much that *I* did them

but that I surrounded myself with those who did; I embrace truly vicious people, I suppose as an antidote to the middle class safe rational spineless world my wives had forced on me. Cut loose from my children and wives I had no responsibilities to anyone but myself, and I wallowed in the gutter; and yet, to be fair to me, drew from that very gutter, lives of young people that might otherwise have been lost. [. . .] I am only out of there because once again I am married and must lock my door each night, lest some one rip off my valuables. I was happier living with those who ripped off (i.e. stole) valuables.

Phil exaggerates for effect here; he was never a "bourgois wage-earner," and he had no real desire to abandon the safe harbor of Tessa and their Fullerton home. But he had *felt* Fred/Bob's craving, and this spurred him to finish what he had begun with Felix Buckman in *Flow*: the creation of a fully sympathetic policeman protagonist. Fred's drive to escape the suburban void leads him to Death. He loves his fellow addicts even as they betray him by slipping him ever more Death. The result is toxic brain psychosis that severs the right and left hemispheres of the brain, terminating gestalt functions in the percept and cognitive systems.

It all adds up to this: Fred stops knowing who Bob is.

He narcs on himself. Listens disdainfully to the Holo-Scanner surveillance tapes of Bob and his friends babbling aimlessly. As the toxicity advances, the world grows ever more murky. His police superiors notice that all is not well and bring in Fred, clad in scramble suit, for testing—just a little too late. The brain hemispheres have begun to compete. And then all but the dimmest awareness fades away. Just before that final stage, Fred/Bob lives out the truth of Paul's words in 1 Corinthians by way of his Scanner self-surveillance:

> It is [the police psychologist explains] *as if one hemisphere of your brain is perceiving the world as reflected in a mirror.* [. . .]
> "Through a mirror," Fred said. A darkened mirror, he thought; a darkened scanner.

Scanner was wrung from late-sixties darkness, from Phil's times of hellish despair. Donna Hawthorne, an undercover cop who loves and betrays Fred/Bob, is based on the dark-haired Donna who saw Phil through hard times and let him go to Vancouver alone. Death addict Jerry Fabin, who cannot fight off the aphids, is drawn from Phil's Santa Venetia housemate Daniel. The maniacal Jim Barris, who may have slipped Fred/Bob the final Death overdose, is based on Peter, the ominous hanger-on whom Phil suspected of burglarizing his house. New-Path, the drug treatment center to which the husk of Fred/Bob is consigned, owes much to X-Kalay. In *Scanner*, New-Path is the clandestine supplier of Death.

203

The police, by contrast, are rendered nobly. Indeed, in February 1973 Phil wrote to the Department of Justice to offer his assistance in "the war against illegal drugs" because "drug-abuse is the greatest problem I know of, and I hope with all my heart to accomplish something in this novel in the fight against it." Phil even proposed to dedicate *Scanner* to Attorney General Richard Kleindienst—a remarkable exception to Phil's otherwise implacable opposition to the Nixon administration. But in daily life Phil adopted a less adamant approach to drugs, even smoking an occasional joint or bowl of hash.

In the service of its antidrug theme, *Scanner* nails down the hazy, twisting weirdness of sixties doper dialogue perfectly. In novels such as *The Soft Machine* and *The Wild Boys*, William Burroughs employs a junkie patois that is part forties Times Square, part private eye, part laconic Beat Burroughs. Vivid and sharp, but *not* the way it sounded at the time. What it did sound like, when the dream devoured itself, is Ernie Luckman explaining to Fred/Bob Arctor a new idea for smuggling dope:

> "Well, see, you take a huge block of hash and carve it in the shape of a man. Then you hollow out a section and put a wind-up motor like a clockworks in it, and a little cassette tape [. . .] and it walks up to the customs man, who says to it, 'Do you have anything to declare?' and the block of hash says, 'No, I don't,' and keeps on walking. Until it runs down on the other side of the border."
>
> "You could put a solar-type battery in it instead of a spring and it could keep walking for years. Forever."
>
> "What's the use of that? It'd finally reach either the Pacific or the Atlantic. In fact, it'd walk off the edge of the Earth, like—"
>
> "Imagine an Eskimo village, and a six-foot-high block of hash worth about—how much would that be worth?"
>
> "About a billion dollars."
>
> "More. Two billion."
>
> "These Eskimos are chewing hides and carving bone spears, and this block of hash worth two billion dollars comes walking through the snow saying over and over, 'No, I don't.' "
>
> "They'd wonder what it meant by that."
>
> "They'd be puzzled forever. There'd be legends."

After this strange colloquy, a silence. Then:

> "Bob, you know something . . ." Luckman said at last. "I used to be the same age as everyone else."
>
> "I think so was I," Arctor said.
>
> "I don't know what did it."

"Sure, Luckman," Arctor said, "you know what did it to all of us."
"Well, let's not talk about it."

Phil cried often during the long nighttime stints writing *Scanner*. In the spare bedroom at Quartz Lane, he would type until he collapsed from exhaustion, then sleep an hour or two and go at it again. In a 1977 *Exegesis* entry, Phil provided a fitting coda:

[. . .] I can see what I have done to transmute those terrible days into something worthwhile [. . .] This is what God does; this is his strange mystery: how he accomplishes this. When we view the evil (which he is going to transmute) we can't see for the life of us how he can do it—but later on, & only later on, after it's done, can we see how he has used evil as the clay out of which he as potter has fashioned the pot (universe viewed as artifact).

♦

Even as he worked on *Scanner*, public interest in Dick's work continued to mount. An admiring parody by John Sladek of Phil's pell-mell cosmic style—"Solar Shoe Salesman"—appeared in *F & SF*. In March 1973 the BBC came to Fullerton to shoot Phil acting out a scene from *Counter-Clock World*. That summer, the SF slick *Vertex* conducted an interview, followed in September by a French documentary crew who set Phil and Norman Spinrad to discoursing on Nixon and SF amid the whirling teacups at Disneyland. Then Entwhistle Books, a small independent publisher, announced plans to publish *Confessions of a Crap Artist*—the first of his fifties mainstream novels to make it. On French TV Phil's work was proposed for the Nobel Prize. The year closed with an interview by the *London Daily Telegraph*.

Alas, the subject of all this attention was near broke most of the time. To Ashmead and the Meredith Agency, Phil wrote citing the critical praise, hoping it would make a difference in the New York marketplace. It did not.

Worse yet, the new bout of writing productivity was jeopardizing Phil's health. In April 1973 he wrote to Nancy and Isa:

[T]he doctor says I have serious if not dangerous hypertension (physical high blood pressure, not psychological) and it must be controlled. So I'm on a goddam pill again, after having had no prescriptions for over a full year for anything. [. . .] After sending the novel [*Flow*] to my agent [. . .] I started another one [*Scanner*] [. . .] (a) a 62-page outline; (b) 82 final pages to mail to accompany the outline for submission; (c) 240 pages more in rough. Add that up, for a period from February 20 to April 2, and how many pages of writing do you get? A fatal stroke, that's what. See? *See???* I'm writing more and faster off chemicals than I was on. And—my blood pressure is higher. Does not compute.

One source of the intense pressure Phil was feeling was also a source of great joy: Tessa was pregnant. In April they were married. Tessa recalls:

> I don't know why I married Phil. He asked, and I said I would think about it. We were already living together. I wanted to have a baby, although I didn't really care whether it was out of wedlock. The next thing I knew, Phil thought I had said yes. [. . .] When he got a check in April, from his agent, he called a minister and had him come to our apartment and marry us. I was five months pregnant, my feet too swollen to wear anything but sandals, and I thought it would be a good idea to marry the baby's father.

On July 25, 1973, Phil's son, Christopher, was born. It was a relief to Phil, who had feared that twins were on the way. Life with a son changed things between Phil and Tessa, but differently from the changes that followed the birth of Isa. Tessa writes:

> Phil was a model father. [. . .] He loved his son a great deal, probably more than he loved me. [. . .] Where Phil and I had been "partners in crime," pulling off little pranks and practical jokes, I found myself gradually cut out in favor of Christopher. It was wonderful, for me, to watch the two of them together. It was okay to be cut out, because I enjoyed seeing their relationship blossom.

There were two practical limits to Phil's parenting: He never did diapers, and he insisted on quiet while he wrote. Quiet proved elusive, as Christopher cried loudly through most nights.

For all his joy, Phil found himself in a deep depression. To Dorothy he wrote in September: "Right after Christopher's birth I had a post partum, and nearly did myself in (as I often nearly do). I contacted Orange County Mental Health, and their therapist pulled me out in three weeks." But the depressions recurred; later in the year, Phil considering entering the LaHabre Psychiatric Hospital, but family and finances precluded this move.

There was, that September, one bright moment of career recognition that actually translated into an immediate $2,000. United Artists picked up the film option on *Do Androids Dream of Electric Sheep?* and was interested enough to continue option payments for some years. Phil was excited and took to taping to the walls photographs of young actresses (such as Victoria Principal) who he felt would be right for the part of Rachael Rosen (ultimately played, in the 1982 film *Blade Runner*, by Sean Young).

Nonetheless, fears over the responsibilities of a new baby, coupled with an erratic income, troubled Phil sufficiently that he put forward, in another September letter to Dorothy, a self-justification that would address what Phil was certain she was thinking:

There is, in this country, a tendency to look down with contempt on people who are in financial trouble, who lose their house, their possessions; I fight that attitude and take pride in the fact that, for example, as I said in my previous letter, Stanislaw Lem considers me to be the sole artist working in the field. Who would there be, then, were I to quit?

The growing recognition of his work was a balm when Phil badly needed and deserved one. Just a few days before his self-justification to Dorothy, Phil had written to French critic Marcel Thaon in response to Thaon's queries on the direction of his future novels. Phil explained that he now saw "authentic reality as being amazingly simple: the rest, perhaps, has been generated by our own inner problems, and by the power aspirations of ruling classes."

Amazingly simple? Somewhere someone or something was laughing.

10 Annus Mirabilis: *Information-Rich Pink Light, The Black Iron Prison And The Palm Tree Garden Superimposed, Christopher's Life Saved, A Meta-abstraction Of Ultimate Infinite Value—But Who KNEW What The Hell It REALLY Meant? Not Phil, Not Even As It Beamed Out Nightly Dreams Explaining It All In Giant Books (February 1974–February 1975)*

Religious experience is absolute. It is indisputable. You can only say that you have never had such an experience, and your opponent will say: "Sorry, I have." And there your discussion will come to an end. [. . .] And if such experience helps to make your life healthier, more beautiful, more complete and more satisfactory to yourself and to those you love, you may safely say: "This was the grace of God."

C. G. JUNG, *Psychology and Religion*

My life has divided this way: survival/cultural/spiritual/postmortem (resurrection as of 3-74)

PHIL, 1978 *Exegesis* entry

Who the hell knows? I don't want to go into this deeply but I've had weird dream experiences myself. God knows what's in our unconscious. What would Phil have said about it? He would have said six different things! I'll say this. Anybody who takes this without a laugh misses it all.

NORMAN SPINRAD, in interview

FOR all the subsequent confusion he sowed, Phil never really doubted that the visions and auditions of February–March 1974 (2-3-74) and after had fundamentally changed his life.

Whether or not they were *real* was another question. As usual. In seeking an answer, Phil hovered in a binary flutter:

Doubt. That he might have deceived himself, or that It—whatever It was—had deceived him.

208

Joy. That the universe might just contain a meaning that had eluded him all through his life and works.

This dialectic lies at the heart of the eight-year *Exegesis* (a largely handwritten journal, some eight thousand pages long, devoted to the solution of 2-3-74) and of *Valis* (p. 1981). And out of it burgeoned the theories—Phil's own and those posed by friends and critics. Many of them can explain almost everything.

But let's put aside theories for now and try first to determine just what happened in 2-3-74 and the months that followed. Be forewarned that Phil's experiences during this time simply do not fall into a neat, over-arching pattern—to fashion one for them is to distort them irrevocably. They include moments of doubt, panic, and anguish such as to make them seem all too human. But there are also times of startling sublimity, not to mention sheer breathtaking wonder. They neither prove that Phil was crazy, nor do they establish the existence of a Saint Phil. In fact, the 2-3-74 experiences resemble nothing so much as a wayward cosmic plot from a Phil Dick SF novel—which is hardly surprising, given who the experiencer was.

In attempting a plain narrative, this biography draws upon the first study ever made of the *Exegesis* in its entirety. Combined with letters, interviews, and the novels, a tentative whole can be formed. Phil never did set it all down in one chronological sequence, not even in *Valis*. And he seldom recounted any of the events without dropping in a new twist. But onward.

In February 1974, *Flow My Tears, the Policeman Said* was published. It was his best-received novel since *High Castle,* earning Nebula and Hugo Award nominations and winning the 1975 John W. Campbell Memorial Award. The money situation had improved somewhat, what with four-figure paperback resales of back titles such as *High Castle.* The family lived in a pleasant little apartment. Nearby U Cal Fullerton proudly housed Phil's papers in its special collections; now and then he even guest lectured. But Phil didn't socialize much. Somehow Tessa and his friends had not meshed, and Phil was always less gregarious when married.

Not a bad life, all in all, but for the fact that deep down Phil was scared silly. Later he would write in the *Exegesis:* "Although I can't prove this, I believe I was programmed to die in 3-74 [. . .]" Programmed by whom or what? Phil wasn't sure, but IRS woes were in there somewhere. He believed that his "civil disobedience"—joining the *Ramparts* tax protest during the Vietnam years—might cost him fifteen years in prison. And the April 1974 filing was coming up. Phil was broke and feared the IRS would seize his assets.

The fears ranged further. He worried that somehow he'd drawn the attention of the ruling authorities—U.S. or Soviet or both—by his writings. The just-released *Flow* could be read as a vision of Gulag-like prisons maintained by a fascist America. And *Ubik* had won the un-welcome praise of Marxist critics as a brilliant ungluing of capitalism. Other past works posed equally dire interpretive possibilities.

Phil needed extrication—grace if you will—fast. And 2-3-74 did the job, call it what you wish. Sometimes, as in this 1978 *Exegesis* entry, Phil went so far as to call it "total psychosis":

> Yes, it was a mercy to me—I went over the brink into psychosis in '70 when Nancy did what she did to me—in '73 or so I tried to come back to having an ego, but it was too fragile & there were too many financial and other pressures; the hit on my house and all the terrors of 1971 had left their mark—& so, esp. because of the IRS matter I suffered total psychosis in 3-74, was taken over by one or more archetypes. Poverty, family responsibility (a new baby) did it. & fear of the IRS.

In February 1974 the fear was heavy within him. He also endured a mundane agony: an impacted wisdom tooth. During oral surgery, Phil received sodium pentothal; afterward the pain remained, though the pentothal seemed to linger. A prescription pain killer was delivered to Phil's door:

> The doorbell rang and I went, and there stood this girl with black, black hair and large eyes very lovely and intense; I stood staring at her, amazed, also confused, thinking I'd never seen such a beautiful girl, and why was she standing there? She handed me the package of medication [Darvon], and I tried to think what to say to her; I noticed, then, a fascinating gold necklace around her neck and I said, "What is that? It certainly is beautiful," just, you see, to find something to say to hold her there. The girl indicated the major figure in it, which was a fish. "This is a sign used by the early Christians," she said, and then departed.

What precisely happened on that February 20 after Phil had gazed upon the golden fish? Phil's accounts are piecemeal, but the long se-quence of visions seems to have started this day, with a sudden triggering of what he experienced as past lives and genetic memories. Phil felt certain for the first time that he was—not as an individual, but as a spiritual entity—immortal:

> The (golden) fish sign causes you to remember. Remember what? This is Gnostic. Your celestial origins; this has to do with the DNA because the memory is located in the DNA (phylogenic memory). Very ancient memo-ries, predating this life, are triggered off. [. . .] You remember your real nature. Which is to say, origins (from the stars). *Die Zeit is da!* [The time is here!] The Gnostic Gnosis: You are here in this world in a thrown condition, but you are not *of* this world.

Phil adopted a term first employed by Plato, *anamnesis*, to describe the experience of recollecting eternal truths, the World of Ideas, within ourselves. But what could account for the sudden anamnesis? Perhaps it was "the combination of the pentothal and the golden fish sign—the latter may have acted hypnotically on me: the combination of the metal and the sunlight." Then too, he'd been taking prescribed doses of lithium regularly.

Phil never settled on a physical cause. What mattered were the "ancient" or "phylogenic" memories. Always, they revealed the Roman world, circa first century A.D. (the period of the Book of *Acts* and the peak of Gnostic activity) as coexisting with our own modern world. It was as if linear time was illusion and true time was layered: simultaneous realities stacked one upon the other, the interpenetration visible to the opened mind. Phil's accounts of the newly revealed Roman realm varied. In this 1978 *Exegesis* entry, he became the Gnostic Simon Magus:

> When I saw the Golden Fish sign in 2-74 *I* remembered the world of *Acts*—*I* remembered it to be *my* real time & place. So I am (esse/sum) Simon reborn—& not in 2-74 or 3-74 but all my life. I must face it: I am Simon but had amnesia, but then in 2-74 experienced anamnesis. I Simon am immortal. & Simon is the basis for the Faust legend.

More often, however, Phil named this ancient personage Thomas (a first-century Christian) or Firebright (a spiritual force/entity of wisdom and light). While Firebright was of a divine nature, Thomas was quite human. Phil felt he knew that Thomas had been tortured by the Roman authorities who relentlessly persecuted the new Logos. Quite clearly, Thomas's plight paralleled Phil's.

Phil never settled on a name for the new, dual consciousness within him. His most frequently used term was "homoplasmate"—a bonding of a human and an information-rich "plasmate" life form. He further felt that this new wisdom or grace had been "programmed" in him by age four, and that it would save him. His "Prologue" to *Radio Free Albemuth* (w. 1976) explores a way this might have happened. A boy (almost four) gives a blind, bearded beggar a nickel and receives a piece of paper, which he hands to his father:

> "It tells about God," his father said.
> The little boy did not know that the beggar was not actually a beggar but a supernatural entity visiting Earth to check up on people. Years later the little boy grew up and became a man. In the year 1974 that man found himself in terrible difficulties, facing disgrace, imprisonment, and possible death. There was no way for him to extricate himself. At that point the supernatural entity returned to Earth, loaned the man a part of his spirit, and saved him from his difficulties. The man never guessed why the supernatural entity came to

rescue him. He had long ago forgotten the great bearded blind beggar and the nickel he had given him.

In late February and early March Phil had a series of nightmares that compounded his dread. Some contained what he described as "flying monsters with horses' necks (dragons)." In one dream these dragons swooped down upon a young Phil who lived, in dreamtime, with a prehistoric tribe. As the dragons drew near Phil *became* his pet saber-toothed cat and hissed defiance—but found himself in a cage without escape. Tessa writes:

> One night I woke to the sound of a large reptile hissing. I sat up and saw Phil lying there, still asleep, hissing. Afraid to touch him, I called out his name. I was scared, and getting more scared with every second that passed. I sensed that it was not Phil who was hissing, but some mindless beast that had taken over his body. I kept on calling his name, more and more urgently.
>
> Finally, he stopped hissing. He cried a little and started praying in Latin, *"Libera me Domine."* [Free me, God.] It was something he learned from an opera. He kept repeating that and other prayers for half an hour, then fell asleep. I was awake for the rest of the night. Phil's dream had been so real to him that he thought it must be some kind of a memory trace rather than a dream.

Phil was living in a psychic caldron. What better way out than to turn up the heat? He'd read of new psychiatric research indicating that massive doses of water-soluble vitamins improved neural firing in schizophrenics. Phil speculated that, for an ordinary person, such vitamin dosages might heighten synchronous firing by the two brain hemispheres, thereby enhancing both left-brain practical efficiency and right-brain imagination. In *Psychology Today* Phil found a "recipe." The almost certain source is an article called "Orthomolecular Psychiatry: Vitamin Pills for Schizophrenics" by psychiatrist Harvey Ross in the April 1974 issue (which appeared, as magazines do, a month before its printed date). Dr. Ross's prescription for a young boy suffering from hypoglycemia and schizophrenic visions: a high-protein, low-carbohydrate diet and, after each meal, 500 mg of niacin (vitamin B_3), increased to 1,000 mg after the first week; 500 mg of vitamin C, increased to 1,000 mg after the first month; 100 mg of vitamin B_6; 100 mg of vitamin B_2; 200 IU of vitamin E; and a multiple vitamin B tablet. All the vitamins were water-soluble. In "experimenting" with the formula, Phil accidentally took seven more grams of vitamin C than called for. The end result, as stated in the *Exegesis:* "both hemispheres came on together, for the first time in my life."

Was it the vitamins that spurred the vivid March visions? Phil never decided on a single cause. The more he speculated, the more "disinhibiting" candidates he found. After all, the vernal equinox was approaching, the time of Easter and Passover and the resurrection of the spirit. And somehow, in the weeks following the golden fish Darvon delivery, Phil found himself moved to burn, day and night, white votive candles before a little shrine he'd assembled in their bedroom, including an old wooden saint figure from the Philippines. Then he and Tessa purchased bumper stickers with the Christian fish sign—metallic silver with a black backing—and placed them on their living-room window. Sometimes, after looking at those stickers while the sun streamed through the window, Phil would see pink rectangular shapes: phosphene afterimages, they seemed.

Pale prefigurings of the fireworks to come. In a July 1974 letter, Phil described the visions that started in mid-March 1974:

Then [. . .] while lying in bed unable to sleep for the fifth night in a row, overwhelmed with dread and melancholy, I suddenly began seeing whirling lights which moved away at such a fast speed—and were instantly replaced—that they forced me into total wakefulness. For almost eight hours I continued to see these frightening vortexes of light, if that's the word; they spun around and around, and moved away at incredible speed. What was most painful was the rapidity of my thoughts, which seemed to synchronize with the lights; it was as if I were moving, and the lights standing still—I felt as if I were racing along at the speed of light, no longer lying beside my wife in our bed. My anxiety was unbelievable.

One week later, under similar circumstances, I began at night to see light once more. But this time quite different [. . .] the little votive candle reassured me, as did the placid face of the 150-year-old wooden figure of a saint which had come from the Philippines.

This time I saw perfectly formed modern abstract paintings, which I later identified from art books as being of the type Kandinsky developed. There were literally hundreds of thousands of them; they replaced each other at dazzling speed [. . .] I did recognize the styles of Paul Klee and one or two of Picasso's various periods. [. . .] So I spent over eight hours enjoying one of the most beautiful and exciting and moving sights I've ever seen, conscious that it was a miracle. [. . .] I was not the author of these graphics. The number alone proved that.

In the following days I felt that [. . .] I must have been the involuntary recipient of an ESP experiment. That was most likely. I knew the dazzling graphics had come to me from outside myself; I sensed that they contained information and that somehow I was to respond. For over a month I sought ways of responding; I even wrote to an ESP lab in Leningrad, asking if they were involved in the long-range transmission by ESP of Modern Art graphics [i.e., paintings in the Hermitage collection]. No response. After that I sort of shut up about it and began reading.

Working by myself, in a total vacuum, with no background or experience or knowledge, I had only my hunches to go on.

213

I was sure someone living was trying to communicate with me. I was sure it came from above—maybe from the sky. Especially the stars; I began to go outdoors at night to watch the stars, with the strong impression that information was coming from them.

Descriptions of these visions, which Phil often termed "phosphene graphics," appear in both *Radio Free Albemuth* and *Valis* and are incorporated into Fred/Bob Arctor's "scramble suit" in *A Scanner Darkly*. Their source remained hidden, but the urgency of their content was unmistakable. Something much more than a stream of pretty pictures was passing through Phil's new consciousness. Perhaps "second self" Thomas was his right hemisphere—or his left? Had the unfamiliar unity of mind opened new realities? But the graphic display indicated an external source with wisdom to bestow:

My first stage of the experience was to undergo the Bardo Thodol [Tibetan Book of the Dead] journey, and was then suddenly surprised to find myself confronting Aphrodite, who Empedocles believed to be the generative principle of all life, of all love and the formation of *krasis* or *gestalts* in the universe, as opposed to the principle of strife. What this meant I did not know at the time.

This contact with Aphrodite was the first of many encounters with divine female aspects—or, Phil sometimes said, his anima—through a voice that came to him in dreams or hypnogogic states. While Phil often called this the "AI" (artificial intelligence) voice, he ascribed to it a feminine quality and termed it not only Aphrodite but also Artemis/ Diana, Athena/Minerva, Saint Sophia (Holy Wisdom, the goddess of Gnosticism), and twin sister Jane—with whom Phil felt he was, at times, in telepathic contact.

Exactly one year later, in March 1975, Phil typed out a paean to these mid-March visions and the unknown "it" behind them:

March 16, 1974: It appeared—in vivid fire, with shining colors and balanced patterns—and released me from every thrall, inner and outer.

March 18, 1974: It, from inside me, looked out and saw that the world did not compute, that I—and it—had been lied to. It denied the reality, and power, and authenticity, of the world, saying, "This cannot exist; it cannot exist."

March 20, 1974: It seized me entirely, lifting me from the limitations of the space-time matrix; it mastered me as, at the same instant, I knew that the world around me was cardboard, a fake. Through its power I saw suddenly the universe as it was; through its power of perception I saw what really existed, and through its power of no-thought decision, I acted to *free myself*. It took on in battle, as a champion of all human spirits in thrall, every evil, every Iron Imprisoning Thing.

On March 20, the action by which Phil freed himself was his handling of what he called, in the *Exegesis*, the "Xerox missive." Accounts of this event are provided in *Radio Free Albemuth* and, far more accurately, in *Valis*. Horselover Fat (who, in *Valis*, is also SF writer Phil Dick) has a dream about a Soviet woman—Sadassa Ulna—who will contact him by mail. "An urgent message fired into Fat's head that he must respond to her letter when it came." Fat confides to his wife, Beth (based on Tessa), his sense of danger. Then comes the fateful day:

On Wednesday, Fat received a plethora of letters: seven in all. Without opening them he fished among them and pointed out one, which had no return name or address on it. "That's it," he said to Beth, who, by now, was also freaked. "Open it and look at it, but don't let me see her name or address or I'll answer it."

Beth opened it. Instead of a letter per se she found a Xerox sheet on which two book reviews from the left-wing New York newspaper *The Daily World* had been juxtaposed. The reviewer described the author of the books as a Soviet national living in the United States. From the reviews it was obvious that the author was a Party member.

"My God," Beth said, turning the Xerox sheet over. "The author's name and address is written on the back."

"A woman?" Fat said.

"Yes," Beth said.

I [Phil] never found out from Fat and Beth what they did with the two letters. From hints Fat dropped I deduced that it was innocent; but what he did with the Xerox one, which really wasn't a letter in the strict sense of the term, I do not to this day know, nor do I want to know. Maybe he burned it or maybe he turned it over to the police or the FBI or the CIA. In any case I doubt if he answered it.

Tessa confirms that for a week or more, Phil had been anticipating a letter that would "kill" him. When it arrived, he gave it to her to read but instructed her not to let him see it. Tessa summarized for him its form and content. She recalls:

Certain words in the article [book review] were underlined, some in red and some in blue. All were what Phil called "die messages." Words like decline, decay, stagnation, decomposition. The book, it seems, was about the decline and fall of American capitalism. There was a return address on the envelope, a hotel in New York, but no name [Fat, in the *Valis* quote above, says there was a name]. As if Phil ought to know who had sent it, and as if he ought to write back to them.

Phil suspected that the Xerox missive was somehow connected to his two-week amnesia episode in Vancouver in March 1972. The Mafia types in black suits had driven him around in the back of a limousine, asking questions he could no longer recall. What had been programmed into him? By whom? He feared that the juxtaposed Xeroxed book reviews were supposed to have triggered off something in him, but somehow failed. He confided his fears and speculations to Tessa, who writes: "I believed him. He always asked me, 'Am I nuts?' I always said no. I still believe he was sane. Crazy people don't ask, 'Am I nuts?' They know they're sane."

Phil's sense of the Xerox missive threat was keen. It forced him into prompt defensive action. In the aftermath, there was a sense of freedom—karma broken—and of intense lingering guilt.

As hinted at in *Valis*, Phil forwarded the Xerox missive to the FBI. In a 1978 *Exegesis* entry he noted that time was of the essence to parry either (1) KGB recruitment or (2) FBI loyalty-test fake KGB recruitment. "It took me 2½ hours to phone the Bureau. That's a *good* (test) score [. . .] Don't tell me there's no God. The phosphenes began the week before; I was all ready for the damn thing when it came."

Phil had an acute sense of *something* taking *control* of him to direct his response to the Xerox missive. In the *Exegesis*, he speculated that it was Thomas—no longer an early Christian but instead a thought-control implant by U.S. Army Intelligence—who guided him. Phil's alternate name for Thomas under this theory was "Pigspurt." Pigspurt or other, Phil's searing sense of his personality's being taken over led him, on March 20, to take the startling step of calling not only the FBI but also the Fullerton police. "I am a machine," he told the officer who answered the phone—and then asked to be locked up. The police took no action.

Phil shortly thereafter regained a sense of self-control. But he continued to believe—by virtue of the wisdom and guidance that he believed had been bestowed upon him—that placating the ruling authorities was essential to preserve his personal safety. And so Phil maintained contact with the FBI, writing several times to its L.A. office from March through September 1974. He was out to negate any possible doubt of his loyalty on the Bureau's part. The letters include defensive explanations as to why leftist critics valued his work and assurances that his letters to Soviet scientists engaged in ESP research were by way of trying to get them to rise to the bait and reveal themselves. (Phil's cautiousness was not entirely unfounded. In 1975, through the Freedom of Information Act, Phil learned that a 1958 letter he had written to a Soviet scientist had been intercepted by the CIA.)

To all his correspondence he received a single response: a March 28,

1974, form letter from FBI director William Sullivan: "Your interest in writing as you did is indeed appreciated and the material will receive appropriate attention." But by the act of proclaiming his loyalty Phil obtained a great measure of comfort and calm. The dread that had afflicted him since the November 1971 break-in now lifted.

But the guilt remained. Memories of the McCarthy era and of FBI agents coming to his and Kleo's Berkeley home in the fifties must have passed through his mind when Phil considered his actions. He had, in many of his SF novels—most recently *Flow My Tears, The Policeman Said*—decried the police state and the informants on which it relied. Had Phil become that which he despised? In a 1979 *Exegesis* entry he raked himself over the coals for his cowardice:

> I cooperated fully with my oppressors. There was no further degree to which I could be turned around—I went all the way, due to the override, & experienced a sense 1) of having done the right thing for God & country; & 2) a total loss of anxiety, of exculpation (naturally). Fred, of Bob/Fred [in *Scanner*] had totally won. I literally narked on myself! [. . .]
>
> Fear killed the rebel in me in 3-74 & I never regretted it, since it gave me freedom from fear. They got me. The intimidation worked—e.g. the hit on my house. [. . .]
>
> I am afraid of 1) the civil authorities (Caesar); & 2) God (Valis). Hence it can be said I am afraid of authority, of whatever is powerful.

In his own defense, Phil would stress the magnitude of the peril and the direct command of a higher intelligence that had compelled him to contact the FBI. From a subsequent 1979 entry:

> So I turned to God & the Bureau, & financial security. Well, *excuse* me. I was a totally desperate person, which I no longer am. I can sleep at night okay [. . .] I may not have done the ideologically right thing but I did the *wise* thing. [. . .] My conversion was not so much a spiritual one as a conversion to the path of wisdom, correctly defined: *how to survive*. That was my goal: survival. I succeeded. In my opinion, Holy Wisdom [Saint Sophia] herself took over my life & directed me [. . .] I lived a wild, unstable, desperate, Quixotic life, & would soon have died. Hence it is not accident that Holy Wisdom came to me; I needed her very badly.

Be it noted that Phil was never so craven with respect to "authority" as he here accuses himself. As to "God," Phil challenged the concept every which way. As to "Caesar," for all his posturing to the FBI, Phil remained outspoken on the abuses of the Nixon administration—in essays such as "The Nixon Crowd" (1974) and in novels such as *Radio Free Albemuth* and *Valis*.

Even after the Xerox missive crisis passed, March 1974 continued to hold its surprises. There were strange alterations in his daily life. Pets (including the beloved Pinky the cat) seemed more intelligent, even somehow attempting to communicate. And then there was the radio that played on even after Phil and Tessa unplugged it and put it in the kitchen.

It all started when the radio began to abuse Phil with obscenities at night. In *Radio Free Albemuth*, protagonist Nicholas Brady undergoes the same treatment: " 'Nick the prick,' the radio was saying, in imitation of the voice of a popular vocalist whose latest record had just been featured. 'Listen, Nick the prick. You're worthless and you're going to die. You misfit! You prick, Nick! Die, die, *die!!*' " In interview with J. B. Reynolds, Tessa recalled: "The thing about that was that we *both* heard the music, and it was always between two and six A.M., and the radio wasn't even *plugged in*. [. . .] But we still got Easy Listening music, only Phil kept hearing it tell him that he was no good, that he should die. And I didn't hear that. We gave up and plugged the radio back in again, because it was easier to sleep with music on."

The most striking of all the changes was the advent of the pink light beams firing information into Phil's brain. While Tessa believes in the genuine mystical nature of Phil's experiences, she suggests that the silver-black Christian fish bumper sticker on their window may have played a physiological role here; but Phil began seeing pink rectangular images on the apartment walls even when he had not looked at the fish sign in sunlight. When it hit, the pink light beam was blinding, like a flashbulb going off in Phil's face. The beam was information-rich and full of spiritual surprises. At one point it instructed Phil in how to administer the Eucharist to son Christopher according to the rites of the early Christians. The ceremony is described in *Valis*:

In March 1974 during the time that VALIS overruled me, held control of my mind, I had conducted a correct and complex inititation of Christopher into the ranks of the immortals. [. . .]

This was an experience which I treasured. It had been done in utter stealth, concealed even from my son's mother.

First I had fixed a mug of hot chocolate. Then I had fixed a hot dog on a bun with the usual trimmings; [. . .]

Seated on the floor in Christopher's room with him, I—or rather VALIS in me, as me—had played a game. First, I jokingly held the cup of chocolate up, over my son's head; then, as if by accident, I had splashed warm chocolate on his head, into his hair. Giggling, Christopher had tried to wipe the liquid off; I had of course helped him. Leaning toward him, I had whispered,

"In the name of the Son, the Father and the Holy Spirit."

No one heard me except Christopher. Now, as I wiped the warm chocolate from his hair, I inscribed the sign of the cross on his forehead. I had now baptized him and now I confirmed him; I did so, not by the authority of any church, but by the authority of the living plasmate in me: VALIS himself. Next I said to my son, "Your secret name, your Christian name, is—" And I told him what it was. Only he and I are ever to know; he and I and VALIS.

Phil felt certain that there was an entity communicating with him throughout 2-3-74, and one of the names he gave it was VALIS, an acronym for Vast Active Living Intelligence System. Valis bestowed information on Phil by means other than pink light. A series of tutelary dreams began in March, continued on nightly into the summer, and returned intermittently for the rest of his life. In a July 1974 letter Phil insisted that "the most eerie—and yet at the same time the most valid proof of what had happened, that indeed something real *had* happened— were my continuing experiences while asleep. Soon after the eight-hour show of dazzling graphics I began to have what I do not think are dreams, since they are not like any dreams I have ever had or even read about." Phil believed that the information they contained had been subliminally encoded during the March 18 graphics display. In a June 1974 letter he described the dream flow:

> [. . .] I was hoping for increased neural efficiency. I got more: actual information about the future, for during the next three months [from March on], almost each night, during sleep I was receiving information in the form of print-outs: words and sentences, letters and names and numbers—sometimes whole pages, sometimes in the form of writing paper and holographic writing, sometimes, oddly, in the form of a baby's cereal box on which all sorts of quite meaningful information was written and typed, and finally galley proofs held up for me to read which I was told in my dream "contained prophecies about the future," and during the last two weeks a huge book, again and again, with page after page of printed lines.

Information from the future? Phil had already, in *Ubik* and *Counter-Clock World*, posited a kind of Logos that moved in retrograde or backward time to bestow knowledge and salvation. And his research on 2-3-74 uncovered tantalizing physics research on tachyons, particles that move faster than light in retrograde time and could, theoretically, carry information from the future. Whatever the source, a basic problem remained: The dreams seldom offered clear guidance. Often the information came in the form of non sequitur language fragments (one of these, "Aramcheck," became a character's name in *Radio Free Albemuth*) or integer sequences. Some words and fragments proved to be Sanskrit roots or phrases of koine Greek (the language of the Near East in the time of Christ), such as *"poros krater"* (limestone bowl), *"crypte morphosis"* (latent shape), and "The *Rhipidon* Society" (*rhipidos:* fan; the Rhipidon Society plays a key role in *Valis*). There were also the terms "Fomalhaut" and "Albemuth," which Phil associated with the distant star—Sirius, he speculated—from which the information might have been transmitted. Then again, the koine Greek indicated that Asklepios, the god of healing, whose father was Apollo and whose stepmother was the Cumaen sibyl (the possible source of the "AI Voice"), might be his nightly tutor.

In one dream appeared "singed pages," as if "the book had gone through a fire but had been rescued." Phil wasn't always sure that he wanted to take in what he felt he was being "forced" to read. Some of the dream texts pointed to ominous "religious fanatics" conspiracies that took in the deaths of Pike, Martin Luther King, Jr., and Robert Kennedy. Meanwhile, hypnagogic voices offered enigmatic oracles. While falling asleep one evening in July 1974, Phil "heard her (you know, my anima, the sibyl), singing along with a choir: 'You must put your slippers on / To walk toward the dawn.' " In January 1975, also in a hypnagogic state, came "Saint Sophia is going to be reborn." (Alternative version: "St. Sophia is going to be reborn again; she was not acceptable before.") Readers of Valis will recognize these oracles.

In addition, there were the dreams of the three-eyed beings. In Valis Phil writes of the dual identity character Fat/Phil:

In March 1974 at the time he had encountered God (more properly Zebra), he had experienced vivid dreams about the three-eyed people—he had told me that. They manifested themselves as cyborg entities: wrapped up in glass bubbles staggering under masses of technological gear. An odd aspect cropped up that puzzled both Fat and me; sometimes in these vision-like dreams, Soviet technicians could be seen, hurrying to repair malfunctions of the sophisticated technological communications apparatus enclosing the three-eyed people.

In the *Exegesis,* Phil drew pictures of these beings and sometimes identified their third eye with the wisdom (ajna) eye of Hinduism and Buddhism. He also explored the possibility that they were aliens of superior intelligence who had, by means of satellite-fired information beams, contacted him. As to such theorizing, narrator Phil concludes, in *Valis:* "By now Fat had totally lost touch with reality." In real life, Phil was equally aware of how his richly associative mode of thought—in which there were no "dead" gods who could not be reborn in the human psyche—would sound to others. From a July 1974 letter which Phil included in the *Exegesis:*

> I can see myself telling my therapist this. "What's on your mind, Phil?" she'll say when I go in, and I'll say, "Asklepios is my tutor, from out of Periclean Athens. I'm learning to talk in Attic Greek." She'll say, "Oh really?" and I'll be on my way to the Blissful Groves, but that won't be until after death; that'll be in the country where it's quiet and costs $100 a day. And you get all the apple juice you want to drink, along with Thorazine.

As this letter indicates, Phil was not one to lose his sense of humor, not even when it came to his own "divine" revelations. On the contrary, Phil always retained the ability to see just how loopy his experiences could seem. Not only could he laugh at them, he could also subject himself to fiercely skeptical questioning—as an *Exegesis* self-interview quoted later in this chapter will establish. Phil was neither credulous nor a fool. He held to no single set of beliefs as to what was happening to him. Yet he possessed the moral courage to treat it all seriously, as a source of possible knowledge, rather than dismiss it outright. In America, if you are unfortunate enough to have a spiritual-seeming vision, it had better conform to the doctrines of an established church. If it doesn't, you're crazy, simple as that. Phil knew full well just how his experiences would seem to others. But he was damned if he was going to deny himself a single avenue of speculation.

By July 1974, Phil was considering the possibility that his psyche had been merged with that of his friend the late Bishop Pike. After all, so many of the little changes in Phil seemed to reflect Pike's tastes:

> Now I am not the same person. People say I look different. I have lost weight. Also, I have made a lot of money doing the things Jim tells me to do, more money than ever before in a short period, doing things I've never done, nor would imagine doing. More strange yet, I now drink beer every day and never any wine. I used to drink only wine, never beer. I chugalug the beer. The reason I drink it is that Jim knows that wine is bad for me—the acidity, the sediment. He had me trim my beard too. For that I had to go up and buy special barber's scissors. I didn't know there even was such a thing.

Also, for no reason attributable to Bishop Pike, Phil began calling the dogs "he" and the cat "she"—the opposite of the facts.

But what were the money-related instructions Jim/Thomas/Valis/Other gave Phil? In a 1979 interview Phil stated: "It immediately set about putting my affairs in order. It fired my agent and publisher." Well, Phil never fired his publisher, Doubleday, though he was extremely angered, in April–May, by having been quoted inconsistent sales figures for *Flow* that seemed to Phil to indicate that Doubleday, aided by the indifference or collusion of the Meredith Agency, was trying to rip him off on royalties. In addition, he resented the low $2,500 paperback advance (from DAW) that Doubleday had negotiated for *Flow*. In a May 5 letter Phil requested an audit of the printing runs of all of his previous novels published by Doubleday. And in a still more vituperative May 7 letter, which Phil may never have sent (editor Lawrence Ashmead, the addressee, doesn't recall receiving it), Phil told the tale of hapless SF author "Chipdip K. Kill" (Phil's name in John Sladek's 1973 parody), author of "Floods Of Tears, The Ripped-Off Author Said," victimized by "Dogshit Books" and agent "Skim Morewithit."

In a May 4 letter, he dismissed the Meredith Agency after twenty-two years. His primary stated reason: The agency had failed to back him in his dispute with Doubleday. Phil proved mistaken in his allegations concerning the *Flow* print runs, which he himself soon recognized. And the $2,500 DAW bid for the paperback rights to *Flow* was the highest received; there was nothing to be done. In a letter dated May 12, Phil reinstated his client status with the agency. In the meantime, however, he'd opened negotiations with agent Robert Mills, which he didn't terminate until October, keeping his options open. For Phil had placed one condition on the May 12 rehiring that vindicates to an extent his claims of increased practical acumen—and earnings—as a result of 2-3-74.

Phil insisted that the agency pursue the total back royalties due him from Ace Books. In the early seventies, the Science Fiction Writers of America was successfully pursuing Ace royalty claims on behalf of a number of writers. The clamor Phil raised effectively heightened the efforts of the Meredith Agency on his behalf in checking out Ace royalty reports—by May 28, it had forwarded to Phil over $3,000 in back royalties.

But all the dreams, visions, and hard-nosed acumen exacted a severe physical toll. Phil had suffered from hypertension for years; at the time of their marriage, April 1973, Tessa recalls, his blood pressure was roughly 200/160. Phil's 2-3-74 experiences seem to have exacerbated the hypertension. In early April, he was hospitalized after a blood-pressure reading (as stated in *Valis*) of 280/178: "The doctor had run every test possible, during Fat's stay in the hospital, to find a physical cause for the elevated blood pressure, but no cause had been found." Uppers had been out of the picture since 1972. Tessa is convinced that Phil experienced a series of minor strokes during this time, and notes that Phil's doctor offered this as a probable diagnosis:

> The times I think of as "minor strokes" are the times when he stumbled for no apparent reason, when he suddenly turned livid or flushed, when he would blank out in mid-sentence. These were stressful times, and I believe that he was having strokes, although very minor ones. If the spirit had not told him to go to the doctor, he might have died. Although he was supposed to have his blood pressure checked regularly, he would not go to the doctor. There would always be some excuse (usually the flu) for staying at home. The spirit, however, insisted that he go. When he went, the doctor told him to check into the hospital.

Tessa adds: "Were his experiences nothing more than a series of minor strokes? I doubt it, although I have no doubt that he was also having strokes."

During his five days in the hospital, Phil purchased gifts for fellow patients—little girls suffering from muscle disease. In addition, he spoke of his experiences with one Roman Catholic and two Episcopal priests who came to his bedside at his request. During one of Tessa's visits, some of Phil's papers were stolen from their apartment. A disquieting sign— shades of Santa Venetia.

Phil recovered sufficiently from his hypertension to attend, in early May, the local SF Carsacon for high school students. Tim Finney, who arranged for Phil and other SF luminaries such as Bradbury, Spinrad, and Sturgeon to appear, recalls that Phil went over best of all with the young audience. Despite this public triumph, he canceled out attending the July 1974 SF Westercon, of which he had been named guest of honor. But even in the safety of his own apartment, what with the visions and an infant who often cried through the night, exhaustion was setting in. Tessa recalls:

> It [2-3-74] made Phil more fun to be with. Every day brought an adventure. It also wore us out. You can only keep your adrenaline up for so long. [. . .] Phil had more severe periods of depression, more often than I did. He would lie in bed for a week at a time, needing to have his meals brought to him three times a day, plus snacks. Sometimes his appetite was dull, but most often he ate ravenously. He would get up every few hours and type—letters, notes, his latest novel.
>
> He would doze off, then wake up frantic, run to the bathroom, try to get a drink of water. You see, during his sleep, sometimes the juices from his stomach would come up and he would choke on them. I would have to drop whatever I was doing—or wake up—and get him a drink, hold him and comfort him, talk to him as if he were a very small child, in order to get him through the trauma.

223

During May 1974, Phil was paid what he regarded as an unwelcome visit by Marxist-oriented French literary critics; he reported the visit to the FBI. These critics found in the *Ubik* force a metaphor for the decay of capitalism. To Finney Phil complained: "To me it [the novel's setting] is in Cleveland or Des Moines—I don't think of it as a capitalist nation. [. . .] To them—they are materialists; to me, I am *this* person. I saw it as a spiritual journey away from this world."

Phil's visionary experiences continued apace. One of the most notable was his repeated sighting of the "Golden Rectangle" (based upon the golden mean ratio of Greek art; numerically expressed in the Fibonacci constant of 1.618). In *Radio Free Albemuth*, Nicholas Brady describes the vision:

> What I was seeing now was a door, proportioned by the measure which the Greeks had called the Golden Rectangle, which they had considered the perfect geometric form. I repeatedly saw this door, marked with letters of the Greek alphabet, projected onto natural formations that resembled it: a dictionary stand, a basalt block, a speaker cabinet. And one time, astonishingly, I had seen Pinky [Phil's cat] pressing outward from beyond the door into our world, only not as he had been: much larger, more fierce, like a tiger, and, most of all, filled to bursting with life and health. [. . .] [Brady] glimpsed beyond the door: a static landscape, nocturnal, a quiet black sea, sky, the edge of an island, and, surprisingly, the unmoving figure of a nude woman standing on the sand at the edge of the water. I had recognized the woman; it was Aphrodite. I had seen photographs of Greek and Roman statues of her. The proportions, the beauty and sensuality, could not be mistaken.

In a July 1974 *Exegesis* entry Phil observed, concerning the Greco-Roman content of his dreams and "Golden Rectangle" visions:

> If it [his unconscious] shows me the Golden Rectangle it does so in order to calm me with that ultimate esthetically balanced sight; it has a firm therapeutic purpose. There is a utilization of all its abstract material for genuine purposes, for me, by and large. It is a tutor to me as Aristotle was to Alexander [. . .] I sense Apollo in this, which is consistent, since the Cumaen sibyl was his oracle. Moderation, reasonability and balance are Apollo's virtues, the clear-headed, the rational. *Syntosis* [self-harmony].

The events surrounding the death of Pinky from cancer in the fall of 1974 were a further visionary confirmation to Phil. Two years earlier, when Phil had contracted pneumonia during the completion of *Flow*, Pinky had lain across his stomach to care for him as best a cat could. Phil had recovered, but now came Pinky's time to die:

> That Sunday night, four days before Pinky died, he and Tessa and I were lying on the bed in the bedroom, and I saw pale white light filling the room,

evenly distributed, and I saw Pinky inert and exposed, like a decoy duck, floating forever, and I got incredibly frightened and kept saying, "Death is in the room! I'm going to die!" I began to pray frantically, in Latin, for almost half an hour. I knew Pinky couldn't see it; I alone could. Death was there, but I thought it was for me. I knew Pinky and I would be separated. "Within the next four days," I said to Tessa. "Death will strike." She said, "You're nuts." Later that night I dreamed that a terrific gunshot was fired at me, deafeningly; I was okay but a woman, close by me, lay torn open and dying. I went for help. Three days later Pinky was dead [. . .] And the evening he died, while I was in the bathroom, I felt a firm hand on my shoulder; I was sure Tessa had come into the room behind me, and I turned to ask her why. No one was there. It was the touch of my friend, on his departure; he paused a moment to say goodbye.

Prior to Pinky's death, Phil had undergone a physical crisis of his own. In early August, during an argument with Tessa, Phil flung a seashell against the wall and painfully separated the shoulder he'd previously injured in 1964 and 1972. Following corrective surgery, Phil was forced to plot his novel in progress—*Valisystem A*—by dictating into a small tape recorder. (*Valisystem A* and a second proposed novel, *To Scare the Dead*, eventually blossomed into *Radio Free Albemuth* and *Valis*; this sequence is detailed in Chapter Eleven.)

It was in this weakened condition, in late summer, that Phil was zapped by the "pink light" information that Christopher suffered from a potentially fatal inguinal hernia. This diagnosis was confirmed by their physician and corrective surgery was performed in October. From an *Exegesis* entry c. 1977:

I am thinking back. Sitting with my eyes shut I am listening [in 1974] to "Strawberry Fields [Beatles song]." I get up. I open my eyes because the lyrics speak of "Going through life with eyes closed." I look toward the window. Light blinds me; my head suddenly aches. My eyes close & I see that strange strawberry ice cream pink. At the same instant knowledge is transferred to me. I go into the bedroom where Tessa is changing Chrissy & I recite what has been conveyed to me: that he has an undetected birth defect & must be taken to the doctor at once & scheduled for surgery. This turns out to be true.

What happened? What communicated with me? I could read & understand the secret messages "embedded within the inferior bulk." [Quotation from Gnostic text.]

Phil relished the fact that a pop song, of all things, had bestowed the needed wisdom. From a 1980 *Exegesis* entry: "God talked to me through a Beatles tune ('Strawberry Fields'). [. . .] A random assortment of trash blown by the wind, & there is God. Bits & pieces swept together to form a unity." But Phil being Phil, he posed contrary views with equal conviction. From a 1981 entry: "The beam of pink light fired at my head—as discussed in VALIS—is, I have always believed deep down underneath, not God but technology, and technology from the future at that."

In September, fellow SF writer Thomas Disch paid Phil a visit. Each admired the other's work; Disch recalls that Phil looked to him as "the great rationalist who was going to be sympathetically but objectively examining his theory for flaws. These are unusual social circumstances for meeting somebody for the first time." Their talk, fueled by beer, went on for twelve hours. At stake, it seemed, was Phil's probity. Says Disch:

> We talked about whether the dreams were of an external source. He wanted to say, how else could I have heard ancient Greek? But I said that the part of the mind used in dreams is unlikely to decide that we're hearing Greek. He didn't fancy my argument.
>
> I was fascinated. He was determined to make me say, yes, this is a religious experience. It was like arm wrestling for hours, and neither one of us got the other's arm down on the table.
>
> I was being lightly skeptical and affirming his imaginative side of it. At the same time I thought: Interesting—a masterful con that works. He's a professional entertainer of beliefs—in other words, a con man. He wants to turn anything he imagines into a system. And there was his delight in making people believe—he LOVED to make you believe. It made for great novels—but when he overdid it it became delusions of reference. The urge to translate every imagined thing into a belief or suspended belief is a bit of a jump. Yet it was probably his ability to sew these things together that was his strength as a novelist.

For his part, Phil was heartened by their talk; in particular, he valued Disch's suggestion that 2-3-74 resembled the *enthusiasmos* of prophecy, as when one is filled with the spirit of Elijah. Long passages in the *Exegesis* explore this theory, which bore fruit in *Valis* and *The Divine Invasion*.

But in the final months of 1974, Hollywood and Fame came a-calling, and Phil had exciting possibilities other than those posed by 2-3-74 to consider.

In September, French director Jean-Pierre Gorin met with Phil to negotiate a film option on *Ubik*. Phil had, at this point, three other novels optioned out to various Hollywood-based producers: *Time Out of Joint*, *The Three Stigmata of Palmer Eldritch*, and *Do Androids Dream of Electric Sheep?* But Gorin, who'd previously collaborated with Jean-Luc Godard, was an outsider in the Hollywood world. After a day of happy brainstorming, Gorin and Phil struck an agreement by which Gorin paid Phil, out of his own meager pocket, $1,500 down to produce a first-draft screenplay by December 31, 1975, with an additional $2,500 due on delivery. Things were looking bright: Francis Ford Coppola had expressed interest in producing the film. But the Coppola deal fell through. And then Phil went and finished the screenplay within a *month* instead of a year, which Gorin had never expected, producing an instant cash-flow crisis (Phil was eventually paid). In the end, despite great effort, Gorin failed to win financial backing for the project.

To interviewer D. S. Black, Gorin recalled his September 1974 meeting with Phil:

> He was a very broadshouldered, enthusiastic guy, who was from first contact very easy and very much fun. Apparently from the dialogue we had he was very much taken with the fact that some French dude talked to him as a writer. He was very fond of spinning out a thousand and one references a minute, ranging from what I learned to be one of his hobbies—Elizabethan poetry—to all sorts of considerations. [. . .] There was this very strange woman he was living with at the time—had this sort of bizarre look to herself, a Squeaky Fromme quality. Short skirt, long hair; he kept bantering with her. There was talk of women, sex and literature. A big, big guy like a bouncer; a low-culture Hemingway figure in some ways. Very, very warm and genuine in the way he interacted.

Two other visitors with movie-making aspirations paid calls in November. Robert Jaffe, son of producer Herb Jaffe, had written an *Androids* scrrenplay, which Phil roundly detested, though he enjoyed Jaffe's raffish Tinseltown gossip; Herb Jaffe let the *Androids* option expire. The second visitor, Hampton Fancher, was also interested in *Androids*. He paid two visits to Phil's Fullerton apartment, once accompanied by actress Barbara Hershey, who dazzled Phil. Fancher recalls that Phil treated him like a "cigar-chomping Hollywood producer after plunder." Despite this tension, Fancher remained fascinated:

> He was baronial, expansive, wall-to-wall effusiveness—come into my home, make dinner, "my dear," and so on. Germanic almost. There was no room for two-way conversations, no room for another ego in the same room. He was a brilliant guy. His eyes twinkled, he was congenial.
>
> I began to think that he was a little . . . that he lied. He told me things which I didn't know if he believed or not. Some of these things, if he *did* believe them, I thought that he might be, not clinically, but a touch paranoid. That the FBI is after him. And he would dramatize with physical, facial characteristics that were a little "over the top," as they say in acting. Telling a story of how the FBI came down on him, he would look around and demonstrate the position he was in, and enjoyed being watched.

Meanwhile, the publicity ground swell that had been building since 1973 was reaching its apex. Paul Williams conducted an interview in November 1974 for *Rolling Stone*. Shortly afterward, *New Yorker* staff writer Tony Hiss interviewed Phil for two sequential "Talk of the Town" pieces (January 27 and February 3, 1975), in which Phil was referred to as "our favorite science fiction writer," which was not to be taken to mean— nor did the Meredith Agency so take it—that the *New Yorker* would have published a trashy Phil Dick story on a bet.

One of the subjects that Phil discussed with Williams—within days of Fancher's visit—is alluded to by Fancher above. Paranoia. Phil didn't like the term, but conceded that it used to fit: "Okay. I used to believe the universe was basically hostile. [. . .] Now, I had a lot of fears that the universe would discover just how different I was from it." Phil then wove a fascinating premise—that religious belief pulls paranoia "inside out" and spiritually redeems it:

> [. . .] you see a pattern of events, and if you have no transcendent viewpoint, no mystical view, no religious view, then the pattern must emanate from people. Where else can it come from, if that's all . . .? [. . .] Turn it inside out, rather than just abolish it. That it's benign, and that it transcends our individualities and so on. The way I feel is that the universe itself is actually alive, and we're in it as a part of it. And it is like a breathing creature, which explains the concept of the Atman, you know, the breath, *pneuma*, the breath of God . . .

Phil was vouchsafed, in this *annus mirabilis*, one last key vision, of a Palm Tree Garden, in January and February 1975. In a 1981 *Exegesis* entry he wrote of "that other way of being-in-world that I associate with 2-74 to 2-75, what I call the Palm Tree Garden, or as I now term it, the Spacial Realm [. . .]" In the *Exegesis*, the Palm Tree Garden (PTG) is contrasted with the Black Iron Prison (BIP) of the Empire (reigning Authority) that never ended. Phil included his PTG vision in *Deus Irae*, his collaboration with Roger Zelazny. To Dorothy he wrote: "I walked about in it [the PTG] for several hours, enjoying it exactly as Dr. Abernathy does [. . .]" The passage was written solely by Phil:

> Dr. Abernathy felt the world's oppression lift but he did not have any insight as to why it had lifted. At the moment it began he had taken a walk to the market for the purchase of vegetables. [. . .]
>
> Somewhere, he thought, a good event has happened, and it spreads out. He saw to his amazement palm trees. [. . .] And dry dusty land, as if I'm in the Middle East. Another world; touches of another continuum. I don't understand, he thought. What is breaking through? As if my eyes are now opened, in a special way. [. . .]
>
> Somehow goodness has arrived, he decided. As Milton wrote, "Out of evil comes good." [. . .]
>
> Then, he thought, possibly the world has been cleared of its oppressive film by an evil act . . . or am I getting into subtleties? In any case, he sensed the difference; it was real.

I swear to God I'm somewhere in Syria, he thought. In the Levant. [. . .]
    To his right, the ruins of a prewar [the novel is set in SF future time] U.S.
Post Office substation.

Tessa recalls that spring day: "We were walking to the post office—a
regular habit, with us. [. . .] The post office [. . .] was a Byzantine-looking
brick building with archways and a false front that made it appear to be
domed. During the day, the city around us took on more and more of the
appearance of a first-century Roman colony. Phil kept seeing stone walls
and iron bars where more modern structures and barriers actually stood."
    In an undated typed page found among Phil's 1975 correspondence,
there is a fitting overview to the year of visions and voices, wisdom and
perplexity:

This is not an evil world, as Mani [founder of Manichaeanism, which
equates earthly matter with evil] supposed. There is a good world under the
evil. The evil is somehow superimposed over it (Maya), and when stripped
away, pristine glowing creation is visible.

One day the contents of my mind moved faster and faster until they ceased
being concepts and became percepts. I did not have concepts about the world
but perceived it without preconception or even intellectual comprehension. It
then resembled the world of UBIK. As if all the contents of one[']s mind, if
fused, became suddenly alive, a living entity, which took off within one's
head, on its own, saw in its own superior way, without regard to what you had
ever learned or seen or known. The principle of emergence, as when nonliv-
ing matter becomes living. As if information (thought concepts) when pushed
to their limit become metamorphosed into something alive. Perhaps then in
the outer world all the energy or information when pushed far enough will do
the same. Fuse into something everywhere (the force Ubik) that is sentient and
alive. Then inner-outer, then-now, cause-effect, all the antimonies will fade
out. We will see only a living entity at its ceaseless building: at work. Creating.
(Has continual creation almost reached completion?) (Such dichotomies as
big-small, me-notme will be transcended.)

The universe as unified information is, of course, a favorite metaphor of
quantum physics theorists.

◆

    Those skeptics who would dismiss 2-3-74 as the symptomology of a
stroke or the delusions of a psychotic should bear in mind (among other
limitations of reductive explanations) that Phil could be as skeptical as
themselves.
    Consider this *Exegesis* self-interview by Phil, just after having been
interviewed by Charles Platt in May 1979 for Platt's book *Dream Makers*.
Phil made his own tape of the Platt interview; upon reviewing it, he was

provoked into high courtroom drama, a cross-examination designed to impeach Phil's own integrity:

Listening to the Platt tape I construe by the logic presented [by himself] that Valis (the other mind) which came at me from outside & which overpowered me from inside was indeed the contents of my collective unconscious, & so technically a psychosis (it certainly would explain the animism outside, & the interior dissociated activity). But—well, okay; it would account for the AI voice, the 3 eyed sibyl, & the extreme archaism of the contents, & seeing Rome c. AD 45 would simply be psychotic delusion—I did not know where or when I really was.

Q: What about the resemblance to my writing?
A: The content was originally in my unconscious, e.g. "Tears" & "Ubik."
Q: What about external events? The girl? The letters?
A: Coincidence.
Q: & the written material? Huge books held open?
A: Verbal memory.
Q: Why would I believe that my senses were enhanced i.e. I could see for the first time?
A: Psychotomimetic drugs indicate this happens in psychosis.
Q: & *kosmos?* Everything fitting together?
A: "Spread of meanings" typical of psychosis.
Q: Foreign words I don't know?
A: Long term memory banks open. Disgorging their contents into consciousness.
Q: Problem solving—i.e. the Xerox missive?
A: There *was* no problem; it was harmless.
Q: Why the sense of time dysfunction?
A: Disorientation.
Q: Why the sense that the mind which had taken me over was wiser than me & more capable?
A: Release of psychic energy. [. . .]
Q: If 2-3-74 was psychosis, then what was the ego state which it obliterated.
A: Neurotic. Or mildly schizophrenia [sic]. Under stress the weak ego disintegrated.
Q: Then how could the phobias associated with my anxiety neurosis remain? e.g. agoraphobia?
A: It does not compute. Something is wrong. They should have gone away or become totally overwhelming. The impaired ego must have still been intact.
Q: Was my "dissociated" behavior [e.g., the Xerox missive, diagnosis of Christopher's hernia] bizarre?
A: No, they were problem-solving. It does not compute.
Q: Perhaps there were no real problems.
A: Not so. It was tax time.

From this point on, Phil, having considered the worst, rallied to his own defense. It cannot be said that he is convincing either in condemning his sanity or in exalting 2-3-74. Finally, the answer seems to lie in Phil's first and lasting loss:

A: Then the enigma remains.
Q: We have learned nothing.
A: Nothing.
Q: After finishing listening to the tape do you have any intuition or guess as to who & what the Valis mind is? (Later.)
A: Yes. It is female. It is on the other side—the post mortem world. It has been with me all my life. It is my twin sister Jane. [. . .] The other psyche I carry inside me is that of my dead sister.

For those yearning for a diagnosis to slap onto 2-3-74, good news: Temporal lobe epilepsy can induce seizures that are neither disabling nor obvious for purposes of medical diagnosis or the individual's own sense of something amiss. It can't be disproven that Phil may have had such seizures during 2-3-74—or other times throughout his life. And if he did, *everything* is explained—from the AI Voice to the endless *Exegesis*. Consider this eerily on-the-money description from a medical study:

Such "psychic" or "experiential" phenomena activated by epileptic discharge arising in the temporal lobe may occur as complex visual or auditory or combined auditory-visual hallucinations or illusions, memory "flashbacks," erroneous interpretations of the present in terms of the past (e.g. as an inappropriate feeling of familiarity or strangeness, the "déjà vu" and "jamais vu" phenomena), or as emotions, most commonly fear. Penfield [. . .] called these phenomena "experiential," an appropriate term considering the fact that to the affected patients they often assume an astonishingly vivid immediacy, which they liken to that of actual events. Nevertheless, the patients are never in doubt that these phenomena occur incongruously, that is, out of context, as if they were superimposed upon the ongoing stream of consciousness, with the exception of fear, which is sometimes interpreted as fear of an impending attack. This insight clearly distinguishes these phenomena from psychotic hallucinations and illusions.

Not bad as a skeptic's schematic of 2-3-74. A standard psychiatric textbook includes the following as behavioral traits of patients suffering from temporal lobe seizures:

Hypergraphia is an obsessional phenomenon manifested by writing extensive notes and diaries. [. . .] The intense emotions are often labile, so that the patient may exhibit great warmth at one time, whereas, at another time, anger

and irritability may evolve to rage and aggressive behavior. [. . .] Suspicious-
ness may extend to paranoia, and a sense of helplessness may lead to passive
dependency. [. . .] Religious beliefs not only are intense, but may also be
associated with elaborate theological or cosmological theories. Patients may
believe that they have special divine guidance. [. . .]

There are, of course, also listed traits that miss Phil by a mile, such as
"stern moralism" and "humorless sobriety."

For those seeking a reasonable diagnosis, temporal lobe epilepsy does
the trick. One can even go so far as to group writers who may have been
influenced—in their spiritual concerns—by the *possible* presence of temporal lobe epilepsy. Dostoevsky, who suffered from epileptic seizures,
is one prominent example. But how far do such speculative diagnostics
and groupings take us? William James draws the line this way: "To
pass a spiritual judgment upon these states, we must not content ourselves with superficial medical talk, but inquire into their fruits for
life."

What "fruits" were there for Phil's personal life? Phil seldom doubted
that 2-3-74 was a blessing. But he never claimed to have become a saint.
A 1975 *Exegesis* entry makes this plain:

[. . .] I am in no customary sense—maybe in no sense whatsoever—
spiritualized or exalted. In fact I seem even more mean and irascible than
before. True, I do not hit anybody, but my language remains gunjy and I am
crabby and domineering; my personal defects are unaltered. In the accepted
sense I am not a better person. [. . .]

But as to the lack of proper spiritual refurbishing in me . . . perhaps we have
too clear an attitude toward pious transformations as being the ones He wishes
in us. Perhaps these are our standards for the very pure; after all, He would
retain the individual, I think, and not force us all into one proper mold. I have
been changed, but not in all ways; I have been improved, but not according to
human standards. I can only hope I am obeying His will and not my own.

I do not conform to my own views of goodness, but maybe I do to His.

Tessa's perspective is similar:

I saw no personality change in Phil. If anything, he was more of what he
had been before the experience. It did hold our relationship together, but it
also tore us apart, in the end [the marriage ended in 1976]. Just as Phil
believed that someone was out to get him, to kill him, he came to believe that
someone was out to kill his wife and child. Phil was so intense, immediately
following a vision, that his presence in the room became a tangible thing, a
thickness of the atmosphere. But he was only quantitatively different, not
qualitatively different. There were brief periods, however, when Phil was not
himself the way an apple is not a rectangle.

The events of 2-3-74 and after are unusual, even bizarre. There are scenes of tender beauty, as when Phil administered the eucharist to Christopher. There are instances of inexplicable foresight, as when he diagnosed his son's hernia. And there are episodes, like the Xerox missive, that foster skepticism. For some, the visions and voices will constitute evidence of grace. Others, both atheists and religionists, will doubt 2-3-74 for those very reasons. Saint John of the Cross warned:

> It often happens that spiritual men are affected supernaturally by sensible representations and objects. They sometimes see the forms and figures of those of another life, saints or angels, good and evil, or certain extraordinary lights and brightness. They hear strange words, sometimes seeing those who utter them and sometimes not. [. . .] we must never delight in them nor encourage them; yea, rather we must fly from them, without seeking to know whether their origin be good or evil. For, inasmuch as they are exterior and physical, the less is the likelihood of their being from God.

There are, of course, eminent examples through the ages of persons who did not fly from such signs. One such is Blaise Pascal. On the night of November 23, 1654, Pascal experienced a vision that he transcribed, sewing the account into the lining of his coat so as to keep it by him constantly:

> From about half past ten in the evening until about half past twelve
> FIRE
> God of Abraham, God of Isaac, God of Jacob, not of the philosophers and scholars.
> Certitude. Certitude. Feeling. Joy. Peace.

And here we come to the heart of Phil's 2-3-74 experiences. Certitude had he none. Oh yes, one can find numerous passages—in interviews, the novels, and the *Exegesis*—in which Phil advances a theory with the sound of certitude. But always (and usually quite soon thereafter) he reconsidered and recanted.

Indeterminacy is the central characteristic of 2-3-74.

And how fitting that is. Mystical experiences are almost always in keeping with the tradition of the mystic. Julian of Norwich, a Catholic, perceived "great drops of blood" running down from a crown of thorns. Milarepa, a Tibetan Buddhist, visualized his guru surrounded by multifold Buddhas on lotus seats of wisdom.

Phil adhered to no single faith. The one tradition indubitably his was SF—which exalts "What IF?" above all.

In 2-3-74, all the "What IFs?" were rolled up into one.

As *Valis* proved, it was, say whatever else you will, a great idea for a novel.

11 As 2-3-74 Ripens Into Valis, Phil Fashions New Theories Nightly Yet Wonders—Meta-abstractions Be Damned—If Ever He'll Find The True Love He Deserves (Who Doesn't?), While Slowly He Discovers (Sometimes) Something Like Happiness Anyway (1975–1978)

Year after year, book after book & story, I shed illusion after illusion: self, time, space, causality, world—& finally sought (in 1970) to know what was real. Four years later, at my darkest moment of dread & trembling, my ego crumbling away, I was granted dibba cakkhu *[enlightenment]—& although I didn't realize it at the time, I became a Buddha. ("The Buddha is in the park") [AI voice message]. All illusion dissolved away like a soap bubble & I saw reality at last—&, in the 4 ½ years since, have at last comprehended it intellectually—i.e. what I saw & knew & experienced (my exegesis). We are talking here about a lifetime of work & insights: from my initial satori when, as a child, I was tormenting the beetle. It began in that moment, forty years ago.*

PHIL, September 1978 *Exegesis* entry, just before writing *Valis*

My God, my life—which is to say my 2-74/3-74 experience—is exactly like the plot of any one of ten of my novels or stories. Even down to the fake memories & identity. I'm a protagonist from one of PKD's books, USA 1974 fades out, ancient Rome fades in & with it the Thomas personality & true memories. Jeez! Mixture of "Impostor," "Joint" & "Maze"—if not "Ubik" as well.

PHIL, earlier 1978 *Exegesis* entry

(It is also obvious that I have let the world know [in Valis] that I went through some bad years, during the last decade. Future biographers will find their job done for them before they start. My life's an open book and I myself wrote the book.)

PHIL, February 1981 letter to agent Russell Galen

YOU'D suppose that, with 2-3-74 to ponder, life would be anything but dull.

But dull was precisely Phil's complaint as New Year's Eve 1975 rolled around. Next door in their Fullerton apartment building, a neighbor was throwing a big loud bash. Meanwhile, Tessa used the night to catch up on laundry, while Phil was left to pop Christopher's balloon with a cigarette as midnight arrived. In a letter two days later he railed: "I hadn't realized before how fucking dumb and dull and futile and empty middle class life is. I have gone from the gutter (circa 1971) to the plastic container. As always, I got it wrong once again."

It wasn't that their life was all that secure. Phil would take in roughly $19,000 in 1974 and $35,000 in 1975, but a good chunk of that income was advances on royalties made by the Meredith Agency to keep Phil afloat between irregular royalty checks. Foreign sales were his mainstay: British, French, Italian, German, Swedish, Dutch, and Japanese rights accounted for the bulk of Phil's real earnings in 1975. Tentatively, Phil and Tessa were beginning to nibble at the bottom end of the good life. Phil treated himself to the new *Encyclopaedia Britannica 3*, in which he read voraciously; citations to it in the *Exegesis* are legion. For Tessa, there was a new guitar and a fee-stabled horse. In March they moved from Cameo Lane to a rented house—Phil's credit rating didn't allow for a purchase—at 2461 Santa Ysabel in Fullerton. In April 1975, Phil popped for a red Fiat Spyder—his first sports car since Anne.

It felt good. And it gnawed at him. There was *more*. Phil wrestled with it in the *Exegesis*—handwritten as if to emphasize its provisional nature. In his fiction, Phil balanced his themes of "What is Human?" and "What is Real?" As to the former, Phil felt he knew the answer: kindness. But as to the latter, he never made up his mind. On this question, the *Exegesis* gave him room to fly—creating and banishing worlds at will.

From the nightly sessions certain key ideas began to emerge. One of these is "orthogonal time," which Phil discusses in a 1975 essay, "Man, Android and Machine." Orthogonal time is "rotary," moving perpendicularly to "linear" time. It contains "as a simultaneous plane or extension everything which was, just as the grooves on an LP contain that part of the music which has already been played; they don't disappear after the stylus tracks them." In a March letter to Ursula Le Guin Phil honed the concept: Orthogonal time was "Real Time"—"without it, there would be nothing but illusion, nothing but Maya, so to speak."

In the spring, Phil received some welcome visits from friends and family. His daughter Isa was a brief houseguest, as was Loren Cavit, his loyal friend from the dark days of 1971. Cartoonist Art Spiegelman, who was then editing *Arcade*, made an overnight stop. He and Phil had first met in 1973, after Phil had written a glowing fan letter in response to a Spiegelman comic strip about Walt Disney coming back to life in a Tomorrowland world of robot presidents. Phil now proposed a collaboration; but the story Phil submitted in March 1975—"The Eye of the

Sibyl"—was, like the 1974 *Ubik* screenplay, too intricate for adaptation to the intended (comic book/movie) medium.

In this same month came an unfortunate rift with Harlan Ellison. The circumstances were ideally suited to hurt Ellison's feelings. Phil and Ellison had socialized on an occasional basis since Phil's 1972 move to Orange County, but the friendship had grown uneasy. Ellison felt that Phil was jealous of his financial success and Hollywood connections. For Phil, there was some lingering, if unjustified, resentment over the reference to Phil's LSD use in Ellison's 1967 anthology *Dangerous Visions*. Personal frictions aside, Phil had proclaimed that Ellison's story "The Deathbird" "will be read for centuries to come." It was hardly surprising that Ellison thought of Phil as an apt writer to contribute an essay to an Ellison tribute issue planned by *F & SF*. Nor is it surprising that, after telling Ellison he'd be glad to oblige, Phil declined in a letter to *F & SF* editor Edward Ferman (a friend of Ellison's), explaining that he hadn't been fully awake when Ellison called, didn't care for most of Ellison's work, and didn't do freebies. Ferman wrote back explaining that he'd intended to pay. Ellison, who regarded Phil's concerns over being paid as an affront to Ferman's editorial integrity, sent Phil a vituperative termination-of-friendship notice.

But all this fury with Ellison was by way of the mails. In daily life, tender feelings and reasonably good tidings prevailed. The long collaboration with Roger Zelazny finally bore fruit when *Deus Irae* was completed in July. The Entwhistle Books edition of *Crap Artist* also appeared that month: a published mainstream novel at long last. Driving himself full bore, Phil finished revisions to *Scanner* by August. This effort was fueled in part by Phil's desire to collect the final advance installment from Doubleday and repay a loan from Robert Heinlein, who'd already been an SF giant back when Phil first started reading the pulps. Heinlein and Tessa had established a friendship after meeting at a 1974 SF gathering. Phil hadn't attended, but a warm correspondence between the two writers ensued. During summer 1975, as the bank account bottomed out, Tessa asked Heinlein for a loan. While Phil was grateful, his wife's going asking for money shamed him. After Heinlein turned down a second loan request, the letters stopped. (When the two finally met in 1977, the encounter was brief and awkward.)

Meanwhile, Phil remained publicly circumspect on 2-3-74. When he learned that an essay on his work by Thomas Disch would appear in the December 1975 *Crawdaddy*, Phil wrote to Disch requesting silence as to 2-3-74. "I'm still having mystical visions and revelations (but that's our little secret, not for the readership of *Crawdaddy* who really wouldn't want to know anyhow, would they?)."

The dramatic visions of the first months had not reappeared, but visionary dreams and the hypnogogic AI voice continued. To comprehend as best he could, Phil searched through the *Britannica*, the

Encyclopedia of Philosophy, works on Orphic, Gnostic, Zoroastrian, and Buddhist thought, *The New Testament Decoded*, studies on bicameral brain research—no philosopher's stone was left unturned. In a July 1975 *Exegesis* entry he took stock:

> I feel a great peace now, at last, for the first time in my life. This whole period, including 3-74, has been arduous; [. . .] I believe I've worn myself out more with this than with any previous writing, any novel or group of novels. [. . .] What does it all add up to (at this point in my knowledge)? I passed through the narrow gate in mid-74, and now I am told that he will come back for the world itself, fairly soon.

When not immersed in night-shift *Exegesis* speculations, Phil was reestablishing contact with his original circle of Fullerton friends, including Mary Wilson and Tim Powers. Powers, who kept a journal, is the Boswell of Phil's life in Orange County. Here is Powers's account of "The Most Brilliant SF Mind on Any Planet" (as *Rolling Stone* had billed him in November 1975) imagining all the possibilities while graciously autographing his latest work:

> One time Phil was signing a book for a young lady who always, despite being the steady girlfriend of a friend of ours, managed to give an impression of lighthearted promiscuity. Phil scribbled in the book for a little while, then looked up at the young man and asked, "How do you spell 'gorgeous'? Our friend told him, and Phil scribbled some more. Then, "How do you spell 'anticipate'? Our friend spelled it out for him, not quite as cheerfully as before. Finally Phil paused again and asked, "How do you spell 'consummate'?", and the young man burst out, "Goddammit, Phil . . ."

Phil enjoyed playful flirtations, but they grew increasingly painful for Tessa. Phil himself, in a 1975 *Exegesis* entry, confessed that he felt like a "dirty old man" after one party flirtation. To exacerbate matters, Tessa would tend Phil during his bedridden bouts of depression and agoraphobia, but was left behind when Phil arose ready for the world again. She writes:

> In late 1975 and early 1976, he found himself able to go out more often, but not with me. He could go with the guys, or even with another woman, but not with me. He assured me that these relationships were purely platonic, but I didn't care. I was tired of being confined to the house with a small baby. I did not enjoy going out alone. If I went out for more than half an hour, Phil became depressed. It upset him terribly when, in September 1975, I began school. I took two classes at the junior college: German and biology. The German was so I could understand Phil when he spoke it. The biology interested me because I had wanted to be a veterinarian.

Phil had been getting counseling since 1973, and in addition to his psychotherapy, we had marriage counselling. The psychologists and the psychiatrist had tried all sorts of therapy and medication, all to no effect. Phil was diagnosed as manic depressive. I always disputed that. I felt that it all went back to his twin sister's death. He never got over that loss, and he was always looking for a substitute for that sister. As his wife, I would not do, because that would make our relationship incestuous. Therefore, he had to surround himself with women who were just friends. That was why he could go out with another woman, and not with me.

While Phil griped about the marriage to friends, he felt an acute need for a stable family setting. In July 1975, Tessa and Christopher paid a weeklong visit to her family. For the prior three years, Phil and Tessa had seldom spent a night apart. Now Phil surprised himself by gritting it out. From a July letter:

I've always thought of people who liked to be alone as sick, as schizoid. Now I find that I am having difficulty adjusting to other people in the house—my adjustment to solitude was that good, that complete. [. . .] Secretly, in my own head, I thought my own thoughts and began to settle down and enjoy myself. It is, I believe, a permanent change in me. The lessons beaten into me in all that therapy at X-Kalay [survival as part of a group] burst into fragments last week; they had to; they no longer applied.

It was not, in fact, a "permanent change," though it did mark the beginning of a changed attitude. In the last years of his life, Phil lived alone and came to appreciate solitude. But in 1975, life alone—for however brief an interval—could be outright anguish. Tessa and Christopher went off on another family visit over Labor Day; just prior to their departure, Phil grew depressed enough to contemplate suicide. While they were gone, he vented his anger and misery in the *Exegesis*:

If she does return this time she will leave again [. . .]; this is the fledgling practice flights. [. . .]

It is important (to me anyhow) to note that I have achieved for Tessa just about every material thing she ever named as wanting [. . .] I have the hollow shell built to enclose this family, but the family is dead. [. . .] I equipped Nancy the same way and she left; in each case I took a young girl who lived at home and had nothing, gave her what she wanted; whereupon she left, with my child. It is as if I am a bridge for fledgling girls, taking them to womanhood and motherhood, whereupon my value ends and I am discarded.

As it happened, it was Phil who finally left Tessa, in the summer of 1976, after further struggles and "fledgling practice flights" on Tessa's part. But Phil was clearly aware of the difficulties his fifth marriage was facing, and he was, moreover, distracted by his deepening feelings for another woman.

Phil first met Doris Sauter in 1972, while she was dating Norman Spinrad. Then in her early twenties, Doris was attractive and intelligent, a brown-haired California native with a love for SF and a growing commitment to her Christian beliefs. Their friendship intensified in the spring of 1974, when Doris confided to Phil about her recent conversion experience. Naturally, Phil was delighted, and in turn told Doris all about 2-3-74.

Doris—the principal inspiration for Sherri Solvig in *Valis* and Rybys Romney in *The Divine Invasion*—believes that, at root, Phil was Christian in outlook. "Christianity helped him to integrate aspects of his personality. The life of Christ helped Phil put his own past poverty in perspective, and he became even more ethical and caring for the poor." Would Phil have felt comfortable being defined as Christian in belief? Doris replies:

> If you had asked him what he believed, his answer would have depended on what kind of theoretical fever he was running at the time. When the rubber hit the road, he wanted a priest to talk to. One of the first places Phil went after his March religious experiences was an Episcopal church in Placentia—not a Moony parlor.
>
> In a sense, religion became Phil's business when he started to write theological novels in the seventies. Not that he wasn't religious. But it also had this quality of being useful—as material for the next book. Imagination was his stock in trade, and he tried out theories to see how people reacted.

Phil and Doris planned, for spring 1975, to help *The Agitator*, a liberal-left Catholic newspaper, by subscribing to fifty copies, which they would hand out free to Cal State Fullerton students. They also contacted the House of Hospitality soup kitchen in Los Angeles, to which Phil had previously donated funds. It was to be a time of commitment and high adventure.

But then everything changed. And their bond grew stronger.

In May 1975 Doris was diagnosed as suffering from cancer. She lost weight, her eyesight diminished, and she was in the last stage of lymphatic cancer. Even prior to her cancer, Phil had been struck by the fact that Doris, like himself, had undergone a premature birth. He explained his own barrel-chested physique as the result of struggling for air as an infant. Doris recalls during her cancer sufferings that Phil would insist that her struggle "started with that first struggle to breathe. Premature birth was an important determinant, and metaphor, to Phil. He would attach to certain women because he was looking for his twin."

During the latter half of 1975, Phil repeatedly urged Doris and two of her friends to move into the house with his family. Fortunately, her cancer had gone into remission by the end of 1975, though Doris continued to suffer from *grand mal* seizures. But Phil's yearning to live with Doris continued apace. In January 1976, Phil asked Doris to marry him. Doris refused: She loved him but did not wish to disrupt his marriage to Tessa. Also, she was skeptical: "Phil had a way of bonding to people who were in trouble. One of the reasons I never wanted to marry him was that I felt that might be operative in our relationship, and that it wasn't healthy. But he really did *want* to help—some of that could be manipulative, but most was genuine."

Meanwhile, the domestic harmony Phil and Tessa had known was increasingly punctuated by fierce quarrels. Their marriage was spiraling into precisely the scenario Phil feared most—his wife, their child in her arms, leaving him alone in a house filled with memories. In February 1976, after a bad fight, Tessa took Christopher and left. Powers, in his journal, recalls visiting Phil while Tessa was packing—she took the coffee table on which their wineglasses rested. "Never oversee what they take," Phil advised his friend. "It is better to let them take what they like and inventory afterwards." Tessa states that Phil had demanded that she leave. However it all went down, what happened next is undisputed.

Chapter 4 of *Valis* opens with a droll, hellish, and largely accurate account of, thankfully, the last serious suicide attempt Phil would ever make; Powers's journal is an invaluable complementary source. Phil ingested forty-nine high-grade digitalis tablets (over twelve times the daily dose prescribed to him for his arrhythmia), assorted Librium, Quide, and Apresoline (an antihyperintensive, used to treat high blood pressure) pills, and half a bottle of wine. For good measure, he slashed his left wrist and sat in his Fiat in a closed garage with the engine running. "Fat was technically dead," explains *Valis* narrator Phil Dick. How did he survive? The wrist bleeding coagulated, the Fiat stalled, he vomited up some of the drugs. In the morning he somehow made it to the mailbox: There was the typescript of *Deus Irae*. He put out water for the cat. And suddenly Phil no longer wanted to die. He phoned his therapist, who told him to call the paramedics. Time was of the essence; the digitalis had all but depleted the potassium in Phil's body. He was rushed to Orange County Medical Center and was shortly thereafter transferred—by an armed cop pushing him in a wheelchair—from cardiac intensive care to the psych ward.

Beth, Fat's wife in *Valis*, is based upon Tessa. It is, for the most part, an unpleasant and accusatory portrait. Tessa writes: "He was angry; so was I. I do not take offense at the portrayal of Beth." In *Valis*, Beth refuses to visit Fat in the hospital. Tessa visited twice, once with Christopher, and brought clothing. Snuff and a Bible were provided by Powers. The amenities were nice, but winding up in a lockup nut ward after barely surviving a suicide that by all rights should have succeeded scared the hell out of Phil. Lying on his cot, he went through his dark night of the soul in true American style: "Fat could see the communal TV set, which remained on. Johnny Carson's guest turned out to be Sammy Davis, Jr. Fat lay watching, wondering how it felt to have one glass eye. At that point he had no insight into his situation." Where was the higher wisdom of 2-3-74? "Either he had seen God too soon or he had seen him too late. In any case, it had done him no good at all in terms of survival. Encountering the living God had not equipped him for the tasks of ordinary endurance, which ordinary men, not so favored, handle."

Phil did rouse himself by the time his fourteen-day hospital stay— under observation, with the prospect of ninety days more being tacked on—ended. One frequent visitor was Doris Sauter, who recalls that one day "Phil looked up at me and asked, 'Now will you move in with me?' But I played hardball with Phil. I didn't want to be manipulated, and I told him to 'get up off your butt.' The paramedics were staring, but Phil admired me for how I handled him that day." Phil also felt a new respect for his own body—its will to live even at the height of the digitalis convulsions—which helped him to refrain from future attacks upon it.

After his discharge, Phil and Tessa stayed together through May. But he had resolved to live with Doris. His arguments to Doris focused on mutual need: Doris was in a weakened state and in danger of suffering further grand mal seizures; Phil had high blood pressure and was subject to unexpected collapse. He pledged to end his marriage even if she refused him. Despite his ardor, breaking up marriage and family troubled Phil. There were memories of father Edgar's traumatic departure to dispel. "I was not roaming off into fields of pleasure, like my father did," Phil avowed in one letter.

The move took them from Fullerton to Santa Ana: 408 East Civic Center Drive #C1, which would remain Phil's address for the rest of his life. It was still Orange County, but there were important differences. The building featured an elaborate security system—a reassurance to Phil, who'd had more than his share of uninvited guests. Also, it was situated on the edge of the barrio. Across the street was the Catholic St. Joseph's Church—the pealing bells delighted him. Down the block was the Episcopal Church of the Messiah. Nearby was a twenty-four-hour Trader Joe's, where, during nighttime shifts, Phil could break for roast beef sandwiches and Orange Crush. Also nearby was Tim Powers's apartment, where Phil was always welcome.

Money Phil had in something like abundance for the first time. Mark Hurst, a young editor at Bantam Books, was a staunch Phil Dick advocate. Publicity in *Rolling Stone* and other venues gave Hurst the leverage to strike the best deals in Phil's career to date. In May 1976, Bantam acquired three novels—*Palmer Eldritch, Ubik*, and A *Maze of Death*—for $20,000, a far cry from Phil's typical $2,000-per-title reprint advances. Still more dazzling was a $12,000 Bantam advance for a novel to be called *Valisystem* A (finally published, in 1981, as *Valis*). Of course, SF in the mid- to late seventies was enjoying a boom. Phil's big money paled beside the six-figure advances less talented peers raked in—but then, his sales hardly rivaled theirs. No matter. Phil was flush, and the novel targeted for so long in the *Exegesis* had a contract.

Phil enjoyed a summer of happiness with Doris. Their new apartment had two bedrooms and two bathrooms, assuring him privacy for writing. He'd brought along his cat Harvey and his massive record collection. One album cover depicting an alien being (probably the Starship album *Dragonfly*) led to a startle for Doris during their first week together. Phil confided to her that, while looking at this cover, he'd realized that, fundamentally, his being was not of this Earth. Was he sincere or testing the limits of future readers' credulity? Both, most likely. Doris confirms that Phil seemed sincere when he said it—and that such speculations came and went.

Together they explored the barrio neighborhood, but Phil continued to be troubled by agoraphobia. To Doris, he ascribed his anxieties to his chronic mourning for Jane. In restaurants, Phil was careful to take large enough mouthfuls to provide an adequate bolus for easy swallowing. In their apartment, Doris recalls, "Phil only had two switches: 'I'm not writing now and I want your attention entirely' and 'I'm writing now and I want no one's attention.' " In the first mode, Phil was a charming man with a sly, weird sense of humor that could pull Doris out of her blackest moods. They would cook dinner together and then sit down to a cable movie. In the second mode, you wanted to stay clear.

He went at it eighteen to twenty hours a day by this schedule: Wake up at 10:00 A.M., write all day, down some quick "swill" at 5:00 P.M., and then back at it till 5:00 to 6:00 A.M. Stories took one or two days, novels ten days to two weeks. His concentration was intense—no noise allowed but for his own music. Phil would joke that he had to write fast, as his notes were so lousy he'd otherwise forget his plot. But Phil was great at making detailed notes he never followed. Fast was essential: The book took hold of him as it was written, flowing from his fingers. Phil avoided playing the piano, as he feared it might decrease his typing speed. Not that Phil would refuse to revise: under the guidance of Ballantine editor Judy-Lynn Del Rey, he undertook painstaking revisions to *Scanner* in 1975. He would bemoan the fact that his pulp past had trained him to churn it out to stay alive. But even when Phil could afford to take his time, that first draft had to come in a flash.

It didn't take long for problems to arise. When Phil wasn't writing, his intense demands made Doris feel that no privacy was left to her. Writing or not, Phil writhed when Doris spent time away from him with other friends—male *or* female. And there was the nasty image of "cohabitation." Phil canceled, in August, a planned visit by Isa (now nine years old) on the grounds that she shouldn't be exposed to such an arrangement. Then there were money hassles. Phil generously paid for their food and rent and gave Doris his old Dodge. But he was also prone to pointing out just how generous he was, making himself seem victimized (to his friends) and manipulative (to Doris). Doris recalls offering several times to pay half the expenses; Phil refused her money. In August, Doris decided to return to college in the fall, a necessity for her goal of Episcopal priesthood. Phil offered to pay two thousand dollars in tuition, then backed out at the last moment on grounds of financial necessity. Doris barely managed to make alternate arrangements—and she was furious.

In September, the apartment next door opened up, and Doris took it. She saw it as a move that would preserve the good times while giving her needed privacy. To Phil, it was a devastating confirmation that his "rescuer" role would backfire forever. In June he'd walked out on a marriage, and here it was September and he was living alone again. Gak. In late September Phil asked Powers to drive him to his analyst's office. The reason: Phil had recently gone the wrong way against traffic, turning into a gas station at the last minute to avoid a suicidal crash; now he didn't quite trust himself to drive. Thankfully, as his depression persisted, Phil checked into the mental ward of St. Joseph's Hospital in Orange on October 19. Powers's journal records: "Doris drove him to the hospital and she took delight in him telling everyone, 'This is Doris—she drove me here.' He told her he loved her so much it made him crazy."

Two days after his admittance, Powers paid Phil a visit:

> He was entirely cheerful (unlike the aftermath of the [February] suicide attempt), and he told me about a girl he'd met in the hospital, a Dylan fan and ex-doper; he had vague plans to look her up after he checked out. He told me he'd "flipped out" in Trader Joe's on Tuesday while buying kitty litter, but I think to some extent Phil used to buy therapy just to cheer himself up.
>
> One of the doctors there had told Phil that he (Phil, not the doctor) picked remarkably unsuitable girls to fall in love with. Phil told me this and shrugged. "It's true, Powers," he admitted. "The way I get girls is to put two rocks in a sack and go out in the woods with a flashlight, then I bring the rocks together and close up the mouth of the sack after something's run into it."

The jest does no justice to Doris. Phil's fierce attachment to her endured even after he left the hospital and they made the adjustment to neighborly relations. And he grieved when, in December, Doris lost her remission. Ultimately, she would regain full health. But during a difficult first year of recovery, Phil bought Doris a bed, looked after her fondly, and endured the painful vomiting noises that came through their adjoining wall (the same is endured, to a humanizing end, by Herb Asher in *The Divine Invasion*). Phil also gave roughly $2,400 to fund Doris's social work job at the Episcopal Church of the Messiah. He'd help Doris and the poor at the same time: perfect. Except that the money wound up funding a higher-up bureaucratic committee. The diversion from immediate needs did not please Phil, who had long been skeptical of the Church as an institution. But his feeling for Episcopal teachings had run deep since the *Palmer Eldritch* days. And he followed doctrinal disputes sufficiently to take a position against female priests, because during the mass the priest becomes Christ—a man.

In late 1976, editor Hurst asked for minor revisions in the *Valisystem A* manuscript (which would ultimately be published, in the form in which Phil submitted it to Hurst, as *Radio Free Albemuth* in 1985). Unbeknown to Hurst, this set Phil to thinking of a completely new novel (as opposed to mere revisions) that would grapple with 2-3-74 more completely. After all, the *Exegesis* was yielding ever more startling ideas. In December 1976 came the "Zebra Principle." Back in the sixties, Phil had read *The Mask of Medusa*, a study of insect mimicry which suggested that humans could be as deceived by a hypothetical "high-order mimicry" as birds are by insect mimicry (or lions by zebras' stripes). Phil's Zebra Principle asks: What if the "high-order mimicry" were that of a higher, or even divine, intelligence? To Hurst, Phil explained:

> Zebra, if it can be said to resemble the contents of any religion, resembles the Hindu concept of Brahman:
>
> *"They reckon ill who leave me out,*
> *When me they fly I am the wings.*
> *I am the doubter and the doubt,*
> *And I the hymn the Brahman sings."*
> [quotation from *Bhagavad Gita*]

Creating a worthy new novel seemed to necessitate that Phil reread and analyze all of his past SF to determine what, in light of 2-3-74, he had already accomplished. (*Crap Artist* alone among the mainstream works receives attention in the *Exegesis.*) Here's one stab at a summation, from a 1977 entry:

> So one dozen novels & too many stories to count narrate a message of one world obscuring or replacing another (real) one, spurious memories, & hallucinated (irreal) worlds. The message reads "Don't believe what you see; it's an enthralling—& destructive, evil snare. *Under* it is a totally different world, even placed differently along the linear time axis. & your memories are faked to jibe with the fake world (inner & outer congruency).["]

In another 1977 entry, Phil underscored that kindness is the sole means we possess to ascertain the truth of this world:

> If this [the influence of occluding satanic powers] be so, then my writing has been of value, beyond the obvious contribution of indicting the universe as a

forgery (& our memories also) & present the most accurate and stringent—rigorous—*revised* criteria to pull the truly real as set out of ground (Love, making exceptions, humor, determination, etc. The *little* virtues).

Exegesis ferment was one reason Phil could make a successful adjustment to living alone. Another was the peaceful and friendly relations he had established with Tessa, who came with Christopher for a visit two or three times a week, even as the divorce was finalized in February 1977. Though legal custody of Christopher had been given to Tessa, Phil could continue to be with his son.

Then too, Phil had the good fortune to live within walking distance of Powers, whose good humor, calm outlook, and broad reading made him an ideal confidant. Powers was hosting Thursday-night gatherings that solidified into a tradition. Informality was the rule, and the core group, aside from Phil, consisted of budding authors Powers, K. W. Jeter, and James Blaylock, who have since become three of the most prominent SF writers of their generation. Also often present were Steve Malk, who worked in a bookstore and supplied Phil with the latest in philosophy and religion; Roy Squires, a bibliophile and small-press publisher; and brothers Chris and Greg Arena, whose street smarts fascinated Phil. Thursday nights had a decided men's club feel: Women were excluded (Serena Powers became the exception after her marriage to Tim in 1980). Guidelines were established as necessity dictated: no firearms, no coming or going through the window of the second-floor apartment. As Powers was working at a tobacconist's, there were pipes and aromatic blends to sample, while others brought fine malt Scotches.

But Phil usually kept to snuff and Orange Crush. He was one of the guys and writing was what he did for a living. Says Powers, in interview: "I think Phil's very emotional side that his girlfriends saw was not one he dragged out among his male friends. He looked at his sessions with his friends as a kind of relief from that." Phil's typical topics were health worries, car worries, the Bible and anything metaphysical, music, politics, and his big crushes on Victoria Principal, Kay Lenz, and, most of all, Linda Ronstadt. Blaylock recalls:

> It wasn't his writing that made me admire him so much, it was his sheer depth of goodness. He had this idea that a person you didn't know would help you for no reason at all—and Phil was that person. And he was very funny. The laughter seldom stopped.
>
> He would always be eager to discuss whatever idea in the *Exegesis* he was working on at the moment—he was fascinated with Fibonacci [the discoverer of the golden rectangle ratio] and the Gnostics. We would sit there gaping while Phil spun out big extravagant relationships between these seemingly random things in such a convincing way. By the end of the evening . . . I won't swear I believed it, but I was scared shitless sometimes, or in awe other times.

K. W. Jeter, the third young writer of the triumvirate, was equally fascinated by Phil's speculations but always more skeptical than Blaylock or Powers. Phil and Jeter had first met in 1972 after Professor McNelly showed Phil the manuscript of a novel Jeter, then a student, had written. (The novel, *Dr. Adder*, was finally published in 1984, with an "Afterword" by Phil.) But Phil had been suspicious that Jeter might be a government agent and so resolved to break off personal contact. But they resumed their friendship in late 1976, after a three-year hiatus, and now Jeter played the gadfly role to perfection. A former antiwar activist in the Socialist Workers Party, Jeter was little drawn to the religious theories Phil fashioned from his 2-3-74 experiences. But Jeter knew how to stoke the theoretical fires, adding complexities on top of Phil's own. He called attention to the similarities between Phil's novels and those of William Burroughs—such as an invading alien virus occluding human faculties (for Burroughs, the virus is language). Jeter and Phil even performed their own Burroughs-influenced "cut-up" writing experiment, scrambling texts from Roderick Thorp's *The Detective*, Melville's *Moby Dick*, and the New Testament Book of Acts.

Jeter held down a graveyard-shift watchman job at the Orange County Juvenile Hall, which allowed time for late-night phone calls from Phil, who would interrupt his *Exegesis* stints to test out the latest possibilities on his friend. To interviewer Andy Watson, Jeter emphasizes that, for all his theoretical enthusiasms, Phil retained a skeptical outlook: "[I]n his other hand, out of sight, is always kept what we would call [. . .] the *minimum hypothesis*. Which is that it [2-3-74] was nothing." In interview with the author, Jeter suggests that, even in his most fervent *Exegesis* passages, "Phil is getting inside a belief and walking around it and testing it out by the measure of absolute truth." Jeter also allows that, as Phil knew of Jeter's skepticism and would sometimes adapt to his listener's expectations, Phil's own skepticism may have played a larger role in their talks.

Friends to confide in and his work to take him through the night, an established career and a safe place to live—when last had Phil known such calm?

But there was something missing, and Phil knew what it was. "In February of 1977 I began to hallucinate (if that is the right word) during nocturnal states, hypnogogic, sleep, hypnopompic, etc., the presence of a woman, very close to me; in my arms, in fact, as close as could be. Once begun this sensation persisted."

The woman Phil was destined to meet was Joan Simpson, then thirty-two, a psychiatric social worker at Sonoma State Hospital in the Valley of the Moon. Through her book dealer friend Ray Torrence, Joan had discovered Phil's work and became a collector of the lovely, lurid Ace Doubles of the fifties. Personally and financially independent, Joan was sharp, funny, and sensual, with curly brown hair and large brown eyes.

When Torrence once asked Joan to name the two people she most wanted to meet, Phil edged out rock promoter Bill Graham for first place. Unbeknown to Joan, Torrence wrote a letter of introduction on her behalf to Phil, who phoned to invite her to visit. Joan recalls her April 1977 arrival:

> It's a twelve-hour drive. I got down there at nighttime and phoned—Phil said, "Come on over." You had to buzz the gate to get in. He lived upstairs—and there around a corner of the staircase a head was poking out. Turns out it was Phil. He saw me, went, "Oh! Oh!" and ran away. Actually, he said, "Are you Joan Simpson?" I said, "Yes, are you Philip K. Dick?" and that's when he went, "Oh! Oh!" I went up after him, and when I got to his apartment he was on the phone to Jeter, saying, "She's a fox, she's a fox . . ."
>
> I was so relieved. He certainly was not the severe or scary person I thought he might be. Crazy maybe, but also boyish and nonthreatening. That sort of describes many things about Phil—he was naturally very childlike and naïve. That, coupled with a lot of craziness, physical and emotional trouble, and so much mental energy and genius, made him the most unusual person I'd ever met.
>
> We talked a long time. He told me how relieved he was my knuckles weren't dragging along the ground. Wanted to know if I was married, had a boyfriend. At the same time, very gentlemanly, no hanky-panky. He was just awful at hustling—it really wasn't his style. He told me, "Here is your room, you can stay here, lock the door if you like." Yeah, I did stay there. For a week. That was the beginning of our relationship.
>
> That very first night Phil talked about Zebra and things like that—he was a living actuality of his novels. It was amazing. I told him that when I first began reading his stuff I thought it wasn't fiction in the normal sense of the word. I still think that. There wasn't this person who had this inspirational idea for a story or novel and wrote it down. It was a person's experience.

During Joan's visit, Chez Phil was in typical disarray. The cats were depositing flea eggs over the two glass-topped coffee tables, and there was snuff everywhere—numberless little tins of Dean Swift, shipped in by the case each month from San Francisco, as well as brown coatings of snuff dust. Piles of books and records and *Exegesis* pages. Enough pill bottles to stock a pharmacy. Phil was taking several prescribed medications daily—muscle relaxers, blood-pressure controls, antidepressants. The food on hand was mainly frozen dinners and pot pies.

Their time together went wonderfully. Life was a P.M. shift, with lots of sleeping in late. Activity commenced in mid- to late afternoon. The daily pile of mail to contend with. Friends dropping by. And Phil wrote every day—letters and the *Exegesis*. Says Joan: "I wanted to be around him to learn from him. I never loved him in that young lover heart-throbbing way. I loved him like you would a great master. After three weeks I came back up to Sonoma, and he came with me—which was *amazing!"*

Indeed. Phil's willingness, on the spur of the moment, to leave behind his Orange County home (on which he kept up the rent) and return to the Bay Area—the scene of the break-in and so many other past sorrows and dangers—is the greatest possible testimony to the joy he took in the new relationship. Phil and Joan were extremely close, but they never became lovers in the strict sense. Phil, at this time, was not capable of sex; the reasons are unclear (one possible theory is that loss of interest in sex is a symptom of temporal lobe epilepsy), and by the early eighties Phil was sexually active again. With Joan, it was hugs and warmth that mattered.

Together, in May, they rented a house on 550 Chase Street in Sonoma and established a circle of friends that included Ray Torrence and fellow book dealer Nit Sprague, Paul Williams, SF writer Richard Lupoff, and psychologists David and Joan May. Lupoff conducted an interview with Phil over Berkeley's KPFA FM; they also talked casually at the Chase Street house. One exchange recalled by Lupoff shows the humorous protective coloring Phil employed to ward off fruitless debates:

> Phil and I were sitting on the floor and he was wearing a crucifix—a big hand-carved wooden one. And I asked him why he was wearing it and how seriously did he take it? He said, "Listen, I live in Santa Ana and Joan lives in Sonoma. That means I spend a lot of time on I-5 in my car. And on occasion I get stopped by the highway patrol and they will come over to my car and lean in my window and say, 'Sir, do you realize you were exceeding the speed limit?' And I'll fondle my crucifix and say, 'Why, no, Officer, I didn't know that.' " Phil said he never got a ticket.

To begin with, Phil did not in fact commute regularly on I-5. Once he moved up to Sonoma with Joan he stayed put there. More to the point, friends such as David May recall numerous spiritual talks with Phil. Writes May: "I am certain that his prime directives were to await faithfully the Grace he sought, and on a day to day basis, to do good deeds—acts of loving kindness toward his fellow humans."

However high his aspirations, Phil could not evade his bouts of severe depression. Joan recalls:

> Whoever was with him at this time would have to be a full-time . . . I was going to say nursemaid—but companion, housekeeper. And not expect the same from him. A lot of it was housekeeping, nursing care—Phil would really go into states of collapse where he would be nonfunctional. He'd be so depressed or physically ill that he'd have to take to bed, and God knows when he'd come out again.

248

Phil suffered from palpitations, sweats, high blood pressure, sometimes quite elusive things. He has been accused of malingering by everyone in the book. But psychological states of unease can manifest physical symptoms— headaches, ulcers; I think everyone agrees with that. Phil's depressions took on a multitude of forms.

I had to give him lots of TLC [tender loving care] and let him be. You couldn't, like, say, "Come on, get out of bed, you'll feel better." He didn't respond well to reality therapy. It was more like "I will take care of you, you don't have to do anything, don't worry."

That summer, Phil wrote a story as a gift for Joan: "The Day Mr. Computer Fell Out of Its Tree." Composed in a childlike tone, "Mr. Computer" is a dress rehearsal of certain key themes in *Valis*. It is also a declaration of love that both delighted and frightened Joan, who feared she might not be up to the task of keeping the world intact, as the female protagonist in "Mr. Computer" must:

Not only does that take a lot of time and energy—it takes away from anything you might want to do for yourself as a singular entity. It calls for total twenty-four-hour devotion—make sure the computer and everything else is okay.

Phil, it seems, always was with women who were strong, and yet there was that about him that wanted to make women little girls, buy things for them. That was his form of caring and devotion. If something was bothering me and I wanted to climb in his lap and be comforted, that was okay. But if it was something more profound, he wasn't good at that, because that always carries a responsibility to it. It can be a burden.

I really couldn't let him pamper me in a little-girl way. I had my own car, money, life—I was in many ways the antithesis of what he wanted me to be.

That pampering also had a backlash effect. If things weren't working out, or there was a divorce, that same woman he'd wanted to buy things for turned into the flip side—"She wants my house, my novels."

That summer in Sonoma, Phil resumed his acquaintance with fellow SF writer Robert Silverberg. They had first met in 1964, but since then Silverberg had gone on to garner numerous Hugos and Nebulas and to earn advances that dwarfed Phil's. In interview he recalls: "Phil did feel competitive with me in some fashion—a nice fashion. But there was always an edge on Phil, whether because I was the hot new kid on the block or maybe because he resonated with something in my character. He would always duel with me in a playful way—defying me to keep up in banter." The humor could serve as a façade. Silverberg writes: "Once we held a long public conversation in fractured Latin in the cocktail lounge of a convention hotel; it was wildly funny, but I would rather have been speaking English with him. I figured he was lost to me."

In early 1977, Silverberg had favorably reviewed *Scanner* in *Cosmos*. A correspondence ensued, in which Silverberg confided to Phil the anguish of his then-ongoing divorce. To Silverberg, Phil was a man who had lived on the edge long enough to serve as a worthy guide through hard times. Indeed, Phil did offer solace and advice, and the competitive edge vanished. In their private talks, Phil seemed to Silverberg "much quieter and much more authentic—less the performer. Mainly he sounded very troubled and frightened. His publishers, health, women, the break-in. Always something."

In June–July 1977, D. Scott Apel and Kevin Briggs conducted interviews with Phil, which are included in Apel's excellent *Philip K. Dick: The Dream Connection* (1987). Apel writes: "Photos do not do him justice. He was large, physically imposing and hairy. He was wearing slacks and an open shirt, as if his hairy barrel chest and barrel belly couldn't stand being confined." Apel notes that when Phil took phone calls, he would often break off to consult his Rolodex. "When he came back on the line, it was always with some personal comment, like, 'How'd the surgery go on your cat?' or 'How come you haven't called in six months?' After ringing off, he'd make a note of the conversation on the caller's card, and then continue with the interview."

Phil battled depressions throughout the summer—his failure to find a novel to fit 2-3-74 left him feeling woefully unproductive, and his unfulfilled contract with Bantam weighed heavily upon him. But the relationship with Joan had infused him with new confidence. Proof of this was his willingness to travel with her, in September 1977, to Metz, France, for an SF festival of which he had been named guest of honor. Phil was nervous enough about the trip to score a supply of speed—the only time he resorted to amphetamines in his final decade.

Nonetheless, for Phil, the Metz Festival was a triumph over long-standing fears. He enjoyed the fine architecture of the city, relished sampling French food and wine, and was understandably thrilled to find that in France he was regarded by fans and the press as the greatest SF writer in the world. Meanwhile, Joan came down with stomach flu and was largely confined to their hotel room. During their breakup two months later, Phil would claim that she'd had a "nervous breakdown" in France—a claim he denied when Joan confronted him about it. The reality was that it galled Phil not to have her by his side throughout the festivities, though it did leave him free to flirt madly.

Roger Zelazny, who also attended the Metz Festival, recalls that Phil's sixties reputation had preceded him. At one dinner, a young Frenchman popped the pill that Phil had placed alongside his plate, then asked what to expect. Phil explained that he'd soon feel better if he happened to have a sore throat.

There was a perfect Phildickian mix-up with regard to Phil's guest of honor speech, "If You Find This World Bad, You Should See Some of the Others." The speech raised a number of speculations derived from 2-3-74, such as our world seen as a Gnostic computer chess game: "God, the Programmer-Reprogrammer, is not making his moves of improvement against inert matter; he is dealing with a cunning opponent. Let us say that on the gameboard—our universe in space-time—the dark counterplayer makes a move; he sets up a reality situation." All of this would have been startling enough if Phil had read the speech as he'd written it (with simultaneous translation into French). But at the last moment the festival organizers asked Phil to shorten it by twenty minutes. Phil made some hasty deletions, which were not, alas, the same deletions made by his translator. The resulting bilingual hybrid, coupled with Phil's delight in sowing tongue-in-cheek chaos, left the audience in a daze. Zelazny recalls:

[. . .] Several hours after the time the talk was scheduled, people began drifting in from the hall where Phil had been speaking. A man came up to me with a book and said, "Monsieur Zelazny, you have written a book with Monsieur Dick [*Deus Irae*]. You know his mind. I have just come from his talk. Is it true he wishes to found a new religion, with himself as Pope?"

I said, "Well, he has never mentioned that ambition to me. I don't know how these things come through in translation. He has a very peculiar sense of humor. It might not have carried through properly. But I don't think he meant it to be taken literally."

The fellow who was behind me said, "*Non*, I think you are wrong. I rode back to the hotel in a taxi, and Monsieur Dick gave me the power to remit sins and to kill fleas."

I said, "I'm sure that was meant to be taken with a grain of salt. I wouldn't be too concerned about it."

A little later, another fellow came in [. . .] "Well, in the lecture he said that there are many parallel time tracks and we are on the wrong one, because of the fact that God and the Devil are playing a game of chess and every time one makes a move, it reprograms us to a different time track, and that whenever Phil Dick writes a book, it switches us back to the proper track. Would you care to comment on this?"

I begged off.

Harlan Ellison was also in attendance at Metz. He and Phil hadn't been in contact since their 1975 break, and Ellison avoided attending Phil's speech. He recalls that the audience, as it wandered back to the hotel bar where Ellison sat nursing a Perrier, "looked like they had been stunned by a ball peen hammer. They couldn't describe it to me except that they thought he was either drunk or doped. After the speech Phil was, if not ostracized, then treated differently. I felt very bad for him, but I couldn't get near him or want to get near him to help."

The two did encounter each other a few days later in that same hotel bar. Neither had been drinking, but the verbal pyrotechnics lasted better than an hour. Ellison recalls:

> Phil looked like hell physically. Pale, dark bags under his eyes, haunted look. I didn't know what he had been going through. By the time Metz came along, I was convinced he was a loony—unreliable and not fit to deal with as a friend.
>
> It started off with him making an introductory jibe at me and just took off from there. Phil would say something that was intended to hurt you, but he delivered it with such cleverness that it came off as light and frivolous. I was not about to be made an ass of by any damn body.

Joan, who witnessed the fray, remembers it this way:

> Phil was very antithetical to Harlan. Harlan is very cocky, glib, cool, and here is Phil going clunk clunk clunk. Phil was not a very debonair or self-assured man. Snuff falling out of his nose, ninety-two spots on his tie—you know. And Harlan thought Phil treated people very badly because he wandered away, got lost, had people support him rather than be master of his own ship.
>
> Anyway, they got into this huge debate. Phil does very well in those kinds of situations. Here is Harlan banging his chest, and Phil was more a philosopher. Phil was just great—more dynamic and sexy than I'd ever seen him be.

The bar crowd relished the bloodletting, but the rift between the two friends was now final—to the lasting regret of both.

On their return to the States, the plan was that Phil would wrap up affairs in Santa Ana and then rejoin Joan in Sonoma. In October, Phil did attend the SF Octocon in Santa Rosa, where he mingled with kindred spirits Theodore Sturgeon and Robert Anton Wilson. But Phil now balked at a permanent move back to Northern California, and Joan would not consider Orange County residence. The relationship ended. For years to come Phil would miss Joan—the last woman with whom he lived in a serious relationship.

But friendships and *Exegesis* labors sustained him. He and Jeter drew ever closer through their night-shift collaborations. In late 1977, Jeter introduced Phil to *Discreet Music*, an album of tape loop minimalist music by Brian Eno—the inspiration for the "Synchronicity Music" of composer "Brent Mini" in *Valis*. Phil adored the album, playing it constantly. Recalls Jeter: "And I thought, 'Jesus, Phil. You may be off drugs, but you still have the drug user's personality. Give you anything good, and the first thing you do is go out and abuse it.' "

Jeter's barbed wit had the salutary power to shake Phil free from his periodic depressions. During one funk in March 1978, Jeter told him that if he was too fucked up to go out and buy something that would cheer him up—a good stereo system—then he was a loser and might as well end it all. Together they went to an audio store, where Phil happily plunked down for an excellent system. In May, Phil paid full cash purchase price for a new red Mercury Capri. He could afford to make such moves because the foreign and reprint sales of his cumulative work were conferring upon Phil upper-middle-class status for the very first time in his life. In 1977 he grossed roughly $55,000; in 1978 he exceeded $90,000. Phil gave to several charities, including Care, Save the Children, and the Crusade for Life, an antiabortion group. And he took pride and comfort in the success he'd achieved at long last. But the money didn't change the basic pattern of his life: shared dinners with neighbor Doris, snuff, Thursday nights at Powers's place, and the *Exegesis*.

Jeter sometimes drove Phil to group therapy sessions at Orange County Medical Center. Phil disliked these sessions, but was required to attend in order to receive his prescribed medications. He tried to make the best of a bad situation. Recalls Jeter:

> He would come out with *phone numbers!* Of these very weird people.
>
> I said, "Phil, you want to go to a bar and meet people? Whatever you want to do. Church even. That's fine. But don't go to the mental ward of the Orange County Hospital and come out with phone numbers. These people are not the kind you need to get involved with."
>
> He'd go, "Yeah, I suppose you're right."
>
> He's the one person I ever knew who seriously cruised those kinds of places for dates.

Phil was now long overdue on his promised novel for Bantam. He was bursting with metaphysics, but the shape of the plot would not come. Meanwhile, from his handwritten *Exegesis* notes, he attempted a synthesis of his key ideas. In January 1978, he typed out in one long night an essay titled "Cosmogony and Cosmology," which posited an "Urgrund" (fundamental Being) that, for the sake of self-awareness, "constructed a reality-projecting artifact (or demiurge; cf Plato and the Gnostics)," which had in turn created our own spurious empirical world. We are, at one and the same time, instructed and enslaved by the artifact. To progress spiritually, we must learn to break free from false reality—to disobey our teacher. Our spur to do so is suffering:

> What can one say in favor of the suffering of little creatures in this world? Nothing. Nothing, except that it will by its nature trigger off revolt or disobedience—which in turn will lead to an abolition of this world and a return to the Godhead.

In an essay written later that year—"How to Build a Universe That Doesn't Fall Apart Two Days Later"—Phil explored similar themes with greater skepticism and a lighter hand. Its title playfully sums up the *Exegesis*, which now numbered several thousand pages.

In August 1978, Dorothy died in a Bay Area hospital. During her final illness, Phil had phoned Lynne Cecil, who knew what agony travel was for Phil and so dissuaded him from flying up to pay a last visit. At first, Phil's reaction to his mother's death was shock and grief. Second wife Kleo recalls that (much to her surprise) Phil called her long-distance to tell her the news, his voice distraught and anguished. But then a chill set in again. In his address book, by Dorothy's name, he inscribed simply "*todt*" (German: dead). And in the *Exegesis*, in late 1978, Dorothy's passing is seen as a favorable turn—enhancing Phil's personal growth:

> Only now, as I become for the first time in my life financially secure, am I becoming sane, free of psychotic activity [. . .] Also, my accomplishments last year—traveling, being with Joan—did wonders for my psychological health. I learned to say no, & I conquered most of my phobias. I think they lessened as I learned to enjoy living alone for the first time in my life. [. . .] The death of my mother has helped, because I can see what a malign person she was in my life & how I feared and disliked her—which she deserved.

What is most startling about this passage is the offhand manner in which Phil introduces the subject of Dorothy's death—it is no more nor less than one of a list of recent developments cited to demonstrate Phil's psychological progress. His hatred for her, as expressed here, was complete and unrepentant. Of all the aspects of Phil's personality, this is perhaps the most startling and saddening. For Dorothy did love her son, and at many points in Phil's life—the early writing years, the breakup with Anne, the dark days in Santa Venetia—he had drawn heavily on that love. But it had never been enough—not for Phil, and surely not for sister Jane. Now, at last, they both were avenged.

In a September 1978 entry, Phil was far less sanguine about his prospects. The form for a novel to encompass 2-3-74 still eluded him. He was lost in his own questionings. And soon, he sensed, he was to die:

> My books (& stories) are intellectual (conceptual) mazes. & I am in an intellectual maze in trying to figure out our situation (who we are & how we look into the world, & world as illusion, etc) because the *situation* is a maze, leading back to itself, & false clues show up, such as our "rebellion." [. . .]
>
> The fact that after 4½ years of strenuous exegete, whereupon I have reached these conclusions (not to mention 27 years of published writing) I now find myself signalled to die—which effectively makes it impossible for me to put this gnosis in a form that I can publish—is a condition which can be deduced from my exegesis itself, & shows I'm on the right intellectual path, but to no avail.

In late September, "Thérèse"—a young woman whom Phil had met at Metz the year before—came to stay for a month at his Santa Ana apartment. Phil was a gracious host, providing financial help and emotional encouragement. According to Phil, on the last night of her visit Thérèse offered to make love with him by way of repayment for his kindness. Her whorish ways appalled Phil even as they caught at his lust. He turned her down. In an anguished *Exegesis* entry, the enticements of sex were stripped away to show the skull of death beneath the skin. Lust—like art and the *Exegesis* itself—is a stratagem of the maze:

> I now know sin & evil, I know myself and what went wrong—what *Genesis* is about. I know that without Christ's help I am damned. [. . .] Obviously I cannot punish myself for this original sin by killing myself, or being killed; my punishment is that which I don't want: life. & a lonely and pointless life, a life I loathe. What I really want is what I wanted from [Thérèse]. But the price is too great: humiliation, to be degraded & know I was degraded. It's like being addicted to some hideous drug.

In his vehemence here, Phil returns to the tone of suspicion and loathing that marked his descriptions of sex in his earliest mainstream novels of the late forties, such as *Gather Yourselves Together* and the notes for the unfinished *The Earthshaker*. Phil was no prude, but he did bear within himself a visceral sense of disgust over sex, which his pleasurable adult sexual experiences never did quite strip away. Then too, his temporary bout of impotence during his time with Joan Simpson in 1977 may have contributed to his anxieties with Thérèse.

Another problem that would not go away was the long-overdue novel for Bantam. A young newcomer to the Meredith Agency played a role in helping him solve it. Russell Galen was an ardent admirer of Phil's work and had Phil assigned to him as a client. He recalls: "Things could have been done on Phil's behalf that weren't being done, and I simply started doing them. Nobody objected, because it brought in considerable income to the agency." Under Galen's aegis, Phil's back titles were kept steadily in print, and it was Galen who would negotiate the *Blade Runner* film deal. But none of Galen's efforts proved more fateful than his unsuccessful attempt, in September 1978, to market a book of Phil's nonfiction. Phil, delighted at being so championed, sent a glowing letter of thanks—Galen had convinced him that he had a novel in him after all.

On November 29, Phil mailed off the *Valis* manuscript—dedicated "To Russell Galen, who showed me the right way"—to the Meredith Agency. The cover letter read: "Here is VALIS for Bantam. My work is done."

◆

Galen's encouragement was crucial. But it came at the end of a four-year struggle with the narrative shape of 2-3-74. How do you fictionalize when you're not sure what really happened? How do you dramatize events that sound crazy to nearly everyone else?

The questions were sufficiently difficult to force Phil to try out a number of possibilities over the years. From April to November 1974, Phil had pondered a novel called *Valisystem A* that would take up the story of *High Castle* character Hawthorne Abendsen—the author of *The Grasshopper Lies Heavy*, the alternative-world novel (within an alternative-world novel) that claimed that the Allies, not the Axis, had won World War II. In *Valisystem A*, Phil planned for Abendsen to be captured by the Nazis; but Abendsen cannot tell them what they want to know—is the *Grasshopper* vision true?—because he isn't sure himself.

The transition to a new vision—entitled *To Scare the Dead*—was described in a February 1975 letter. *Valisystem A* had been allowed to lie fallow. It now became part of a new whole:

> I combine VALISYSTEM A and TO SCARE THE DEAD.
> Every novel of mine is at least two novels superimposed. This is the origin; this is why they are full of loose ends, but also, it is impossible to predict the outcome, since there is no linear plot as such. It is two novels into a sort of 3-D novel.

The title *To Scare the Dead* derives from the shock experienced by early Christians (such as Phil's own "Thomas") when they are reborn inside the brains of modern-day Californians such as protagonist Nicholas Brady. In a March 1975 letter, Phil sketched out the new plot. Brady (Abendsen is long gone) discovers that "there are two of him: his old self, at his secular job and goals, and this Essene from the Qumran wadi back circa 45 A.D." Phil played with the notion of turning Brady into a government agent who spies upon a character based upon Bishop Pike and then realizes that Pike's researches bear on his own "Experience."

Returning to the title *Valisystem A*, Phil wrote, in summer 1976, the novel ultimately published in 1985 as *Radio Free Albemuth*. *Albemuth* pits Brady, a Berkeley record store clerk turned record company A & R man, against the Black Iron Prison ruled by President Ferris Fremont (inspired by Richard Nixon). Brady's life resembles Phil's in many respects, but "Phil Dick" shows up as an entirely separate character—a sympathetic but quite rational SF writer. Ultimately Brady is killed, while "Phil" is interned in a government detention camp. The hope for the future lies with the "kids" who must find, in trashy song lyrics, vital hints as to the truth of this world. *Albemuth* has its moments but stands, at last, as an unsuccessful trial run. Its cloak-and-dagger plot, with Brady leading a pop-song conspiracy against the ruling tyranny, is impossible to take seriously. Phil himself showed little regard for *Albemuth*. It was seldom mentioned in the *Exegesis*—in which every other seventies novel was subjected to detailed analysis.

In his September 1977 Metz speech, Phil alluded to a new novel in progress called *Valis*, with three key characters: Nicholas Brady (who undergoes 2-3-74 experiences), government agent Houston Paige (who understands "Zebra" theoretically but lacks confirming experience), and Phil Dick (who needs a good SF plot quick). Paige meets Brady and goes mad from seeing his theory confirmed.

But Phil's ideas simply would not settle down into a cohesive plot. How could a novel contain the key to the structure of being? Phil girded himself for the challenge in this 1978 *Exegesis* entry:

This novel *must* be written, & I have the redeemed state of 2-74/2-75 to base it on, but God, what a task: to depict 1) that which redeems; 2) the process of redemption; 3) the redeemed (restored) state of man—in contrast to the occluded state (described in "Scanner"). It could take the rest of my life to do it. I don't know if I can. [. . .] But it must be done. & it must [. . .] point to the 5th Savior whose coming is imminent.

Rays of light emerged from odd sources. Phil had recently written two autobiographical pieces—the introduction to the *Golden Man* story collection and a short reminiscence on "Roog," his first SF story sale. Their informality felt somehow right—the writing flow had returned. Those heavy *Exegesis* ideas might yield some ground to a style that stayed loose and funny, as Phil could be when posing "What Ifs?" to Jeter and Powers. And then came the Galen letter—a true ally at last at the Meredith Agency.

In a two-week burst in November 1978, Phil solved the problem of how to contain the recalcitrant 2-3-74 beast within a novel's skin. Phil began *Valis* in the middle of an *Exegesis* session—page 115 of a lengthy streak of speculation. The long years of "research" were over. Once the flow was sure, Phil switched back to his typewriter and pounded it out.

What triggered the release? At root, it was Phil's realization that all he could do was write it down as it happened.

You admit outright that all your big theories don't prove a thing—and how important can 2-3-74 be if you can't make up your mind as to what it was? Then, to prove you know damn well how crazy it all sounds, you split yourself in two: "Phil Dick" and "Horselover Fat" (*Philip*, in Greek, is "a lover of horses"; *Dick* is German for "fat"). The reader is told right off that Fat is insane, the victim of a nervous breakdown. Who is the narrator? Phil Dick, who confides: "I am Horselover Fat, and I am writing this in the third person to gain much-needed objectivity."

Right off we have the Epimenides paradox—"All Cretans are liars. I am a Cretan."—that Phil first used with protagonist/fool Jack Isidore in *Crap Artist*. The paradox is insoluble, an infinite regress. In *Valis*, the reader can't be sure if "Fat" is really crazy—for if he is, then how can

"Phil" be objective? And from whom springs this lucid, funny narrative? Is *Valis* autobiography or novel? Both. As Phil explained in a March 1979 letter: "Oddly, the most bizarre of events in it are true (or rather—and this is a crucial difference—I *believe* they are true)."

Character Phil's first-person asides wind in and out of the *Valis* narrative, which tells of the quest of Fat the perfect funny Fool to find God. Unlike Parsifal of the Grail myth, Fat lives in modern-day Orange County, where people who want what Fat wants so stubbornly—God, Truth, The Works—are nuts. Phil keeps trying to explain this to Fat. But deep down Phil and the reader both know that the hope of the world lies in Fat's never being convinced. The "Tractates Cryptica Scriptura" that concludes *Valis* consists of distillations from Fat's *Exegesis*. Character Phil scoffs at them. (Real-life Phil confirmed that "Tractates" entries 7 and 9 were revealed to him by the "telepathic" AI voice.)

Throughout the novel Fat is surrounded by friends and lovers who draw strength from his faith even as they deride his speculations. As previously mentioned, Fat's wife, Beth, was inspired by Tessa, and his cancer-stricken girlfriend, Sherri Solvig, was based largely on Doris. Maurice—Fat's bighearted therapist, who tries an aggressive approach to shake Fat out of his suicidal despondency—owed much to psychotherapist Barry Spatz, who treated Phil after his February 1976 suicide attempt. Fat's friend David—naïve, good-natured, and Catholic—was drawn from Powers. And friend Kevin—acerbic, derisive, but gallant in his own longing for truth—was a portrait of Jeter. In interview, Jeter stresses the stylized nature of the *Valis* characters:

> It wasn't as if Tim was a complete religious no-doubts fundamentalist or Catholic person. I wasn't a complete scoffing church-burning skeptic, and Phil wasn't this completely befuddled person. Actually each of us incorporated segments of that, so that there was an overlapping body of things that we talked about. But for the book, Phil separated out those characters so that the relationships would be clearer. [. . .] And in terms of veracity, going to see the movie is really the point at which the book differs from reality. Although there was a movie that we all went to see.

That movie was *The Man Who Fell to Earth*, directed by Nicholas Roeg and starring David Bowie. Phil loved it, and for a short time he and Jeter listened closely to Bowie albums, hoping to discern a sly pop sign from God/Valis/Zebra. No luck. But a failed experiment can be a useful plot device, and in *Valis* Fat and Kevin go to see a movie called *Valis*, which portrays the struggle between *Albemuth* characters Nicholas Brady (who is zapped by the pink light force) and evil President Ferris Fremont. Fat gets in touch with rock star Eric Lampton and his wife, Linda, who both star in the film. Fat is convinced that they know about Valis—the

Vast Active Living Intelligence System—and can rescue him from his spiritual isolation.

The Lamptons live in Sonoma, a setting fresh in Phil's mind from his summer with Joan. In honor of their proposed visit, Fat, Kevin, and David form the "Rhipidon Society"—a phrase bestowed to real-life Phil by the AI voice in a 1974 dream. *Rhipidos* is Greek for "fan," and due to their fanlike fins "Fish cannot carry guns." Fat believes that this motto contains the essence of Christianity. In Sonoma, they learn that Valis is an information-firing device from the "Albemuth" star system and, still more startling, that Valis and Linda have made a baby daughter: Sophia. The fifth Savior, by Fat's count, and the first to incarnate in female form.

At their very first meeting, Sophia dispels character Phil's need to project a "Horselover Fat." She bestows sanity, wisdom, kindness. But "Valis" film soundtrack composer Brent Mini, whose own past exposure to the Valis information beam has left him ill and facing a slow death, accidentally kills Sophia with a laser in an effort to extract the maximum information from her.

Horselover Fat returns. Stricken with grief, Fat vows to travel the world in search of further signs from Valis. And character Phil, in his lonely apartment, scans the TV channels for hidden clues.

Bantam was more than a little freaked out by *Valis*. Hurst had left the scene, and Bantam didn't resolve to publish the novel until the very end of the contract period. In the *Exegesis*, poor Phil was posing worried queries to the *I Ching*: Would any other house take it if Bantam turned it down?

Valis puzzled many of Phil's longtime readers; it earned a reputation as a *difficult* book.

But *Valis* stands alongside *Palmer Eldritch* as Phil's greatest work—a breviary of the spiritual life in America, where the path to God lies through scattered pop-trash clues. Unsanitized by sanctity, loopy as a long night's rave, it breaks the dreary chains of dogma to leave us, if not enlightened, freely roaming.

What's it all mean? In *Exegesis* entries to the end of his life, Phil went at *Valis* again and again—startled by each new interpretation, as if it had been written by someone else.

12 Big Bucks And Condo Comfort, First Mainstream Sale To A New York House, The Gosh Wow Hollywood Dazzle Of Blade Runner—None Of These Are Enough, Not Nearly, Not With A World Crying Out For Redemption And Stubborn Reality Still Undefined; But Time Is Running Out And Phil Knows It (1979–1982)

I am looking for clues to an invisible being of great size, whose outline is dim but, to me, real. I call this being Christ. But I do not know what its real name is (at one time I called it Ubik, then later Valis). These are names I made up. [. . .] That is my quest: to know its name. And to learn that I will have to encounter it and hear it tell me; it alone knows. I saw it once; I will see it again. If I keep looking.

PHIL, November 1981 journal entry

◆

I have willed this condition for myself, here in the final glide pattern of my life. I know it and I take responsibility for it. The only thing is, Why? Why do I want to be isolated? What do I get out of it? Lots of time to write and think. BFD—big fucking deal. [. . .] I think of people I have loved ("dilexi," the Latin word is: "I have loved") but where are they now? Scattered, dead, unknown to me as to where they are and how they are. [. . .] This is dreadful; I should live in the now, and time-bind into the future. Well, I do time-bind; I anticipate the publication of VALIS. "He's crazy," will be the response. "Took drugs, saw God. BFD. Harlan Ellison is right about him."

PHIL, December 1980 letter

◆

His philanthropy, his warmth, his loyalty, his devotion to his art, and his moodiness.

MARY WILSON, in response to interview query:
Name five aspects of Phil that remained constant

PHIL enjoyed the afterglow of his tour de force completion of *Valis*. The novel that had plagued him for four years had taken sudden shape in two weeks. Naturally, he was already conceiving a sequel, to be entitled *Valis Regained*, after Milton. But Phil needed fallow time—he no longer had the bodily stamina to plunge from one novel to the next, as in the sixties. The nightly *Exegesis* "research" sessions continued apace, however.

Meanwhile, Phil's worth in the New York market had climbed impressively. Back-title royalties and resales enabled Phil to gross $101,000 in 1978 and $75,000 in 1979. In January 1979, a lucrative package deal for three of his least distinguished Ace titles—$14,000 for *The Cosmic Puppets*, *Dr. Futurity*, and *The Unteleported Man*—prompted Phil to send this telegram to the Meredith Agency: "Russ Galen's sale to Berkley Books the best of my career. Please congratulate him. He has enormously enhanced my career." Phil's shrewd intent was to enhance young Galen's career as well. At last, after nearly thirty years, Phil had found a truly enthusiastic ear in the agency. He meant to keep it.

Along with financial success came the reassurance that the counter-culture young continued to relish his effects. Two different punk bands took their names from his novels in 1979: Eye in the Sky and JJ-180 (the drug in *Now Wait for Last Year*). Then, in May, Phil learned that *A Scanner Darkly* had won the Grand Prix du Festival de Metz. In June, he completed a new story, "I Hope I Shall Arrive Soon," which Galen sold to *Playboy*. Phil didn't care for the *Playboy* philosophy and gave his four-figure fee to Cambodian famine relief. At the same time, he was proud of this major market sale, and prouder still when the story (published in December 1980 as "Frozen Journey") earned him a "Best New Contributor" award. Another coup came when "Rautavaara's Case" appeared in the October 1980 *Omni*. A third new story, "The Exit Door Leads In," was featured in the fall 1979 *Rolling Stone College Papers*. (For discussion of these stories, see *I Hope I Shall Arrive Soon* in the Chronological Survey.)

To his great joy, Phil was able now to reestablish close ties with Laura and Isa. Both paid him visits during this time. Isa, who came to stay three times in the late seventies, recalls:

> We didn't see enough of each other, but I sort of understood he just couldn't do it. What would happen when I'd go down there is that we would be so close. We'd snuggle and talk, and when I had to go home it was awful. I'd cry, and I know he would too. So pretty soon it was better not to see each other, because it was too hard to deal with parting.
>
> He told me once that while he and Tessa were married, he saw an angel over Christopher's head while he was playing in the sandbox. He started crying, saying, "It's true, I really saw this." It was important to him that I believed he saw this angel.

He had so much anxiety that he couldn't really take me anywhere. The only place we could walk every day was to a little market that sold sandwiches. He didn't exercise at all. We'd play kickball, but after five or ten minutes his heart would start to pound from the running and he'd have to rest. Day after day he'd sit in the dark apartment. He'd stay up late and get up late and take an afternoon nap. He didn't care about his clothes or appearance. I didn't see him as an author. He never told me about his writing. He was just my dad.

Phil and Laura had not spent any extended time together for fifteen years prior to her February 1979 visit. Rumors of Phil's excesses had made Anne mistrustful. But Phil and Laura had managed to correspond and talk by phone throughout the seventies, and now that she was of college age there could be no objection to her flying down to Santa Ana. Laura recalls:

He was so funny, an incredible sense of humor. And also so polite—his manners were impeccable. When he walked with women he walked on the outside, nearest the street. He opened doors for me, helped me pick out clothes. And he was so witty and quick. Half the time when he gave interviews he was laughing inside at the things he said. People didn't seem to know that, though.

His apartment was full of Bibles and religious books, encyclopedias, and books of science fiction. Lots of records, especially Wagnerian opera. It was disordered, cluttered, and dirty—I didn't want to use the bathtub. There was mold and mushrooms in the corners in the shower. It didn't bother him.

He was one of the most frightened people that I have ever known. He wanted to make people happy. He was brilliant and empathetic. But he was trapped by his fears. Crowds, cars, freeways, travel, speaking in front of people. All the times he'd say he would do things and then didn't. Tickets to go places that were never used—I found them while cleaning up his apartment after he died.

He said that I could move in with him and attend U.C. Irvine instead. I didn't take him seriously about that. I couldn't see him being thrilled by my being there day after day. The distance contributed to our having a good relationship.

He did his best—he did very well. I never felt he wasn't a good father. He was who he was.

Certain aspects of fatherhood did cause Phil difficulty. Both Isa and Laura concur that coming to their father for financial help was touch and go. Phil contributed over $5,000 in 1979 to charities such as Children, Inc., and Covenant House (a New York shelter for runaways). But, for whatever reasons, Phil was on his guard when either Isa or Laura brought up money. Recalls Isa: "Lots of times when we'd ask him for money he'd get very paranoid and say, 'No, I'm broke.' He was very

262

generous when he wanted to be. But if you'd ask, he'd get suspicious and weird."

Spontaneity appears to have been the key. Phil promptly sent Laura a check for $4,000 when he learned of her acceptance by Stanford. Later he promised her $200 per month, which he soon discontinued; the sense of obligation killed the joy. Phil's reluctance here is striking, given that he continued to carry a grudge against his own father for failing to provide help with tuition expenses when Phil attended U Cal Berkeley in 1949. Says Laura: "Like many things he said, his intentions were good but the follow-through was lacking. He would send me a Christmas card that said he'd given to the children of Biafra in my name. And I became furious—I told him that *I* would give to that charity, or to something else, if I wanted to. He was kind to a lot of people, but he turned me down when I asked for a $1,000-to-$2,000 loan, and I was working three jobs at Stanford."

By contrast, Tessa stresses Phil's generosity in assisting her and Christopher. Phil not only kept up his legally required $200-per-month child-support payments, but also voluntarily upped the sum to $400 per month. He further helped Tessa purchase a house, and made substantial contributions for private school and toys for his son. Then too, Tessa (unlike his prior wives and daughters) was there in Santa Ana to persistently plead her case.

If Phil was sometimes wary of financial contributions to his out-of-town daughters, he nonetheless anguished over his own self-acknowledged failings as a father.

In a May 1979 letter to Laura, he describes the ceaseless, obsessive *Exegesis* labors, which he felt kept him from his children:

I am neglecting entire parts of my life such as my relationships with my children because of my worry and exhaustion. I have become a machine which thinks and does nothing else. It scares me. How did this come about? I posed myself a problem and I cannot forget the problem but I cannot answer the problem, so I am stuck in fly paper. I can't get loose; it's like a self-imposed karma at work. Every day my world gets smaller. I work more, I live less. [. . .]

Phil did not always find his *Exegesis* stints so disheartening. Tim Powers confirms that while Phil saw himself first and foremost as a fiction writer, he considered the *Exegesis* perhaps his most significant writing. James Blaylock recalls that Phil the writer was happiest composing letters and *Exegesis* entries. On the other hand, K. W. Jeter relates that he once intercepted Phil on the way to the incinerator with a stack of *Exegesis* pages. Phil's confidence in the worth of his speculations may have wavered, but his will to set them down night after night did not. Its publication did not matter to him. It was a means to an end: fashioning theories for novels that poked indelible holes in official reality. And with his friends Phil could share the fun of his speculations and sudden visions. Powers recalls a March 1979 episode when Phil, despairing of the truth, decided to *demand* some answers:

> [. . .] Monday night he called me and said that the night before—Sunday—he'd been smoking some marijuana that a visitor had left, and felt himself entering that by-now-familiar state in which he had visions (generally not dope-related—unless you count Vitamin C as dope), and he said, "I want to *see* God. Let me *see* you."
>
> And then instantly, he told me, he was flattened by the most extreme terror he'd ever felt, and he saw the Ark of the Covenant, and a voice (Voice?) said, "You wouldn't come to me through logical evidence or faith or anything else, so I must convince you this way." The curtain of the Ark was drawn back, and he saw, apparently, a void and a triangle with an eye in it, staring straight at him. (How prosaically I put this all down, especially when I pretty much believe it's true!) Phil said he was on his hands and knees, in absolute terror, enduring the Beatific Vision from nine o'clock Sunday evening until 5 A.M. Monday. He said he was certain he was dying, and if he could have reached the telephone he'd have called the paramedics. The Voice told him, in effect, "You've managed to talk yourself into disbelieving everything else (more gentle and suited for human consumption) I let you see, but *this* you'll never be able to forget or adapt or misrepresent."
>
> Phil said that during the ordeal he said, "I'll never do dope again!" and the Voice said, "That's not the issue."

Spurred by encounters of this kind, Phil's *Exegesis* labors were yielding remarkable fruit. The quality of the entries varied considerably, of course. But Phil's gift for startling speculation—grant him his initial premises and he would weave of them remarkable worlds—lend select portions of the *Exegesis* a power akin to that of his best novels. His most persistent starting point was the "two-source cosmogony" discussed in *Valis*: our apparent but false universe (*natura naturata, maya, dokos,* Satan) is partially redeemed by its ongoing blending with the genuine source of being (*natura naturans, brahman, eidos,* God). Together the two sources—set and ground—create a sort of holographic universe that deceives us. Disentangling reality from illusion is the goal of enlightenment, and the essence of enlightenment is Plato's anamnesis (as in 2-3-74): recalling the eternal truths known to our souls prior to our birth in this realm. But enlightenment is a matter of grace. God bestows it at the height of our extremity, in response to our need and readiness to receive the truth. These are Phil's basic themes in the *Exegesis*. Of course, the variations he fashioned are near infinite.

Occasionally Phil would type out formulations that particularly pleased him. One of the finest of these is a 1979 parable on the apparent lack of divine wisdom in our world:

Here is an example of hierarchical ranking. A new ambulance is filled with gasoline and parked. Then next day it is examined. The finding is that its fuel is virtually gone and its moving parts are slightly worn. This appears to be an instance of entropy, of loss of energy and form. However, if one understands that the ambulance was used to take a dying person to a hospital where his life was saved (thus consuming fuel and somewhat wearing the moving parts of the ambulance) then one can see that through hierarchical outranking there was not only no loss but in fact a net gain. The net gain, however, can only be measured outside the closed system of the new ambulance. Each victory by God as intelligence and will is obtained by this escalation of levels of subsumation, and in no other way.

Phil often called long-distance to confide in Galen at the lower early-morning rate after being up all night during *Exegesis* stints. During a vacation in September 1979, Galen finally paid the writer he so admired a visit. Galen recalls:

Phil ordered in Chinese food and Cokes and we talked from 6:00 P.M. to 6:00 A.M., and at that point I was exhausted and had to leave. I was just not up to it—I could not adjust to Phil in person. It came so fast and thick I didn't know what he was talking about. I was fascinated, but it was such a rush of ideas and I got so sleepy. Phil showed no signs of tiring. I don't think I said anything for two or three hours at a stretch. He talked about 1974, politics, technology—it could be ten topics in a few minutes or one topic for two hours. I could handle small doses: letters or a half-hour phone call. But twelve hours. . . .

In October, Phil's apartment building was converted to condominiums. Phil felt secure there and had no desire to relocate. He took a $10,000 loan from the Meredith Agency, which, coupled with his savings, enabled him to make a $52,000 lump sum purchase of his premises. But the condo conversion forced friend Doris Sauter to move out; the next August she moved from Orange County completely, a wrenching separation for Phil.

Other residents were also forced to move out. Phil, who knew well the vertigo of losing one's home, responded with an essay, "Strange Memories of Death" (included in *I Hope I Shall Arrive Soon*), detailing the crisis of his neighbor the "Lysol Lady": "What bothers me is that I know the only thing separating me from the Lysol Lady, who is crazy, is the money in my savings account. Money is the official seal of sanity."

Phil's grief at no longer having Doris Sauter next door was intense. Their warm neighborly relations had inspired a 1979 story, "Chains of Air, Webs of Aether," which portrays two crotchety Earth colonists living in separate domes on a remote asteroid. Leo McVane wants to lose himself in fantasies of singer Linda Fox (inspired by Linda Ronstadt), but

Rybus Romney suffers from multiple sclerosis and needs Leo's help to survive. Leo, in turn, comes to see that in the capacity for kindness lies salvation.

Phil plundered the first half of this story to serve as the beginning to *Valis Regained*, his sequel to *Valis*, and upped the plot ante considerably in the process. Phil completed the new novel in a two-week rush that concluded on March 22, 1980, and it was bought by Simon and Schuster, which published it in 1981 as *The Divine Invasion*.

The Divine Invasion brings Phil's religious ideas together in an SF invasion story. Rybus—respelled Rybys—Romney has been impregnated by Yah (from Hebrew *YHVH* or Tetragrammaton: the God of the Torah). Leo, now named Herb Asher (from Hebrew *Ehyeh asher ehyeh*: "I Am That I Am," God's declaration in *Exodus*), serves as a sort of Joseph figure to accompany Rybys back to an Earth under the spiritual domination of Belial (Hebrew *beli ya'al*: without worth).

Yah works in strange ways. Within Rybys—if only she and Herb can survive—is the divine boy child Emmanuel (Hebrew: God aids us), who alone can restore truth and meaning to an occluded world. To guide the unlikely parents, Yah sends a seedy old wanderer, Elias Tate, who is Elijah the prophet, the eternal friend of humankind. But through tragic accident (or the work of Belial?) Rybys dies. Emmanuel is born in a synthowomb, brain-damaged and unable to remember that he is God. Zina Pallas, a young girl who is the feminine aspect of God, restores Emmanuel's memory. She completes him; the cosmos is healed.

Phil wavered as to the worthiness of *The Divine Invasion* as a sequel to *Valis*. Although there is mention in *The Divine Invasion* of a Vast Active Living Intelligence System and of the film *Valis*, the two novels must be viewed highly abstractly indeed (as Phil himself viewed them in several *Exegesis* entries) to form a convincing union.

After completing *The Divine Invasion*, Phil considered moving on to a new "alternate world novel," *The Acts of Paul*, for which he'd produced a brief plot synopsis in January 1980. The "alternate world" is set in our own present, as in *High Castle*. Manichaeism, with its dualistic good and evil gods, is the dominant world religion. By contrast, Christianity all but died out in the third century (as did Manichaeism in our world). The proposed narrator, a scholar out to locate the "secret Christians" who carry on the faith, resembles Phil's later portrait of Bishop Timothy Archer.

Exegesis aside, Phil did not undertake any sustained writing projects for the remainder of 1980. And while he was a regular at Powers's Thursday-night sessions, Phil chose carefully his forays into the outside world. When Powers and Serena asked Phil to serve as best man for their June wedding, Phil regretfully declined. Powers understood: "He wasn't a recluse—he just didn't like going where there would be crowds of people he didn't know."

As a wedding gift, Phil repeatedly offered to purchase the couple a condominium in his building—an offer they graciously declined. Phil's close friends were aware of what a soft touch he was and took care not to take advantage. But there was no curbing Phil's sudden acts of generosity, like the $1,000 he gave to a bank teller who'd confided in him as to her financial difficulties. Phil's kindness went beyond writing checks. On walks, he would worry over children playing in the street and seek out their parents to alert them. And he had the gift of empathy for troubled souls from whom others would steer clear. In interview with Andy Watson and J. B. Reynolds, Powers recalls:

> [. . .] Phil and I had taken a friend to [. . .] Orange County Medical Center, to the mental wing to have this friend committed. The friend was just sitting there like this (catatonic stare, frozen pose). And then some stranger shambles up and, looking at us in that not-in-focus way, says, "You could do a lung transplant." Phil says, "Yeah, you could." Phil tended to agree with anything anybody said in stress situations. So the guy lurches away and then comes back in a while and says, "A vasectomy is a simple operation. You could do it on yourself." Phil says, "Possibly so." The guy comes back in a while again and says, "I'm going to do it on myself." A vasectomy. "Who do I talk to to get permission?" And Phil says, "Those ladies over at the desk. Get the permission *in writing*." (Laughter) And the guy leaves. I said, "Why in writing, Phil?" And he said, "He'll hear the voices saying it's okay, but it'll take an extra psychosis to imagine a piece of paper okaying it."

Even though *Valis* was not due to come out until early 1981, Phil continued to attract a steady stream of interviewers, who found in him a sure source for stimulating copy. *Slash*, a punk music magazine, sent Gary and Nicole Panter to conduct an interview for the summer 1980 issue. In it, Phil managed to outpunk the punks by declaring that a youth revolution that would dismantle the inhuman government apparatus was both possible and desirable: "That's my dream. Not that kids would rule, but that they would make it impossible for the sophisticated technology to function. I have this impulse that comes to me when I'm drinking orange soda. That is to pour half a can of orange soda into my television set."

Phil and Nicole struck up an enduring friendship. She recalls:

> Phil really took a shine to me during the interview, maybe because I was dumb to it, hadn't read his books at all. The questions in the interview like "What's in the fridge?" are mine. He liked that. He didn't look down on me because my intelligence was in a different direction from the analytical nerdy guys who were at his place a lot.
>
> He tested you in a way, to see what you really liked him for. I think he found it hard to believe anyone could like him for himself. Once he offered me a job, being his buffer from other people. I don't know if it was because I

was cute—he was sort of lecherous to me—but there were apparently lots of people coming around to see him for movie deals and other things and he just couldn't deal with all of them.

I turned it down, told him working for him would be like baby-sitting—I could get away with murder. Also, there'd have been the kick-in-the-back-of-the-head result. Phil would put you in a position where you could take advantage. And if you did, you were a shit.

We had a good sick friendship. We'd talk about medication, frozen foods, depression, manic phases. He was wacky—he knew he was. He didn't think like other people. He wasn't embarrassed about it, though. Did he have a "visionary" quality? Fuck no—he was this slobby middle-aged man.

He did this kind of attention-getting thing—like he'd call and say, "I'm not going to take my heart medicine anymore." So for forty-five minutes I'd have to talk him into it. He was sick of taking medicine. If he wasn't physically strong enough to live without heart medicine, he'd rather not take it. To me, it was a kid thing to get attention. That was fine. Talented individuals are often fucked up and weird.

Attention-getting it surely was, but Phil's efforts to reduce his dependence on prescription medications were also quite sincere and arduous. During this period, Phil was variously prescribed antihypertensives such as Apresoline and Dyazide for high blood pressure, Inderal for his heart arrhythmia, Darvon for pain relief, and Elavil, Sinequan, and Tranxene as antidepressants. At one point, Phil vowed to get off the antidepressants, despite their sanction by his psychiatrists. Jeter recalls:

Phil finally decided that prescription drugs were no different from street drugs in terms of creating a real dependency. So he put down the mood elevators cold turkey—and suffered terribly. He fell into a deep depression and called me up, and I went over.

He could barely talk. It was Phil's "death" voice—he was so close to the bottom he could barely speak above a forced whisper. I knew he was really desperate when he sounded like that. But Phil had made his mind up that he would have to put an end to mood elevators, and that he would rather die than go back on that decision. He had tremendous willpower.

Phil's analytical willpower was also a source of wonder to Jeter: "You could see him getting inside a belief and walking around it and testing out its absolute truth. He believed in God and he had some conventional religious beliefs. He also felt that his experiences had given him a greater authority to talk on certain religious matters than most priests possessed. But I don't think he ever forgot, at any point in the *Exegesis*, that he was accepting a given hypothesis." In Jeter's fine 1985 SF novel *The Glass Hammer*, the character Dolph Bischofsky—who tries to reassemble a shattered cathedral window for which the original pattern no longer exists—is a tribute to Jeter's friend and mentor.

In August 1980 Phil outlined yet another novel that he never came to write: *Fawn, Look Back*. The protagonist, based on Phil, is named Nasvar Pflegebourne. Nasvar's work (as an artist) and life have "disbanded"—split in two—thereby inducing schizophrenia. Wrote Phil of Nasvar, of himself:

It was his salvation and his doom both, this disbanding.

In a sense he is twins (inside him) and one twin flourished and one twin sickened and died (expressed by the irreparable loss of Jardi who represents all his loved ones—women—since Eryns [a character to be styled after third wife Anne]).

At the end, then, he is not schizophrenic but so-to-speak half schizophrenic: half disbanded. His work still bands him to reality.

Phil's search for a suitable new novel had a unique urgency. He was worried because the AI voices that had come so regularly since 2-3-74 had ceased altogether since he'd finished *The Divine Invasion*. In an October 1980 interview feature in the *Denver Clarion*, Phil set forth a flat either/or: "you have a direct relation with the divine or you have no relation with the divine." By November, the absence of a direct relation was gnawing at him.

At 11:00 A.M. on November 17, Phil was hanging out in his kitchen, very stoned, chatting with friend Ray Torrence (who recalls absolutely nothing unusual about the occasion).

Zap. Riproaring direct contact.

That same day Phil typed it out first-draft hot in the *Exegesis*—a five-page Phildickian vision, fable and wistful elegy, never before published. The full text follows.

11-17-80

God manifested himself to me as the infinite void; but it was not the abyss; it was the vault of heaven, with blue sky and wisps of white clouds. He was not some foreign God but the God of my fathers. He was loving and kind and he had personality. He said, "You suffer a little now in life; it is little compared with the great joys, the bliss that awaits you. Do you think I in my theodicy would allow you to suffer greatly in proportion to your reward?" He made me aware, then, of the bliss that would come; it was infinite and sweet. He said, "I am the infinite. I will show you. Where I am, infinity is; where infinity is, there I am. Construct lines of reasoning by which to understand your experience in 1974. I will enter the field against their shifting nature. You think they are logical but they are not; they are infinitely creative."

I thought a thought and then an infinite regress of theses and countertheses came into being. God said, "Here I am; here is infinity." I thought another explanation; again an infinite series of thoughts split off in dialectical antithetical interaction. God said, "Here is infinity; here I am." I thought, then, of an infinite number of explanations, in succession, that explained 2-3-74; each single one of them yielded up an infinite progression of flipflops, of thesis and antithesis, forever. Each time, God said, "Here is infinity. Here, then, I am." I tried for an infinite number of times; each time an infinite regress was set off and each time God said, "Infinity. Hence I am here." Then he said, "Every thought leads to infinity, does it not? Find one that doesn't." I tried forever. All led to an infinitude of regress, of the dialectic, of thesis, antithesis and new synthesis. Each time, God said, "Here is infinity; here am I. Try again." I tried forever. Always it ended with God saying, "Infinity and myself; I am here." I saw then, a Hebrew letter with many shafts, and all the shafts led to a common outlet; that outlet or conclusion was infinity. God said, "That is myself. I am infinity. Where infinity is, there am I; where I am, there is infinity. All roads—all explanations for 2-3-74—lead to an infinity of Yes-No, This or That, On-Off, One-Zero, Yin-Yang, the dialectic, infinity upon infinity; an infinity of infinities. I am everywhere and all roads lead to me; *omniae [v]iae ad Deum ducent*. Try again. Think of another possible explanation for 2-3-74." I did; it led to an infinity of regress, of thesis and antithesis and new synthesis. "This is not logic," God said. "Do not think in terms of absolute theories; think instead in terms of probabilities. Watch where the piles heap up, of the same theory essentially repeating itself. Count the number of punch cards in each pile. Which pile is highest? You can never know for sure what 2-3-74 was. What, then, is statistically most probable? Which is to say, which pile is highest? Here is your clue: every theory leads to an infinity (of regression, of thesis and antithesis and new synthesis). What, then, is the probability that I am the cause of 2-3-74, since, where infinity is, there I am? You doubt, you are the doubt as in:

They reckon ill who leave me out;
When me they fly I am the wings.
I am the doubter and the doubt . . .

"You are not the doubter; you are the doubt itself. So do not try to know; you cannot know. Guess on the basis of the highest pile of computer punch cards. There is an infinite stack in the heap marked INFINITY, and I have equated infinity with me. What, then, is the chance that it is me? You cannot be positive; you will doubt. But what is your guess?"

I said, "Probably it is you since there is an infinity of infinities forming before me."

"There is the answer, the only one you will ever have," God said.

"You could be pretending to be God," I said, "and actually be Satan." Another infinitude of thesis and antithesis and new synthesis, the infinite regress, was set off.

God said, "Infinity."

I said, "You could be testing out a logic system in a giant computer and I am—" Again an infinite regress.

"Infinity," God said.

"Will it always be infinite?" I said. "An infinity?"

"Try further," God said.

"I doubt if you exist," I said. And the infinite regress instantly flew into motion once more.

"Infinity," God said. The pile of computer punch cards grew; it was by far the largest pile; it was infinite.

"I will play this game forever," God said, "or until you become tired."

I said, "I will find a thought, an explanation, a theory, that does not set off an infinite regress." And, as soon as I said that, an infinite regress was set off. God said, "Over a period of six and a half years you have developed theory after theory to explain 2-3-74. Each night when you go to bed you think, 'At last I found it. I tried out theory after theory until now, finally, I have the right one.' And then the next morning you wake up and say, 'There is one fact not explained by that theory. I will have to think up another theory.' And so you do. By now it is evident to you that you are going to think up an infinite number of theories, limited only by your lifespan, not limited by your creative imagination. Each theory gives rise to a subsequent theory, inevitably. Let me ask you; I revealed myself to you and you saw that I am the infinite void. I am not in the world, as you thought; I am transcendent, the deity of the Jews and Christians. What you see of me in world that you took to ratify pantheism—that is my being filtered through, broken up, fragmented and vitiated by the multiplicity of the flux world; it is my essence, yes, but only a bit of it: fragments here and there, a glint, a riffle of wind . . . now you have seen me transcendent, separate and other from world, and I am more; I am the infinitude of the void, and you know me as I am. Do you believe what you saw? Do you accept that where the infinite is, I am; and where I am, there is the infinite?"

I said, "Yes."

God said, "And your theories are infinite, so I am there. Without realizing it, the very infinitude of your theories pointed to the solution; they pointed to me and none but me. Are you satisfied, now? You saw me revealed in theophany; I speak to you now; you have, while alive, experienced the bliss that is to come; few humans have experienced that bliss. Let me ask you, Was it a finite bliss or an infinite bliss?"

I said, "Infinite."

"So no earthly circumstance, situation, entity or thing could give rise to it."

"No, Lord," I said.

"Then it is I," God said. "Are you satisfied?"

"Let me try one other theory," I said. "What happened in 2-3-74 was that—" And an infinite regress was set off, instantly.

"Infinity," God said. "Try again. I will play forever, for infinity."

"Here's a new theory," I said. "I ask myself, 'What God likes playing games? Krishna. You are Krishna.' " And then the thought came to me instantly, "But there may be a god who mimics other gods; that god is Dionysus. This may not

271

be Krishna at all; it may be Dionysus pretending to be Krishna." And an infinite regress was set off.

"Infinity," God said.

"You cannot be YHWH Who You say You are," I said. "Because YHWH says, 'I am that which I am,' or, 'I shall be that which I shall be.' And you—"

"Do I change?" God said. "Or do your theories change?"

"You do not change," I said. "My theories change. You, and 2-3-74, remain constant."

"Then you are Krishna playing with me," God said.

"Or I could be Dionysus," I said, "pretending to be Krishna. And I wouldn't know it; part of the game is that I, myself, do not know. So I am God, without realizing it. There's a new theory!" And at once an infinite regress was set off; perhaps I was God, and the "God" who spoke to me was not.

"Infinity," God said. "Play again. Another move."

"We are both Gods," I said[.] And another infinite regress was set off.

"Infinity," God said.

"I am you and you are you," I said. "You have divided yourself in two to play against yourself. I, who am one half, I do not remember, but you do. As it says in the GITA, as Krishna says to Arjuna, 'We have both lived many lives, Arjuna; I remember them but you do not.' " And an infinite regress was set off; I could well be Krishna's charioteer, his friend Arjuna, who does not remember his past lives.

"Infinity," God said.

I was silent.

"Play again," God said.

"I cannot play to infinity," I said. "I will die before that point comes."

"Then you are not God," God said. "But I can play throughout infinity; I am God. Play."

"Perhaps I will be reincarnated," I said. "Perhaps we have done this before, in another life." And an infinite regress was set off.

"Infinity," God said. "Play again."

"I am too tired," I said.

"Then the game is over."

"After I have rested—"

"You rest?" God said. "George Herbert wrote of me:

Yet let him keep the rest,
But keep them with repining restlessnesse.
Let him be rich and weary, that at least,
If goodness leade him not, yet wearinesse
May tosse him to my breast.

"Herbert wrote that in 1633," God said. "Rest and the game ends."

"I will play on," I said, "after I rest. I will play until finally I die of it."

"And then you will come to me," God said. "Play."

"This is my punishment," I said, "that I play, that I try to discern if it was you in March of 1974." And then thought came instantly, My punishment or my reward; which? And an infinite series of thesis and antithesis was set off.

"Infinity," God said. "Play again."

"What was my crime?" I said, "that I am compelled to do this?"

"Or your deed of merit," God said.

"I don't know," I said.

God said, "Because you are not god."

"But you know," I said. "Or maybe you don't know and you're trying to find out." And an infinite regress was set off.

"Infinity," God said. "Play again. I am waiting."

Phil was so forcefully struck by this "theophany" (divine encounter) that he resolved to abandon what he now called the "hell-chore" of the *Exegesis*. On December 2, after a few good stints at analyzing 11-17-80 ("God said that I couldn't know with certainty, but, instead, to watch where the computer punch cards piled up. Okay. [. . .]"), he inscribed, "END," and fashioned a title page for the thousands of sheets piled all about him:

3/20/74
12-2-80

THE DIALECTIC:
God against Satan, & God's
Final Victory foretold & shown

Philip K. Dick

AN EXEGESIS

Apologia Pro Mia Vita

But by December 12 he'd filled an envelope with new notes. And then Phil was back at the *Exegesis* again. Hadn't he told God that he'd play the game again as soon as he'd rested?

For a guy who had just been granted a theophany, Phil had a downright dismal Christmas. He was blue because it seemed there was no one to talk with about the ideas that mattered to him. In the *Exegesis*, Phil acknowledged that his talk sometimes sounded like "religious nonsense & occult nonsense"—but somewhere in it all was the truth. And he would never find it. God Himself had assured him of that. So come Christmas Eve 1980 he was alone—by choice—watching the Pope's Midnight Mass on TV and seeing no sign of Christ in the ritual display.

By the New Year, Phil had recovered some of his zest for speculation. And he grappled with his sense of declining energy by dieting severely. Within a relatively short time, Phil was thin for the first time since the early sixties. He found the dietary discipline easy—what he called his "self-denial trip" allowed him to relish giving up favorite foods like canned steak-and-kidney pies from Ireland. The change in physical image suited Phil. Chris Arena, a Thursday Night Group regular, recalls Phil's prior vulnerability about his weight:

> One night Phil and I were having this chop session with each other and I told him, "You're just a fat old man." Phil gets up like okay, now I'm going to kick your ass. And then he sits down and says, "I *am* a fat old man." The doctor told him to lose weight and not drink, and that prompted Phil to go on the diet. But even before that, he knew that I was telling him the truth.

The new slim Phil took on a surprising role in his condominium association. Juan and Su Perez, who became Phil's new neighbors and close friends after Doris Sauter moved out, recall that the new condo occupants enjoyed having a "creative kook" in the building but suspected that Phil smoked a lot of weed. Those few who ventured to read his books were horrified. So how the hell did Phil become chairperson of the Rules and Grievances Committee? "He was always home," Juan explains. "And Phil was concerned that anyone else would be too strict about cats and loud music."

Phil and Juan, who was working on his master's in psychology (he'd been assigned two of Phil's novels for a class on delusional thought), would fantasize out a book project that would blend Juan's background in chemistry and psychology with Phil's philosophical and religious knowledge. Su recalls that Phil, a frequent guest at dinnertime, would often bemoan his bad luck with women and request her advice. "I would say to him, 'Don't tell them so much about yourself so fast.' "

But in early 1981 there arose an event that eclipsed even the longing for a woman: A Major Hollywood Motion Picture!

At long last, negotiations to adapt *Androids* for the screen had resulted in a solid deal. Producer Michael Deeley took up the project, with the Ladd Company to handle distribution. Ridley Scott *(Alien)* would direct the film—to be titled *Blade Runner*—and Harrison Ford (of *Star Wars* and *Raiders of the Lost Ark*) would play Rick Deckard, whose job it is to kill "replicants" (as Phil's "androids" are called in the film) who escape their colony planets. Shooting would commence in Hollywood— just a short jaunt up the freeway from Phil's place—in the first half of 1981.

To understand the impact all this had upon Phil, it's important to realize that in the early production stages *Blade Runner* was the odds-on candidate to be the next *Star Wars*. No two names were then hotter than Ridley Scott and Harrison Ford. The budget ultimately reached $25–$30 million, a heavy wager by the firm's backers. *Blade Runner* only gradually earned the profits to justify the gamble—at the outset, reviews were mixed, the box office so-so, the merchandising spin-offs were a total flop. In the long run, the film has made substantial earnings through international distribution and the video sales and rental markets. In Japan, *Blade Runner* is regarded as a cult classic and it is a key factor behind Phil's towering literary status in that country. But in America, the film never quite took hold in first-run distribution—though it's not hard to see why Phil was so excited at the time.

Phil was also duly skeptical that the film would do justice to his novel. But no one is immune to Hollywood dreams, and Phil had his fantasies of fame and glory. Reality obtruded quickly enough, though. Phil loathed Hampton Fancher's screenplay, which he read in December 1980. His response was to declare war on the project. In a piece for the February–March 1981 issue of *SelecTV Guide*—the magazine of Phil's cable service—he took a potshot at Ridley Scott's biggest hit: "For all its dazzling graphic impact, ALIEN (to take one example) had nothing new to bring us in the way of concepts that awaken the mind, rather than the senses."

It's extremely doubtful that any of the *Blade Runner* principals ever took notice of Phil's little piece. David Peoples, who in early 1981 was called in to do a rewrite of the Fancher script, doesn't recall Phil's name ever coming up in meetings. Peoples thought Fancher's initial script excellent and never read *Androids*, before or after his rewrite—which Phil (making a 180-degree shift from his previous disdain for the entire project) praised to the skies when he read it in August 1981. The final screenplay, jointly credited to Fancher and Peoples, recasts or eliminates key elements of the *Androids* plot (see Chronological Survey); the Mercer empathy religion is entirely absent, for example. But Phil was well aware of the differences between the print and film media and never thought an exact transposition possible or even desirable.

While the screenplay struggles ended happily, a more painful and personal misunderstanding arose, by way of the mails, between Phil and Ursula Le Guin. In February 1981 Le Guin gave talks at Emory University, at which SF writer Michael Bishop was in attendance. Bishop had written admiring essays on both *Ubik* and the just-released *Valis* and was corresponding with Phil. (Since then, Bishop has published a 1987 novel, *The Secret Ascension*—subtitled *Philip K. Dick Is Dead, Alas*—in which the late mainstream author Philip K. Dick could not, in his lifetime, find acceptance for his subversive SF works.) Bishop informed Phil of certain of Le Guin's comments, the substance of which Phil considered offensive enough to warrant a public response in *Science Fiction Review*, a fanzine in which quarrelsome correspondence is an entertainment staple:

> I'm looking at a recent letter to me from Michael Bishop. Michael likes my new novel VALIS, but learned that Ursula Le Guin had been tremendously

upset by it, "not only for its examination of perhaps unresolvable metaphysical matters (into which she seems to fear you are plunging at the risk of never emerging again) but for its treatment of female characters—every one of which, she argued, was at bottom (I cannot remember her exact phrase) a hateful and not to be trusted death figure [. . .] she had the utmost admiration for the work of Philip K. Dick, who had been shamefully ignored in this country and who appeared to be spiraling into himself and going slowly crazy in Santa Ana, California." Her dismay, Michael says, "Results solely from a genuine human concern about your intellectual and emotional well-being."

Phil's letter also cites Le Guin's complaint that he had failed to portray the redemptive power of art in his *Valis* self-portrait.

For her part, Le Guin deeply regretted Phil's hurt feelings. She had long been a staunch public advocate of Phil's talent, and her 1971 novel *The Lathe of Heaven* was, by her own acknowledgment, markedly influenced by his sixties works. A letter from her offering apologies and clarification is included in that same summer 1981 issue of *SFR*. In interview, Le Guin explains that she never seriously feared for Phil's sanity and does not recall terming his themes "unresolvable." "I would say 'crazy' about both Phil and Virginia Woolf. But I don't like those books of his later period through *Valis*. I think there is a madness in those books that he didn't come out of—Virginia Woolf comes out, Phil doesn't always. It is not always transmuted into art." Le Guin reaffirms her dislike of the female characters in the decade preceding *Valis*. "The women were symbols—whether goddess, bitch, hag, witch—but there weren't any women left, and there used to be women in his books."

Phil and Le Guin did come to an ultimate reconciliation through subsequent private letters. But it remains useful to trace just where Phil stood firm or gave way in response to her criticisms. As to her alleged dislike for unresolvable metaphysical speculations, Phil pointedly replied, in his *SFR* letter, "I have never drawn the line between ideas that could and could not—should and should not—be looked into. That, to me, is a dangerous idea: that some ideas are better left alone, for the good and the sanity of all concerned." The issue of his sanity was a more painful matter, of course. In the *SFR* letter, Phil insisted that *Valis* be taken as picaresque fiction and not as a self-portrait: "The fact that my protagonist, Horselover Fat, is a madman does not prove that I, the author, am a madman even if I say, 'I am Horselover Fat', because this is the way you write certain kinds of books. There are scenes of violent arguments between Phil Dick and Horselover Fat in the novel."

As for the redemptive role of the artist, this had always been one of Phil's least favorite themes. In the *SFR* letter, Phil proudly restated his proletarian writer's credo, unchanged since the Berkeley days. "My answer: My novel is my justification, not anything I arrogate to myself as a person, as a novelist. [. . .] This [writing] talent [. . .] does not make me superior to people who repair shoes or drive buses." Phil's defiance here is surely related to his longtime sense of the differences between his status and that of Le Guin. He was the trashy writer, she the elegant stylist who had far outdistanced him in garnering SF awards and even mainstream acceptance—stories in the *New Yorker*, novels published by Knopf. Back in a 1978 *Exegesis* entry, Phil had offered an explanation of their respective fates:

> Taking a pop form [SF] as "serious" is what you do if it won't go away. It's a clever tactic. They welcome you in [. . .] This is how the BIP [Black Iron Prison] handles it if they can't flat out crush it. Next thing, they get you to submit your S-F writing to them to criticize. "Structured criticism" to edit out the "trashy elements"—& you wind up with what Ursula writes.

As to the woman problem in his work, Phil's *SFR* response—that women and men alike in *Valis* are portrayed as picaresque rogues—isn't to the point, and Phil himself wasn't convinced by it. In a subsequent letter to Galen, Phil acknowledged that in his work prior to *The Divine Invasion* "my depiction of females has been inadequate and even somewhat vicious." In May 1981, upon completing *The Transmigration of Timothy Archer*, with its loving portrait of Angel Archer, Phil would write to Le Guin in joy and triumph: "This is the happiest moment of my life, Ursula, to meet face-to-face this bright, scrappy, witty, educated, tender woman, [. . .] and had it not been for your analysis of my writing I probably never would have discovered her."

But new troubles were brewing on the *Blade Runner* front. The film's backers badly wanted a novelization of the screenplay to market in conjunction with the film's release. Galen took the position that *Androids* itself, and not a hastily written rehash, ought to be reissued as a tie-in with the *Blade Runner* title. The backers' May bargaining response was classic carrot and stick. Carrot: If Phil agreed to a novelization, he could write it himself for a $50,000 advance plus a 50 percent cut of net profits from *all* print media tie-ins—souvenir magazines, posters, comic books, etc. If the film was a smash, Phil could stand to earn $250,000 to $400,000 in total royalties. But *Androids*, his own novel, would be shunted aside. Stick: If Phil refused, the backers still had the right to issue print tie-ins of 7,500 words or less *without* Phil's consent—and Phil wouldn't see a dime. And if some publisher chose to reissue *Androids*, it would be under its original title—no mention permitted of its relation to *Blade Runner*.

As it turned out, Phil would, by Galen's estimates, have earned roughly $70,000 on the proposed novelization deal, with only $20,000 or so coming from print media tie-ins. But at the time that Phil and Galen were talking over their strategy, a gross of $400,000 seemed at stake. And the offer had come at a most pivotal moment. For David Hartwell, the editor who had purchased *The Divine Invasion* for Simon and Schuster, had just contracted with Phil for a *mainstream* novel. In fact, in the course of a single day's visit with Phil in April 1981, Hartwell had agreed to terms for three Phil Dick novels: a $7,500 advance for the mainstream novel, *Bishop Timothy Archer* (Phil's working title), $17,500 for an SF novel to be called *The Owl in Daylight* (never written), and $3,500 for a Timescape paperback reissue of *Crap Artist*. Hartwell's trust in Phil's talent was unconditional. In interview he recalls:

> Phil talked for nearly six hours in enormous detail on what became *Timothy Archer*. The whole structure was there—all he had to do was sit down and write it.
>
> As for *Owl*, I never got a formal written proposal. Phil once told me that he could pitch anything to editors and agents before two in the afternoon and make it sound like a convincing plot—two was when his mail came, and he had a fetish about his mail, couldn't get any writing done until he had seen it. The plot description of *Owl* I got the day I visited was something like Dante, like Thomas Mann, like *Valis*, like *The Divine Invasion*, and at that point I didn't push. Later I did get a letter with a few paragraphs of description, but it was the vaguest kind of Philip K. Dick description.
>
> By late that day I had decided to buy all three books, and I told him so. Phil picked up his cat and said to him, "Boy, do we have a hot one here." We went to dinner and had a great time.

So here Phil was with a first ever New York mainstream deal worth all of $7,500, while Hollywood dangled a fat $400,000 cigar between its lips for a gimcrack novelization. Phil often described these two options as a vital either-or test of his integrity. Galen recalls the course of the negotiations this way:

> Phil told a lot of people that I said there were two offers—*Timothy Archer* for $7,500 or the novelization for $400,000—which do you want to do? His version makes a better story, but it's not true. He didn't have to choose. He could have done both.
>
> Really, his initial reaction was, it sounds great, let's explore it. I told him no, it's terrible, if you do a novelization no one will read *Androids*. He wanted to know how much they were offering—and this is what people try not to remember, that Phil came out of the hack world and the money definitely mattered. He couldn't understand why I'd say no to a lucrative deal. We talked, and he finally said, "I guess you're right."

The final deal saw *Androids* reissued under the title *Blade Runner*, with the film backers getting a one percent royalty. In an interview before final terms were agreed to, Phil decried the idea of novelization, but also pointed out that, had he been willing to write one, "financially, as my agent explained it, I would literally be set up for life. I don't think my agent figures I'm going to live much longer."

But it was Phil, not Galen, who was having premonitions of death. This was nothing new: Phil had sensed himself signaled to die several times over the past decade, as during the Xerox missive episode of March 1974. The difference now was that Phil felt himself not so much endangered from without as, simply, bone weary. Galen's point that Phil could have done both projects is true enough from a contractual standpoint; but as a matter of will and energy Phil knew better.

He turned to writing *The Transmigration of Timothy Archer* in April and May of 1981, and experienced a powerful sense of having endured temptation: "my spiritual aspirations endured white-hot iron testing[. . .] Finally, I am right now triumphing, as I write the 'Archer' book," Phil wrote in the *Exegesis*. He emphasized: "Literature is not the issue. Forging a vision of *anokhi* [Hebrew: I am the Lord] as I write *is the issue*. For me there is no other issue. Pure consciousness." While Phil's literary aims were exalted, his manner of fueling this new writing stint was not. To Paul Williams, he confided that he drank significant quantities of Laphroaig Scotch each night he worked on the novel—and felt that he was thereby jeopardizing his health.

Timothy Archer is an exploration of the soul of a man for whom, like Phil, "vision" and "consciousness" are the essence of life. No other of Phil's novels delineates so clearly the radical difference between Phil the thinker and Phil the artist. For in telling the story of Bishop Archer's failed existence—his unhappy family life, bitter extramarital affair, and soulless intellectual justifications—Phil is in essence rejecting the abstractions of his own *Exegesis* in favor of the simple, day-to-day virtues of human warmth and kindness.

Timothy Archer is also, more markedly than is typical for Phil, a straightforward *roman à clef*. Bishop Archer, who dies in the Judean desert in search of *anokhi* in the form of the *Vita verna* mushroom, is a psychological portrait of Bishop Pike. A letter on the bishop's life, sent by Angel Archer to "Jane Marion" in Chapter 2, closely resembles a February 1981 letter by Phil to Joan Didion (who wrote an essay on Pike in *The White Album*). Jeff Archer commits suicide, as did Bishop Pike's son, Jim junior, but the key models for Jeff were two of Phil's friends, Tom Schmidt and Ray Harris. Archer's mistress Kirsten Lundborg is limned from Maren Hackett. Teacher Edgar Barefoot is based on Alan Watts.

And Bill Lundborg, Kirsten's schizophrenic son, who believes Bishop Archer's soul has come to inhabit him, is based in part on Phil himself. The notion that Bishop Pike was somehow within him had continued to haunt Phil, as in this 1981 *Exegesis* entry: "2-3-74: I was bewitched. The purpose: to re-create Jim so he could continue [. . .] speaking (through my writing, & not just the 'Archer' book)." But the Jim Pike re-created in *Archer* is a most ambiguous portrait. His desert quest for *anokhi* is the act of an unwise, driven man. Angel Archer, the narrator, writes of him:

That this trying out of every possible idea to see if it would finally fit destroyed Tim Archer can't be disputed. He tried out too many ideas, picked them up, examined them, used them for a while and then discarded them . . . some of the ideas, however, as if possessing a life of their own, came back around the far side of the barn and got him. [. . .] But he died hard, which is to say, he died hitting back. Fate had to murder him.

Though the plot focus of the novel is ostensibly on Bishop Archer, it is his daughter-in-law Angel Archer, practical and tender, a widow in her thirties who manages a Berkeley record store, who quietly dominates the narrative. A key inspiration for Angel was daughter Laura (whose middle name is Archer). Donna, Phil's great love from the Santa Venetia days, was another model for the character, according to the *Exegesis*. But these real-life models emerged into something more. Angel's simple transcendence over the bishop's abstract speculations gave Phil a sense of having at last reconciled with the feminine, the anima, within himself. In the *Exegesis*: "When God looks at me he sees Angel Archer because this is what Christ has made me: new life: reborn. The [feminine] AI voice is the voice of my own soul."

His delight in creating Angel Archer led Phil to yearn anew for mainstream status. If *Timothy Archer* was well received, there was a chance that the doors would open at last. To Galen, in a June 1981 letter, Phil allowed that exclusion from the mainstream "has been the tragedy—and a very long-term tragedy—of my creative life." He proposed to devote himself to further mainstream efforts and asked for his agent's advice. Galen's letter in response was guarded: He loyally urged Phil to abandon SF if he so desired. But Galen's heart wasn't really in it. In interview Galen recalls:

What I was trying to say in that letter was, don't stop writing science fiction. I just couldn't say it. I felt it would break his heart. If he had lived to see *Archer* not be a success—and *Archer* did poorly—it would have been very difficult, 1958 all over again. I would have had to submit his next mainstream novel to twenty-five houses and get twenty-five rejections.

To my mind, his mainstream stuff wasn't one-tenth as good as his science fiction. It's not something you could say to his face. Now he's dead and a martyr, and it's convenient to look at Phil as this man who could have been a mainstream writer but the dirty rotten publishing industry never gave him a chance. I don't think that's the case.

Timothy Archer didn't sell out its modest print run, even though it was published in spring 1982, just after Phil's death. A 1983 paperback reissue made a small profit. His subsequently published mainstream works have garnered the same low profits and quiet esteem.

Did Phil suspect the worst? In an August 1981 letter to Galen, Phil seemed to shake himself free of the mainstream dream. "Yes, I think I will continue to write SF novels. It's in my blood, and I feel no shame about being an SF author." He was wrestling with *The Owl in Daylight*, posing different plots in letters to Galen and Hartwell and pondering a "lamination" of them all. In one version, a Dantesque Inferno-Purgatorio-Paradiso structure forms the backdrop to the tale of a scientist imprisoned in an amusement park by an angry computer. Only by solving ethical dilemmas can the scientist—trapped in a boy's body—reach Paradiso and recollect his true self. The park includes a Berkeley milieu with a Tony Boucher figure who helps the boy become an SF writer.

Another element in the *Owl* plot stew was "Ditheon," a word that came to Phil in a June 1981 dream: A beneficent medication appeared on a dream cylinder labeled—shades of *Ubik!*—"DITHEON." In the morning Phil hit the reference books and parsed out the Greek words *di* (two) and *theon* (God). In the *Exegesis* Phil exulted: "The term—the concept—Ditheon is the complete, absolute, total, accurate, definitive, final, ultimate explanation of 2-3-74." A person possessed by Ditheon has fused the two prior forms of divine wisdom, the justice of the Torah and the grace of Christ, into a third and higher spiritual wisdom—a return to pure being as expressed in Plato's concept of ideas. In a July letter Phil explained: "As human is to android, Ditheon is to human."

What role would Ditheon play in *Owl?* Phil never quite nailed that down. Had he lived, the time would have come for the feverish two-week stint that would have put such questions to rest. In an interview conducted by friend Gwen Lee in February 1982—just days before the first of the strokes that killed him—Phil offered what must stand as a final version of the *Owl* plot. The protagonist is a composer loosely inspired by Beethoven, who composed what Phil believed to be his finest music after becoming deaf. This is possible, Phil reasons, because music is a conceptual act processed by the right brain.

Phil's composer, Ed Firmley, lives out in the boonies, maybe Oregon. He's a strange loser type—musically ungifted, he earns a good living writing scores for cheap SF flicks. Then comes his big break: "They have this really rotten science fiction film about this detective who is tracking down these androids." (A parody of *Blade Runner*.) Firmley "is writing a schmaltzy score to go with this movie. [. . .] Now it's easy to track him down, because he is well known." Who's tracking Firmley down? Aliens from a planet on which music—or any sound—is unknown. Color is the basis of their language. One such alien discovers music by way of a religious experience and travels to Earth to learn how it is composed. "I have to write from the standpoint of the creature who is using color for language and for whom this is a sacred planet—like finding God." Firmley is the unwitting object of this sacred quest. "The alien decides to biochip himself and insert himself as a symbio into the human host brain." Phil doesn't provide an ending for *Owl* but does pose its ultimate theme:

The problem here is does a human want an alien in his brain as a symbio? I intend to make that a major question. You're catching me when I'm actually organizing a novel. This is the most essential part of writing a book, what I'm doing now. We switch viewpoints. A human being who is a composer would be the ideal host for this alien. [. . .] It's there to enjoy music. It's a transcendental religious experience.

Why the title? "Owls cannot see in daylight, they become confused. It simply means a person whose judgment is clouded over."

Ideas for *Owl* came and went, but Phil couldn't bring himself to start it. In a letter Phil confided: "I'm afraid I bit off more than I can chew; I exhausted myself writing THE TRANSMIGRATION OF TIMOTHY ARCHER [. . .] and just can't keep up the pace." Phil feared he would follow the fate of Herb Hollis and a Point Reyes friend, western writer Bill Cook, both of whom died in early middle age from heart attacks. Then, in early September, Phil read in a Berkley Books newsletter that two of its writers had suffered heart attacks, one fatal. His response was desperate:

After I read the news [. . .] I stopped taking notes on my novel-in-progress, lay down for a nap, got up, drove to the grocery store, drove home and rammed a support column in our underground parking area. My unconscious was saying, *Enough*. I knew I was going to hit the support column and even after I hit it I kept on moving; I wanted to hit it. I wanted to protest the two heart attacks [. . .]; I wanted to protest my own enslavement to decades of writing in order to pay spousal support, child support, send my older daughter to Stanford, my youngest boy to a private school, buy my ex-wife Tessa a $150,000 house—meet deadlines, rent a tux for the gala premier showing of BLADE RUNNER, all the long-distance phone calls, all the answering letters from readers who plan to commit suicide and want me to talk them out of it, because I wrote about my own suicide attempt in VALIS and they know I'd understand. I do understand. I understand that the payoff for writers—and editors as well!—who work day after day, sixteen hours a day, seven days a week [. . .] is not happiness but sudden death or total disability; they are, as Jesus said, like "your ancestors who ate manna in the wilderness; they are all dead."

The crash left him with an injured leg that made even walking about his condominium difficult. Intense physical expressions of empathy and rage were part and parcel of Phil's makeup. When he learned of the 1981 assassination of Egyptian president Anwar Sadat, Phil crushed an aluminum pop can so that it cut into his wrist. These were protests that verged upon suicide but stopped short. Phil wanted to live. He was looking forward to the *Blade Runner* premier, scheduled for mid-1982, and despite his complaints, money wasn't really an issue. But Phil *was* tired—and more than tired. He craved redemption for himself and for the world.

The endless explanations of 2-3-74 had left him high and dry, and he knew it. A week after the accident he wrote to Galen enclosing a one-page "final statement" on the *Exegesis*. His cover letter explained that 2-3-74 was real "but what it is I simply do not know, nor do I expect ever to know." The "final statement" admits his ignorance but argues that knowledge—not mere faith—as to the true "hyper-structure" of the universe *is* possible. A new species with a higher level of awareness than humans may be evolving, and the "hyper-structure" is "actively involved" in this evolution. "[I]t is a meta-entity in the truest sense, and poses a vast, urgent mystery deserving of our profoundest attention."

Which all sounds like something that skeptical Angel Archer could have assented to. But Phil had met the "hyper-structure" head on in 2-3-74 and had played for infinite stakes with God on 11-17-80. Acknowledgment of the mystery could not satisfy him; only actual contact would do. As for a better world, the prospect of slow evolution over the centuries wasn't much of a solace.

In 1979 the AI voice had told Phil: "The time you've waited for has come. The work is complete; the final world is here. He has been transplanted and is alive." The AI voice added that the savior would be found on an island. On the night of September 17, 1981, Phil was just about to fall asleep when he was startled awake by a hypnagogic vision of this savior, named Tagore, who was living in Ceylon. In a September 19 letter to Galen he avowed that "I got more than information, more than words by the AI voice; I actually saw Tagore, although imperfectly. The vision will remain with me forever." In the *Exegesis*, Phil termed it a teaching (*kerygma*) that he must communicate. And so on September 23 he mailed a letter to *Niekas* fanzine editor Edmund Myskys (who published it) and some eighty-five others—friends and distant contacts—describing Tagore and his teachings. According to Phil, Tagore was dark-skinned, Hindu or Buddhist, and worked in the countryside with a veterinary group. "Although Tagore is the second incarnation of Christ he is taken to be Lord Krishna by the local population." Religious labels hardly matter—at stake is the survival of the earth and of the spirit of man:

Tagore is burned and crippled; he cannot walk but must be carried. As near as [Horselover] Fat could make out, Tagore is dying, but he is dying voluntarily: Tagore has taken upon himself mankind's sins against the ecosphere. Most of all it is the dumping of toxic wastes into the oceans of the world that shows up on Tagore's body as serious burns. Tagore's *kerygma*, which is the Third Dispensation (following the Mosaic and Christian) is: the ecosphere is holy and must be preserved, protected, venerated and cherished—as a *unity*[. . .]

Tagore teaches that when the ecosphere is burned, God himself is burned, [. . .] Thus a macro-crucifixion is taking place now, in and as our world, but we do not see it; Tagore, the new incarnation in human form of the Logos, tells us this in order to appeal to us to stop. If we continue we will lose God's Wisdom and, finally, we will lose our own physical lives.

The letter notes the similarity between Tagore's teachings on the ecosphere as Cosmic Christ and those of Teilhard de Chardin in *The Phenomenon of Man*. But for Chardin the sacred reveals itself in evolution; Tagore comes by way of a divine invasion of our world.

In this public letter (and not in his earlier letter to Galen) Phil attributed the vision to Horselover Fat: "He got me to write this letter as a way of telling the world—the readership of *Niekas*, more precisely— about it. Poor Fat! His madness is complete, now, for he supposes that in his vision he actually *saw* the new savior." Phil never denied to friends or interviewers that he had seen Tagore. But there was a comfort in the irony of alter ego Fat's voice. In the February 1981 debate with Le Guin, that irony had served to fend off the charge of madness. In a 1981 *Exegesis* entry he acknowledged: "All these 7 years I've feared I was nuts (hence H. Fat is so described)."

How did Phil regard the Tagore vision? *Village Voice* critic Greg Sandow visited Phil in early October and recalls their talk over drinks at a neighborhood bar: "He said that he had been receiving several communications from God and that they confused and troubled him. He spoke very matter-of-factly and directly, not trying at all to awe me. Phil identified with Tagore—what was happening to the savior was happening to himself by way of the injured leg. He was preoccupied with death, but it also seemed to him to be natural, in the sense that the savior himself dies when the world is in bad shape." In the *Exegesis*, Phil posed the struggle: "I must ask what God wants of me. To promulgate Tagore's *kerygma*? Or to sacrifice myself? As of today I see only the latter as lying within my power; I do not have the strength left for the former, so he cannot want the former. I must emulate Tagore."

The Tagore vision became one more piece of the puzzle that would never fit together. It didn't stop Phil in his tracks any more than 11-17-80 had. And a concentration on the new *kerygma* didn't mean putting on self-righteous airs or forgetting to have fun. One week after Phil sent off the Tagore letter, he dashed off a scathing self-parody (in the form of a review of *The Divine Invasion*) for a fanzine named *Venom*. The review concludes:

It is glib enough, but apparently Dick is trying to work off the bad karma he allegedly acquired during his year or years with street-people, criminals, violent agitators and just by and large the scum of Northern California (this all took place, apparently, after the collapse of one of his many marriages). This reviewer suggests that a better way to make amends would be to take some much-deserved R & R: stop writing, Phil, watch TV, maybe smoke a joint—one more bite of the dog won't kill you—and generally take it easy until both the Bad Old Days and the *reaction* to the Bad Old Days subside in your fevered mind.

◆

Phil still enjoyed weaving wild late-night tales of Gnostic mysteries and KGB counterplots with Jeter, Blaylock, and Powers. All three would receive urgent phone calls from Phil apropos of anything. Recalls Blaylock:

One time he'd gotten a check for around $20,000 as a partial payment for *Blade Runner*. So he calls and says, "Jeez, it's eleven at night and I've got $20,000, what can I do with it?" I said, "What do you want most?" and he said, "I'd kill for a ham sandwich." I told him, "That's asking a lot in Orange County at eleven at night." He said, "What about a girl?"

Back in 1978, a girl—Thérèse—who had offered her body had disgusted Phil to the core. Phil's joke touched on this pain and betrayed his loneliness. Hadn't he always known that even God wasn't enough without the love of a good woman? But it had been a four-year dry spell.

But then his luck changed, or so it seemed.

In October he met "Susan," the wife of an acquaintance. She was in her late twenties, intelligent and striking. Her marriage was shaky, her husband living out of state. Phil was drawn to her; Susan returned his feelings. Time to fall in love: "I remember that night still, how I felt: the world came alive for me, as if I had been reborn. I had come out of my shell, into which I had withdrawn back in 1977 when Joan and I split up." They had a brief, passionate affair. But early on Susan confided that she would soon move to the northern Bay Area. This news cast a blight upon Phil's hopes. He saw a classic double bind: love me/I'm leaving. Her married status gnawed at him: Adultery was not a "right act" by Tagore's standards. And Phil would not follow her north, as he had Joan four years before. In a November letter to Susan he drove the point home. Career, friends, family, and stable home came before passion:

Anything that jeopardizes these *as a package* is on a collision course with my life, and that is the name of that tune. My mode of being (*Dasein*) is accumulative; I add on—this after decades of disorder and intoxication and smashing and leaving and just plain wandering the face of the Earth. For nine years I have systematically built up steadily, and I project all that years into the future. I intend to keep on building.

Brave and sensible as this sounds, calling off the relationship proved tremendously painful for Phil. A lengthy typed self-analysis from this November details the struggle. One night Phil experienced "oceanic dread" and asked Tessa to come over; she comforted him through the night, and he felt the bonds that still held them together. At the same time, Phil was appalled that both Susan and Tessa were mother figures to him: "It is very bitter, painful and terrible to be forever searching for the good mother (the tender, kind, loving mother) you never had, think that at last you have found her—and then discover that you are right back where you started: involved with the cruel, hateful, suspicious, judgmental mother, the bad mother, all over again."

Phil next entered into a brief platonic romance with a fellow condo owner. There were moments of bliss in which, as he wrote, "because of you I re-entered reality, from which I fled years ago." But she had a younger lover, and Phil's old yearning for love at all costs was changing: "I asked myself, Am I in love [. . .]? No I am not. Nor am I in love with [Susan] any more. With Tessa? Perhaps. It's the work, the writing."

Nonetheless, relations with Tessa were warming. Their joint care of Christopher provided the sense of family that Phil craved. They discussed the possibility of remarrying. Phil's approach to the question was typical of his handling of difficult emotional issues—he played out different sides at different times. To his friends he posed it as Tessa's desire, with which he would not comply. With Tessa he talked about getting a house together.

In the midst of all this high drama, Phil did enjoy one stable and comfortable friendship with a woman. Mary Wilson had been a trusted confidante since 1972; now, in the last six months of his life, they were in contact nearly every day. Mary, an actress, could handle the Hollywood glitter and hype, and Phil did have occasion to deal with Hollywood now and then. *Blade Runner* had finished shooting in September 1981, and there were strong rumors that the Disney Studios would exercise its option on *Total Recall*, a screenplay based on Phil's 1966 story "We Can Remember It for You Wholesale." (Since Phil's death, this film project has become a reality—see the discussion of *The Preserving Machine* in Chronological Survey.) There were even occasional Hollywood parties, such as the one thrown for prospective backers of *Claw* (a screenplay based on the 1953 novella *Second Variety*).

But the big event was the November invitation from the *Blade Runner* people to come see a reel of special effects devised for the film. Back in June, Phil had through sheer chance seen a short clip from *Blade Runner* on the local news and been pleased with the techno-*noir* beauty of the film. Now he was to receive a private showing. Mary told him to request a limousine and driver—and the studio complied! Phil posed with

286

Ridley Scott for publicity stills in which Phil, not the big-time director, is wearing a tie.

Phil and Mary would conduct marathon late-night talks at his condominium. Phil's thorough analyses of all possibilities—be the subject Hollywood, God, art, or women—accounted for most of the conversation. He fueled himself with strong Blue Sumatra coffee and frequent snorts of Dean Swift snuff. With Mary, Phil planned to make a triumphant return to France. The organizers of the Metz festival had invited him to come again as guest of honor, all expenses paid, in 1982. On the way they would stop in New York, and Phil would finally visit the city that published him. After Paris and Metz, perhaps they would take in Germany. Mary recalls that they began to discuss their relationship as a "partnership" and that Phil wanted to draw up formal papers to that effect. If he died—and he seemed to sense that he had little time left—a partnership would give her a fair share of the estate. But the idea of papers troubled Mary. "I didn't want to do it—it was like by signing that I'd want his money, not him." To other friends, Phil denied that he ever intended a formal partnership.

In late December daughter Isa called long-distance. Now fifteen years old, she was very nervous about being called on by the teachers at school, and Phil comforted her. Immediately after the call he wrote her a long letter that he asked her to save—she would understand it better as she grew older. In it he spoke of the human soul that is not at home in this world. The answer to the soul's plight lies in God's grace. God intervenes when our burden becomes too great, but only if we call out to God—"this is why not all humans are saved, because not all humans see, ever, in their entire lives, that they live by and through God, and God alone; [. . .]"

In January 1982, according to Tessa, Phil proposed and she accepted. She writes: "Phil had convinced me, this time, that I did not have to be afraid of finding his dead body some day when I came home from the supermarket. That was always my greatest fear, that Phil would successfully attempt suicide, and that I would find the body, or maybe our baby would find it. Phil convinced me that he wanted to live, would go on living. He was wrong." To other friends, Phil denied that he had ever proposed.

One night in late January, Phil was listening to a KNX FM talk show. The guest was Benjamin Creme, a British artist and mystic who proclaimed the world advent of a godlike teacher—at once the second coming of Christ and the arrival of the future Buddha, Maitreya. This teacher lived somewhere in Europe and was an important spokesman in his community, but he had kept his spiritual identity a secret. He would manifest himself to the world in late spring, and a new spiritual Age of Aquarius would be ushered in.

Creme's predictions were not so very far removed from Phil's Tagore vision. Phil was thrilled by the show and sent copies of *Valis* and the Tagore letter to Creme's Tara Center headquarters in Hollywood. He then followed up with the purchase of two Tara Center books, which Phil studied and thought excellent, and a $150 donation. In a February 12 letter to *Childworld* magazine Phil avowed the Creme teachings as truth: "The central doctrine of his new dispensation is that we of the industrial nations must take primary responsibility for feeding and caring for the poorer people, of the Third World per se; we must share the wealth, energy and resources of the world with all mankind. Our own lifestyles must become more simple; we must not only cease to hoard the resources of the world, we must also cease to waste them." To interviewer Gregg Rickman, he spoke at length concerning his faith in the coming of Maitreya; this interview appears in *Philip K. Dick: The Last Testament*.

Rickman writes that, when the interview was completed and the tape recorder shut off, Phil confessed to some doubts as to Creme's prediction of a new spiritual age. When he traveled to Europe he planned to investigate the matter further by checking up in Belgium and the Netherlands. Mary recalls these plans: "Phil said that even if you aren't sure it's true, it doesn't hurt to be included—he would rather be one of the bosses deciding who would pick beans than be one of the bean pickers. I think it was the scenario of his next book—I really do." The *Exegesis* confirms that Phil took Creme to task over the true nature of the divine invasion. And one 1982 entry suggests why Phil waited until the tape recorder was off to express doubt—such doubt might undermine his goal of exercising an influence on public opinion:

> I've realized: I'm into power. In terms of my writing & in terms of what I do with the money I earn from my writing. The key term is: *effective*.
>
> I am interested in only one thing: instead of society molding me, I mold it: (1) in my writing; (2) in what I do with the money; (3) in interviews; (4) in the movie [. . .] Vast thematic doctrines are emerging [. . .] *This* is what the whole opus adds up to: anticipation of the coming kingship of God. In other words, the kerygma.

To Gwen Lee, in an interview conducted in Phil's final week of consciousness, Phil blended the burdens of prophecy and the plot of *Owl* and confessed to great weariness:

> I wanted to write about a guy who pushes his brain to its limit, is aware he has reached his limit, but voluntarily decides to go on and pay the consequences. I realized that this is simply a restatement of the whole prophecy thing. It could be the same with money, acquisition of property. It's really the striving—the person becomes aware that whatever he is striving for becomes the cost.

The cost is riding higher and closing the gap all the time. Eventually the cost line goes higher. This is something I didn't realize about myself. Although I think my writing is getting better all the time my physical stamina is nothing like it used to be. [. . .] I can still write well but the costs—I can see the graph in my mind where the cost line is going to meet and then pass the use line. It's inevitable.

On the night of February 17, Phil called up therapist Barry Spatz. He was worried because during his interview with Rickman that evening he had frequently contradicted himself on and off tape, and not only with respect to Creme. He also was experiencing failing eyesight. Was this a psychological symptom—the avoidance of some truth he didn't want to see? Spatz advised Phil that these sounded like serious physical symptoms and that he should go to a hospital immediately. Phil promised to do so, but he didn't.

The next day a neighbor saw Phil pick up his newspaper. He had an appointment scheduled with Spatz, and he missed it. Mary tried to reach him by phone and couldn't. It was his neighbors Juan and Su Perez who found Phil unconscious on the floor of his apartment and called for the ambulance. In the hospital Phil was diagnosed as having had a stroke, but one from which he could, over time, recover. He could not speak, but he could smile and his eyes found the faces of the friends and loved ones who came to visit. But further strokes followed, accompanied by heart failure.

Phil died in the hospital on March 2, 1982. Age fifty-three.

The gravesite, chosen by Phil's father, Edgar, is in Fort Morgan, Colorado, a town Phil passed through as a baby boy moving with his family to California.

Buried beside him is sister Jane.

CHRONOLOGICAL SURVEY AND GUIDE

It is one of the cardinal errors of literary criticism to believe that the author's own views can be inferred from his writing; Freud, for instance, makes this really ugly error again and again. A successful writer can adopt any viewpoint which his characters must needs possess in order to function; this is the measure of his craft, the ability to free from his work his own prejudices.

PHIL in *Double:Bill*, SF Writers' Symposium (1969)

People have told me that everything about me, every facet of my life, psyche, experiences, dreams and fears, are laid out explicitly in my writing, that from the corpus of my work I can be absolutely and precisely inferred. This is true.

PHIL, "Introduction" to *The Golden Man* (1980)

PHIL Dick was far too prolific to allow for discussion of all of his works in the course of a biographical narrative.

This Chronological Survey offers a guide to the Phildickian world as a whole for those interested in exploring it further. The books are discussed in the order they were written. To ensure pointless arguments, I've rated each of the works that survive intact on a scale of 1 to 10. That scale is internally based: 10 equals the best work Phil produced, which is, in my view, very good indeed. May readers confronted by over fifty titles to choose from derive benefit thereby. Where the works have been previously discussed in the main narrative, I've provided chapter references.

Underwood/Miller provided a great service by publishing, in 1986, an elegant five-volume *Collected Stories* (which includes previously unpublished tales). Nonetheless, I've approached the stories in this survey by way of the separate collections—*A Handful of Darkness* (1955), *The Variable Man* (1957), *The Preserving Machine* (1969), *The Book of Philip K. Dick* (1972), *The Best of Philip K. Dick* (1977), *The Golden Man* (1980), and *I Hope I Shall Arrive Soon* (1985)—because they contain the best of the stories. (Phil helped with the selection process for *Best of* and *Golden Man.*)

In *Only Apparently Real*, Paul Williams chronologically orders Phil's novels based upon the dates manuscripts were received by the Scott Meredith Literary Agency (SMLA). I vary from Williams in estimating (on the basis of textual clues) the writing of *Gather Yourselves Together* as 1949–50 and *Mary and the Giant* as 1953–54. Both the estimated year(s) of writing (w.) and the year of publication (p.) are indicated where they differ.

◆

1. *Return to Lilliput* (w. 1941–42). See Chapter 2. Williams reasonably speculates that "There are probably other early novels of which neither manuscript nor name survive."

2. *The Earthshaker* (w. 1948–50). See Chapter 4. It's possible, as Williams notes, that this is the "long ago straight novel" that Phil mentioned as a precursor of *Dr. Bloodmoney*. Another possible candidate is *Pilgrim on the Hill*, a lost 1956 mainstream novel that survives only in the form of an agent's synopsis on an SMLA index card. (Phil might have enjoyed this strange state of affairs.) See *Pilgrim*, below, for the synopsis.

3. *Gather Yourselves Together* (w. 1949–50). Three isolated Americans in a newly Communist mainland China find that their personal lives are devoid of genuine values. See Chapter 3 for further plot details. This is likely the first novel Phil completed. At 481 pages, it cries out for cutting. Young, innocent Carl keeps a notebook that prefigures the *Exegesis*. There's a dead-cat-as-indictment-of-Being story much like the one in *Valis*. And the first "dark-haired girl" in any of Phil's novels appears in a flashback reverie by Carl. One of Verne's past lovers, a woman named Teddy, was surely inspired by young Phil's imaginary sister Teddy (see Chapter 1). At the end of *Gather* America/Roman Empire and China/Early Christians parallels are tentatively drawn. But this novel isn't really about politics, despite the superficial plot framework. It's about sex, betrayal, and the slow, hard dying of love's ideals. Rating: Phil paying apprenticeship dues.

4. *Voices from the Street* (w. 1952–53). A young man, struggling with an unsatisfying job and a dreary marriage, falls into total despair when the supposed ideals of both politics and religion fail him. This unpublished mainstream novel meanders in its surviving 547-page draft form, but it features a strong set of characters. Jim Fergesson, the Hollis-inspired owner of Modern TV Sales and Service, has a paternal, quarrelsome relationship with salesman Stuart Hadley, a would-be dandy in his mid-twenties who is, for all his pretensions, a lost and frightened soul whom Fergesson nicknames "Stumblebum." Hadley's wife, Ellen, with whom he has a son, bores him; once he has even struck her. Hadley adores his beautiful older sister Sally, who would protect him from the

world if she could (twin sister Jane figures in this portrait). His friends the Golds, a Jewish socialist couple, disgust him (despite himself) with their victimlike ways. Hadley is drawn to strong, extreme types like Marsha Frazier, the tall, gaunt editor of the fascist literary quarterly *Succubus*, and Theodore Beckheim, the charismatic black preacher who heads the Society of the Watchmen of Jesus. Hadley has a bitter affair with Marsha, who resembles mother Dorothy in physique and forceful temperament. Stuart Hadley is not Phil's self-portrait, but there are similarities: Both attended special schools in Washington, D.C., for example. Fergesson fires Hadley when he wanders off on an identity quest once too often. This spurs a drunken spree (likely influenced by the "Nighttown" sequence in *Ulysses*) and then disaster. Fergesson appeared briefly in *Gather* and returns along with Stuart Hadley (as a black man) in *Dr. Bloodmoney* (p. 1964). Hadley also shows up in *The Crack in Space* (p. 1966), where he and boss Darius Pethel parallel Hadley-Fergesson here. Rating: 2.

5. *The Cosmic Puppets*, originally titled A *Glass of Darkness* (w. 1953, p. 1956 in *Satellite*, p. 1957 in slightly expanded form as half of an Ace Double). A small Virginia town becomes the unexpected site of the battle for ultimate control of the universe. This is Phil's only pure fantasy novel. The original title was inspired by Paul's troubled observations in 1 Corinthians; twenty years later, in A *Scanner Darkly*, the metaphor returns in more striking form. Ted Barton's home town of Millgate is split asunder in the ongoing struggle between Good and Evil, as personified by the warring deities of Zoroastrian dualism: Ormazd and Ahriman. The book is blandly written and woodenly plotted, but it foreshadows ideas Phil would put to better use in later works. Barton must remind Ormazd (who dwells in Millgate in human form) of his divinity. The god who forgets his nature returns again as young Emmanuel in *The Divine Invasion* (p. 1981). And Mary, the wise little girl who assists Barton and is in reality Armaiti, the only daughter of Ormazd, is a precursor of Sophia in *Valis* (p. 1981) and Zina in *The Divine Invasion*—both youthful female incarnations of the divine spirit. In letters written in July 1974, Phil affirmed his then conviction that the events of 2-3-74 were Zoroastrian in spirit. Rating: 3.

6. A *Handful of Darkness* (w. 1952–54, p. 1955). Phil's first hardcover, a selection of early stories published by Rich & Cowan in London. At the time Phil considered his fantasy stories to be his best, but R & C held that fantasies were for children. Only two made it: "The Cookie Lady" (w. 1952, p. 1953), a variation on the Hansel and Gretel theme, and the haunting "Upon the Dull Earth" (w. 1953, p. 1954), Phil's take on the Orpheus legend, with a lover seeking to rescue his Eurydice from life-thirsting angels. For "Colony" (w. 1952, p. 1953) and "Impostor" (1953), the two best tales in the book, see Chapter 4. Rating: 4.

7. *Solar Lottery*, originally titled *Quizmaster Take All* (w. 1953–54,

p. 1955). In the twenty-third century, anyone may become absolute leader of the world if the magnetic lottery bottle "twitches" his or her "power-card." But this random system, which is supposed to preclude undue concentration of power, fails miserably, and it's up to the disenfranchised working class to take desperate measures to regain their rights. This was Phil's first SF novel, half of an Ace Double. The 1955 British hard-cover, titled *World of Chance*, differs slightly in form due to editorial changes. *Solar Lottery* owes a great deal to the tilt-a-whirl societal-upheaval plots of A. E. van Vogt and just a tad to fifties game-theory strategies. Until *Do Androids Dream of Electric Sheep?*, retitled *Blade Runner*, was reissued as a tie-in to the movie, *Solar Lottery*—at over 300,000—was Phil's biggest seller. Ace editor Wollheim explains that the limited number of fifties SF titles had something to do with that. The plot: Ted Benteley, like Ted Barton in *The Cosmic Puppets*, is an idealistic young man, with a straight-ahead quality that disappears in the sixties novels. His world is ruled by the despotic Quizmaster Verrick, who presides over a corrupt society (deprived of purpose by so much random bottle twitching) of exalted white-collar Classifieds and disdained blue-collar Unclassifieds. Leon Cartwright, the Phildickian repairman hero, replaces Verrick by rigging the bottle game, but his nerves can't take being stalked by the "Pellig-thing"—an android assassin powered in random sequence by a dozen different human minds in order to madden Cartwright's protective telepathic Corps. Meanwhile, the Prestonite cult (to which Cartwright belongs) tries to locate a "mythical" tenth planet discovered by its founder, cranky old astronomer John Preston. Flame Disc is the planet's name, and Preston's *Flame Disc* is the first of many book-within-a-book alternative realities in Phil's novels. Rating: 5.

8. *The World Jones Made*, originally titled *Womb for Another* (w. 1954, p. 1956). A fanatic gains power through his ability to see ahead one year into the future, but then learns that limited foresight may be worse than none at all. In *Solar Lottery* rule by random forces was the falsehood by which society deemed itself protected from tyranny. In *Jones* the twenty-first-century post–nuclear holocaust falsehood is "Relativism," which deadens the human spirit by denying all ideals that cannot be objectively proven. (There is a similar world in "Stability," a story Phil wrote in high school. See Chapter 3.) Floyd Jones, a disgruntled carny fortune-teller (born in Greeley, Colorado—mother Dorothy's home town), can see exactly one year into the future. He becomes a Hitler-like demagogue by whipping up the ideal-starved populace against the threat of the "drifters"—enormous single-cell protoplasms that may be landing on Earth soon. Jones proves a tragic leader: His limited precognition ultimately renders him helpless because he cannot bring himself to fight against what he knows will happen. *Jones* is Phil's first SF work to include a drug subculture; here, a twenty-first-century North Beach

nightclub serves heroin and marijuana and features dancing hermaphrodite mutants who transform their sexes as they copulate onstage. Rating: 4.

9. *The Book of Philip K. Dick* (w. 1952–55, p. 1973). In an interview with D. Scott Apel and Kevin Briggs (published in Apel's *Philip K. Dick: The Dream Connection* [1987]), Phil recalled that Don Wollheim was "grumpy" about the stories in this DAW selection, complaining that the cream had gone to Ballantine for their *Best of* volume (contracted for in the early seventies and published in 1977). Well, Wollheim was right. "Shell Game" (w. 1953, p. 1954) is the best of the bunch, prefiguring a burning issue in *Clans of the Alphane Moon* (1964): How do you defend against an alien invasion when everyone on the planet is clinically insane? In "Shell Game" a group of paranoids proves that you can never *disprove* that everyone's out to get you; only human trust will do, and who's stupid enough to rely on that? Rating: 3.

10. *The Variable Man and Other Stories* (w. 1952–55, p. 1957). The best story in this early Ace collection is "Second Variety" (w. 1952, p. 1953), set during a future U.S.–Soviet war (which resembles the World War I trench warfare described to young Phil by Edgar). But the human-looking killer "claws" produced by U.S. autonomic underground factories threaten the survival of Russians and Americans alike, as the factories have begun to create new claw varieties on their own—in forms most likely to induce human empathy: a wounded soldier, a little boy with a teddy bear, a sympathetic ally, and an attractive woman (Tasso, an early malevolent "dark-haired girl"). "Second Variety" has inspired some Hollywood feelers, and Dan O'Bannon has completed a screenplay which was to be produced by Capitol Pictures before it folded. In "Autofac" (w. 1954, p. 1955) (which uses the name Phil devised for the autonomic factories of "Second Variety"), the autofacs won't stop producing (and consuming) all raw materials. Thomas Disch termed "Autofac" one of the earliest SF ecology warnings. Rating: 5.

11. *Mary and the Giant* (w. 1953–55, p. 1987). A young woman comes to grips with her fears, ideals, and emergent sexuality in a small Northern California town of the fifties. See Chapter 4. *Mary* is a flawed but fascinating work that elicited interest from mainstream publishers back in 1955–56. Mary Anne Reynolds is Phil's most sympathetic female character prior to Angel Archer in his last novel, *The Transmigration of Timothy Archer.* Mary is twenty, thin, with brown hair and "straw-colored" eyes. Her father abused her and now, coming of age, Mary wants much and believes little. She's frigid, but takes several lovers in hopes of finding a haven. Carleton Tweany, a black singer, initiates her into the mean old night world of the blues. Joe Schilling, the Hollis-inspired record store owner who hires Mary and falls in love with her, is the "Giant" of the title—too old, however, and lacking in the courage Mary requires. To Gregg Rickman (in *Philip K. Dick: In His*

Own Words [1984]) Phil described the novel as a retelling of Mozart's *Don Giovanni,* with Schilling seduced and destroyed by a young woman. But Schilling is more seducer than seduced, and losing Mary spurs him to greater self-awareness. The last chapter—a flash-forward blissful marriage to young bop pianist Paul Nitz—is utterly unconvincing. Sure enough, in response to his publisher's requests, in 1955 Phil changed a previous bitter ending (now lost) as well as Nitz's color—from black to white. This novel wastes much of its force on lame secondary characters, but Tweany, Schilling, and Mary are a powerful triumvirate. Schilling and a wayward Mary Anne (last name now McClain) appear in modified form in *The Game-Players of Titan* (p. 1963). Mary Anne Dominic in *Flow My Tears, The Policeman Said* (p. 1974) has a purity of heart prefiguring Angel Archer. Rating: 5.

12. *Eye in the Sky,* originally titled *With Opened Mind* (w. 1955, p. 1957). See Chapter 4. Rating: 7.

13. *The Man Who Japed* (w. 1955, p. 1956). A futuristic propaganda wizard grows tired of propping up his dreary government and decides to bring it to its knees through satire. *Japed* is the only SF novel of the fifties that was published with the title Phil gave it. Unfortunately, it is also the worst novel of the bunch. In the post–nuclear holocaust twenty-second century, society is ruled by Morec (Moral Reclamation): conventional morality carried to brittle, prudish extremes and enforced by citizens spying on each other. The only alternative to the dreary Morec regime is the escapist Other World planet run by manipulative psychiatrists. Allen Purcell, who becomes head of Telemedia, the propaganda arm of Morec, travels to Other World's Mental Health Resort and is diagnosed as having a rare psionic talent: a sense of humor. Purcell, who takes on the pseudonym "Coates" while in therapy, is surprise-gassed by his shrink and enters a world in which Coates is real. A more harrowing split-identity crisis befalls Robert Arctor in *A Scanner Darkly* (p. 1977). Purcell's big TV "jape" is a rip-off of Jonathan Swift's "Modest Proposal"—but, after all, Phil's lost first novel was called *Return to Lilliput*. Rating: 2.

14. *A Time for George Stavros* (w. circa 1955). This lost mainstream novel was recast, in part, into *Humpty Dumpty in Oakland* (w. 1960, p. 1987). A plot summary of *Stavros* survives in this cheery 10/24/56 index card synopsis by "jb" of SMLA after Phil had submitted a rewrite: "Didn't like this before, & still don't. Long, rambling, glum novel about 65 yr old Greek immigrant who has a weakling son, a second son about whom he's indifferent, a wife who doesn't love him (she's being unfaithful to him). Nothing much happens. Guy, selling garage & retiring, tries to buy another garage in new development, has a couple of falls, dies at end. Point is murky but seems to be that world is disintegrating, Stavros supposed to be symbol of vigorous individuality now a lost commodity." In a February 1960 letter, Phil commented on title character Stavros: "Contact with vile persons does not blight or contaminate or doom the

really superior; a man can go on and be successful, if he just keeps struggling. There is no trick that the wicked can play on the good that will ultimately be successful; the good are protected by God, or at least by their virtue."

15. *Pilgrim on the Hill* (w. 1956). Lost. (See *The Earthshaker*, above.) Here's another index-card synopsis (11/8/56) by "jb" of SMLA, who's having a hard day: "Another rambling, uneven totally murky novel. Man w/psychosis brought on by war thinks he's murdered his wife, flees. Meets 3 eccentrics: an impotent man who refuses to have sex w/his wife, the wife—a beautiful woman who's going to a quack dr. for treatment, an animalistic worker w/ambition but no talent. Man has affair w/wife, is kicked out by husband, tries to help slob. Finally collapses, is sent to hospital, recovers, returns home. BUT WHAT DOES IT ALL MEAN? Try Miss Pat Schartle at Appleton." Hello, Pat? Have I got a book for you!

16. *The Broken Bubble of Thisbe Holt* (w. 1956, p. 1988 as *The Broken Bubble*). The lives of an older and younger couple intertwine, and all four learn valuable lessons as to their true ideals and weaknesses. Jim Briskin is a character name in three other SF stories and two other SF novels (most notably *The Crack in Space*). All of the Briskin guys are empathic, *human*. In this mainstream work he's a classical music DJ divorced from ex-wife Pat because he's sterile, though they're still in love. They meet a teenaged married couple, Art and Rachael. Pat has a passionate affair with Art and loves him as she would a newborn baby, even though he belts her in the eye. Jim and Rachael also become involved, and she offers to raise her baby with Jim in Mexico. At novel's end, as in Shakespearean comedy, the wayward players are reunited with their original partners. The incredibly weird cast of secondary characters includes Ferde Heinke, a fledgling SF author (a Heinke SF story, "The Peeping Man"—a parody of the psionic premises favored by *Astounding* editor John Campbell—is included in *Bubble*), and Thisbe Holt herself, a large-breasted woman whose unfortunate livelihood is to entertain scuzzy optometrist conventioneers by stepping naked into a large plastic bubble (with breathing holes) that they can kick and roll about at will. In a February 1960 letter Phil observed of this novel: "It is full of fear, apprehension, and hate. I identify with the most helpless, the most defenseless and weak persons in society—the kids." Rating: 2.

17. *Puttering About in a Small Land* (w. 1957, p. 1985). See Chapter 5. Rating: 5.

18. *Nicholas and the Higs* (w. 1957, rew. 1958). Lost. In a February 1960 letter Phil gave this overview: "This is an odd one, half 'straight,' half science fiction. An inferior man can destroy a superior one; a Robert Hig can move in and oust Nicholas because he, Hig, has no morals [. . .] Only by relying on base techniques can Nicholas survive; [. . .] Awareness of this is enough to drive Nicholas out; he must give up because to

win is to lose; he is involved in a terrible paradox as soon as Hig puts in his appearance. In other words, you can't really beat the Adolf Hitlers; you can only limit their success." The SMLA synopsis (1/3/58) by "hm" provides plot details: "Very long, complex story, usual Dick genius for setting. Future society wherein trading stamps have replaced currency and people live hundreds of miles from work (drive at 190 mph), have set up living tracts. Cars often break down, so they have tract mechanic on full-time basis. Mechanic old, has bad liver, seems to be dying. People of tract use general fund to buy pseudo-organ but man is dead for a few days and 'comes back' a bit touched. Sub plot concerns man from whom tract got organ (which is illegal), and how his presence causes moral break-down of people in tract." SMLA marketed *Higs* as mainstream. The old mechanic who needs an artificial organ reappears in *The Penultimate Truth* (p. 1964) (as do character names "Robert Hig" and "Nicholas"); there's a Christ-like robot in need of repair parts in Phil's 1954 SF story "The Last of the Masters."

19. *Time Out of Joint* (w. 1958, p. 1959). See Chapter 4. Rating: 7.

20. *In Milton Lumky Territory* (w. 1958, rew. 1959, p. 1985). A true *noir* novel in which three characters—an isolated bachelor and a young married couple—struggle to find their souls and fail. Bruce Stevens is a young salesman without much depth. He marries Susan Faine, an older divorcee with kids, who was his fifth-grade teacher in 1945 (the year Phil, a high-school sophomore, had a crush on English teacher Margaret Wolfson). Milton Lumky, a middle-aged salesman who clings to higher ideals, is in love with Susan but befriends the younger man anyway. They go on a road trip together, during which Lumky urges the younger man to seek God and spirituality. Bruce laughs in his face. Yet the friendship persists. We learn that Lumky is dying from Bright's disease (the kidney ailment from which Dorothy suffered). Bruce learns a moral lesson in the course of trying to make a quick profit on cheap typewriters; but this new insight cannot save his faltering marriage. In the final chapter, Bruce imagines a future in which his marriage is rekindled; in that future, Lumky's death leads him to realize that "There was not enough contact." True enough—and *Lumky* fails as a result. Rating: 3.

21. *Dr. Futurity* (w. 1953 as novelette, "Time Pawn," p. 1954 in *Thrilling Wonder Stories*; rew. 1959 for its fitting destiny as half of a 1960 Ace Double, with John Brunner's *Slavers of Space*). The medical skills of a twenty-first-century physician are needed to save the life of a twenty-fifth-century rebel leader who would topple the sterile world dystopia. Ahem. In 1959, as Phil was padding out this bland time-travel tale, his interest in SF had reached its nadir. It shows. Dr. Jim Parsons is snatched from his comfy world to 2405, where eugenics reigns (when someone dies, out comes a new zygote from the "Soul Box"—good-bye over-population) and medical treatment is illegal. Parsons is summoned

to heal the leader of a rebel group, falls in love with the goddesslike Loris (of pure Iroquois blood), and experiences the bliss of bigamy across the centuries. A potboiler that barely bubbles. Rating: 1.

22. *Confessions of a Crap Artist* (w. 1959, p. 1975). See Chapter Five. Rating: 8.

23. *Vulcan's Hammer* (w. 1953–54, p. 1956 as novelette in *Future*, rew. 1959–60 for deserved purgatory as half of a 1960 Ace Double, with John Brunner's *The Skynappers*. Both Phil and Brunner went on to better things, and Brunner promoted Phil's work within British SF circles). Humankind has placed too much trust in computers, and now the damn things are fighting with each other. See *Dr. Futurity*, above, as to Phil's lack of interest in SF at this time. In the post–nuclear holocaust future, white-collar technocrats and their power-crazed computer Vulcan 3 keep the blue-collar "Healers' Movement" in check. Turns out the Healers were founded by former big cheese Vulcan 2. Vulcan 3 bites the dust in a scene that defines *anticlimax*. Phil never set out to write a bad book, but anyone who has tried to make a living at SF has cranked out drek like this to pay the bills. Okay? Okay. Rating: 1.

24. *The Man Whose Teeth Were All Exactly Alike* (w. 1960, p. 1984). See Chapter 5 as to the Harcourt Brace contract under which *Teeth* (and *Humpty Dumpty in Oakland*, below) was produced. *Teeth* is Phil's most thoroughgoing exploration of the lusts, grudges, and terrors that preside in the hell of an unhappy marriage. A shifting third-person focus takes in the lives of two very different yet equally miserable West Marin couples: Walt and Sherry Dombrosio, who have a competitive marriage (resembling that of Phil and Anne), and Leo and Janet Runcible (inspired by a neighboring Point Reyes Station couple who are no longer alive). When sharp-tongued Sherry takes a PR job in Walt's company, the territorial violation drives Walt to rape her in order to make her pregnant and take her out of the work force. The subsequent fight over Sherry's desire for an abortion is as pitiless a marital quarrel as you will find in any novel. Leo and Janet Runcible dwell in a different purgatory: Janet is an obedient wife broken in spirit, and Leo a driven realtor with moral courage. His act of conscience, taking him to the brink of bankruptcy, is to establish a sound water system for "Carquinez" (based on Phil's work on a petition campaign to improve the Point Reyes Station water system). Contacts between the two couples are minimal, but, as is the way with neighbors who hate, they make those contacts count. Late in life, Phil agreed with editor David Hartwell, who had expressed interest in *Teeth*, that it needed a rewrite—he would get to it after finishing *The Owl in Daylight*. Rating: 6.

25. *Humpty Dumpty in Oakland* (w. 1960, p. 1987). The bitter lives of two Bay Area working-class men are depicted in unflinching detail; the worst toll of poverty, it seems, is that it corrodes the capacity to love and trust. See Chapter 5 as to the Harcourt Brace contract under which

Phil recast his lost 1955 novel, *A Time for George Stavros*, to produce this book. He told third wife Anne: "*Humpty Dumpty in Oakland* is a novel about the proletarian world from the inside. Most books about the proletarian world are written by middle-class writers." Aging Jim Fergesson, who owns a car-repair garage, fears having a heart attack (Phil had like fears at the time of writing) and decides to sell the biz. Along comes slick capitalist Chris Harman to talk the old guy into investing the proceeds in a Marin County development. Jim is a gnarly but decent working stiff (inspired by Herb Hollis). Al Miller, the moody young used-car dealer next door to the old man's garage, pops goofballs when his nerves fail him—which is often enough to confine him to an impoverished, powerless existence. Jim and Al are almost friends, but their mutual despair is too deep. Their wives, who cannot help them, are minor figures in the narrative. The plot descends into Al's murky, fearful world, while sleazy Chris turns out to be a great guy. Jim dies of that heart attack he was worrying about. A straight-up bourbon novel. Rating: 4.

26. *The Man in the High Castle* (w. 1961, p. 1962, Hugo Award 1963). See Chapter 5. Rating: 9.

27. *We Can Build You*, originally titled *The First in Your Family* (w. 1962; p. November 1969 as *A. Lincoln, Simulacrum* in *Amazing*, with the final chapter written by editor Ted White; p. 1972 by DAW minus White's final chapter. White contends that Phil approved his chapter, which Phil denied; surviving letters support White's position). Two Phildickian entrepreneurs resolve to get rich quick by building robot simulacra modeled after famous Americans, but they soon learn that their simulacra know more about reality than they do. See also Chapter 5. *Build* is an odd SF/mainstream blend set in the no-longer-future of 1982. Partners Maury Rock (based on Berkeley friend Iskandar Guy) and Louis Rosen decide Civil War nostalgia is hot and build simulacra of Edwin M. Stanton, Lincoln's secretary of war, and of Lincoln himself. *Build* was written just after the Civil War Centennial; Phil's friend Will Cook, a western writer, was a Civil War buff, and Phil had just visited Disneyland and seen its Lincoln simulation. One of *Build*'s highlights is the debate between the Lincoln sim and greedy tycoon Sam Barrows on what is human—with the human, not the machine, denying the existence of the soul. But Phil's real focus, plot smokescreens aside, is the tormented affair between Louis and Maury's young daughter, Pris Frauenzimmer. *Build* is Phil's most intense exploration of his "dark-haired girl" obsession. Pris Frauenzimmer ("womankind" and "whore" is Louis's dual translation from the German) is that obsession full-blown. But *Build* is frequently funny and wise, and the Lincoln sim ranks with Mr. Tagomi as one of Phil's finest characters. Rating: 6.

28. *Martian Time-Slip*, originally titled *Goodmember Arnie Kott of Mars* (w. 1962, p. August 1963 in shorter form as *All We Marsmen* in *Worlds of Tomorrow*, p. 1964). Life in the bleak Martian colonies bears a

striking resemblance to business as usual on modern-day Earth. See Chapters 2 and 5. In the parched Martian colonies, grasping Arnie Kott is the chief of the powerful plumbers' union (based on the fifties Berkeley Co-op Phil despised for its wrangling politics). The little guy, repairman Jack Bohlen, is a onetime schizophrenic who still lives with schizophrenia's aftereffects. An autistic kid, Manfred Steiner, slipslides helplessly forward and backward in time, into realms of entropy and death. The key source for Phil's ideas on schizophrenia—in *Time-Slip* and throughout his last two decades—was Swiss analyst Ludwig Binswanger, whose study of a schizophrenic, "The Case of Ellen West," terrified Phil when he read it in the early sixties. Phil used Binswanger's term *tomb world* (schizophrenic self-entrapment) in several sixties SF works; Jack Bohlen describes mental illness as "a moldering, dank tomb, a place where nothing came or went." In an October 1976 letter to Dorothy, Phil wrote: "In the hospital I had the occasion to reread my '64 novel MARTIAN TIME-SLIP. I found it weak dramatically (weak in plot) but extraordinary in its ideas. I stripped the universe down to its basic structure. I guess I always do that when I write: analyze the universe to see what it's made over. The floor joists (sp?) of the universe are visible in my novels." Phil made contradictory claims for most of his works, but this assessment strikes me as just. Rating: 9.

29. *Dr. Bloodmoney, or How We Got Along After the Bomb* (w. 1963, p. 1965. Phil had proposed two titles: *In Earth's Diurnal Course* and *A Terran Odyssey*). A post–nuclear holocaust idyll that is one of Phil's warmest and most accessible novels. See Chapter 1; also see *The Earthshaker*, above, as to possible mainstream antecedents. Of course, the garish title was Ace editor Wollheim's attempt to cash in on Kubrick's film *Dr. Strangelove*. Strange to say, *Dr. Bloodmoney* bears some resemblance to Hardy's Wessex novels—a rich tableau of pastoral life in West Marin County. The details, from mushroom gathering to town meetings, are direct takes from Phil's early-sixties days in Point Reyes Station. Kindly shrink Doctor Stockstill is based on Dr. X, Phil and Anne's psychiatrist. The "labyrinthitis" suffered by teetering Doctor Bluthgeld (blood money—inspired by A-bomb father Edward Teller) as he walks across U Cal Berkeley was drawn from Phil's own high school classroom horrors. Set in a 1981 post–nuclear holocaust world, *Dr. Bloodmoney* resolutely avoids realism as to the effects of the blasts and fallout. Rating: 9.

30. *The Game-Players of Titan* (w. 1963, p. 1963). After aliens take over Earth, the surviving humans are governed by a cosmic version of Monopoly that determines not only which lands they occupy but also whom they will sleep with. See also *Mary and the Giant*, above. *Game-Players* is a twisting, gripping tale that borrows certain plot elements of *Solar Lottery* (a societal Game; evasion of telepathic probes) but replaces straight-arrow *Solar* protagonist Ted Benteley with Pete Garden, a typical

leading man in Phil's sixties SF: suicidal, overly fond of pills and alcohol, compulsively drawn to destructive women. It's the twenty-second century; a war between America and China, in which Hinkel radiation (designed by Nazi Bernhardt Hinkel) was used as a weapon, has left most of the survivors sterile. And Earth has been conquered by the "vugs" from the Saturn moon Titan. To spur population growth, the vugs have designed The Game, which mates humans randomly. Only Bindmen (property owners) can play; wagering deeds on the spin of the Game wheel is what the action's all about. Phil got the deeds from Monopoly and the spinning wheel from Life. Pete Garden (Marvin Gardens would have been too obvious?) is the first to realize that among his fellow humans might be simulacra spies for the vugs. Unfortunately, this realization comes shortly after Pete has ingested "five Snoozex tablets," "a handful of methamphetamine tablets," and a few drinks. When Pete sees that his shrink (who is asking him when the world first started to seem unreal) is a vug, is it psychosis brought on by the speed-liquor mix, or is it the truth we humans are afraid to face? And don't overlook the possibility that psychosis lowers defenses and may have given Pete involuntary telepathic powers. In the big final Game, speed helps Pete pull off the ultimate bluff. Rating: 6.

31. *The Simulacra*, originally titled *The First Lady of Earth* (w. 1963, p. 1964; a portion of this novel was adapted for use in "Novelty Act," a story p. February 1964 in *Fantastic*). Of all Phil's novel plots, this may be the most complex. To say that a German drug cartel manufactures simulacra presidents who hold figurehead power while beautiful Nicole Thibodeaux, the first lady, really runs the show is only to hint at its intrigues and capers. Alas, *The Simulacra* is a fascinating work that wastes too many of its best ideas. In the twenty-first century the United States of Europe and America—essentially, Germany and America merged—is ruled by a delightful couple: Rudy Kalbfleisch (cold flesh) *der Alte* (the Old One), a simulacrum, and Nicole Thibodeaux, the glamorous, cultured First Lady (inspired by Jacqueline Kennedy) who struggles against plots to topple her benignly indifferent autocratic regime. Among the plotters are two German cartels that show up often in Phil's sixties SF: the A. G. Chemie pharmaceutical house and the Karp u. Sohnen Werke, which manufactures the finest in sims (including *der Alte*). The Earth population is divided between the elite Ges (*Geheimnis*), bearers of the truth about *der Alte*, and the Bes (*Befehaltrager*), who merely believe and carry out instructions. (Similar truth-based elite/masses distinctions occur in *The Zap Gun* and *The Penultimate Truth*, both w. 1964.) Loony Luke is making a fortune selling rocket jalopies that allow desperate families to emigrate to Mars. Al Miller runs a Loony Luke lot; his friend Ian Duncan is in love with Nicole's TV image. Meanwhile, Richard Kongrosian, the virtuoso schizoid psychokinetic piano player, can't cope with public appearances anymore. So many balls

in the air—all dropped by the novel's abysmal fade-out ending. But certain scenes, as when Kongrosian's psyche is engulfed by the outside world, rank among the best of Phil's sixties work. Rating: 7.

32. *Now Wait for Last Year* (w. 1963, rew. circa 1965, p. 1966). A tottering but lovable world leader utilizes his all-too-human wits and wiles to stave off the takeover of Earth by Nazi-like aliens. See Chapters 2 and 6. The hypochondriacal, heart-of-gold world dictator, Gino Molinari, held a special place in Phil's heart, alongside Glen Runciter in *Ubik* and Leo Bulero in *Palmer Eldritch*. According to Phil, Molinari was a composite of Christ, Abraham Lincoln, and, most prominently, Mussolini. Mussolini? Phil saw him as a precursor of existentialism: putting the deed above ex post facto justifications. To Phil, for whom theorizing was life, the contrary position was heady food for thought. But Phil had no sympathy for fascist rule; *High Castle* speaks for itself. Rating: 7.

33. *Clans of the Alphane Moon* (w. 1963–64, p. 1964). *Clans* answers the age-old question, what would happen if the inmates ran the asylum? In this case, the asylum happens to be a remote moon in the Alphane system, but that's no reason to overlook the remarkable resemblance of the goings on there to life on our officially sane Earth. See Chapter 6. Norman Spinrad observes of *Clans*: "[T]he psychotic inmates of a lunar mental hospital revolt and manage to form a functional society that runs by a clinical caste system. [. . .] Partly it is parody, but it is also a description of how divergent and even crippled individual consciousnesses can synergize into a functional whole. It could be Dick's bedrock paradigm for the human condition." The lunatic clans include the Pares (rigid paranoids: the leaders, who live in Adolfville); Manses (manics: inventors and cruel warriors, who live in Da Vinci Heights); Skitzes (schizophrenics: visionary mystics, who live in Gandhitown); Heebs (hebephrenics: manual laborers and ascetic mystics, also in Gandhitown); Polys (polymorphic schizophrenics: the most cheerful and even-tempered, because at times their fluctuations bring them close to normality); Ob Coms (obsessive-compulsives: useful functionaries); and Deps (depressives: listless souls who live in Cotton Mather Estates; no clan likes the Deps). Unfortunately, too little of *Clans* is devoted to the clans, and too much to cumbersome plotting between the Terran CIA and the alien Alphanes. Tossed about in all this is Chuck Rittersdorf, the archetypal hapless Phildickian protagonist, whose brilliant psychiatrist wife, Mary, shows contempt for his job as a hack programmer of CIA propaganda simulacra (a job with a strange resemblance to writing SF for a living). The most memorable character is Lord Running Clam, a telepathic Ganymedean slime mold (inspired by Phil's Marin County mushroom hunting) who holds, with Saint Paul, that *caritas* is the greatest virtue. *Clans* is an uneven novel, but there's nothing else like it. Rating: 7.

34. *The Crack in Space* (first half w. 1963 and p. July 1964 as "Cantata 140," in *F & SF*; second half w. 1964; entire novel p. 1966). In the future, politicians develop a truly radical means of combating overpopulation and underemployment: They freeze excess citizens and await better times. But a strange crack in space may or may not have opened the way to an alternate world that could be populated by thawing the multitudes. *Crack* is a rarity among Phil Dick novels—a truly dull book. Not that there aren't some interesting ideas: Phil's throwaways could serve as an entire plot for lesser writers. Take the entity George Walt—mutant twins with two bodies but joined by a single brain (George gets the right hemisphere, Walt the left). One of the twins (which one is uncertain) died at birth, and the other was so lonely that he constructed a synthetic replacement. As in *Dr. Bloodmoney*, the trauma of Jane's death is transposed into a remarkable mutant life form. The main plot of *Crack* concerns the perils faced by black presidential candidate (and former "newsclown") Jim Briskin. Phil's title for the first-half novelette, "Cantata 140," refers to a Bach work entitled "Wachet auf" ("Sleepers, awake"). The sleepers here are millions of people (mostly blacks) living in suspended animation because there are no jobs. A well-intentioned liberal tale. Rating: 2.

35. *The Three Stigmata of Palmer Eldritch* (w. 1964, p. 1965). See Chapter 6. Rating: 10.

36. *The Zap Gun* (w. 1964, serialized November 1965 and January 1966 as "Project Plowshare," in *Worlds of Tomorrow*, p. 1967 in book form). Government leaders of both the East and the West finally get wise to the notion that you don't need real weapons systems to keep populations subjugated under the yoke of cold war terror. Seeing is believing, so why not scrap expensive weapons research and just come up with some dazzlingly devastating videos? See Chapter 2. *The Zap Gun* was written concurrently, in March–April 1964, with *The Penultimate Truth* (see below). Both novels portray governments that deceive their people through ersatz media reality, with grave psychic costs for both the deceivers and the deceived. Both novels were written at high speed (Phil claimed that during this period he produced twelve hundred pages in three weeks—fifty-seven pages a day) with the aid of amphetamines during the final breakup of his marriage to Anne. And both novels are wayward, sometimes careening out of control. But they are utterly different in tone. *The Penultimate Truth* is somber, while *The Zap Gun*, for all its plot loopholes and clunking stylistic constructions, is hilarious and wildly brilliant. One reason for the tone shift lies in how *The Zap Gun* came to be written: An editor at Pyramid Books, a paperback house, decided to commission two novels bearing the archetypal—and marketable—SF titles *Space Opera* and *The Zap Gun*. Jack Vance took on the former; Phil, eager for a new project with which to cash in on his Hugo Award, grabbed *Zap*. The plot: Wep-fash (weapons-fashion) designer

Lars Powderdry's role in creating ersatz shows of military might to dupe the "pursap" (pure sap) populace undermines him both morally and sexually, leading him into a desperate liaison with his female counterpart from enemy Peep-East, Lilo Topchev. Both Lilo and Maren Faine, Lars's other mistress, were inspired by Anne. Ol' Orville, the missile guidance system "plowshared" (cf. Isaiah) into a talking toy, tries its best to help Lars out. The Empathic-Telepath Pseudononhomo Ludens Maze is a game so *literally* absorbing that it saves Earth from invasion. Surley G. Febbs, the paranoid pursap catapulted into dizzying power, gets my vote as the funniest character Phil created. Phil described Febbs to interviewer Charles Platt as "the black side of Jack Isidore [of *Crap Artist*]." Rating: 7.

37. *The Penultimate Truth*, originally titled *In the Mold of Yancy* (w. 1964, p. 1964.) Cynical world leaders keep their populations huddled in underground bomb shelters when in fact the war is long over; the leaders would rather continue to occupy immense baronial estates than let out the truth. See also *The Zap Gun*, above. *The Penultimate Truth* draws upon four of Phil's stories: "The Defenders" (1953), "The Mold of Yancy" (1955), "War Veteran" (1955), and "The Unreconstructed M" (1956). *Penultimate* is Phil's most pointed examination of the lies woven by government. But the seriousness of its theme is blunted by its clunking style and wayward plot. Stanton Brose, the purely evil leader of the "yance-men" (propagandizing speechwriters and filmmakers, who keep the underground populace deceived), is made up entirely of mechanized "artiforg" organs except for his brain; he's a cousin of sorts to Palmer Eldritch. Thomas Disch writes that Phil "knew himself to be a yance-man—albeit one employed in the lower levels of the power structure—as a hack writer producing sci-fi paperbacks. By way of signalling that fact and of sharing it with the unhappy few who could be counted on to read his hack novels as a phantasmal form of autobiography, Dick gave the Agency that is responsible for this global deception the then-current address of his own literary agent, Scott Meredith, at 580 Fifth Avenue." Disch notes that Phil's theme of pervasive deception parallels Orwell's *1984*. As it happens, in *The Zap Gun* (written concurrently with *Penultimate*) Lars Powderdry, under Big Brother–type surveillance, asks himself: "But who can blame them? Orwell missed that point. *They* may be right and we may be wrong." Phil always considered all the possibilities. Rating: 4.

38. *The Unteleported Man* or *Lies, Inc.* (w. 1964–65, p. 1966, 1983, 1984 in differing book forms). A fascistic megacorporation lures colonists to a mysterious far-off planet named Whale's Mouth through a one-way-only teleportation system. Protagonist Rachmael ben Applebaum decides to investigate by illicitly commandeering an interstellar spaceship. After numerous twisted drug trips, Rachmael alerts Earth to the Nazi-like terrors on Whale's Mouth. *Lies* has the most tangled publishing history of

any of Phil's novels. In December 1964 he published a novelette, *The Unteleported Man*, in *Fantastic*. Ace editor Wollheim expressed interest in an expanded version; Phil wrote thirty thousand additional words, which he submitted to SMLA in May 1965. This part two consists largely of acidlike explorations by protagonist Applebaum (inspired by Phil's own short period of LSD use). Alas, these reality bends have damn near nothing to do with the part-one colonization plot. Wollheim rejected part two, infuriating Phil, who wrote to SMLA in May 1965 that the "far-out" elements were necessary for a "true novel" as opposed to the hackneyed "space opera" form of part one. (By 1977 Phil would concede that the part-two writing was weak.) Ace published part one as *The Unteleported Man*, half of an Ace Double, in 1966. In 1983 Berkeley published parts one and two together under the same title. In 1984, after the discovery of further 1979 revisions by Phil, Gollancz published a third version as *Lies, Inc.* (with two brief gap-filling passages by John Sladek). A summary of the whole: The part-one tale of overpopulation and migration to an alternate world is transformed into a part-two horror story of invasive irreality like *Palmer Eldritch* and then back again, with some 2-3-74 reflections (by way of the 1979 revisions) for good measure. Two stock elements of the sixties SF make an appearance: nefarious time-traveling Nazis and an *I Ching*–like book-within-a-book: *The True and Complete Economic and Political History of Newcolonizedland*, by Dr. Bloode. Damn weird. Rating: 5.

39. *Counter-Clock World*, originally titled *The Dead Grow Young* and *The Dead Are Young* (w. 1965, p. 1967). Time suddenly flows backward, the dead awaken, and all adults must face death in their infancy. When a powerful black leader, the Anarch Peak, ascends from his tomb, the powers that be fear all hell will break loose. Expanded from the story "Your Appointment Will Be Yesterday" (*Amazing*, August 1966), *Counter-Clock* was Phil's first return to sustained novel writing after a long dry spell that included the badly glued together *Unteleported Man* and the uneven *Ganymede* collaboration with Ray Nelson. In the *Counter-Clock* world of 1998, time is flowing backward due to the Hobart Phase, pseudo-scientifically described (in the best SF tradition) as "one of the most vast of sidereal processes, occurring every few billion years." Lives progress from revival in the tomb to regression to the womb. "Future" ideas and inventions disappear or, rather, are "eradicated" by the Erads, who run the People's Topical Library and have as their futile aim the preservation of an eternally receding status quo. Protagonist Sebastian Hermes is the owner of the Flask of Hermes Vitarium (an allusion to alchemical psychic rebirth), one of many Vitariums in the business of digging up and then selling the reviving dead who find themselves trapped in the horror of the "Tiny Place" (the tomb; cf. schizophrenic entrapment in the "tomb world" of Swiss psychiatrist Ludwig Binswanger, discussed under *Martian Time-Slip*, above). Sebas-

tian is torn between his goodhearted but dependent wife, Lotta (drawn from fourth wife Nancy), and the unscrupulous Ann McGuire (inspired by third wife Anne). The Anarch Peak—revived by the Hobart Phase and rescued from the tomb by the Flask of Hermes—is an inspired black religious thinker who (based upon Bishop James A. Pike) had been expelled from the Episcopal Church after a heresy trial. Peak is more sympathetic than Bishop Timothy Archer, the Pike-inspired character in Phil's last novel. Phil did not, in *Counter-Clock*, meet the plot challenge of a retrogressing world; *Ubik*, written a year later, would remedy that failure with a vengeance. Rating: 5.

40. *The Preserving Machine* (w. 1953–66, p. 1969). This fine story collection, assembled and edited by the late Terry Carr, won Phil's praise when it first appeared. But it has since been superseded in quality by two later collections—*The Best of Philip K. Dick* (1977) and *The Golden Man* (1980) (see entries)—each of which includes stories that also appear in *The Preserving Machine*. But *The Preserving Machine* is the only one to feature "We Can Remember It for You Wholesale" (1966), a looping tale of memory implants and undercover spy activity on Mars that is, at the time of this writing, under film production by Carolco under the working title *Total Recall*; the film stars Arnold Schwarzenegger, is directed by Paul Verhoeven (*Robocop*), and has a projected budget of $50 million; the scheduled release date is summer 1990. Another story unique to this volume, "Retreat Syndrome" (1965), is a chilling SF invasion tale that also employs the implanted-memory theme and somehow manages to interweave Phil's marital tensions of the time into the espionage plot. Rating: 6.

41. *The Ganymede Takeover*, in collaboration with Ray Nelson; originally titled *The Stones Rejected* (w. 1964–66, p. 1967). The Ganymedeans, telepathic worms, have occupied Earth and hold their power with the help of craven human underlings. But resistance is building, and a future of freedom is possible if only black leader Percy X can overcome his intense mistrust of potential white allies. See also Chapter 7. Nelson writes that *Ganymede* represented a "preliminary sketch" for *Ring of Fire*, a proposed sequel to *High Castle*, which would portray a hybrid Amerasian culture. In *Ganymede* the worms who occupy Earth are a "comic metaphor" for the machinations of the Japanese Imperial Court, while protagonist Joan Hiashi is a composite portrait of the authors' wives Nancy Dick and Kirsten Nelson. Joan Hiashi becomes the "Nowhere Girl" as a result of the nefarious therapy of Nazi-like Terran shrink Rudolph Balkani, chief of the Bureau of Psychedelic Research. Percy X, the separatist black leader who spurs Earth's revolt against the Ganymede invaders, falls victim to his longing for power in the final showdown, in which the empathy of humanistic shrink Dr. Paul Rivers prevails. An intelligent potboiler. Rating: 3.

42. *Do Androids Dream of Electric Sheep?*, originally titled *The Elec-*

tric Toad; Do Androids Dream?; The Electric Sheep; The Killers Are Among Us! Cried Rick Deckard to the Special Man (w: 1966, p. 1968). Rick Deckard makes a living hunting runaway androids. When he starts to feel for them, he learns the true difference between the human soul and the machine. *Androids* inspired the 1982 film *Blade Runner* (see Chapter 12 for the story of Phil Meets Hollywood) and has been reprinted under that title. *Androids* is an excellent novel from the same vintage year—1966—that produced *Ubik*. Rick Deckard is a bounty hunter who earns his living, in 1992, by killing "andys" (androids) who have escaped from their labors in the Martian colonies and are trying to pass as humans on bleak post–nuclear holocaust Earth (Andys Roy and Irmgard Baty are modeled after Ray and Kirsten Nelson). Two results of the radioactive fallout have been to make virtually all species of animals extinct (owning a real live owl or sheep—as opposed to a simulacrum thereof—is the height of status) and to create a new category of humans known as "specials" (mutants, including low-IQ "chickenheads"). John Isidore, named for the wise fool in *Crap Artist*, is a lonely chickenhead whose compassion for lovely andy Pris Stratton proves sadly misplaced. Meanwhile, Rick Deckard and his wife, Iran (inspired by Nancy), are having hard times and take recourse in Penfield mood-organ settings such as 888: "The desire to watch TV, no matter what's on it." Deckard has a crisis of conscience, leading to a soulless affair with andy Rachael Rosen (in the film, Deckard and Rachael overcome their differences and fall in love). Both Deckard and Isidore fall into "tomb world" despair due to their failure to touch the heart of an andy. Both are restored by the salvific intervention of Wilbur Mercer (left out of the film), who is contacted by gripping "empathy box" handles (cf. "The Little Black Box" [1964] and the empathic Ludens Maze in *The Zap Gun)*. Mercer is exposed by TV personality–jerk Buster Friendly as being none other than two-bit actor Al Jarry (a tribute to pataphysician Alfred Jarry). It doesn't matter: Agape surmounts surface trappings. The Phildickian neologism *kipple*— accumulating junk that exemplifies "the final disorder of all forms"— debuts here (it was coined by Phil's friend Miriam Lloyd). *Androids* is one of Phil's best. Rating: 9.

43. *The Glimmung of Plowman's Planet* (w. 1966, p. 1988 in Britain by Gollancz as *Nick and the Glimming*). A boy and his family fight for freedom and dignity on a strange new colony planet. *Glimmung*, intended as SF for children, was originally rejected by twenty publishers. Back in 1962, a juvenile SF novel outline, *The Thrasher Bashers*— schoolboys ward off an alien invasion—also went unsold. *Glimmung* has its charms—primarily, the odd fauna of Plowman's Planet, to which boy hero Nick and family emigrate because an overcrowded Earth slights human dignity and makes pets illegal. Horace the cat (named for Phil's cat Horace Gold) and Nick fight for the forces of light (led by the "printers," shapeless creatures who duplicate all physical

forms) against the forces of darkness (led by Glimmung). Glimmung's festering spear wound recalls the Fisher King of the Grail legend. Rating: 2 for adults, 7 for kids.

44. *Ubik*, originally titled *Death of an Anti-Watcher* (w. 1966, p. 1969). See Chapter 7. Rating: 10.

45. *Galactic Pot-Healer* (w. 1967–68, p. 1969). The semidivine alien Glimmung has summoned a motley band of unemployed Earth artisans, including pot-healer Joe Fernwright, to the remote Plowman's Planet to raise the sunken cathedral Heldscalla from the dark sea Mare Nostrum. But the Glimmung asks for more than mere manual skills from his followers: He demands faith, and it is faith that Fernwright most desperately lacks. See Chapter 7. Phil frequently disparaged *Pot-Healer* in later years. Unfairly, I would contend. *Pot-Healer* is a gem, a finely crafted, ironic, and delightfully ludicrous parable of little craftsman Joe Fernwright's path toward, and fall from, deliverance from his isolated, meaningless life. The Glimmung (who bears little relation to the deity of the same name in *The Glimmung of Plowman's Planet*, above) may not rival in profundity and power fellow divinely charged forces in such works as *Palmer Eldritch*, *Ubik*, and *Valis*, but then again, none of them have the Oz-like bluster and fun (and Phil loved the Oz books as a child) of the semi-all-powerful Glimmung. If Chesterton had written SF, it would have read like this. Rating: 8.

46. *A Maze of Death*, originally titled *The Name of the Game Is Death* (w. 1968, p. 1970). A group of colonists encounter inexplicable doings—including brutal murders—on the supposedly uninhabited planet Delmark-O. They then learn the truth of Milton's maxim that the mind creates its own heavens and hells. See Chapter 6 as to Phil's LSD experience (described in Chapter 11 of *Maze*) and Chapter 7 for the Phil–Bishop Pike relationship. In his "Foreword" to *Maze* Phil cites the help of William Sarill in creating the "abstract, logical" religion posed in the novel; Sarill, in interview, says he only listened as Phil spun late-night theories. The plots of *Eye*, *Ubik*, and *Maze* are strikingly similar: A group of individuals find themselves in a perplexing reality state and try to use each other's individual perceptions *(idios kosmos)* to make sense of what is happening to them all *(koinos kosmos)*. Only in *Eye*, written ten years earlier, is this effort successful. In *Ubik* and *Maze*, by contrast, individual insight and faith are the only means of piercing the reality puzzle. In *Maze*, Seth Morley alone escapes the dire fate of his fellow twenty-second-century Delmark-O "colonists" (who are, in truth, the trapped crew of a damaged rocket ship, dreaming a polyencephalic dream to stay sane), through his faith in the Intercessor. There is a quaternity of gods in *Maze*—an admixture of Gnosticism, neo-Platonism, and Christianity: the Mentufacturer, who creates (God); the Intercessor, who through sacrifice lifts the Curse on creation (Christ); the Walker-on-Earth, who gives solace (Holy Spirit); and the Form Destroyer,

whose distance from the divine spurs entropy (Satan/Archon/Demiurge). The tench, an old inhabitant of Delmark-O, is Phil's "cypher" for Christ. Rating: 7.

47. *Our Friends from Frolix 8* (w. 1968–69, p. 1970). A repressive Earth police state tries to keep the people down, but some mighty powerful aliens from Frolix 8 have other ideas. Phil dismissed *Frolix* as a potboiler. In plot, it's a throwback to his fifties work, especially *Solar Lottery*. In *Frolix*, solitary genius/space traveler Thors Provoni (leader of the Undermen) tries to find help for an oppressed Earth on far-off Frolix 8—a parallel to the journey to Flame Disc by John Preston (leader of the Prestonites) in *Solar*. But Preston, a craftsman, stands for individuality and hard work, while Provoni (a freak combination of ultra-high-intelligence New Man and psionically gifted Unusual) wins the support of the wise Frolixians through empathy. Meanwhile, the New Men and the Unusuals tyrannize the genetically mediocre Old Men (us) on twenty-second-century Earth. Nick Appleton, one such Old Man, is an anxiety-ridden, pill-popping tire regroover (Jack Isidore's profession in *Crap Artist*), who loves dark-haired girl Charley. *Frolix* is a fast-paced *policier* without the reality shifts that dominate the other late-sixties novels. Willis Gram, the Unusual police chief, prefigures the sympathetic police protagonists to come: Felix Buckman in *Flow My Tears, The Policeman Said* and Robert Arctor in *A Scanner Darkly*. Rating: 4.

48. *Flow My Tears, The Policeman Said* (w. 1970, rew. 1973, p. 1974, won John W. Campbell Award). See Chapter 7. Rating: 7.

49. *The Best of Philip K. Dick* (w. 1952–73, p. 1977). This selection of nineteen stories, in which Phil played an active part, lives up to its title, including two moving tales of childhood, "Foster, You're Dead" and "The Father-thing" (see Chapter 2); tales from Phil's Berkeley salad days, like "Roog," "Beyond Lies the Wub," "Second Variety," "Colony," and "Impostor" (see Chapter 4 and *A Handful of Darkness*, above); and the best of all of Phil's stories, "The Electric Ant" (see Chapter 7). Rating: 10.

50. *The Golden Man* (w. 1952–1973, p. 1980). An admirable story collection assembled by editor Mark Hurst with Phil's input. The "Introduction" and "Story Notes" by Phil are alone worth the price of admission. The best story is "Precious Artifact" (w. 1963, p. 1964), in which the all-too-human need for hope gives the conquering Proxmen the edge they need. "The Little Black Box" (1964), originally part of *The Ganymede Takeover* but removed from the final version, introduces the empathic religion of Mercerism, which plays such a major role in *Do Androids Dream of Electric Sheep?* "The King of the Elves" (1953) (see Chapter 4) is a gem—Phil's best fantasy story. Rating: 8.

51. *A Scanner Darkly* (w. 1973, rew. 1975, p. 1977). See Chapters 8 and 9. Rating: 9.

52. *Deus Irae*, in collaboration with Roger Zelazny; originally titled

The Kneeling Legless Man (w. 1964–75, p. 1976). Can an artist ever render ultimate truth? It is painter Tibor McMasters's impossible task to try, as he sets out in pursuit of the great god Carlton Leufteufel, who in his wrath called down nuclear devastation on Earth. See Chapters 6 and 10. Phil's first collaborator on *Deus Irae* was Ted White, who lost enthusiasm but suggested, in 1967, that Zelazny take it on. The collaborative marriage was a happy one: Working primarily through the mail, with peak years of productivity in 1970 and 1975, Phil and Zelazny at last produced a moving novel on the harrowing spiritual "pilg" (pilgrimage) by armless, legless "inc" (incomplete) Tibor McMasters, the master artist of the post–nuclear holocaust twenty-first century. Zelazny, whose Hugo-winning *Lord of Light* (1967) Phil admired, was a gracious collaborator who says he treated the project as "Phil's book"; when Zelazny learned of Phil's financial straits in 1975, he voluntarily reduced his royalty share from one-half to one-third. *Deus Irae* is, at root, a Phil Dick novel, with a plot that follows (unusually closely) an outline Phil submitted to win the Doubleday contract in 1964. Two of Phil's early stories, "The Great C" (1953) and "A Planet for Transients" (1953), were drawn upon for plot parts, but a greater influence was *Dr. Bloodmoney*— the post-holocaust setting and the resemblances between Dr. Bluthgelt and Hoppy Harrington in *Dr. Bloodmoney* and Carlton Leufteufel and Tibor McMasters in *Deus Irae*. Leufteufel (sky devil), the onetime government advocate of nuclear war as rational policy, is disfigured and driven mad by the engines of destruction he has unleashed and becomes the human embodiment of the God of Wrath (Deus Irae). McMasters's pilg ends in apparent glory, with a divine vision, but he dies in bitter isolation, having made "certain diary-like entries" on the subject of whether or not his portrait of the Deus Irae is genuine. The parallel to the *Exegesis* is plain. *Deus Irae* is a fascinating blend of sixties Phil (such as Pete Sands, in Chapter 3, citing drugs as a valid means of inducing visions) and seventies Phil (the Palm Tree Garden in Chapter 18—the *natural* vision conferred at last). Rating: 7.

53. *The Dark-Haired Girl* (w. 1972, 1975, p. 1988). See Chapter 8 for discussion of *The Dark-Haired Girl*, "The Evolution of a Vital Love," and "The Android and the Human," the three major pieces included in this volume. This eclectic collection of letters, essays, a story, and a poem will fascinate those who crave a front-seat roller-coaster ride through the psyche of Phil the lover. The romantic letters included in *The Dark-Haired Girl* run the gamut from breathtaking ecstasy to vicious spleen. As Paul Williams notes in his astute "Introduction," the judgments passed by Phil on the personalities of the women he adored are not necessarily trustworthy. At his most bitter, Phil could merge— briefly—with the uncomprehending android state he normally despised. At his most adoring, he is irresistible—to the reader, at least, if not always to the women he courted. This volume is as naked a portrayal of a writer's

inner life as you will find. As noted in Chapter 8, Phil later had reservations as to the worth of the *Dark-Haired Girl* letters. "Man, Android and Machine" (1975), a twisting, sophisticated essay (originally intended to be delivered as a speech at a London SF conference that Phil never attended) that explores the concept of "orthogonal" or "layered" time, is a good introduction to this key theme of the *Exegesis*. Rating: 6.

54. *Radio Free Albemuth*, originally titled *Valisystem A* (w. 1976, p. 1985). Record producer Nicholas Brady and SF writer Phil Dick do battle against the Empire that never ended. See Chapters 2, 10, and 11. *Albemuth* was purchased in 1976 by Bantam editor Mark Hurst, a staunch ally of Phil's work. When Hurst suggested changes in the manuscript, he had no idea that Phil, never one for minor rewrite tinkering, two years later would produce an entirely new and different novel, to wit, *Valis*, his masterwork, as to which *Albemuth* stands as a preliminary study. In *Albemuth*, Phil appears as an explicitly named autobiographical character for the first time. But fellow protagonist Nicholas Brady is also Phil: the Phil of his Berkeley youth, who never became an SF writer but instead took that A & R job Phil said he was offered by a record company back then. Nicholas sees himself standing beside his bed, just as Phil did in the early fifties, and has a vivid, eight-hour vision of Mexico, just as Phil did in 1971. The events of 2-3-74 are spread through the fifties and sixties for Nicholas, who is contacted (controlled?) by Valis (God? a satellite constructed by Extra-Terrestrial Intelligence? other?) as part of the battle of light against the darkness of Ferris Fremont (Richard Nixon) and the oppressive Empire that has never ended. Brady's handling, in Chapter 15, of the Xeroxed shoe ad parallels Phil's handling, in March 1974, of the "Xerox missive"; Brady's prior agonies of conscience over how much to cooperate with the Friends of the American People (FAP) parallel Phil's own with respect to his 1974 communications to the FBI. Rating: 6.

55. *Valis* (w. 1978, p. 1981). See extensive discussion in Chapters 10 and 11. Rating: 10.

56. *I Hope I Shall Arrive Soon* (w. 1953–80, p. 1985). This posthumous collection, edited by Mark Hurst and Paul Williams, includes, most notably, an entertaining 1978 speech with the aptly Phildickian title "How to Build a Universe That Doesn't Fall Apart Two Days Later" (in which Phil confesses that he rather enjoys creating universes that *do* fall apart), as well as three first-rate stories published in 1980: "Chains of Air, Webs of Aether" (adapted into *The Divine Invasion*), "Rautavaara's Case" (in which the brain activity of a dying human astronaut is utilized by research-oriented Proxmen as a window into the next world), and "I Hope I Shall Arrive Soon" (first published as "Frozen Journey"—a spaceship computer tries without success to find happy life memories to occupy the mind of an astronaut awakened from cryogenic slumber during a ten-year space voyage). Rating: 7.

57. *The Divine Invasion,* originally titled *Valis Regained* (w. 1980, p. 1981). See Chapter 12. Rating: 7.

58. *The Transmigration of Timothy Archer,* originally titled *Bishop Timothy Archer* (w. 1981, p. 1982). See Chapter 12. Rating: 8.

59. *The Owl in Daylight.* Phil's last novel project. See Chapter 12.

SOURCES AND NOTES

I have thought it best to avoid the clutter of tiny endnote reference numbers throughout the narrative. These endnotes should allow interested readers to readily trace primary sources. Specific references (by page number) are provided for all direct quotations. Sources that provided especially useful bits of information or inspiration (but were not directly quoted in the text) are listed generally for each chapter.

Much general information in the narrative comes from unpublished PKD manuscripts, letters, and other material in both the PKD Estate Archives (in Glen Ellen, California; Paul Williams, literary executor) and the Special Collections of the University of California–Fullerton Library (Linda Herman, chief librarian), as well as the over one hundred personal interviews conducted by the author. Specific citations of these sources are provided only when they are directly quoted. In the case of all direct quotations, all *bracketed* material is my own. In the case of quotations from the *Exegesis* and other unpublished manuscripts, I have taken the occasional liberty of correcting obvious misspellings.

As there are many different editions of most of the novels of Philip K. Dick, I have, for uniformity's sake, referenced quotations from all of them by chapter rather than by page number, along with the year of first publication. For the same reason, quotations from stories are referenced simply by the title and year of first publication. As to the *Exegesis*, references are to the numbers assigned to the manila folders in which the pages are presently being stored in the PKD Estate Archives; as most of Phil's entries are undated, the years of composition provided are often my estimates based on internal textual evidence.

In the case of Phil's unpublished letters, journals, and manuscripts (copies of all such, with noted exceptions, are in the PKD Estate Archives), the reference is to the date and (for letters) the intended recipient. Quotations from all unpublished works by authors other than PKD are referenced by manuscript title and chapter. In all cases where published works by other authors are used, references are to page numbers in a specific edition.

I am grateful to all fellow authors and interviewers whose labors I have drawn upon in this work. Although I have made no specific citations thereto, I must acknowledge, as an invaluable fact-checking source, *PKD A Philip K. Dick Bibliography*, compiled by Daniel J. H. Levack (San Francisco: Underwood/Miller, 1981). Out of the welter of previous writings on PKD, four books were of special help in the overall biographical map-making process: D. Scott Apel, ed., *Philip K. Dick: The Dream Connection* (San Diego: The Permanent Press, 1987); Anne Dick, *Search For Philip K. Dick* (written 1982–85 and as yet unpublished—which is a shame); Gregg Rickman, *Philip K. Dick: In His Own Words* (Long Beach, Calif.: Fragments West/The Valentine Press, 1984); and Paul Williams, *Only Apparently Real: The World of Philip K. Dick* (New York: Arbor House, 1986).

Introduction: If Heraclitus Is Right

Books and articles: Stanislaw Lem, "Science Fiction: A Hopeless Case—With Exceptions," in Bruce Gillespie, ed., *Philip K. Dick: Electric Shepherd* (Melbourne, Australia: Nostrilla Press, 1975).

Author's interviews: With Norman Spinrad, February 1986; with Harlan Ellison, March 1986.

Quotations listed by page number:

3 First discovered SF: PKD "Self Portrait," written in 1968 (perhaps at the request of a publisher, for publicity purposes), published in Philip K. Dick Society (PKDS) Newsletter #2, December 1983.

4 Write about people I love: PKD "Introduction" to story collection *The Golden Man* (New York: Berkley, 1980), xviii.

5 Fictionalizing philosopher: *Exegesis* 075 (1981).

6 On Pierre Menard: Jorge Luis Borges, "Pierre Menard, Author of Don Quixote," *Ficciones* (New York: Grove Press, 1968), pp. 54–55.

6–7 I speak of: Typed single page dated March 21, 1975, in PKD Estate Archives.

7 Discrediting states of mind: William James, *The Varieties of Religious Experience* (New York: Collier-Macmillan, 1970), p. 29.

8–9 Charles Freck: C. 11 of *A Scanner Darkly* (1977).

9 He's crazy: Letter, PKD to Patricia Warrick, December 27, 1980.

Chapter 1: This Mortal Coil

Books and articles: Double Feature, Canada's Newsletter for Parents of Twins, Triplets and Quads, Vol. 7, No. 2 (Spring 1984); Helen J. Landy, Louis Keith, and Donald Keith, "The Vanishing Twin," in *Acta Genet Med Gemellol* 31: 179–94 (1982).

Author's interviews: With Anne Dick, February 1986; with Kleo Mini, March 1986; with Barry Spatz, March 1986; with Nancy L. Segal, Ph.D. (specialist in psychology of twins), September 1986.

Quotations:

11–12 First six weeks: Letter, Dorothy Hudner to PKD, August 2, 1975.

12 Got all the milk: C. 9 of Anne Dick, *Search for Philip K. Dick*.

13 Bessie: "Life On Hilly Farm," in J. Edgar Dick, *As I Remember Them* (unpublished family memoir).

13 Difficult time: "People, More People," in *As I Remember Them*.

14 Got away; corporal: Interview of J. Edgar Dick by Gregg Rickman, 1982 (tape transcribed by author).

14 Gas attacks: Unpublished PKD "Headnote" (probably written in 1976 for potential use in the *Best of Philip K. Dick* story collection; a much shorter note was used instead) for the 1963 story "The Days of Perky Pat." In Dick Estate Archives.

15 Special event: Elizabeth M. Bryan, "The Death of a Newborn Twin: How Can Support for Parents Be Improved," *Acta Genet Med Gemellol* 35: 115–18 (1986).

15 Germ phobias, kissing: Letter, Dorothy Hudner to PKD, August 1975.

16–17 Get very mad: Paul Williams, *Only Apparently Real* (New York: Arbor House, 1986), pp. 58–59.

17 I fear that death: "A dream, from St. Sophia," in *Exegesis* 005 (1975).

17 Jane-in-me-now: Ibid. Twinning: Dr. George Engel, "Death and Reunion: The Loss of a Twin," *Dartmouth Alumni Magazine*, June 1981.

18 I wish I could come out: C. 10, *Dr. Bloodmoney* (1965).

18 Do me: C. 12, *Dr. Bloodmoney*. She (Jane) fights: *Exegesis* 013 (1978–79).

19 The changing information: "Tractates Cryptica Scriptura," in *Valis* (1981).

Chapter 2: Coming Of Age

PKD's works: Exegesis 005 (1975).
Books and articles: Interview of Tessa Dick by J. B. Reynolds and Tim Powers, 1986 (a complete transcript of which was kindly provided by Reynolds to the author). A slightly edited version of this interview appeared in PKDS Newsletter #13, February 1987.
Author's interviews: With Lynne Cecil, February 1986; with Neil Hudner, February 1986; with Barry Spatz, March 1986; with Laura Coehlo, September 1986.

21 No physical contact: Letter, Dorothy Hudner to PKD, August 2, 1975.

21 Friendly youngster: Letter, Child Welfare Institute to Dorothy Hudner, August 12, 1931 (Dick Estate Archives).

21 Handsome little fellow: Interview of J. Edgar Dick by Gregg Rickman, 1982 (tape transcribed by author).

22 Reactions quickly displayed: Mental Test Report, June 1933 (Dick Estate Archives).

22 Promoter: Interview of J. Edgar Dick by Rickman. Jane as cowgirl: Letter, Tessa Dick to author, July 21, 1986.

22   Psalms: Interview of J. Edgar Dick by Rickman.

22–23   White-haired beggar: Letter, PKD to Tessa Dick, August 18, 1976.

23   Edgar's disciplinary approach: C. 9 of Anne Dick, *Search for Philip K. Dick*.

23   Jingle snake and trapped rabbits: C. 9 of Anne Dick, *Search*.

23   Football game: Interview of J. Edgar Dick by Rickman. Physically lazy: Interview of J. Edgar Dick by Rickman. Illness and Dorothy's care: C. 9 of Anne Dick, *Search*.

24   Ted Walton: "The Father-thing" (1954). Two fathers: "Afterthoughts of the Author," in *The Best of Philip K. Dick* (1977).

24   Clear blue sky: C. 9 of Anne Dick, *Search*. Jealousy: Author's interview with Lynne Cecil, February 1986.

25   Dorothy's fight for custody: Letter, Dorothy Hudner to PKD, August 2, 1975.

25   Meemaw: Letter, Dorothy Hudner to PKD, August 2, 1975. Meemaw's disciplinary approach; Earl: Letter, Tessa Dick to author, July 21, 1986.

25–26   Molestation as child: C. 4 of Anne Dick, *Search*.

26   Mike in shelter: "Foster, You're Dead" (1955).

26   Separation from Meemaw: Letter, Dorothy Hudner to PKD, August 2, 1975.

27   PKD's reaction to pamphlet: Cs. 3 and 9 of Anne Dick, *Search*. Country-side School: School brochure in PKD Estate Archives.

27   Washington, D.C.: PKD "Self Portrait" (w. 1968), in PKDS Newsletter #2, December 1983.

27   Grief and loneliness: C. 9 of Anne Dick, *Search*.

28   "Song of Philip": Single-page typed MS. in PKD Estate Archives. Mother Dorothy preserved this poem along with other examples of Phil's youthful writing. My editor, Michael Pietsch, has suggested that this poem is too mature to have been written by a five-year-old, and that its author may be Dorothy. That is, of course, possible, but it seems unlikely to me—the poem seems too *immature* for an adult woman, and further, if Dorothy had written and titled it, surely she would have described her son in it. I believe the MS. to be Dorothy's typed transcription of the words of a precocious child.

28   Wrong one died: Author's interview with Kleo Mini, February 1986.

29   Faith in women: Letter, PKD to J'Ann Forgue, November 23, 1970.

29   Story telling: Report card in PKD Estate Archives.

29   Beetle satori: Rickman, *Philip K. Dick: In His Own Words*, pp. 49–50.

29–30   Childhood reading: "Self Portrait" (1968).

31 Great change: Rickman interview with J. Edgar Dick.

32 Jim's behavior: Report cards in PKD Estate Archives. Bored in school: Letter, Dorothy Hudner to Tessa Dick, August 10, 1977.

32 Concord: C. 9 of Anne Dick, *Search*.

33 "Daily Dick": In PKD Estate Archives.

33 Visit to father: Letter, PKD to Dorothy Hudner, May 1940 (undated).

34 Phil and father: Author's interview with Kleo Mini, February 1986.

34 "He's Dead": Poem in PKD Estate Archives.

34 *Oz* books: PKD "Self Portrait" (1968).

35 Lure of SF: PKD, "Notes Made Late at Night by a Weary SF Writer" (w. 1968), in *Eternity Science Fiction*, July 1972.

35 Pearl Harbor: Letter, PKD to Laura Coehlo, April 2, 1979.

36 Girls: Author's interview with Leon Rimov, February 1986. Condoms and homosexuals: Author's interview with George Kohler, March 1986.

36 First girlfriend: Letter, PKD to Laura Coehlo, October 29, 1974.

37 "The Truth": In PKD Estate Archives.

38–39 *Gather Yourselves Together:* C. 15 of unpublished PKD novel in PKD Estate Archives.

39 Introvert: Author's interview with Leon Rimov.

39–40 *Return to Lilliput:* Interview of PKD by Mike Hodel for the Los Angeles–based *Hour 25* radio program, June 13, 1976. Tape transcribed by Janice Jacobson for PKD Estate Archives.

40–41 All quotations from PKD's writings (1942–44) for the "Young Authors' Club" column of the *Berkeley Gazette* come from articles pasted in a softbound composition notebook (presumably by PKD, given that they are accompanied by his youthful written comments, such as the one quoted on page 41) in the PKD Estate Archives.

Gregg Rickman, in correspondence with the author, has suggested that several other poems and prose pieces published in the same column in 1944 under the pseudonym "Teddy"—some of which deal with Christian themes in a devout, traditional manner, and one of which examines the Faust legend—may be the work of PKD. Rickman's hypothesis is that "Teddy" enabled PKD to express religious sentiments that otherwise would have been awkward for him in the irreligious Berkeley climate; Rickman sees the name "Teddy" as a clue, given that PKD's father's familiar name was "Ted" and that "Teddy" was (according to Tessa Dick) the name given by PKD to an imaginary playmate (perhaps inspired by Jane). Rickman deserves credit for his research efforts here, but I am skeptical of the hypothesis for the following reasons: (1) PKD consistently described his childhood and adolescence as lacking in Christian (or other religious) convictions—see, for example, the *Exegesis* quote serving as an epigram for my Chapter 10, where that period of his life is described as "cultural." (2) PKD tried to start a

Bible Club in junior high school—he was not afraid to show an interest in religious matters, though his friends saw him as an agnostic, not a believer. (3) Why, in the privacy of his own notebook, did he not paste in the "Teddy" contributions as well? (4) In the *Exegesis*, PKD sometimes looked back on his life in hopes of finding spiritual events precursing (and thus somehow confirming) those of 2-3-74. He recalled the old, bearded beggar, the beetle satori, and the voice that gave him answers to the physics test (see my Chapters 2 and 3 for descriptions of these events). Why would he have omitted mention of the devout "Teddy" poems? (5) Finally, the "Teddy" poems don't read like PKD to me.

41 Ojai catalogue: In PKD Estate Archives.

42 Life at Ojai: Letters, PKD to Dorothy Hudner, October 1942 and May 1943 (undated).

42–43 PKD on schools: Letter, PKD to Laura Coehlo, March 17, 1974.

43 Vertigo: C. 10 of Anne Dick, *Search*. Seventh-grade anxieties: Letter, PKD to Isa Dick, December 26, 1981.

44 Little Jackie: C. 5 of *Martian Time-Slip* (1964).

Chapter 3: Forward Into The "Real" World

PKD's works: "Stability," unpublished short story from high school days, in PKD Estate Archives. *Gather Yourselves Together*, unpublished novel written c. 1949–50, in PKD Estate Archives.

46 House and Dorothy: Gerald Ackerman, "Remembrances of Philip K. Dick," October 1983, eight-page typed memoir in PKD Estate Archives.

46 Disembarrassed state: Interview of Dick Daniels by Anne Dick, 1982 or 1983 (tape transcribed by author). On Margaret Wolfson: PKD handwritten notepad journal, 1970, in PKD Estate Archives. PKD in high school: author's interview with Margaret Wolfson, February 1986.

46–47 Super hard in high school: Letter, PKD to Laura Coehlo, October 29, 1974.

47 Polio: Author's interview with George Kohler, March 1986. Musical interests: PKD "Self Portrait" (1968). Devising tricks and *amour propre*: Interview of Dick Daniels by Anne Dick, 1982 or 1983 (tape transcribed by author). Concert hall fears: Author's interview with Dick Daniels, February 1986.

47–48 Complaints against others: Interview of Dick Daniels by Anne Dick, 1982 or 1983 (tape transcribed by author).

48 *Idios kosmos:* PKD essay, "Schizophrenia & The Book of Changes," *Niekas*, No. 11, March 1965.

48 Hand-holding: Gerald Ackerman, "Reminiscences of Philip K. Dick," October 1983.

49 Physics test voice: *Exegesis* 001 (1980).

49 Not confused: Author's interview with George Kohler, March 1986. Over-

worked intuitive processes: Author's interview with Barry Spatz, March 1986.

50   Teen experience with psychiatrist: D. Scott Apel, ed., *Philip K. Dick: The Dream Connection* (San Diego: Permanent Press, 1987), p. 63.

50   Rorschach test: Letter, PKD to J'Ann Forgue, November 23, 1970. Diagnosis of agoraphobia: Author's interview with Barry Spatz, March 1986. PKD's use of *schizophrenia* and his "hypochondriacal" tendencies: Author's interview with Anne Dick, February 1986.

51   Admired control of outside world: Author's interview with Kleo Mini, February 1986.

52   Twenty-first birthday: Letter, PKD to Herb Hollis, December 16, 1949, in PKDS Newsletter #11, May 1986.

52   War over: Letter, PKD to Laura Coehlo, February 20, 1975.

52–53   Phil not loose around Hollis: Author's interview with Dick Daniels, February 1986.

53   KSMO copy: Typed MS. page in PKD Estate Archives. Much of PKD's work "palpably autobiographical": *Exegesis* 014 (1978).

54   Fergesson opens shop: Part 1, "Morning," in *Voices from the Street*, unpublished PKD mainstream novel written c. 1952–53, MS. in PKD Estate Archives.

54   Bulero memo: Opening epigram for *The Three Stigmata of Palmer Eldritch* (1965).

54–55   Anti-hero and ultimate surrealism: Interview of PKD by Uwe Anton in Metz, France, August 1977 (transcript in PKD Estate Archives).

55   Radio speakers and traffic lights: Gregg Rickman, *Philip K. Dick: The Last Testament* (Long Beach, Calif.: Fragments West/The Valentine Press, 1985) pp. 3–4.

55   No bill for labor: Interview of PKD by Uwe Anton in Metz, France, August 1977. Moving out of house: Letter, PKD to Laura Coehlo, October 29, 1974.

55–56   Dorothy's version of move: Letter, Dorothy Hudner to Tessa Dick, August 10, 1977.

56   Oedipal conquest: C. 1 of Anne Dick, *Search*. 1981 journal entry: From typed thirteen-page MS. written on November 13, 1981, in PKD Estate Archives.

56   Duncan, opera, and marijuana: Gerald Ackerman, "Reminiscences of Philip K. Dick," October 1983.

57   Disc recordings: Ackerman quoted in Ekbert Faas, *Young Robert Duncan: Portrait of the Poet as Homosexual in Society* (Santa Barbara, Calif.: Black Sparrow Press, 1983), p. 253.

57   Advance up the ladder: PKD "Self Portrait" (1968). PKD on Berkeley and

SF fans: Interview with PKD by Richard Lupoff on KPFA, November 1977 (tape transcribed by author).

57   Concern over homosexual flirtations: Author's interview with Gerald Ackerman, September 1986.

58   Phil as erratic driver: Author's interview with Vincent Lusby, February 1986.

58–59   Getting Phil laid: Author's interview with Vincent Lusby, February 1986.

59   Edgar on Jeanette: Interview of J. Edgar Dick by Gregg Rickman, 1982 (tape transcribed by author).

59   Phil and Jeanette's apartment: Gerald Ackerman, "Reminiscences of Philip K. Dick," October 1983.

59–60   Treasure sold dearly: C. 5 of *Gather Yourselves Together*.

60   Tessa on his first marriage: Letter, Tessa Dick to author, July 21, 1986.

60   Connie Barbour: Interviews with Kleo Mini by author, February and July 1986.

61   Consciousness and freedom of expression: Letter, Phil to Mary, undated. Betty Jo, turning green, movie-type romance: Author's interview with Betty Jo Rivers, February 1986.

61   PKD didn't fit into her circles: C. 11 of Anne Dick, *Search*. Inscriptions in books: Author's interview with Betty Jo Rivers, February 1986. German myth: C. 11 of Anne Dick, *Search*. Phil's attraction: C. 11 of Anne Dick, *Search*.

62   Fantasizing someone to share the pressure: Author's interview with Betty Jo Rivers.

62   Expelled from U Cal: "Introduction" to PKD story collection *The Golden Man* (New York: Berkley, 1980), p. xvi.

63   Horrible experiences at U Cal: Author's interview with Iskandar Guy, February 1986.

63   On nervous breakdown: Paul Williams, *Only Apparently Real* (New York: Arbor House, 1986), pp. 52–54.

64   Treatment notes for *The Earthshaker*, written c. 1947: From typed MS. pages in PKD Estate Archives.

64   Carl's sexual disillusionment: C. 16 of *Gather Yourselves Together*.

Chapter 4: A Real Writer At Last

Books and articles: Michael Ashley, ed., *The History of the Science Fiction Magazine, Vol. 2: 1936–1945* (Chicago: Henry Regnery Company, 1975) and V*ol. 3: 1946–1955* (Chicago: Contemporary Books, 1976); Richard Lupoff, "Introduction" to reprint of PKD story collection A *Handful of Darkness* (Boston: Gregg Press, 1978); Jeff Wagner, "In the World He Was Writing About: The Life of Philip K. Dick," *Foundation* 34, Autumn 1985.

PKD's works and letters: Interview with PKD included in Russell Hill, *Reflections of the Future* (Ginn and Company, 1975); correspondence between PKD and Horace Gold, 1954, in PKD Estate Archives.

Author's interviews: With Richard Lupoff, February 1986; with Evelyn Glaubman, February 1986; with Harlan Ellison, March 1986; with Norman Spinrad, March 1986; with Alexandra Apostolides, August 1986; with Gladys Fabun, August 1986.

Quotations:

67–68 Restaurant date and marriage proposal: Author's interview with Kleo Mini, February 1986.

68 On Dorothy and the wedding ceremony: Ibid.

68–69 Francisco Street house: C. 2 of *Radio Free Albemuth* (1985).

69 Rejections and kitchen mice: Author's interview with Kleo Mini, February 1986.

70 On Anthony Boucher: PKD "Self Portrait" (1968).

70 One initial premise: Author's interview with Ron Goulart, May 1986.

70 Success of fantasy story: PKD "Self Portrait" (1968).

70–71 Boris barking: "Roog" (1953).

71 PKD on "Roog": PKD contribution (along with Michael Moorcock and Fritz Leiber) to "First Sale," *Unearth*, Winter 1979. Letter instead of rejection slip: "Afterthoughts by the Author" in story collection, *The Best of Philip K. Dick* (New York: Ballantine, 1977), p. 446. Mailing off stories: PKD "Self Portrait" (1968).

72 Mini pun: Author's interview with Kleo Mini, February 1986.

72 Second nervous breakdown: Paul Williams, *Only Apparently Real* (New York: Arbor House, 1986), p. 55. Sense of stuffiness: Author's interview with Kleo Mini, February 1986.

73 SF never had it so good: Michael Ashley, ed., *The History of the Science Fiction Magazine, Vol. 3: 1946–1955* (Chicago: Contemporary Books, 1976), p. 84.

74 Stories written when life simpler: "Afterthoughts by the Author," *The Best of Philip K. Dick*, p. 444.

74 Towel attack: "Colony" (1953).

74–75 On "Colony": "Afterthoughts by the Author," *The Best of Philip K. Dick*, p. 447.

75 Refusal to sell to Gold: PKD "Memoir," in Frederik Pohl, Martin H. Greenberg, and Joseph D. Olander, eds., *Galaxy: Thirty Years of Innovative Science Fiction* (New York: Playboy Press, 1980), p. 239.

75 Shadrach carried: "The King of the Elves" (1953). SF and fantasy: PKD, "My Definition of SF," *Just SF* 1 (1981): 1.

75–76 Inner-projection stories: Interview of PKD by Richard Lupoff on KPFA, November 1977 (tape transcribed by author).

76 Private love: Letter, PKD to Mr. Haas, September 16, 1954.

76 Olham robot: "Impostor" (1953). On "Human Is": "Afterthoughts of the Author," *The Best of Philip K. Dick* (New York: Ballantine, 1977), p. 449.

76 Archetypal Campbell story: John W. Campbell quoted in Frederik Pohl, *The Way the Future Was: A Memoir* (New York: Ballantine, 1978), pp. 87–88.

76 Campbell on Phil's fiction and psionics: PKD "Memoir," in Pohl, Greenberg, and Olander, eds., *Galaxy*, pp. 238–39.

77 Publishers unable to find distributors: Frederik Pohl, *The Way the Future Was*, pp. 233–34. Movies difficult: Author's interview with Kleo Mini, February 1986.

78 Doesn't dress well: Letter, PKD to Laura Coehlo, May 27, 1978.

78 Lucky Dog Pet Store: PKD "Introduction" to *The Golden Man* (New York: Berkley, 1980), pp. xv–xvi.

78 Kleo on Phil's sense of humiliation: Author's interview with Kleo Mini, February 1986.

79 James Joyce but not blind: Ibid. Reading Maimonides: Gregg Rickman, *Philip K. Dick: The Last Testament* (Long Beach, Calif.: Fragments West/ The Valentine Press, 1985), p. 2. Kleo on Maimonides story, mystical unity, and animism: Author's interview with Kleo Mini, February 1986.

79–80 Figure standing by bed: Interview of PKD by Richard Lupoff on KPFA, November 1977 (tape transcribed by author). Kleo's memory of it: Author's interview with Kleo Mini, February 1986.

80 Marion's illness: Author's interview with Lynne Cecil, February 1986.

80–81 Dorothy on Marion's death: From two typed journal pages by Dorothy dated November 18, 1952 (copies of these pages provided to author by Lynne Cecil).

81 PKD and Joseph Hudner: Author's interview with Iskandar Guy, February 1986.

81 Visit to Edgar: Author's interview with Kleo Mini, February 1986. Droves of small boys: PKD pulp magazine author's note, September–October 1953, quoted in "Introduction" by Richard Lupoff to reprint of PKD story collection *A Handful of Darkness* (Boston: Gregg Press, 1978), p. viii.

82 Fans as trolls: PKD note quoted in Lupoff, "Introduction," *A Handful of Darkness*, p. x. SF writer in Cassandra role: PKD, "Pessimism in Science Fiction," *Oblique*, December 1955.

82 Van Vogt's advice: "Waterspider" (1964). Van Vogt's suit: Author's interview with Kleo Mini, February 1986. SF writer's lot: Author's interview with Poul Anderson, February 1986.

83 PKD analyzed everything: Author's interview with Virginia Lusby, February 1986. Bad party experience: Author's interview with Vincent Lusby,

February 1986. Herb Gold autograph: PKD "Introduction" to *The Golden Man* (New York: Berkley, 1980), p. xxv.

83–84 FBI agents and seeing the U.S.A.: Author's interview with Kleo Mini, February 1986.

84 Phil on his parents: Interview of Iskandar Guy by Anne Dick, 1982 (tape transcribed by author).

85 Phil's affair: Author's interview with Kleo Mini, February 1986. Proud of his ex-mistress: Author's interview with Anne Dick, February 1986.

85–86 Switch from stories to novels: PKD "Self Portrait" (1968).

86 Mainstream dream: Author's interview with Kleo Mini, February 1986.

86–87 Wrote SF because it was happening: Author's interview with Iskandar Guy, February 1986.

87 Perfect works: Author's interview with Vincent Lusby, February 1986. Falling back on SF tricks: Interview of John Gildersleeve by Gregg Rickman, c. 1985 (tape transcribed by author). Making Gildersleeve a character, PKD's typing speed: Interview of John Gildersleeve by Anne Dick, 1982 (tape transcribed by author).

87 Strange behavior: Author's interview with Chuck Bennett, February 1986.

88 On *Solar Lottery*: Author's interview with Kleo Mini, February 1986. SF stories and novels: Unpublished typed MS. "Foreword" to PKD story collection *The Preserving Machine* (1969), in PKD Estate Archives.

89–90 Wollheim on SF, PKD, their 1969 encounter, and life at Ace: Author's interview with Donald Wollheim, June 1986.

91 Marxist sociological view: *Exegesis* 011 (1979–80).

91 Blurbs: From back cover and front inside page of first edition of *Eye in the Sky* (1957). The eye: C. 7 of *Eye in the Sky*.

92 Wyn's requested changes: Author's interviews with Poul Anderson, February 1986, and Donald Wollheim, June 1986. Hallucinated worlds: *Exegesis* 019 (1978). *Captain Video* and Kleo's response: Author's interview with Kleo Mini, February 1986.

93 Wollheim on PKD mainstream efforts: Author's interview with Donald Wollheim, June 1986.

93–94 Love scene: C. 17 of *Puttering in a Small Land* (w. 1957, p. 1985).

95 Soft-drink stand: C. 3 of *Time Out of Joint* (1959).

95–96 Same novel written over and over: *Exegesis* 015 (1978).

96 Einstein's theory: Letter, PKD to Alexander Topchiev, February 4, 1958.

Chapter 5: Phil Falls In Love

Books and articles: Above and beyond direct citations, I am indebted to Anne Dick's unpublished biography, *Search for Philip K. Dick*, which contains much fascinating material on her years with PKD. See also Ludwig Binswanger, "The Case of Ellen West," in Rollo May et al., eds., *Existence* (New York: Basic Books, 1958), and the essay "Extravagance," in *Being-in-the-World: Selected Papers of Ludwig Binswanger* (New York: Harper and Row, 1968).

PKD's works: *Exegesis* 013 (1978).

Author's interviews: With Hatte Blejer, January 1986; with Miriam Lloyd, February 1986; with Lynne Cecil, February 1986; with Vincent and Virginia Lusby, February 1986; with Iskandar Guy, February 1986.

Quotations:

98   Minor SF writer: C. 1 of Anne Dick, *Search for Philip K. Dick.*

98–99   Conversationalist: Ibid.

99   Say things straight-faced: Author's interview with Kleo Mini, August 1988.

99   Declaration of love: C. 1 of Anne Dick, *Search.* Charisma: Author's interview with Anne Dick, February 1986.

100   Namby-pamby: Author's interview with Kleo Mini, February 1986. Nat Anteil in court: PKD mainstream novel *Confessions of a Crap Artist* (w. 1959, p. 1975). One thing too much: Author's interview with Kleo Mini, February 1986.

101–101   PKD after phone call: Letter, PKD to Anne Dick, December 27, 1958.

101   Intolerance: Ibid. On San Francisco Renaissance: Letter, PKD to Walter Lanferman, December 30, 1958.

101–102   Don't read crap: Author's interview with Jayne Brown, February 1986.

102   Adults don't feel well: Ibid. Perfectly good wife: C.1 of Anne Dick, *Search.* You don't throw away good friends: Author's interview with Kleo Mini, February 1986. I am punished: *Exegesis* 013 (1978).

103   Ace, the lowest of the low, preferred fantasy: C. 1 of Anne Dick, *Search.* Twenty-year effort: Ibid.

103   Lunchtime talks: Ibid.

104   PKD's life: Letter, PKD to Eleanor Dimoff, February 1, 1960, published as PKDS pamphlet #1 (1983).

104   Scrubbing the lights: Author's interview with Jayne Brown, February 1986. Jane made up for: C. 2 of Anne Dick, *Search.* Honeymoon: Author's interview with Anne Dick, April 1984.

104   Not able to rewrite: C. 2 of Anne Dick, *Search.*

105   Borderline surrealism: C. 1 of Anne Dick, *Search.* On Jack Isidore: Letter, PKD to Paul Williams, January 19, 1975, published in Williams's "Introduction" to *Confessions of a Crap Artist* (Glen Ellen, Calif.: Entwhistle Books, 1975), p. viii.

105   Comments on *Crap Artist* (w. 1959, p. 1975): Margin notes made by PKD in September 1980 in the Entwhistle Books edition of *Crap Artist* he gave to Chris Arena, who kindly allowed the author to copy its contents, February 1986.

106   Wind up hitting her: C. 11 of *Crap Artist*.

106   Involved because husband dying: C. 11 of *Crap Artist*. Getting away from mother: Ibid. Fay's voice: C. 5 of *Crap Artist*. Fay's speech patterns: Margin notes to Arena copy of *Crap Artist*.

106   Anne on Fay: C. 2 of Anne Dick, *Search*.

106–107   On Jack Isidore: Letter, PKD to Paul Williams, January 19, 1975, supra.

107   Anne's response: C. 2 of Anne Dick, *Search*. Beware the person from Porlock: C. 2 of Anne Dick, *Search*.

107   Words come from hands: C. 2 of Anne Dick, *Search*. Intuitive method: Letter, PKD to Eleanor Dimoff, February 1, 1960, supra. Die or have baby: C. 2 of Anne Dick, *Search*.

108   Mediterranean family: C. 2 of Anne Dick, *Search*.

108   The abortion: Author's interview with Anne Dick, February 1986.

109   Fantasy life with Pris: C. 18 of PKD novel *We Can Build You* (w. 1961–62, p. 1972). Pris as life and anti-life: C. 12 of *Build*. A man's wife won't help: Letter, PKD to Eleanor Dimoff, February 1, 1960, supra.

109   Castrating females: PKD story "The Pre-Persons" (1974). Love, not anger: PKD "Afterword" to story collection *The Golden Man* (New York: Berkley, 1980), p. 337.

109   Fix the *I Ching*: Author's interview with Iskandar Guy, February 1986.

110   UFOs don't seem as crazy: Margin notes to Arena copy of *Crap Artist*, supra.

110   Streak of black in sky and Anne's response: C. 3 of Anne Dick, *Search*.

111   PKD and Dorothy: C. 1 of Anne Dick, *Search*.

111   Mother abandoning: Ibid. Voodoo stares: Author's interview with Jerry Kresy, February 1986. Silver triangle: C. 14 of PKD novel *The Man in the High Castle* (1962).

111   Anne on jewelry business: Author's interview with Anne Dick, April 1984.

111–112   Third nervous breakdown: Paul Williams, *Only Apparently Real* (New York: Arbor House, 1986), pp. 60–61.

112   Decided to give up writing: Interview of PKD by Daniel DePrez, *Science Fiction Review* (September 10, 1976), pp. 7–8.

112   Never chew cud twice: C. 2 of Anne Dick, *Search*.

113   Dedication: In the first edition of *High Castle* (1962).

114   Castle metaphors: Letter, PKD to Patricia Warrick, October 8, 1977.

114   Multiple narrative viewpoint: Letter, PKD to Patricia Warrick, July 31, 1978.

115   Tagomi going mad: C. 6 of *High Castle*.

116   Baynes on Nazis: C. 3 of *High Castle*.

116   Inner Truth hexagram: C. 15 of *High Castle*. *I Ching* as malicious spirit: Interview of PKD by Daniel DePrez, supra, p. 8.

117   *High Castle* ending: Letter, PKD to Joseph Milicia, August 7, 1978.

117   *High Castle* and *Martian Time-Slip* (1962): Paul Williams, *Only Apparently Real*, pp. 92–93.

118   Wollheim rejection: Author's interview with Donald Wollheim, June 1986.

Chapter 6: Phil's Marriage Mimics "Reality"

Books and articles: Anne Dick, *Search for Philip K. Dick.*
Author's interviews: With Hatte Blejer, January 1986; with Nancy Hackett, March 1986; with Ann Montbriand, February 1986; with Mike Hackett, February 1986.
Quotations:

120   Powerfully brilliant: Author's interview with Anne Dick, April 1984.

120   Bitchy tongue: Author's interview with Anne Dick, February 1986.

121   Killed first husband: C. 4 of Anne Dick, *Search*. Bolting from car: C. 4 of Anne Dick, *Search*.

121   Just wanted a husband: C. 4 of Anne Dick, *Search*.

122   Javelina pig hunt: Author's interview with Harlan Ellison, March 1986.

122   Outrageous stuff: Author's interview with Iskandar Guy, February 1986.

122–123   PKD exaggerated: Author's interview with Lynne Cecil, February 1986.

123   Lock on medicine chest: Author's interview with Lynne Cecil, February 1986. Kill himself with drugs: C. 4 of Anne Dick, *Search*.

123   Diagnosed as manic-depressive: C. 4 of Anne Dick, *Search*. Rooted in marriage: Author's interview with Anne Dick, February 1986.

124   Hatte's memory of drive: C. 4 of Anne Dick, *Search*.

124   Clinic records: Ibid. Effect of Stelazine: Ibid.

125   Chuck and Mary: C. 13 of PKD novel *Clans of the Alphane Moon* (1964). Korsakow's syndrome: C. 12 of PKD novel *Now Wait for Last Year* (1966).

125–126   Talking cab: C. 14 of *Now Wait* (1966).

126   Took arm forcibly: C. 4 of Anne Dick, *Search*. Attend religiously: Ibid. Social climbing: Interview of PKD by Charles Platt in Platt's *Dream Makers* (New York: Berkley, 1980), p. 152.

127   Face in the sky: Unpublished PKD "Headnote" in PKD Estate Archives (probably written in 1976 for potential use in *The Best of Philip K. Dick* story collection; a much shorter note was used instead) for 1963 story "The Days of Perky Pat." Certain chemicals: PKD essay, "Will the Atomic Bomb Ever Be Perfected, and If So, What Becomes of Robert Heinlein?", *Lighthouse* fanzine, October 1966. Psychedelic drugs: Letter, PKD to Rich Brown, August 21, 1967.

326

127 Gas mask memories: Unpublished PKD "Headnote" for "The Days of Perky Pat," supra. *Idios kosmoses* needed to stay sane: Letter, PKD to Bruce Gillespie, June 8, 1969, published in Gillespie, ed., *Philip K. Dick: Electric Shepherd* (Melbourne, Australia: Nostrilla Press, 1975), p. 32. What Anne might have said: C. 4 of Anne Dick, *Search*.

128 Mass symbolism: C. G. Jung, "Transformation Symbolism in the Mass," in Joseph Campbell, ed., *The Mysteries: Papers from the Eranos Yearbooks* (Princeton, N.J.: Princeton University Press, 1978), p. 334. Baptismal devil: C. 4 of Anne Dick, *Search*.

130 Day at the beach: C. 3 of PKD novel *The Three Stigmata of Palmer Eldritch* (1965).

131 Bulero's reassurances: C. 6 of *Palmer Eldritch*.

131–132 It's all the same: C. 11 of *Palmer Eldritch*.

132 PKD's father as Eldritch and Bulero: PKD "Headnote" to "The Days of Perky Pat," supra.

132 Chew-Z: Paul Williams, "The True Stories of Philip K. Dick," *Rolling Stone*, November 6, 1975, included in Williams's *Only Apparently Real* (New York: Arbor House, 1986).

133 Eucharist: Jung, "Transformation Symbolism," supra, p. 290. Arrogant one: *Exegesis* 014 (1978). Bulero as Son of Man: *Exegesis* 021 (1978).

134 Love-blast: Author's interview with Grania Davis, February 1986. Gun and violence: Ibid.

135 Bladder capacity, crazy and complex: Author's interview with Grania Davis, February 1986.

135 Separated from children: Letter, Grania Davis to Cymphia, July 17, 1964.

135 Beautiful letters: Author's interview with Grania Davis, February 1986. Bay Area loudspeaker: Letter, co-written by PKD and Grania to Terry and Carol Carr, October 9, 1964.

136 Advanced schizophrenic paranoid: Letter, PKD to Terry and Carol Carr, October 4, 1964.

136 Nelson on *High Castle* sequels: Ray Nelson, "A Dream of Amerasia," in D. Scott Apel, ed., *Philip K. Dick: The Dream Connection* (San Jose, Calif.: Permanent Press, 1987), p. 136.

137–138 PKD on SF novel construction: Letter, PKD to Ron Goulart, undated but written in spring-summer 1964, according to Goulart, who kindly furnished the author with a copy.

139 Goulart on PKD: Author's interview with Ron Goulart, May 1986. Glancing at him: Interview source wishes to remain anonymous.

139–140 Con flirtation: Author's interviews with Terry and Carol Carr, February 1986.

140 Changing belief systems and three-piece suit: Author's interview with Dick Ellington, February 1986.

140–141   Communion: Letter, PKD to Carol Carr, jokingly dated "Nov. 12, 1902 (the day President Gump was done in by a rotting, poisoned carrot, right between the eyes)"; real date almost certainly November 12, 1964.

141   Monogamous sex: Author's interview with Grania Davis, February 1986. Insurance policy: Letter, J. G. Newkom to author, January 20, 1987.

141   Acid trip in *A Maze of Death:* Letter, PKD to Claudia Bush, July 15, 1974.

142   Acid vision: Letter, PKD to Rich Brown, August 21, 1967.

142   On hallucinations: PKD essay, "Drugs, Hallucinations, and the Quest for Reality," *Lighthouse*, November 1964.

143   Kirsten and PKD: Author's interview with Kirsten Nelson, March 1986.

143   Poem "To Nancy": MS. in PKD Estate Archives. I love you for what you are: Letter, PKD to Nancy Hackett, December 16, 1964.

143–144   Move in for my sake: Letter, PKD to Nancy Hackett, December 19, 1964.

144   She will break me: Letter, PKD to Carol Carr, December 25, 1964.

Chapter 7: A New Start

PKD's works: Exegesis 003 (1977–78), 010 (1977–78), 018 (1978), 019 (1978), 021 (1978), 029 (1978), 032 (1977).

Author's interviews: With Anne Montbriand, February 1964; with Anne Dick, April 1984 and February 1986; with Kirsten Nelson, March 1986; with Terry and Carol Carr, February 1986.

146   More and more out of it: Author's interview with Nancy Hackett, February 1986.

147   Nancy on PKD: Ibid. Rhapsodizing: Letter, PKD to Carol Carr, December 25, 1964.

147   Latest doings: Letter, PKD to Carol Carr, February 28, 1965. Nancy's consort: C. 5 of Anne Dick, *Search.*

148   Experiences without LSD: Author's interview with Nancy Hackett, February 1986. Humorous, Snug and Fuzzy: Author's interview with Nancy Hackett, February 1986.

148   How they talked: Interview of Nancy Hackett by Jeff Wagner c. 1985 (author's transcription of tape kindly supplied by Wagner). Crisis junkie: Author's interview with Miriam Lloyd, February 1986.

149   *On the I Ching:* PKD essay, "Schizophrenia and the Book of Changes," *Niekas*, No. 11, March 1965. Party pooper and acid colors: Letter, PKD to Jack Newkom, November 17, 1965.

150   Séance notes: PKD, "Transcript of a Séance," PKDS Newsletter #12, October 1986, p. 5.

150   Instant after death: Letter, PKD to James A. Pike and Maren Hackett, February 17, 1966 (extant in two different drafts). Giving communion: *Exegesis* 020 (1978).

151   Jim tried for heresy: Letter, PKD to Claudia Bush, July 15, 1974 (letter included in *Exegesis* 004 [1974] file, indicating that PKD kept it with his *Exegesis* papers, as he did several other of his letters written in 1974–76 that dealt in some detailed way with his 2-3-74 experiences). PKD's speculations on his possible cross-bonding with Pike in 1974 are included in *Exegesis* 004, as well as other *Exegesis* sections. Nothing to say: *Exegesis* 054 (1981).

152–153   Joe Chip and the door: C. 3 of PKD novel *Ubik* (1969).

153–154   Runciter commercials: C. 10 of *Ubik*.

154   Ubik on Ubik: Epigram to C. 17 of *Ubik*. *Book of John:* Peter Fitting, "Ubik: The Deconstruction of Bourgeois SF," included in Joseph D. Olander and Martin Harry Greenberg, eds., *Writers of the 21st Century Series: Philip K. Dick* (New York: Taplinger, 1983), p. 152. Though Fitting notes the resemblance to John, he does not suggest that *Ubik* is a Christian work; rather, he attempts to draw from the narrative a Marxist view of decomposing bourgeois realities and (Fitting's language) "new collective possibilities." Be it noted that PKD, in the *Exegesis*, many times considered the true meaning of *Ubik*—he would do this with his novels, as though someone else had written them—and never approached anything like a Marxist formulation of *Ubik* or, for that matter, of any other of his novels of the sixties and after. The nature of ultimate reality, as PKD came to conceive of it, was not subject to fundamental change on the basis of economic reorderings. Particularly in the seventies, in the aftermath of the November 1971 break-in, PKD would become quite uncomfortable with Marxist interpretations of his work, though he did acknowledge, in the *Exegesis*, elements of Marxist sociological critique (drawn in part from his reading of C. Wright Mills) in certain of his fifties novels. See my Chapter 4 and notes thereto.

154   *Ubik* and *Palmer Eldritch*, salvific information: *Exegesis* 032 (1977).

154   I don't write beautifully: *Exegesis* 039 (1978).

154–155   Attracted to trash: *Exegesis* 014 (1978).

155   On *Galactic Pot-Healer: Exegesis* 054 (1981).

156   Didn't believe in marriage: Author's interview with Nancy Hackett, February 1986. Well people: Letter, PKD to Cynthia Goldstone, February 27, 1967.

156   File case: Letter, PKD to Cynthia Goldstone, February 27, 1967. Trip to hospital: Author's interview with Mike Hackett, February 1986.

157   Sensitive person, rescuer, wanted her at home: Author's interview with Nancy Hackett, February 1986. Focus on Nancy, weren't mature: Author's interview with Lynne Cecil, February 1986.

157   Relationship changed after Isa: Author's interview with Mike Hackett, February 1986.

157   Breast-feeding contest: Author's interview with Nancy Hackett, February 1986.

158 Unwelcome Wagon: Author's interview with Grania Davis, February 1986. PKD and Dorothy, medicating himself, money: Author's interview with Nancy Hackett, February 1986.

159 Depressions, writing *Androids:* Ibid. Clever dope fiends: Author's interview with Miriam Lloyd, February 1986. Terrible fear of being crazy: Author's interview with Nancy Hackett, February 1986.

159 PKD's house a known locale: Author's interview with Hatte Blejer, January 1986.

160 1967 nervous breakdown: Letter, PKD to Carol Carr, July 7, 1967 (see also letter, PKD to Rich Brown, July 18, 1967).

160 How can it go on?: Letter, PKD to Mr. Wardlaw (IRS agent), September 2, 1967. Tax protest petition: *Ramparts*, February 1968.

161 PKD reflects on petition: *Exegesis* 040 (1979).

161 Ellison's introduction: Harlan Ellison, ed., *Dangerous Visions* (New York: Berkley, 1967), pp. 213–14.

161–162 Ellison on PKD: Author's interview with Harlan Ellison, March 1986.

162 Throwing away her stash: Author's interview with Miriam Lloyd, February 1986.

162 Drug scene: Author's interview with Miriam Lloyd, February 1986.

163 Status had climbed: Letter, PKD to Lawrence Ashmead, September 7, 1968.

163 No important book since 1964: Letter, PKD to stepdaughter Tandy, May 7, 1969. Garson Poole: PKD story "The Electric Ant" (1969). Writing slump: Letter, PKD to Lynne Cecil, March 21, 1969.

163–164 Plot and writing method: Letter, PKD to Ray Browne, March 21, 1969.

164 Dual loss: Paul Williams, *Only Apparently Real* (New York: Arbor House, 1986), p. 100.

164 Nancy's fears, trying to quit speed: Author's interview with Nancy Hackett, February 1986.

165 PKD on amphetamine use: Williams, *Only Apparently Real*, pp. 132–33.

165 Mescaline: Letter, PKD to Jim, September 17, 1970.

166 Greatest weakness of SF: PKD written response to questionnaire circulated to ninety-four SF writers, all responses published in Bill Mallardi and Bill Bowers, eds., *The Double:Bill Symposium* (D:B Press, 1969), p. 103.

166 Mystical love: Letter, PKD to Anne Dick, September 18, 1970.

167 Nice guy, a little loony: Author's interview with Honor Jackson, February 1986. Driving away: Author's interview with Isa Dick, March 1986.

Chapter 8: Dark Night Of The Soul

PKD works and letters: "Cadbury, the Beaver who Lacked," 1972 story, MS. in PKD Estate Archives; letters to FBI, October 28, 1972, November 4, 1972; letters to Inspector Shine, November 4, 1972, November 9, 1972; letter to William Wolfson, October 6, 1972; letter to Bank of Marin, April 21, 1973.

Books and articles: C. 6 of Anne Dick, *Search for Philip K. Dick,* was especially valuable as to the doings of the young crowd who made PKD's Santa Venetia house their hangout.

169   Fear in Phil: Author's interview with Bernie Montbriand, February 1986. Fearful about the police: Author's interview with Mike Hackett, February 1986.

170   Up for three days: Author's interview with Bernie Montbriand, February 1986. Documented the struggle: PKD 1970–71 notepad journal in PKD Estate Archives.

170   Life in Hermit House: Letter, PKD to J'Ann Forgue, November 25, 1970.

170–171   Made you feel involved: Author's interview with Tom Schmidt, February 1986.

171   Fun and difficult: Author's interview with Mike Hackett, February 1986.

171   Troubled women: Author's interview with Tom Schmidt, February 1986.

172   Frustrating to Phil: Author's interview with J'Ann Forgue, February 1986. J'Ann stepped in: PKD 1970–71 notepad journal.

172   His mother, he requires J'Ann to live, turned bitter: PKD 1970–71 notepad journal.

172–173   Look, Dorothy: Journal entry in the form of a letter, PKD to "Cassie" (fictitious name), which PKD never (by his own statement therein) intended to send, December 15, 1970.

173   Like Jane, turned to fear: PKD 1970–71 notepad journal.

174–176   All quotations from holographic diary of Joseph Hudner as transcribed by author (Hudner's daughter, Lynne Cecil, kindly made the diary available).

176   Astute: Stanford University Hospital records as read aloud by Dr Harry Bryan in an interview with the author, February 1986. People-oriented: Author's interview with Dr. Bryan.

176   Very dramatic, paranoid: Author's interview with Lynne Cecil, February 1986.

177   Guru: Paul Williams, *Only Apparently Real* (New York: Arbor House, 1986), p. 19.

178   Didn't consider himself old: Author's interview with Loren Cavit, February 1986.

178   Fantasized: Ibid.

179   Donna: Letter, PKD to Claudia Bush, July 14, 1974.

179 In bed for eight days: PKD essay, "The Evolution of a Vital Love," w. 1972, in PKD letter/essay collection, *The Dark-Haired Girl* (Willimantic, Conn.: Mark V. Zeising, 1988), p. 172. Taco stand experience: *Exegesis* 039 (1978). FBI or CIA: C. 6 of Anne Dick, *Search for Philip K. Dick*. All right: Author's interview with William Wolfson, February 1986.

180–182 All "Sheila" quotes are from the author's interview with an anonymous source, February 1986.

180 Militant blacks: Paul Williams, *Only Apparently Real*, pp. 37, 106.

181 Journal entry: PKD spiral notebook journal, 1971–72, in PKD Estate Archives.

182 Avram Davidson: Paul Williams, *Only Apparently Real*, p. 168.

182 Locks systematically damaged: Typed journal pages, probably August–September 1971, in PKD Estate Archives. Maybe Phil did it: Author's interview with Tom Schmidt, February 1986.

182–183 Police sergeant: PKD eleven-page typed journal sequence, October 30, 1972, in PKD Estate Archives.

183 Police report: Paul Williams, *Only Apparently Real*, p. 119.

184 Secret police: Letter, PKD to editor, June 7, 1973, published in *The Alien Critic*, August 1973.

184 Everything turned out to be true: Author's interview with Norman Spinrad, March 1986.

185 Most effective forms of sabotage: C. 6 of PKD novel *A Scanner Darkly* (1977).

185 Listening to *Sticky Fingers:* Tim Powers, "Some Random Memories of Philip K. Dick," in PKDS Newsletter #2, December 1983.

185–186 Confirmed someone after him: PKD spiral notebook journal, 1971–72.

186 Entropy, isolation: PKD spiral notebook journal, 1971–72.

186 When you lose someone you love: PKD spiral notebook journal, 1971–72.

Chapter 9: Contemplating Suicide In A Foreign Land

PKD works: The PKD letter/essay collection *The Dark-Haired Girl* (Willimantic, Conn.: Mark V. Zeising, 1988); *Exegesis* 003 (1978), 042 (1979).

PKD letters: To Edward Ferman, February 15, 1973; to Merry Lou Malone, March 7, 1973; to "Donna," March 9, 1972; to Center Point, March 9, 1972; to Terry and Carol Carr, March 9, 1972; to Willis McNelly, March 9, 1972; to Anne Dick, March 12, 1972; to Goran Bengtson, May 4, 1973, and December 7, 1973; to Patrice Duvic, May 2, 1973; to Laura Coehlo, September 28, 1973; to Meredith Agency, October 26, 1973; to Nancy and Isa, December 5, 1973.

Author's interviews: With Harry and Nita Busby, March 1986; with Tim Powers, March 1986; with K. W. Jeter, May 1986; with Norman Spinrad, March 1986; with Harlan Ellison, March 1986; with Art Spiegelman, June 1986; with Doris Sauter, July 1986; with Laura Coehlo, September 1986.

Quotations:

188   Sum up thought: Letter, PKD to Bruce Gillespie, October 31, 1972.

188–189   Quotations from speech: PKD, "The Android and the Human," in Bruce Gillespie, ed., *Philip K. Dick: Electric Shepherd* (Melbourne, Australia: Nostrilla Press, 1975), pp. 53, 55–58.

189   Title-page description: PKD MS. page, quoted in Paul Williams's "Introduction" to PKD letter/essay collection *The Dark-Haired Girl*, p. ix. (This collection also contains "The Android and the Human," cited in the previous note.) Trying to find a center: *Exegesis* 048 (1979). So pretty: *The Dark-Haired Girl*, p. 32.

190   Horse dream: *The Dark-Haired Girl*, p. 29.

190   Masculine solar deities: Phrase used by PKD in his speech "The Android and the Human," in Gillespie, *Electric Shepherd*, p. 66. Andrea has left: *The Dark-Haired Girl*, p. 43.

190–192   Stay with Michael and Susan Walsh: All quotations are from the author's interview with Michael and Susan Walsh, April 1986.

192   Head in a good place: Letter, PKD to Ursula Le Guin, March 14, 1972.

192   Barely dial the last number, talk with counselor, method acting: Arthur Byron Cover, interviewer, "Vertex Interviews Philip K. Dick," *Vertex*, February 1974, p. 97.

192–193   More somber account, moving experience, self-destructive drive: Letter, PKD to Ray, March 30, 1972.

193–194   Problem here: Letter, PKD to Sue, April 5, 1972.

194–195   Rootless and scared: Tim Powers, "Some Random Notes on *Valis* and Philip K. Dick's Mystical Experiences," PKDS Newsletter #4, September 1984.

195   Lost-puppy quality: Author's interview with Merry Lou Malone, March 1986.

195   Basically happy: Author's interview with Mary Wilson, March 1986. Addicted to flattery: Author's interview with Linda Levy/Taylor, March 1986.

196   Books become more weird: PKD, *The Dark-Haired Girl*, pp. 60–61.

196–197   Courtship, breakup, and aftermath: Author's interview with Linda Levy/ Taylor, March 1986.

197   Seemed more withdrawn: Letter, Tessa Dick to author, July 21, 1986.

197–198   Light shone, entertaining, quarrel at Disneyland: Ibid.

198   Phil's joy: PKD, *The Dark-Haired Girl*, pp. 80–81.

198   Roller coaster: Letter, Tessa Dick to author, June 20, 1986. Went bonkers: Interview of Tessa Dick by J. B. Reynolds in PKD Newsletter #13, February 1987. Mood swings, slept little: Letter, Tessa Dick to author, June 20, 1986.

Chapter 10: *Annus Mirabilis*

PKD works: Exegesis 004 (1974–75), 005 (1975–76), 009 (1978), 015 (1978), 018 (1978), 040 (1979), 041 (1979), 044 (1979); *A Scanner Darkly* (1977); *Valis* (1981); *The Divine Invasion* (1981); *Radio Free Albemuth* (1985).

PKD letters: Be aware that many letters written by PKD in 1974–76 were apparently included by him in the growing mass of *Exegesis* papers. I have, in the end notes for this chapter, noted all cases where copies of quoted letters are presently included in the *Exegesis* folders of the PKD Estate Archives. As so much of PKD's correspondence for 1974 provided useful information for this chapter, I shall not list unquoted source letters individually.

Books and articles: D. S. Black, "Puttering About the Silver Screen," in PKDS Newsletter #11, May 1986.

209   Programmed to die: *Exegesis* 015 (1978). Civil disobedience: Letter, PKD to Dorothy Hudner, September 12, 1976, now part of *Exegesis* 005 (1975–76).

210   A mercy to him: *Exegesis* 018 (1978).

210   Prescription delivery and golden fish: Letter, PKD to Ursula Le Guin, September 23, 1974, now part of *Exegesis* 004 (1974–75).

210   Causes you to remember: *Exegesis* 083 (1980).

211   Combination of pentothal and golden fish: *Exegesis* 088 (1980). Remembered world of *Acts*: *Exegesis* 021 (1978).

211–212   Little boy and beggar: "Prologue" to PKD novel *Radio Free Albemuth* (w. 1976, p. 1985).

212   Flying-monster dreams: *Exegesis* 005 (1975–76).

212   Reptile hissing: Tessa Dick, excerpt from "The Search for Valis," in PKDS Newsletter #6, April 1985.

212   Experimenting, both hemispheres came on: *Exegesis* 004 (1974–75).

213–214   Mid-March visions: Letter, PKD to Louise Zimmerman, July 25, 1974, now in *Exegesis* 004 (1974–75).

214   First stage: Letter, PKD to Dorothy Hudner, September 15, 1976, now in *Exegesis* 005 (1975–76).

214–215   Three days in March: Single-page typed statement by PKD, dated March 21, 1975, in PKD Estate Archives.

215   Xerox missive: C. 7 of PKD novel *Valis* (1981).

215–216   Description of Xerox missive: Letter, Tessa Dick to author, July 21, 1986.

216   Believed him: Ibid. Good test score: *Exegesis* 018 (1978). I am a machine: *Exegesis* 088 (1980).

217   Interest in writing: Letter, William Sullivan, Director of FBI, to PKD, March 28, 1974.

217   Cooperated with oppressors. *Exegesis* 041 (1979), Excuse me: *Exegesis* 042 (1979).

218   Nick the prick: C. 14 of *Radio Free Albemuth* (1985). Both heard the music: Interview of Tessa Dick by J. B. Reynolds in PKD Newsletter #13, February 1987.

218–219   Hot dog Eucharist: C. 12 of *Valis* (1981).

219   Experiences while asleep: Letter, PKD to Louise Zimmerman, July 25, 1974.

219   Information about the future: Letter, PKD to Peter Fitting, June 1974 (no specific date given), now in *Exegesis* 004 (1974–75).

219–220   Language fragments: Ibid.

220 Singed pages, forced to read, religious fanatics, hypnagogic voices: *Exegesis* 004 (1974–75) and 005 (1975–76). Three-eyed beings: C. 7 of *Valis* (1981).

220 Fat lost touch with reality: C. 6 of *Valis* (1981). Telling his therapist: *Exegesis* 004 (1974–75).

221–222 Not the same person: *Exegesis* 004 (1974–75).

222 Putting affairs in order: Interview of PKD by Charles Platt in *Dream Makers* (New York: Berkley, 1980), p. 155. Dogshit Books: Letter, PKD to Lawrence Ashmead, May 7, 1974 (letter may never have been sent).

222 Blood-pressure test: C. 7 of *Valis* (1981).

223 Minor strokes: Letter, Tessa Dick to author, June 20, 1986.

223 More fun to be with: Letter, Tessa Dick to author, July 21, 1986.

224 In Cleveland: Interview of PKD by Tim Finney, May 1974 (tape of interview kindly provided by Finney to the author). Golden rectangle vision: C. 27 of *Radio Free Albemuth* (1985).

224 Ultimate aesthetic sight: *Exegesis* 004 (1974–75).

224–225 Pinky's death: Letter, PKD to Claudia Bush, written in late 1974 but not dated, now in *Exegesis* 004 (1974–75).

225 "Strawberry Fields" and Chrissy: *Exegesis* 050 (1977).

225 "Strawberry Fields" and random trash: *Exegesis* 001 (1980). Beam of pink light: *Exegesis* 090 (1981).

226 Great rationalist, talk on dreams: Author's interview with Thomas Disch, June 1986.

227 Jean-Pierre Goran interview by D. S. Black, in "Puttering About the Silver Screen," in PKDS Newsletter #11, May 1986.

227 Negotiations with Fancher: Author's interview with Hampton Fancher, June 1986.

228 Paranoia and religious belief: Paul Williams, *Only Apparently Real* (New York: Arbor House, 1986), pp. 155, 162–63.

228 Palm Tree Garden: *Exegesis* 090 (1981). Walked about like Dr. Abernathy: Letter, PKD to Dorothy Hudner, September 12, 1986, now in *Exegesis* 005 (1975–76).

228–229 Palm Tree Garden in *Deus Irae*: C. 18 of novel written by PKD and Roger Zelazny, *Deus Irae* (1976); in the author's interview with Zelazny, August 1986, he confirmed that this passage was written by PKD alone.

229 Walking to post office: Tessa Dick, "Letter from Tessa," in PKDS Newsletter #4, September 1984.

229 Not an evil world: Undated single typed page by PKD found among 1975 correspondence in PKD Estate Archives.

230–231 PKD self-interview: *Exegesis* 044 (1979).

231 "Psychic" or "experiential" phenomena: Peter Gloor, Andre Olivier, Luis F. Quesney, et al., "The Role of the Limbic System in Experiential Phenomena of Temporal Lobe Epilepsy," *Annals of Neurology*, Vol. 12, No. 2 (August 1982).

231–232 Temporal lobe seizure symptoms: Harold I. Kaplan and Benjamin J. Sadock, eds., *Comprehensive Textbook of Psychiatry/IV*, 4th ed. (Baltimore: Williams & Williams, 1980), p. 153. I am indebted to my friend William R. Dikel, M.D., for suggesting temporal lobe epilepsy as a plausible diagnosis.

232 To pass a spiritual judgment: William James, *The Varieties of Religious Experience*, quoted in Dom Cuthbert Butler, *Western Mysticism* (New York: Harper and Row, 1966), p. 146.

232 In no customary sense spiritualized: *Exegesis* 005 (1975–76).

232 Tessa's perspective: Letter, Tessa Dick to author, July 21, 1986.

233 Warning by John of the Cross: Quoted in Evelyn Underhill, *Mysticism* (New York: Meridian Books, 1958), p. 280.

233 Pascal's vision: Quoted in Emile Cailliet, *Pascal: The Emergence of Genius* (New York: Harper and Row, 1961), p. 131.

Chapter 11: As 2-3-74 Ripens Into *Valis*

Author's interviews: With Kleo Mini, February 1986; with Miriam Knight, February 1986; with Harlan Ellison, March 1986; with Norman Spinrad, March 1986; with Mark Hurst, June 1986; with Russell Galen, June 1986; with Roger Zelazny, August 1986.

235 Fucking dumb and dull: Letter, PKD to Claudia Bush, January 3, 1975.

235 Orthogonal time: PKD essay, "Man, Android and Machine," in Peter Nicholls, ed., *Science Fiction at Large* (London: Gollancz, 1976), p. 207.

235 Orthogonal time as real time: Letter, PKD to Ursula Le Guin, March 5, 1975, now in *Exegesis* 005 (1975–76).

236 PKD on Ellison's story "The Deathbird": Letter, PKD to Norman Spinrad, February 8, 1973.

236 Still having mystical visions: Letter, PKD to Thomas Disch, July 31, 1975.

237 A great peace now: *Exegesis* 005 (1975–76). Autographing a book: Tim Powers, "Some Random Memories of Philip K. Dick," in PKDS Newsletter #2, December 1983.

237 Dirty old man: *Exegesis* 005 (1975–76).

237–238 Tessa's view: Letter, Tessa Dick to author, June 20, 1986.

238 On being alone: Letter, PKD to Carol Carr, July 7, 1975. Venting anger: *Exegesis* 005 (1975–76).

239 PKD's religious beliefs: Author's interview with Doris Sauter, April 1986.

239 First struggle to breathe: Ibid.

240   Bonding to people in trouble: Ibid.

240   Never oversee: From journal of Tim Powers, transcribed by the author during an interview with Powers in March 1986. Technically dead: C. 4 of PKD novel *Valis* (1981).

240   Tessa as Beth: Letter, Tessa Dick to author, July 21, 1986.

241   Sammy Davis, Jr.'s glass eye, seen God too soon or too late: C. 4 of *Valis* (1981). Doris's visit: Author's interview with Doris Sauter, April 1986.

241   Not roaming off: Letter, PKD to Linda, January 8, 1977.

242   PKD's two switches, swill: Author's interview with Doris Sauter, April 1986.

243   Arrival at hospital: From journal of Tim Powers, transcribed by the author during an interview with Powers in March 1986. Powers's visit: Tim Powers, "Some Random Memories of Philip K. Dick," in PKDS Newsletter #2, December 1983.

244   On the Zebra principle: Letter, PKD to Mark Hurst, February 11, 1977.

244   One dozen novels: *Exegesis* 029 (1977).

244–245 Writing has been of value: *Exegesis* 030 (1977).

245   PKD's emotional side: Author's interview with Tim Powers, March 1986.

245   His depth of goodness: Author's interview with James Blaylock, March 1986.

246   "Minimum hypothesis": Interview of K. W. Jeter by Andy Watson in PKDS Newsletter #5, December 1984.

246   Getting inside belief, Jeter's skepticism: Author's interview with K. W. Jeter, May 1986.

246   Began to hallucinate: Letter, PKD to Joan Simpson, May 20, 1977.

247   First meeting: Author's interview with Joan Simpson, April 1984.

247–248 Learn from him: Ibid.

248   Hand-carved crucifix: Author's interview with Richard Lupoff, February 1986.

248   Prime directives: Letter, David May to author, January 15, 1986.

248–249 Full-time companion: Author's interview with Joan Simpson, April 1984.

249   Time and energy: Author's interview with Joan Simpson, April 1984.

249   PKD competitive: Author's interview with Robert Silverberg, February 1986. Fractured Latin: "Philip K. Dick: A Premature Memoir" by Robert Silverberg, in Gregg Rickman, *Philip K. Dick: The Last Testament* (Long Beach, Calif.: Fragments West/The Valentine Press, 1985), p. xi.

250   Quieter in private talks: Author's interview with Robert Silverberg, February 1986. Photos don't do justice: D. Scott Apel, "Phil As I Knew Him," in

Apel, ed., *Philip K. Dick: The Dream Connection* (San Jose, Calif.: Permanent Press, 1987), p. 17.

250   Phone routine: Apel, "Phil As I Knew Him," supra, p. 19.

250   Claimed nervous breakdown: Author's interview with Joan Simpson, February 1986.

251   God the Programmer-Reprogrammer: PKD speech, "If You Find This World Bad, You Should See Some of the Others," p. 13 of typed MS. in PKD Estate Archives.

251   Zelazny's memories: Roger Zelazny, "Musings From Melbourne (on Dick, *Deus Irae*, and alternate time tracks)," in PKDS Newsletter #16, January 1988.

251–252   Ellison's memories: Author's interview with Harlan Ellison, March 1986.

252   PKD antithetical to Ellison: Author's interview with Joan Simpson, April 1984. Drug user's personality: Interview of K. W. Jeter by Andy Watson in PKDS Newsletter #5, December 1984.

253   Phone numbers: Interview of K. W. Jeter by Andy Watson in PKDS Newsletter #5, December 1984. My interview with Jeter in April 1986 established PKD's motive, in attending the group, of keeping his prescription.

253   Suffering of little creatures: PKD essay, "Cosmogony and Cosmology," written January 23, 1978, typed MS. in PKD Estate Archives.

254   Only now: *Exegesis* 018 (1978). Intellectual mazes: *Exegesis* 022 (1978).

255   Sin and evil: *Exegesis* 022 (1978).

255   Things could have been done: Author's interview with Russell Galen, June 1986. Galen showed the right way: Letter, PKD to Russell Galen, November 29, 1978.

256   Combining plots: Letter, PKD to Claudia Bush, February 25, 1975, now in *Exegesis* 004 (1974–75). Two Bradys: Letter, PKD to Robert Orenstein, March 4, 1975, now in *Exegesis* 005 (1975–76).

257   Novel must be written: *Exegesis* 021 (1978).

257   I am Horselover Fat: C. 1 of *Valis* (1981).

258   Bizarre events true: Letter, PKD to John, March 5, 1979.

258   Tractates 7 and 9 revealed by AI voice: Letter, PKD to Carroll Joy, February 12, 1982. Stylized characters: Interview of K. W. Jeter by Andy Watson in PKDS Newsletter #5, December 1984.

Chapter 12: Big Bucks And Condo Comfort

Author's interviews: With Tim Powers, March 1986; with Nicole Panter, March 1986; with David Peoples, July 1986.

PKD works and letters: To Patricia Warrick, December 27, 1980, January 12, 1981,

July 15, 1981, and August 16, 1981; to Thomas Disch, February 21, 1981; to David Hartwell, May 21, 1981, and July 14, 1981; to Russell Galen, August 28, 1981; to Victoria Schochet, September 4, 1981; to Vincent Evans, September 6, 1981; to "Susan" (fictitious name), November 4, 1981; to Sherie, December 26, 1981; typed outline notes for novel *Bishop Timothy Archer* (published as *The Transmigration of Timothy Archer*), in PKD Estate Archives; PKD pharmacy receipts in PKD Estate Archives.

Books and articles: James Van Hise, "Philip K. Dick on *Blade Runner*," *Starlog*, February 1982.

261–262   Didn't see enough of each other: Author's interview with Isa Dick, February 1986.

262   Laura's memories: Author's interview with Laura Coehlo, September 1986.

262–263   Money: Author's interview with Isa Dick, February 1986.

263   Intentions good: Author's interview with Laura Coehlo, September 1986. Neglecting parts of life: Letter, PKD to Laura Coehlo, May 27, 1979.

264   Monday night: Tim Powers, "Some Random Notes on *Valis* and Philip K. Dick's Mystical Experiences," in PKDS Newsletter #4, September 1986.

265   Parable on hierarchical ranking: *Exegesis* 046 (1979).

265   Galen's visit: Author's interview with Russell Galen, June 1986.

265   Only thing separating him: PKD essay, "Strange Memories of Death," in PKD story/essay collection *I Hope I Shall Arrive Soon* (Garden City, N.Y.: Doubleday, 1985), pp. 98–99.

266   Proposed new novel: PKD eighty-page typed synopsis, dated January 30, 1980, for *The Acts of Paul*, synopsis in PKD Estate Archives.

266   Wasn't a recluse: Author's interview with Tim Powers, March 1986.

267   Taking friend to hospital: Interviews of Tim Powers and James Blaylock by J. B. Reynolds and Andy Watson, in PKDS Newsletter #8, September 1985.

267   PKD's dream: Interview of PKD by Gary Panter, in *Slash*, Vol. 3, No. 5 (1980).

267–268   Friendship with Nicole Panter: Author's interview with Nicole Panter, March 1986.

268   Prescription drugs no different: Author's interview with K. W. Jeter, May 1986.

268   Getting inside belief: Ibid.

269   Nasvar Pflegebourne: PKD typed plot outline, dated August 24, 1980, for *Fawn, Look Back*, outline in PKD Estate Archives.

269   Direct relation with divine: George Cain and Dana Longo, "Philip K. Dick: Confessions of an SF Artist," interview in *Denver Clarion*, October 23, 1980.

269–273   November 17 theophany: *Exegesis* 001 (1980).

273   Hell-chore, title page, new beginning: Ibid.

274   Fat old man: Author's interview with Chris Arena, March 1986.

274   Creative kook, always home, advice on women: Author's interviews with Juan and Su Perez, March 1986.

275   PKD on *Alien:* PKD essay, "Universe Makers . . . and Breakers," *SelecTV Guide,* February–March 1981.

275–276   PKD on Le Guin comments: Letter, PKD to editor, February 20, 1981, published in *Science Fiction Review,* Summer 1981.

276   Le Guin on PKD: Author's interview with Ursula Le Guin, July 1986.

276   Never drawn line, Horselover Fat, novel as justification: PKD to *Science Fiction Review,* supra.

277   PKD on himself and Le Guin: *Exegesis* 016 (1978).

277   Inadequate depiction of women: Letter, PKD to Russell Galen, June 29, 1981. Happiest moment: Letter, PKD to Ursula Le Guin, May 13, 1981.

278   Hartwell's memories: Author's interview with David Hartwell, June 1986.

278   Negotiations: Author's interview with Russell Galen, June 1986. Set up for life: John Boonstra, "TZ Interview: Philip K. Dick," in *Rod Serling's The Twilight Zone Magazine,* June 1982.

279   Spiritual aspirations: *Exegesis* 079 (1981). Bewitched: *Exegesis* 080 (1981).

280   Angel Archer on Timothy Archer: C. 12 of PKD novel *The Transmigration of Timothy Archer* (1982).

280   When God looks at me: *Exegesis* 081 (1981). Mainstream tragedy: Letter, PKD to Russell Galen, June 29, 1981.

280   Trying to say: Author's interview with Russell Galen, June 1986 (letter referred to is Galen to PKD, July 15, 1981, copy in PKD Estate Archives).

281   Continue to write SF: Letter, PKD to Russell Galen, August 1, 1981. Ditheon: *Exegesis* 091 (1981).

281   As human is to android: Letter, PKD to Patricia Warrick, July 15, 1981.

281–282   PKD on *The Owl in Daylight:* Interview of PKD by Gwen Lee, February 1982 (tape of interview kindly provided by Lee to the author, who transcribed quotes therefrom).

282   Bit off more than he can chew: Letter, PKD to Vincent Evans, September 6, 1981.

282   Ramming the car: Letter, PKD to Victoria Schochet, September 4, 1981.

283   Final statement on hyper-structure: Letter, PKD to Russell Galen, September 11, 1981.

283   The time you've waited for, more than information: Letter, PKD to Russell Galen, September 19, 1981.

283–284   Tagore: Letter, PKD to Edmund Meskys, editor of *Niekas,* September 23, 1981.

284 Feared I was nuts: *Exegesis* 090 (1981).

284 Sandow's memories: Author's interview with Greg Sandow, August 1987.

284 What God wants of me: *Exegesis* 062 (1981).

284–285 *Venom* review: Letter, PKD to *Venom*, September 29, 1981.

285 Check for $20,000: Author's interview with James Blaylock, March 1986. Remember that night still: Letter, PKD to "Susan" (fictitious name), November 10, 1981.

285–286 Jeopardizes the package: Letter, PKD to Susan, November 9, 1981.

286 Oceanic dread, searching for mother: PKD typed journal pages, November 13, 1981. Reentered reality: Letter, PKD to "Kate" (fictitious name), December 28, 1981. In love with the writing: Letter, PKD to Sherie, December 26, 1981.

287 Partnership, her reluctance: Author's interview with Mary Wilson, March 1986. Why not all humans are saved: Letter, PKD to Isa Dick, December 26, 1981.

287 PKD convinced her: Letter, Tessa Dick to author, July 21, 1986.

288 Central doctrine: Letter, PKD to *Childworld*, February 12, 1982. PKD's doubts: Gregg Rickman, *Philip K. Dick: The Last Testament* (Long Beach, Calif.: Fragments West/The Valentine Press, 1985), p. 225.

288 Even if you aren't sure: Author's interview with Mary Wilson, March 1986. Into power: *Exegesis* 057 (1982).

288–289 Pushing his brain to its limit: Interview of PKD by Gwen Lee, February 1982, supra.

289 Phone call to Spatz: Author's interview with Barry Spatz, March 1986. Found unconscious: Author's interviews with Juan and Su Perez, March 1986.

Index

347